PRAXIS® CORE POWER PRACTICE
(5712, 5722, 5732)

LEARNINGEXPRESS®

D1502216

Copyright © 2017 LearningExpress.

All rights reserved under International and Pan-American Copyright Conventions.
Published in the United States by LearningExpress, New York.

Cataloging-in-Publication Data is on file with the Library of Congress.

ISBN 978-1-61103-101-0

Printed in the United States of America

9 8 7 6 5 4 3 2 1

For more information on LearningExpress, other LearningExpress products, or bulk sales,
please write to us at:
    224 W. 29th Street
    3rd Floor
    New York, NY 10001

CONTENTS

CHAPTER 1   **About the Praxis® Core Academic Skills for Educators Tests**   1

States Using the Praxis Series of Tests   2

What Is Covered on the Praxis Core Tests?   2

Reading   3

Writing   4

Mathematics   5

The Computer-Delivered Test   6

Scoring   6

Retaking the Tests   7

What to Bring to the Test   7

How Do I Register?   7

Special Arrangements   8

Nonstandard Testing Accommodations   8

Where Do I Begin?   9

CHAPTER 2   **The LearningExpress Test Preparation System**   11

How It Works   12

Step 1: Get Information   12

Step 2: Conquer Test Anxiety   13

Step 3: Make a Plan   15

Step 4: Learn to Manage Your Time   15

Step 5: Learn to Use the Process of Elimination   16

Step 6: Know When to Guess   16

Step 7: Reach Your Peak Performance Zone   20

Step 8: Get Your Act Together   21

Step 9: Do It!   21

CONTENTS

CHAPTER 3   **Praxis® Core Academic Skills for Educators: Practice Test 1**   **23**

Praxis® Core Academic Skills for Educators: Reading Practice Test 1   24

Praxis® Core Academic Skills for Educators: Reading Practice Test 1
Answers and Explanations   40

Praxis® Core Academic Skills for Educators: Writing Practice Test 1   50

Part IIa: Argumentative Essay   58

Part IIb: Source-Based Essay   67

Praxis® Core Academic Skills for Educators: Writing Practice Test 1
Answers and Explanations   78

Sample Responses for the Argumentative Essay   81

Sample Responses for the Source-Based Essay   84

Praxis® Core Academic Skills for Educators: Mathematics Practice Test 1   88

Praxis® Core Academic Skills for Educators: Mathematics Practice Test 1
Answers and Explanations   99

CHAPTER 4   **Praxis® Core Academic Skills for Educators: Practice Test 2**   **113**

Praxis® Core Academic Skills for Educators: Reading Practice Test 2   114

Praxis® Core Academic Skills for Educators: Reading Practice Test 2
Answers and Explanations   129

Praxis® Core Academic Skills for Educators: Writing Practice Test 2   140

Part IIa: Argumentative Essay   149

Part IIb: Source-Based Essay   157

Praxis® Core Academic Skills for Educators: Writing Practice Test 2
Answers and Explanations   167

Sample Responses for the Argumentative Essay   170

Sample Responses for the Source-Based Essay   173

Praxis® Core Academic Skills for Educators: Mathematics Practice Test 2   177

Praxis® Core Academic Skills for Educators: Mathematics Practice Test 2
Answers and Explanations   186

CHAPTER 5   **Praxis® Core Academic Skills for Educators: Practice Test 3**   **193**

Praxis® Core Academic Skills for Educators: Reading Practice Test 3   194

Praxis® Core Academic Skills for Educators: Reading Practice Test 3
Answers and Explanations   209

Praxis® Core Academic Skills for Educators: Writing Practice Test 3   220

Part IIa: Argumentative Essay   227

Part IIb: Source-Based Essay   236

Praxis® Core Academic Skills for Educators: Writing Practice Test 3
Answers and Explanations   247

Sample Responses for the Argumentative Essay   253

Sample Responses for the Source-Based Essay   258

Praxis® Core Academic Skills for Educators: Mathematics Practice Test 3   262

Praxis® Core Academic Skills for Educators: Mathematics Practice Test 3
Answers and Explanations   275

CONTENTS

CHAPTER 6   **Praxis® Core Academic Skills for Educators: Practice Test 4**   **287**

Praxis® Core Academic Skills for Educators: Reading Practice Test 4   288

Praxis® Core Academic Skills for Educators: Reading Practice Test 4
Answers and Explanations   303

Praxis® Core Academic Skills for Educators: Writing Practice Test 4   311

Part IIa: Argumentative Essay   320

Part IIb: Source-Based Essay   327

Praxis® Core Academic Skills for Educators: Writing Practice Test 4
Answers and Explanations   336

Sample Responses for the Argumentative Essay   341

Sample Responses for the Source-Based Essay   346

Praxis® Core Academic Skills for Educators: Mathematics Practice Test 4   350

Praxis® Core Academic Skills for Educators: Mathematics Practice Test 4
Answers and Explanations   362

A NOTE ON SCORING   375

ADDITIONAL ONLINE PRACTICE   377

1 ▶ ABOUT THE PRAXIS® CORE ACADEMIC SKILLS FOR EDUCATORS TESTS

CHAPTER SUMMARY
This chapter familiarizes you with the series of Praxis® Core Academic Skills for Educators tests, which are administered by the Educational Testing Service. You will learn the components of all three Core exams, how to register for the exams, how they are scored, and all about the computer-based testing format.

Welcome to your comprehensive review for the Praxis Core Academic Skills for Educators tests! This series of computer-based mathematics, reading, and writing exams tests your knowledge in these core subjects, and assesses your readiness to enter teacher education programs. As the name suggests, the content tested on these exams aligns with the Common Core State Standards.

This book offers complete review, practice, and preparation for the three Core exams:

- Core Academic Skills for Educators: Reading (5712)
- Core Academic Skills for Educators: Writing (5722)
- Core Academic Skills for Educators: Mathematics (5732)

Inside you will find four practice exams to assess your skill levels, to test what you have learned, and to determine where you need more practice. At the end of the book, you will also find a link to an instantly scored online practice exam.

States Using the Praxis Series of Tests

Each state sets its own requirement for which tests you must take and what score will be accepted as passing. Information regarding specific state or organization requirements may change from time to time. For accurate, up-to-date information, refer to the official Praxis website at www.ets.org/praxis/about/core/ and your state's education department.

IMPORTANT CONTACT INFORMATION

ETS—*The Praxis Series*

Website: www.ets.org/praxis

Phone: 609-771-7395, M–F 8 A.M. to 7:45 P.M. (EST) (except for U.S. holidays)

Phone for the Hearing Impaired: 609-771-7714

E-mail directly through the website at www.ets.org/praxis/contact

Before you begin your review, let's take a closer look at the Praxis Core exams.

What Is Covered on the Praxis Core Tests?

The Praxis Core tests are designed to see whether you have the academic skills to be an effective teacher. Each tests your basic skills in either Reading, Mathematics, or Writing.

Praxis Core at a Glance

CORE TEST	TEST CODE	NUMBER OF QUESTIONS	QUESTION TYPES	TIME ALLOWED
Reading	5712	56	Multiple-choice	85 minutes
Writing	5722	40 + 2	• 40 multiple-choice + two essays	40 minutes for multiple-choice questions; 30 minutes for each essay
Mathematics	5732	56	• Multiple-choice: some ask you to select one answer choice; some ask you to select one or more. • Numeric entry: no choices; type in your own answer.	85 minutes

As you can see, most of the questions on the Praxis Core tests, with the exception of the essay portion of the Writing test, are in multiple-choice format. The Mathematics test also features numeric entry questions, where you supply an answer without being given any choices. Each multiple-choice question has five answer choices and is worth one point. Because test scoring is based only on the number of items answered correctly, you are not penalized for incorrect answers on the Praxis Core tests—so be sure to fill in all the answer blanks rather than leaving difficult questions unanswered. Even a guess is better than leaving an answer blank!

Let's look at each test.

Reading

The Praxis Core Academic Skills for Educators: Reading test measures your ability to comprehend, analyze, and evaluate written information. The skills tested on the exam align with the Common Core State Standards for Reading, and emphasize the skills needed to thrive in a teacher preparation program.

You will be asked to read a number of passages (which may vary in length from a few sentences to 100 to 200 words) and then answer questions accompanying each that test your ability to comprehend what you have read. The genre and reading levels of the passages will vary. You will be tested only on your ability to understand and analyze the selection; you will not be required to have specific knowledge about the topics discussed in the passages.

You will have 85 minutes to read all the passages and answer the 56 multiple-choice questions on this exam. Here is a breakdown of the question types on the Praxis Core Reading test.

QUESTION TYPE	NUMBER OF QUESTIONS	PERCENTAGE OF TEST
Key Ideas and Details	17–22	35%
Craft, Structure, and Language Skills	14–19	30%
Integration of Knowledge and Ideas	17–22	35%

Writing

The Praxis Core Academic Skills for Educators: Writing test is divided into two sections:

1. The first section consists of multiple-choice questions that require you to find and/or correct errors in standard English.
2. The second part asks you to write two 30-minute essays: an argumentative essay and a source-based essay.

The skills tested align with the Common Core State Standards for Writing. The multiple-choice section of the writing test is designed to measure your ability to use standard English correctly and effectively, and is divided into four parts: usage, sentence correction, revision in context, and research skills.

Usage questions test your knowledge of:

- structural and grammatical relationships
- mechanics
- idiom or word choice

Usage questions also test your ability to identify error-free sentences.

Sentence Correction questions test your ability to:

- select the best way to state a given phrase or sentence
- correct sentences with errors in grammar, mechanics, idioms, or word choice

Revision-in-Context questions test your skills in editing a passage to strengthen its word choice, flow, style, and organization.

Research Skills questions ask you to assess the credibility of sources, identify parts of a citation, and recognize parts of a passage that have been pulled from various sources.

The Essays

The essay portion of the Praxis Core Writing test is designed to evaluate your ability to express ideas clearly and effectively in standard written English under time constraints. You will be asked to write two different types of essays: an Argumentative essay and an Informative/Explanatory essay.

The **Argumentative** essay will ask you to draw from personal experiences and observation to support a position. To perform well on this essay, you will need to back up your point of view with examples—either from something you have read or seen, from your real life, or from a combination of both.

The **Informative/Explanatory** essay will begin with two passages, which you should read before you begin. You will then be asked to take information from these two sources to answer a question presented by the prompt given.

The given topics present situations that are generally familiar to all educated people and do not require any specialized knowledge in a particular field. Although you will be posing an argument and drawing conclusions based on examples from personal experience or observation, you will not be graded on your opinion—you will be scored only on how effectively you are able to get across your ideas.

You will have 40 minutes to answer the 40 multiple-choice questions on this exam, and 30 minutes for each essay.

Mathematics

The Praxis Core Academic Skills for Educators: Mathematics test measures your proficiency in math. Generally speaking, the test requires a competency at the high school or first-year college level. All the skills tested on the exam align with the Common Core State Standards for Mathematics. Here are the four main math content areas that will be tested:

Numbers and Operations
- order
- equivalence
- numeration and place value
- number properties
- operation properties
- computation
- estimation
- ratio, proportion, and percent
- numerical reasoning

Algebra and Functions
- equations and inequalities
- algorithmic thinking
- patterns
- algebraic representations
- algebraic reasoning

Geometry and Measurement
- geometric properties
- the xy-coordinate plane
- geometric reasoning
- systems of measurement

Statistics and Probability
- data interpretation
- data representation
- trends and inferences
- measures of center and spread
- probability

You will have 85 minutes to answer the 56 multiple-choice (one-answer and multiple-answer) and numeric entry questions on this exam. Here is a breakdown of the question types on the Praxis Core Mathematics test.

QUESTION TYPE	NUMBER OF QUESTIONS	PERCENTAGE OF TEST
Numbers and Operations	17	30%
Algebra and Functions	17	30%
Geometry and Measurement	11	20%
Statistics and Probability	11	20%

Please note: You *will* have access to an on-screen calculator for the duration of the Praxis Core Academic Skills for Educators: Mathematics test. Note that no other calculator use is allowed—you will not be able to bring a calculator from home. The calculator provided is simple and has four functions (+, −, ×, ÷).

The Computer-Delivered Test

Praxis Core Academic Skills for Educators tests are administered as computer-delivered tests in more than 300 locations throughout the United States. They are given frequently. You don't have to know much about computers to take these computer-based tests—each one begins with a tutorial on the use of the computer. You are encouraged to spend as much time as needed on the tutorial.

With the exception of the essay portion of the writing test and numeric entry mathematics questions, all questions are in multiple-choice format. The questions are presented on the computer screen, and you choose your answers by clicking in the oval next to the correct choice or choices (for multiple-answer math questions). For numeric entry questions, you will be asked to type your answer into the box or boxes provided.

The tests now have a special mark function, which allows you to mark a question that you would like to temporarily skip and come back to at a later time during the same section on the test. Test takers will have a review screen to see whether a question has been answered, not seen yet, or marked.

For the two essay questions, you will type your essay directly onto the screen in the space provided. If you are not comfortable with your typing skills, practice them in addition to making your way through this book. The 30 minutes provided for each essay cover your brainstorming, prep work, *and* typing in the essay.

These computer-based tests are designed to ensure fairness, because each test taker receives

- the same distribution of content.
- the same amount of testing time.
- the same test directions.
- the same tutorials on computer use.

Scoring

Your official score report will be available online about two to three weeks after your test date. Your score report will also be sent to the recipients (for example, schools) you designated on your registration form.

The report shows a separate test score for each Praxis subject that you take. Reading and math test scores are based on the number of items answered correctly. There is no penalty for answering a question incorrectly. The writing test score is based on the number of multiple-choice questions answered correctly combined with the essay score, which is scored on a scale of 1 to 6.

Your score report will show your score, whether you passed, the raw points earned in each content category, and the range of possible scores. If you took any test previously within the past ten years, it will also show your highest scores on each test.

Can I Cancel My Scores?

These computer-based tests give you the option to cancel your scores at the end of your test session before viewing the scores (once you have viewed your computerized scores, you cannot cancel them). All score cancellations are permanent, and refunds are not given.

Passing Scores

Each state or institution determines its own passing score. The first thing you will want to do with your scores is to compare them to the passing scores set by your state. Along with your test scores, you will receive the *Understanding Your Praxis Scores* booklet that gives the passing scores for each state. The Praxis Series website (www.ets.org/praxis/states) also has a complete state-by-state listing of required tests and passing scores.

Retaking the Tests

If you don't pass one or more Praxis Core tests, you will be allowed to take them again. How many times or how often you may retake each test is determined by the policies of individual states or institutions. The ETS does mandate that you may take each of these tests only once per 30-day period and no more than six times in one year. Individual states may have further restrictions. Consult your scores from previous tests to see which areas require more study, so that you will pass the tests the next time you take them.

REMINDER

Again, you may take the test only once a month, and no more than six times over the course of a year. This even applies to situations where you may have canceled your scores. If you violate this rule, your retest scores will not be reported, and your fees will not be refunded.

What to Bring to the Test

You will need your photo identification and your admission ticket. You may not bring calculators, cell phones, smartphones or any other electronic devices, pencils or pens, books, bags, scratch paper, or other people into the test room with you. The test administrator will designate an area where you may keep your personal belongings during the test.

On test day, allow plenty of time in the morning to get to your test location, especially if you are unfamiliar with the area where the test is given. You should arrive at least 30 minutes before your test to sign in, present your identification, and get yourself settled.

How Do I Register?

Usually you will need to register at least four weeks prior to the test date.

To register by mail, you must download and complete the appropriate Praxis Registration Form. Find all updated fees for your Praxis Core exams at www.ets.org/praxis/about/fees.

At least one week before your test date, you will receive a testing admission ticket by mail, which you will need to bring for entrance into the test. If you do not receive your ticket at least one week prior to your test day or if you lose it, or if there is an error on your ticket, contact ETS immediately.

You can also register online at www.ets.org/praxis. To register online, you will need a valid e-mail address, mailing address, and phone number. Order confirmations and test admission tickets will be e-mailed to your e-mail address—you will not be sent a paper admission ticket by postal mail when you register online. Print out the ticket provided for you online. Online registration is available only to those not needing special accommodations such as considerations for disabilities or Monday testing.

If you have previously created a Praxis account online, you can register by phone with a credit card. There will be a nonrefundable $35 surcharge for the transaction, in addition to the standard registration and test fees. To register by phone, call 800-772-9476, 8 A.M. to 7:45 P.M. (EST), Monday through Friday.

Emergency Registration

Those trying to register for a desired test date after the regular and late registration deadlines may still be able to take the test on that date by using the emergency registration service for an additional fee. This service guarantees a seat at a test center. Emergency registration is not available for individuals needing special accommodations.

To Cancel or Reschedule Your Test

If you are absent the day of the test or arrive too late to take the test, you are not eligible for a refund. You may cancel or reschedule a test by logging into your Praxis account online or calling ETS at 1-800-772-9476.

You are eligible to receive a refund of 50% of your test fees if the change is received by ETS at least three days prior to the test date. Special service fees are nonrefundable. Registration deadlines are updated and posted on the website. Refunds are mailed approximately four to six weeks after receipt of your request. If you used a credit card to make a payment, the refund will be credited to your credit card account.

Special Arrangements

Special arrangements may be available for individuals with documented disabilities or for test takers whose primary language is not English (PLNE). Monday test dates are available to those who cannot take the test on a Saturday test date due to religious convictions or military orders. These accommodations may vary from state to state. You should contact the ETS long before the test date to make inquiries.

Nonstandard Testing Accommodations

If you have a documented disability, you may be able to receive nonstandard testing accommodations for the tests. Among a list of accommodations, you may qualify for

- extended test time.
- a test reader.
- a separate location.
- a Braille test.
- someone to record your answers.

Online, you will find the *Bulletin Supplement for Test Takers with Disabilities or Health-Related Needs*, which contains contact information, registration procedures, and special registration forms.

If you are requesting accommodations, you must register by mail. At least six weeks before the registration date, send your completed requests for testing accommodations to:

ETS Disability Services
P.O. Box 6054
Princeton, NJ 08541-6054

Where Do I Begin?

You have already taken the first step by reading this chapter and familiarizing yourself with the Praxis Series of tests. Perhaps you have even started researching to see which tests you need to take, when the tests are offered, and where you would like to take them. Now you should begin your study program: Start with "The LearningExpress Test Preparation System" (Chapter 2). This exclusive system gives you valuable test-taking techniques and will help you devise a study schedule that works best for you. If you stick with your study plan and concentrate on improving the areas in which you need help, you are sure to succeed. Good luck!

CHAPTER

2

THE LEARNING-EXPRESS TEST PREPARATION SYSTEM

CHAPTER SUMMARY

The Praxis Series of tests can be challenging. A great deal of preparation is necessary for achieving top scores and advancing your career. The LearningExpress Test Preparation System, developed by leading experts exclusively for LearningExpress, offers strategies for developing the discipline and attitude required for success.

Fact: Taking the Praxis® Core Academic Skills for Educators tests is not easy, and neither is getting ready for them. Your future career as a teacher depends on getting a passing score, but an assortment of pitfalls can keep you from doing your best. Here are some of the obstacles that can stand in the way of success:

- being unfamiliar with the exam format
- being paralyzed by test anxiety
- leaving your preparation to the last minute
- not preparing at all!
- not knowing vital test-taking skills: how to pace yourself through the exams, how to use the process of elimination, and when to guess
- not being in tip-top mental and physical shape
- messing up on test day by arriving late at the test site, having to work on an empty stomach, or feeling uncomfortable during the exams because the room is too hot or cold

What's the common denominator in all these test-taking pitfalls? One word: control. Who's in control, you or the exam?

Here's some good news: The LearningExpress Test Preparation System puts you in control. In nine easy-to-follow steps, you will learn everything you need to know to make sure that you are in charge of your preparation and your performance on the exams. Other test takers may let the tests get the better of them; other test takers may be unprepared or out of shape, but not you. You will have taken all the steps you need to take to get a high score on the Praxis Core Academic Skills for Educators tests.

How It Works

Nine easy steps lead you through everything you need to know and do to get ready to master your exams. Each of the following steps includes both reading about the step and one or more activities. It's important that you do the activities along with the reading, or you won't be getting the full benefit of the system.

Step 1: Get Information	50 minutes
Step 2: Conquer Test Anxiety	20 minutes
Step 3: Make a Plan	30 minutes
Step 4: Learn to Manage Your Time	10 minutes
Step 5: Learn to Use the Process of Elimination	20 minutes
Step 6: Know When to Guess	20 minutes
Step 7: Reach Your Peak Performance Zone	10 minutes
Step 8: Get Your Act Together	10 minutes
Step 9: Do It!	10 minutes
Total	**3 hours**

We estimate that working through the entire system will take you approximately three hours, although it's perfectly okay if you work faster or slower. If you set aside an afternoon or evening, you can work through the whole LearningExpress Test Preparation System in one sitting. Otherwise, you can break it up, and do just one or two steps a day for the next several days. It's up to you—remember, you are in control.

Step 1: Get Information

Time to complete: 50 minutes
Activity: Read Chapter 1, "About the Praxis® Core Academic Skills for Educators Tests."

Knowledge is power. The first step in the LearningExpress Test Preparation System is finding out everything you can about the Praxis Core tests. Once you have your information, the next steps in the LearningExpress Test Preparation System will show you what to do about it.

Part A: Straight Talk about the Praxis Core Tests

Why do you have to take rigorous exams, anyway? It's simply an attempt to be sure you have the knowledge and skills necessary to be a teacher.

It's important for you to remember that your scores on the Praxis tests do not determine how smart you are, or even whether you will make a good teacher. There are all kinds of things exams like these can't test, such as whether you have the drive, determination, and dedication to be a teacher. Those kinds of traits are hard to evaluate, whereas a test is easy to evaluate.

This is not to say that the exams are not important! The knowledge tested on the exams is knowledge you will need to do your job. And your ability to enter the profession you've trained for depends on passing. And that's why you are here—using the LearningExpress Test Preparation System to achieve control over the exams.

Part B: What's on the Tests

If you haven't already done so, stop here and read Chapter 1, which gives you an overview of the Praxis Core series of tests. Then, go online and read the most up-to-date information about your exam directly from the test developers at www.ets.org/praxis.

Step 2: Conquer Test Anxiety

Time to complete: 20 minutes
Activity: Take the "Test Anxiety Test."

Having complete information about the exams is the first step in getting control over them. Next, you have to overcome one of the biggest obstacles to test success: test anxiety. Test anxiety not only impairs your performance on the exams, but also keeps you from preparing. In Step 2, you will learn stress management techniques that will help you succeed. Learn these strategies now, and practice them as you work through the exams so that they will be second nature to you by exam day.

Combating Test Anxiety

The first thing you need to know is that a little test anxiety is a good thing. Everyone gets nervous before a big exam—and if that nervousness motivates you to prepare thoroughly, so much the better. It's said that Sir Laurence Olivier, one of the foremost British actors of the twentieth century, felt ill before every performance. His stage fright didn't impair his performance; in fact, it probably gave him a little extra edge—just the kind of edge you need to do well, whether on a stage or on an examination.

The Test Anxiety Test follows on page 14. Stop and answer the questions to find out whether your level of test anxiety is something you should worry about.

Stress Management Before a Test

If you feel your level of anxiety getting the best of you in the weeks before a test, here is what you need to do to bring the level down again:

- **Get prepared.** There's nothing like knowing what to expect and being prepared for it to put you in control of test anxiety. That's why you are reading this book. Use it faithfully, and remind yourself that you are better prepared than most of the other people taking the test.
- **Practice self-confidence.** A positive attitude is a great way to combat test anxiety. This is no time to be humble or shy. Stand in front of the mirror and say to your reflection, "I am prepared. I am full of self-confidence. I am going to ace this test. I know I can do it." Record it and play it back once a day. If you hear it often enough, you will believe it.
- **Fight negative messages.** Every time someone starts telling you how hard the exam is or how it's almost impossible to get a high score, tune the person out or ask him or her to not speak negatively around you. Don't listen to the negative messages. Turn on your recorder and listen to your self-confidence messages.
- **Visualize.** Imagine yourself reporting for duty on your first day as a teacher or in your teacher training program. Visualizing success can help make it happen—and it reminds you of why you are doing all this work preparing for the exam.
- **Exercise.** Physical activity helps calm your body down and focus your mind. Besides, being in good physical shape can actually help you do well on the exam. Go for a run, lift weights, go swimming—and do it regularly.

Stress Management on Test Day

There are several ways you can bring down your level of anxiety on test day. They will work best if you practice them in the weeks before the test so that you know which ones work best for you.

- **Practice deep breathing.** Take a deep breath while you count to five. Hold it for a count of one, then let it out on a count of five. Repeat several times.

You need to worry about test anxiety only if it is extreme enough to impair your performance. The following questionnaire will provide a diagnosis of your level of test anxiety. In the blank before each statement, write the number that most accurately describes your experience.

0 = Never
1 = Once or twice
2 = Sometimes
3 = Often

___ I have gotten so nervous before an exam that I simply put down the books and didn't study for it.

___ I have experienced disabling physical symptoms such as vomiting and severe headaches because I was nervous about an exam.

___ I have simply not shown up for an exam because I was afraid to take it.

___ I have experienced dizziness and disorientation while taking an exam.

___ I have had trouble filling in the little circles because my hands were shaking too hard.

___ I have failed an exam because I was too nervous to complete it.

___ **Total: Add up the numbers in the blanks.**

Your Test Anxiety Score

Here are the steps you should take, depending on your score. If you scored:

- **Below 3**, your level of test anxiety is nothing to worry about; it's probably just enough to give you that little extra edge.

- **Between 3 and 6**, your test anxiety may be enough to impair your performance, and you should practice the stress management techniques in this section to try to bring your test anxiety down to manageable levels.

- **Above 6**, your level of test anxiety is a serious concern. In addition to practicing the stress management techniques listed in this section, you may want to seek additional, personal help. Call your local high school or community college and ask for the academic counselor. Tell the counselor that you have a level of test anxiety that sometimes keeps you from being able to take an exam. The counselor may be willing to help you or may suggest someone else you should talk to.

- **Move your body.** Try rolling your head in a circle. Rotate your shoulders. Shake your hands from the wrist. Many people find these movements very relaxing.
- **Visualize again.** Think of the place where you are most relaxed: lying on the beach in the sun, walking through the park, or wherever. Now close your eyes and imagine you are actually there. If you practice in advance, you will find that you only need a few seconds of this exercise to experience a significant increase in your sense of well-being.

When anxiety threatens to overwhelm you right there during the exam, there are still things you can do to manage your stress level:

- **Repeat your self-confidence messages.** You should have them memorized by now. Say them quietly to yourself, and believe them!
- **Visualize one more time.** This time, visualize yourself moving smoothly and quickly through the test, answering every question right and finishing just before time is up. Like most visualization techniques, this one works best if you have practiced it ahead of time.
- **Find an easy question.** Find an easy question, and answer it. Getting even one question finished gets you into the test-taking groove.
- **Take a mental break.** Everyone loses concentration once in a while during a long test. It's normal, so you shouldn't worry about it. Instead, accept what has happened. Say to yourself, "Hey, I lost it there for a minute. My brain is taking a break." Put down your pencil, close your eyes, and do some deep breathing for a few seconds. Then you are ready to go back to work.

Try these techniques ahead of time, and see whether they work for you!

Step 3: Make a Plan

Time to complete: 30 minutes
Activity: Construct a study plan.

Maybe the most important thing you can do to get control of yourself and your exams is to make a study plan. Too many people fail to prepare simply because they fail to plan. Spending hours on the day before the exam poring over sample test questions not only raises your level of test anxiety, but also is simply no substitute for careful preparation and practice over time.

Don't fall into the cram trap. Take control of your preparation time by mapping out a study schedule.

Even more important than making a plan is making a commitment. You have to set aside some time every day for study and practice. Try for at least 20 minutes a day. Twenty minutes daily will do you much more good than two hours on Saturday.

Don't put off your study until the day before the exam. Start now. A few minutes a day, with half an hour or more on weekends, can make a big difference in your score.

Step 4: Learn to Manage Your Time

Time to complete: 10 minutes to read, many hours of practice!
Activity: Practice these strategies as you take the sample tests in this book.

Steps 4, 5, and 6 of the LearningExpress Test Preparation System put you in charge of your exams by showing you test-taking strategies that work. Practice these strategies as you take the sample tests, and then you will be ready to use them on test day.

First, take control of your time on the exams. It's a terrible feeling to know there are only five minutes left when you are only three-quarters of the way through a test. Here are some tips to keep that from happening to you:

- **Follow directions.** You should take your time making your way through the computer tutorial before the exam. Read the directions carefully and ask questions before the exam begins if there's anything you don't understand.
- **Pace yourself.** If there is a timer on the screen as you take the exam, keep an eye on it. This will help you pace yourself. For example, when one-quarter of the time has elapsed, you should be a quarter of the way through the test, and so on. If you are falling behind, pick up the pace a bit.
- **Keep moving.** Don't waste time on one question. If you don't know the answer, skip the question and move on. You can always go back to it later.
- **Don't rush.** Although you should keep moving, rushing won't help. Try to keep calm and work methodically and quickly.

Step 5: Learn to Use the Process of Elimination

Time to complete: 20 minutes
Activity: Complete the "Using the Process of Elimination" worksheet.

After time management, your next most important tool for taking control of your exam is using the process of elimination wisely. It's standard test-taking wisdom that you should always read all the answer choices before choosing your answer. This helps you find the right answer by eliminating wrong answer choices. And, sure enough, that standard wisdom applies to your exam, too.

You should always use the process of elimination on tough questions, even if the right answer jumps out at you. Sometimes the answer that jumps out isn't right after all. You should always proceed through the answer choices in order. You can start with answer choice **a**, and eliminate any choices that are clearly incorrect.

Even when you think you are absolutely clueless about a question, you can often use the process of elimination to get rid of one answer choice. If so, you are better prepared to make an educated guess, as you will see in Step 6. More often, the process of elimination allows you to get down to only two possibly right answers. Then you are in a strong position to guess. And sometimes, even though you don't know the right answer, you find it simply by getting rid of the wrong ones.

Try using your powers of elimination on the questions in the worksheet "Using the Process of Elimination." The questions aren't about teaching; they're just designed to show you how the process of elimination works. The answer explanations for this worksheet show one possible way that you might use the process to arrive at the right answer.

The process of elimination is your tool for the next step, which is knowing when to guess.

Step 6: Know When to Guess

Time to complete: 20 minutes
Activity: Complete the "Your Guessing Ability" worksheet.

Armed with the process of elimination, you are ready to take control of one of the big questions in test taking: Should I guess? The answer is: Yes. Some exams have what's called a "guessing penalty," in which a fraction of your wrong answers is subtracted from your right answers—the Praxis Series of tests does

Use the process of elimination to answer the following questions.

1. Ilsa is as old as Meghan will be in five years. The difference between Ed's age and Meghan's age is twice the difference between Ilsa's age and Meghan's age. Ed is 29. How old is Ilsa?
 a. 4
 b. 10
 c. 19
 d. 24

2. "All drivers of commercial vehicles must carry a valid commercial driver's license whenever operating a commercial vehicle."
 According to this sentence, which of the following people need NOT carry a commercial driver's license?
 a. a truck driver idling his engine while waiting to be directed to a loading dock
 b. a bus operator backing her bus out of the way of another bus in the bus lot
 c. a taxi driver driving his personal car to the grocery store
 d. a limousine driver taking the limousine to her home after dropping off her last passenger of the evening

3. Smoking tobacco has been linked to
 a. increased risk of stroke and heart attack.
 b. all forms of respiratory disease.
 c. increasing mortality rates over the past 10 years.
 d. juvenile delinquency.

4. Which of the following words is spelled correctly?
 a. incorrigible
 b. outragous
 c. domestickated
 d. understandible

Answers

Here are the answers, as well as some suggestions as to how you might have used the process of elimination to find them.

1. d. You should have eliminated choice **a** right off the bat. Ilsa can't be four years old if Meghan is going to be Ilsa's age in five years. The best way to eliminate other answer choices is to try plugging them in to the information given in the problem. For instance, for choice **b**, if Ilsa is 10, then Meghan must be 5. The difference between their ages is 5. The difference between Ed's age, 29, and Meghan's age, 5, is 24. Is 24 two times 5? No. Then choice **b** is wrong. You could eliminate choice **c** in the same way and be left with choice **d**.

2. c. Note the word *not* in the question, and go through the answers one by one. Is the truck driver in choice **a** "operating a commercial vehicle"? Yes, idling counts as "operating," so he needs to have a commercial driver's license. Likewise, the bus operator in choice **b** is operating a commercial vehicle; the question doesn't say the operator has to be on the street. The limo driver in choice **d** is operating

(continues)

a commercial vehicle, even though it doesn't have a passenger in it. However, the driver in choice **c** is not operating a commercial vehicle, but his own private car.

3. **a.** You could eliminate choice **b** simply because of the presence of the word *all*. Such absolutes hardly ever appear in correct answer choices. Choice **c** looks attractive until you think a little about what you know—aren't fewer people smoking these days, rather than more? So how could smoking be responsible for a higher mortality rate? (If you didn't know that mortality rate means the rate at which people die, you might keep this choice as a possibility, but you would still be able to eliminate two answers and have only two to choose from.) And choice **d** is plain silly, so you could eliminate that one, too. You are left with the correct choice, **a**.

4. **a.** How you used the process of elimination here depends on which words you recognized as being spelled incorrectly. If you knew that the correct spellings were *outrageous*, *domesticated*, and *understandable*, then you were home free.

YOUR GUESSING ABILITY

The following are ten really hard questions. You are not supposed to know the answers. Rather, this is an assessment of your ability to guess when you don't have a clue. Read each question carefully, as if you were expected to answer it. If you have any knowledge of the subject, use that knowledge to help you eliminate wrong answer choices.

1. September 7 is Independence Day in
   a. India.
   b. Costa Rica.
   c. Brazil.
   d. Australia.

2. Which of the following is the formula for determining the momentum of an object?
   a. $p = MV$
   b. $F = ma$
   c. $P = IV$
   d. $E = mc^2$

3. Because of the expansion of the universe, the stars and other celestial bodies are all moving away from each other. This phenomenon is known as
   a. Newton's first law.
   b. the big bang.
   c. gravitational collapse.
   d. Hubble flow.

4. American author Gertrude Stein was born in
   a. 1713.
   b. 1830.
   c. 1874.
   d. 1901.

5. Which of the following is NOT one of the Five Classics attributed to Confucius?
   a. *I Ching*
   b. *Book of Holiness*
   c. *Spring and Autumn Annals*
   d. *Book of History*

6. The religious and philosophical doctrine that holds that the universe is constantly in a struggle between good and evil is known as
   a. Pelagianism.
   b. Manichaeanism.
   c. neo-Hegelianism.
   d. Epicureanism.

7. The third chief justice of the U.S. Supreme Court was
   a. John Blair.
   b. William Cushing.
   c. James Wilson.
   d. John Jay.

8. Which of the following is the poisonous portion of a daffodil?
   a. the bulb
   b. the leaves
   c. the stem
   d. the flowers

9. The winner of the Masters golf tournament in 1953 was
   a. Sam Snead.
   b. Cary Middlecoff.
   c. Arnold Palmer.
   d. Ben Hogan.

10. The state with the highest per capita personal income in 1980 was
   a. Alaska.
   b. Connecticut.
   c. New York.
   d. Texas.

Answers

Check your answers against the following correct answers.

   1. c
   2. a
   3. d
   4. c
   5. b
   6. b
   7. b
   8. a
   9. d
   10. a

How Did You Do?

You may have simply gotten lucky and actually known the answer to one or two questions. In addition, your guessing was probably more successful if you were able to use the process of elimination on any of the questions. Maybe you didn't know who the third chief justice was (question 7), but you knew that John Jay was the first. In that case, you would have eliminated choice **d** and, therefore, improved your odds of guessing right from one in four to one in three.

According to probability, you should get two-and-a-half answers correct, so getting either two or three right would be average. If you got four or more right, you may be a really terrific guesser. If you got one or none right, you may be a really bad guesser.

Keep in mind, though, that this is only a small sample. You should continue to keep track of your guessing ability as you work through the sample questions in this book. Circle the numbers of questions you guess on as you make your guess; or, if you don't have time while you take the practice tests, go back afterward and try to remember which questions you guessed at. Remember, on a test with five answer choices, your chance of guessing correctly is one in five. So keep a separate "guessing" score for each exam. How many questions did you guess on? How many did you get right? If the number you got right is at least one-fifth of the number of questions you guessed on, you are at least an average guesser—maybe better—and you should always go ahead and guess on the real exam. If the number you got right is significantly lower than one-fifth of the number you guessed on, you would be safe in guessing anyway, but maybe you would feel more comfortable if you guessed only selectively, when you can eliminate a wrong answer or at least have a good feeling about one of the answer choices.

Remember, even if you are a play-it-safe person with lousy intuition, you are still safe guessing every time.

NOT work like that. The number of questions you answer correctly yields your raw score. So you have nothing to lose and everything to gain by guessing.

Step 7: Reach Your Peak Performance Zone

Time to complete: 10 minutes to read; weeks to complete!
Activity: Complete a physical preparation checklist.

To get ready for a challenge like a big exam, you have to take control of your physical, as well as your mental, state. Exercise, proper diet, and rest will ensure that your body works with, rather than against, your mind on test day, as well as during your preparation.

Exercise

If you don't already have a regular exercise program going, the time during which you are preparing for an exam is actually an excellent time to start one. And if you are already keeping fit—or trying to get that way—don't let the pressure of preparing for an exam fool you into quitting now. Exercise helps reduce stress by pumping wonderful good-feeling hormones called *endorphins* into your system. It also increases the oxygen supply throughout your body, including your brain, so you will be at peak performance on test day.

A half hour of vigorous activity—enough to raise a sweat—every day should be your aim. If you are really pressed for time, every other day is okay. Choose an activity you like and get out there and do it. Jogging with a friend always makes the time go faster, or take a radio.

But don't overdo it. You don't want to exhaust yourself. Moderation is the key.

Diet

First of all, cut out the junk. Go easy on caffeine and nicotine, and eliminate alcohol and any other drugs from your system at least two weeks before the exam. Promise yourself a treat the night after the exam, if need be.

What your body needs for peak performance is simply a balanced diet. Eat plenty of fruits and vegetables, along with protein and carbohydrates. Foods that are high in lecithin (an amino acid), such as fish and beans, are especially good "brain foods."

The night before the exam, you might carbo-load the way athletes do before a contest. Eat a big plate of spaghetti, rice and beans, or whatever your favorite carbohydrate is.

Rest

You probably know how much sleep you need every night to be at your best, even if you don't always get it. Make sure you do get that much sleep, though, for at least a week before the exam. Moderation is important here, too. Extra sleep will just make you groggy.

If you are not a morning person, and your exam will be given in the morning, you should reset your internal clock so that your body doesn't think you are taking an exam at 3 A.M. You have to start this process well before the exam. The way it works is to get up half an hour earlier each morning, and then go to bed half an hour earlier that night. Don't try it the other way around; you will just toss and turn if you go to bed early without having gotten up early. The next morning, get up another half an hour earlier, and so on. How long you will have to do this depends on how late you are used to getting up.

Step 8: Get Your Act Together

Time to complete: 10 minutes to read; time to complete will vary
Activity: Complete the "Final Preparations" worksheet.

You are in control of your mind and body, which means you are in charge of test anxiety, your preparation, and your test-taking strategies. Now it's time to take charge of external factors, like the testing site and the materials you need to take to the exam.

Find Out Where the Exam or Exams Are, and Make a Trial Run

Do you know how to get to the testing site? Do you know how long it will take to get there? If not, make a trial run, preferably on the same day of the week at the same time of day as you will be taking your test. Note, on the Final Preparations worksheet on the next page, the amount of time it will take you to get to the exam site. Plan on arriving 30 to 45 minutes early so you can get the lay of the land, use the bathroom, and calm down. Then figure out how early you will have to get up that morning, and make sure you get up that early every day for a week before the exam.

Gather Your Materials

The night before the exams, lay out the clothes you will wear and the materials you have to bring with you to the exam. Plan on dressing in layers; you won't have any control over the temperature of the examination room. Have a sweater or jacket that you can take off if it's warm. Use the checklist on the Final Preparations worksheet to help you pull together what you will need.

Don't Skip Breakfast

Even if you don't usually eat breakfast, do so on exam morning. A cup of coffee doesn't count. Don't eat doughnuts or other sweet foods, either. A sugar high will leave you with a sugar low in the middle of the exam. A mix of protein and carbohydrates is best: Cereal with milk and just a little sugar, or eggs with toast, will do your body a world of good.

Step 9: Do It!

Time to complete: 10 minutes, plus test-taking time
Activity: Ace the Praxis Core tests!

Fast-forward to exam day. You are ready. You made a study plan and followed through. You practiced your test-taking strategies. You are in control of your physical, mental, and emotional state. You know when and where to show up and what to bring with you. In other words, you are better prepared than most of the other people taking the exam. You are psyched.

Just one more thing. When you are finished with the exam, you will have earned a reward. Plan a celebration. Call up your friends and plan a party, or have a nice dinner for two—whatever your heart desires. Give yourself something to look forward to.

And then do it. Go into the exams full of confidence and armed with test-taking strategies you have practiced until they're second nature. You are in control of yourself, your environment, and your performance on the exam. You are ready to succeed. So do it. Go in there and ace the exam. And look forward to your future career as a teacher!

Getting to the Exam Site

Location of the exam site: _____

Date: _____

Departure time: _____

Do I know how to get to the exam site?   Yes ___   No ___

If no, make a trial run.

Time it will take to get to the exam site: _____

Things to Lay Out the Night Before

Clothes I will wear   _____

Sweater/jacket   _____

Watch   _____

Photo ID   _____

Other Things to Bring/Remember

_____

_____

_____

_____

_____

_____

_____

_____

_____

3 ▶ PRAXIS® CORE ACADEMIC SKILLS FOR EDUCATORS: PRACTICE TEST 1

CHAPTER SUMMARY

This is the first of the four full-length Praxis® Core Academic Skills for Educators tests based on the structure and difficulty level of the Reading, Writing, and Mathematics tests. Use these tests to see how you would do if you were to take the Praxis Core tests today.

This chapter contains three tests that mirror the Reading, Writing, and Mathematics Core exams. Although the actual tests you will take are computer-based, the question types for each exam are replicated here for you in the book.

As you take these first tests, do not worry too much about timing. The actual time you will be allotted for each exam is at the beginning of each test, but you should take these practice tests in as relaxed a manner as you can to find out which areas you are skilled in and in which ones you will need to do extra work.

After you finish taking your tests, you should review the answer explanations. (Each individual test is followed by its own answer explanations.) See **A Note on Scoring** on page 375 to find information on how to score your exam.

Good luck!

Praxis® Core Academic Skills for Educators: Reading Practice Test 1

Time: 85 Minutes

Directions: Read the following passages and answer the questions that follow.

Use the following passage to answer questions 1 and 2.

Of the numerous American automotive pioneers, perhaps among the best known are
Charles and Frank Duryea. Beginning their
work of automobile building in Springfield,
5   Massachusetts, and, after much rebuilding, they
constructed their first successful vehicle in 1892
and 1893. No sooner was this finished than
Frank, working alone, began work on a second
vehicle having a two-cylinder engine. With this
10   automobile, sufficient capital was attracted in
1895 to form the Duryea Motor Wagon Company in which both brothers were among the
stockholders and directors. A short time after
the formation of the company, this second
15   automobile was entered by the company in the
Chicago Times-Herald automobile race on
Thanksgiving Day, November 28, 1895, where
Frank Duryea won a victory over the other five
contestants—two electric automobiles and
20   three Benz machines imported from Germany.

Source: Excerpt from *The 1893 Duryea Automobile* by Don H. Berkebile.

1. Which of the following is the best summary of
the passage?

   a. There were many automotive pioneers in
America, but the best known were the
brothers Charles and Frank Duryea, who
began building automobiles in Springfield,
Massachusetts.

   b. Charles and Frank Duryea were among the
best-known American automotive pioneers,
but Frank was more famous than his brother
Charles because Frank won the *Chicago
Times-Herald* automobile race.

   c. On Thanksgiving Day, November 28, 1895,
Frank Duryea won the *Chicago Times-Herald*
automobile race over five other contestants:
two electric automobiles and three Benz
machines from Germany.

   d. Charles and Frank Duryea were pioneering
automobile builders, and Frank developed a
profitable two-cylinder engine vehicle with
which he won the *Chicago Times-Herald*
automobile race.

   e. Although Frank Duryea developed a two-
cylinder engine vehicle, both he and his
brother Charles profited from it because it
earned them the capital to start the Duryea
Motor Wagon Company.

2. In the passage, the author describes the kinds
of cars Frank Duryea defeated in the *Chicago
Times-Herald* automobile race in order to

   a. show that the best automobiles in the world
are built in Springfield, Massachusetts.

   b. imply that he would later develop an electric
car for the Duryea Motor Wagon Company.

   c. indicate that the quality of automobiles
being developed in Europe was very poor at
the time.

   d. suggest that the kind of car he drove is what
helped him win the race.

   e. help the reader understand the differences
between two-cylinder vehicles and electric
automobiles.

Use the following passage to answer questions 3 through 5.

It is not always easy to identify a stone, even with a fresh surface; in a weathered specimen it is often impossible. For this reason the material of which a specimen is made may not be cor-
5   rectly named; frequently the alteration due to exposure will change the appearance of a rock very much, and in such a case the best that can be done is to tell what it looks most like. The material of a majority of specimens, however, or
10 at least the classes of rock to which they belong, as granite, porphyry, etc., are correctly named; to give a more exact name would be possible only by the destruction or injury of the specimen.

Source: Excerpt from *Stone Art* by Gerard Fowke

3. The author's ideas could best be reinforced with illustrations of rocks
    a. in different stages of weathering.
    b. in the granite and porphyry classes.
    c. procured from the bottom of the ocean.
    d. that have been completely destroyed.
    e. commonly found in most areas of the United States.

4. Which of the following would be the best title for this passage?
    a. "The Names of Various Rocks"
    b. "Why Granite Is Called *Granite*"
    c. "The Classes of Rocks"
    d. "Why Rocks Must Be Destroyed"
    e. "The Difficulties of Identifying Rocks"

5. What is the best definition for the word *fresh* as it is used in line 2 of the passage?
    a. novel
    b. unmarked
    c. bright
    d. clean
    e. airy

Use the following passage to answer question 6.

The Pennsylvania Dutch are a hard working people and as they say, "Them that works hard, eats hearty." The blending of recipes from their many home lands and the ingredients available
5   in their new land produced tasty dishes that have been handed down from mother to daughter for generations.

Source: Excerpt from *Pennsylvania Dutch Cooking*

6. The author of this passage would most likely agree with which of the following statements?
    a. The Pennsylvania Dutch people work harder than any other group of people in America.
    b. One of the distinguishing characteristics of the Pennsylvania Dutch people is their excellent cuisine.
    c. The Pennsylvania Dutch people are known throughout the world for their colorful and amusing sayings.
    d. No group of people blends recipes as well as the Pennsylvania Dutch people do.
    e. If fathers and sons in Pennsylvania Dutch families made food, it would not be as good as the food mothers and daughters make.

Use the following passage pair to answer questions 7 through 10.

Passage 1
The variety of species among the jumping spiders appears almost infinite. The genus, or rather family of Epeira, is here characterized by many singular forms; some species have
5   pointed coriaceous shells, others enlarged and spiny tibiæ. Every path in the forest is barricaded with the strong yellow web of a species belonging to the same division with the Epeira clavipes of Fabricius, which was formerly said
10 by Sloane to make, in the West Indies, webs so strong as to catch birds. A small and pretty kind of spider, with very long forelegs, and which appears to belong to an undescribed genus, lives as a parasite on almost every one of these
15 webs. I suppose it is too insignificant to be noticed by the great Epeira, and is therefore allowed to prey on the minute insects, which, adhering to the lines, would otherwise be wasted. When frightened, this little spider
20 either feigns death by extending its front legs, or suddenly drops from the web.

Source: Excerpt from *Some Wonderful Spiders* by Charles Darwin

Passage 2
There are, among spiders, two forms of protective modification: the first, including all cases of protective resemblance to vegetable and inorganic things—that is, all modifications of color
5   or of color and form that tend to make them inconspicuous in their natural relations—I shall call direct protection. The second form, which I shall call indirect protection, includes two classes, the spiders which are specially pro-
10 tected themselves and those which mimic other creatures which are specially protected.

Spiders are specially protected when they become inedible through the acquisition of hard plates and sharp spines. The modification
15 of form is frequently accompanied by conspicuous colors, which warn their enemies that they belong to an unpalatable class.

Source: Excerpt from *Protective Resemblances in Spiders* by Elizabeth G. Pechham

7. Which of the following best describes the relationship between Passage 1 and Passage 2?
   a. Passage 1 makes an argument and Passage 2 contradicts it.
   b. Passage 1 introduces an idea and Passage 2 expands on it.
   c. Passage 1 introduces a difficult concept and Passage 2 explains it.
   d. Passage 1 states facts and Passage 2 states opinions.
   e. Passage 1 makes a claim and Passage 2 supports that claim.

8. With which of the following statements about the undescribed genus of spider that lives in the West Indies would the author of Passage 1 most likely agree?
   a. It deserves to be named.
   b. It is unimportant.
   c. It is uniquely attractive.
   d. It is an enemy of many animals.
   e. It is cowardly.

9. In what way is Passage 1 different from Passage 2?
a. Passage 1 describes the behaviors of several animals.
b. Passage 1 uses scientific research to support its conclusions.
c. Passage 1 is written from a first-person perspective.
d. Passage 1 includes personal opinions.
e. Passage 1 describes how spiders use their bodies to protect themselves.

10. The primary concern of Passage 2 is
a. establishing a definition of the term *protective modification*.
b. describing how the colors of their bodies help to protect spiders.
c. identifying why certain spiders have sharp spines on their bodies.
d. providing details about the Epeira clavipes of Fabricius.
e. explaining the two main ways spiders use their bodies to protect themselves.

Use the following passage to answer questions 11 and 12.

Frederick Douglass lived so long, and played so conspicuous a part on the world's stage, that it would be impossible, in a work of the size of this, to do more than touch upon the salient
5 features of his career, to suggest the respects in which he influenced the course of events in his lifetime, and to epitomize for the readers of another generation the judgment of his contemporaries as to his genius and his character.
10 Douglass's fame as an orator has long been secure. His position as the champion of an oppressed race, and at the same time an example of its possibilities, was, in his own generation, as picturesque as it was unique; and his

15 life may serve for all time as an incentive to aspiring souls who would fight the battles and win the love of mankind.

Source: *Frederick Douglass* by Charles Chestnutt

11. The passage suggests that Frederick Douglass
a. was most concerned with being loved by other people.
b. mostly influenced matters in his hometown.
c. had a uniquely engaging personality.
d. has been the topic of many long history books.
e. was mostly famous for being a great speaker.

12. In the passage, the word *salient* most nearly means
a. outstanding.
b. factual.
c. silent.
d. minor.
e. proven.

Use the following passage to answer questions 13 through 15.

The account of this second journey of the Polos may be read in the wonderful book which Marco afterwards wrote to describe the wonders of the world. They went from Lajazzo
5 through Turcomania, past Mount Ararat, where Marco heard tell that Noah's ark rested, and where he first heard also of the oil wells of Baku and the great inland sea of Caspian. Past Mosul and Bagdad they went, through Persia, where
10 brocades are woven and merchants bring caravan after caravan of treasures, to Hormuz, on the Persian Gulf, into which port put the ships from India, laden with spices, drugs, scented woods, and jewels, gold tissues and elephants'
15 teeth. Here they meant to take ship, but they desisted, perhaps because they feared to trust

themselves to the flimsy nailless vessels in which the Arabs braved the dangers of the Indian Ocean. So they turned north again and
20 prepared to make the journey by land. They traversed the salt desert of Kerman, through Balk and Khorassan to Badakhshan, where there are horses bred from Alexander the Great's steed Bucephalus, and ruby mines and
25 lapis lazuli. It is a land of beautiful mountains and wide plains, of trout streams and good hunting, and here the brothers sojourned for nearly a year, for young Marco had fallen ill in the hot plains: a breath of mountain air blows
30 through the page in which he describes how amid the clean winds his health came back to him.

Source: Excerpt from *A Short History of the World* by H.G. Wells

13. The passage suggests that Marco Polo was
   a. generally easy to convince of fantastical things.
   b. a man who possessed multiple extraordinary skills.
   c. a coward compared to Arabian sailors.
   d. homesick much of his life.
   e. often in poor health because of his exhausting lifestyle.

14. The passage is primarily concerned with
   a. the written work of Marco Polo.
   b. Marco Polo's experiences in Turcomania.
   c. the landscape of Badakhshan.
   d. the travels of Marco Polo.
   e. the people with whom Marco Polo traveled.

15. In line 1, the word *account* most nearly means
   a. report.
   b. balance.
   c. judgment.
   d. credit.
   e. reason.

Use the following passage pair to answer questions 16 through 18.

Passage 1
American independence, the beginnings of which we have just been considering, was accomplished after a long struggle. Many brave men fought on the battle-field, and many who
5 never shouldered a musket or drew a sword exerted a powerful influence for the good of the patriot cause. One of these men was Benjamin Franklin.
   He was born in Boston in 1706, the fif-
10 teenth child in a family of seventeen children. His father was a candle-maker and soap-boiler. Intending to make a clergyman of Benjamin, he sent him, at eight years of age, to a grammar-school, with the purpose of fitting him for col-
15 lege. The boy made rapid progress, but before the end of his first school-year his father took him out on account of the expense, and put him into a school where he would learn more practical subjects, such as writing and arithme-
20 tic. The last study proved very difficult for him.

Source: Excerpt from *American Leaders and Heroes: A Preliminary Text-Book in United States History* by Wilbur F. Gordy

Passage 2
At ten years old I was taken home to assist my father in his business, which was that of a tallow-chandler and sope-boiler; a business he was not bred to, but had assumed on his arrival
5 in New England, and on finding his dying trade would not maintain his family, being in little request. Accordingly, I was employed in cutting wick for the candles, filling the dipping mold and the molds for cast candles, attending the
10 shop, going of errands, etc.
   I disliked the trade, and had a strong incli-nation for the sea, but my father declared

against it; however, living near the water, I was much in and about it, learnt early to swim well,

15 and to manage boats; and when in a boat or canoe with other boys, I was commonly allowed to govern, especially in any case of difficulty; and upon other occasions I was generally a leader among the boys, and sometimes led

20 them into scrapes, of which I will mention one instance, as it shows an early projecting public spirit, tho' not then justly conducted.

Source: Excerpt from *Benjamin Franklin: His Autobiography* by Benjamin Franklin

16. Based on the information in Passage 2, one can conclude that Benjamin Franklin
   a. wished he could follow in his father's footsteps.
   b. never learned how to make candles.
   c. tended to communicate informally.
   d. preferred making candles to boiling soap.
   e. was not well liked by the other boys.

17. Which of the following is a difference between Passage 1 and Passage 2?
   a. Passage 1 is more humorous than Passage 2.
   b. Passage 1 tells the story of one person's life.
   c. Passage 1 is about the life of an important American.
   d. Passage 1 is more specific than Passage 2.
   e. Passage 1 focuses more on a particular period of time.

18. Which of the following best describes the relationship between Passage 1 and Passage 2?
   a. Passage 1 discusses a topic objectively and Passage 2 discusses it personally.
   b. Passage 1 presents a question and Passage 2 answers it.
   c. Passage 1 describes a method and Passage 2 shows how it is put to use.
   d. Passage 1 presents information that contradicts Passage 2.
   e. Passage 1 describes a specific aspect of Passage 2.

Use the following passage to answer questions 19 through 21.

The steamboat was, if anything, a little ahead of the steam engine in its earlier phases. There was a steamboat, the *Charlotte Dundas*, on the Firth of Clyde Canal in 1802, and in 1807 an Ameri-

5 can named Fulton had a steamer, the *Clermont*, with British-built engines, upon the Hudson River above New York. The first steamship to put to sea was also an American, the *Phœnix*, which went from New York (Hoboken) to Phil-

10 adelphia. So, too, was the first ship using steam (she also had sails) to cross the Atlantic, the *Savannah* (1819). All these were paddle-wheel boats and paddle-wheel boats are not adapted to work in heavy seas. The paddles smash too

15 easily, and the boat is then disabled. The screw steamship followed rather slowly. Many difficulties had to be surmounted before the screw was a practicable thing.

Source: Excerpt from *The Frontier in American History* by Frederick Jackson Turner

A TIMELINE OF EARLY STEAMSHIP HISTORY	
1807	The steamboat emerges as a practical form of travel.
1811	The first steamboat travels the Mississippi River.
1818	First steamboat service on the Mediterranean Sea
1819	The first steamboat crosses the Atlantic Ocean.
1838	First transatlantic steamboat service
1851	John Elder patents compound steam engine.

19. The main purpose of this passage is to
   a. compare the steamboat to the steam engine.
   b. provide information about the early history of the steamboat.
   c. explain why Fulton was an important American.
   d. provide a list of important dates in steamboat history.
   e. describe the flaws in the paddle-wheel boats.

20. Based on information in the passage and the timeline, which of the following is most likely true?
   a. The *Charlotte Dundas* was the first steamboat to travel on the Mississippi River.
   b. The *Phœnix* was the first steamboat to cross the Atlantic Ocean in 1819.
   c. The *Savannah* was the first steamboat service on the Mediterranean Sea.
   d. The screw steamship was identical to the compound steam engine.
   e. The *Clermont* helped demonstrate that the steamboat was a practical form of travel.

21. Which of the following could be a factor in the difference between the steamships described in this passage and the steamships developed after them?
   a. The steamships developed after them could not cross oceans.
   b. The steamships developed after them were the first to use British-built engines.
   c. The steamships developed after them were made in America.
   d. The steamships developed after them probably did not have paddles.
   e. The steamships developed after them were paddle-wheel boats.

Use the following passage to answer questions 22 and 23.

The most ancient materials used for recording events were bricks, tiles, shells, and tables of stone. The modes of writing on these different substances were various. The tiles and brick
5 were impressed with a stamp when in a soft state; the shells and tablets of stone were etched or graven, the figures or characters being cut in their surface, and in some cases also stained with various colors. It was by the ancient art of
10 stamping that the walls, palaces, and towers of Babylon were covered with hieroglyphics, which have but recently been brought to light from under the immense mounds of Mesopotamia by Layard and other explorers.

Source: Excerpt from *Gutenberg, and the Art of Printing* by Emily Clemens Pearson

22. The last sentence in the passage provides
  a. an interesting yet incidental detail not directly related to the rest of the passage.
  b. details that contrast information already provided in the passage.
  c. a description of how a process briefly introduced earlier in the passage was performed.
  d. a personal account of information described objectively earlier in the passage.
  e. an example of how techniques described in the passage were used.

23. The passage suggests that after impressing a stamp on a brick, the brick
  a. was dyed red.
  b. lost its original shape.
  c. was covered in hieroglyphics.
  d. would harden.
  e. was graven.

Use the following passage to answer questions 24 and 25.

A history of architecture is a record of man's efforts to build beautifully. The erection of structures devoid of beauty is mere building, a trade and not an art. Edifices in which
5 strength and stability alone are sought, and in designing which only utilitarian considerations have been followed, are properly works of engineering. Only when the idea of beauty is added to that of use does a structure take its place
10 among works of architecture. We may, then, define architecture as the art which seeks to harmonize in a building the requirements of utility and of beauty. It is the most useful of the fine arts and the noblest of the useful arts.

Source: Excerpt from *A Text-Book of the History of Architecture* by A.D.F. Hamlin

24. The final sentence of the passage makes which of the following errors in logic?
  a. incomplete comparison
  b. faulty generalization
  c. circular reasoning
  d. fallacy of composition
  e. moral equivalence

25. In the passage, the author refers to works of engineering in order to
  a. use them as examples of architecture.
  b. describe the designs common in architecture.
  c. illustrate the different uses of architecture.
  d. contrast them with architecture.
  e. provide a definition of the term *architecture*.

Use the following passage to answer question 26.

A man can live for three days without bread, but no man can live for one day without poetry, was an aphorism of Baudelaire. You can live without pictures and music but you cannot live
5 without eating, says the author of *Dinners and Dishes*; and this latter view is, no doubt, the more popular.

Source: Excerpt from "Review of *Dinners and Dishes*" by Oscar Wilde

26. Based only on the information in the passage, which of the following is a valid conclusion?
  a. Most people would not agree with Baudelaire's aphorism quoted in the passage.
  b. *Dinners and Dishes* is a more poetic piece of writing than Baudelaire ever created.
  c. The author of the passage thinks that poetry is more important than pictures and music.
  d. *Dinners and Dishes* is more concerned with pictures and music than eating.
  e. The author of the passage believes that there is nothing poetic about pictures and music.

Use the following passage to answer questions 27 through 29.

Wood exhibits its greatest strength in tension parallel to the grain, and it is very uncommon in practice for a specimen to be pulled in two lengthwise. This is due to the difficulty of mak-
5 ing the end fastenings secure enough for the full tensile strength to be brought into play before the fastenings shear off longitudinally. This is not the case with metals, and as a result they are used in almost all places where tensile
10 strength is particularly needed, even though the remainder of the structure, such as sills, beams, joists, posts, and flooring, may be of wood. Thus in a wooden truss bridge the tension members are steel rods.
15   The tensile strength of wood parallel to the grain depends upon the strength of the fibres and is affected not only by the nature and dimensions of the wood elements but also by their arrangement. It is greatest in straight-
20 grained specimens with thick-walled fibres. Cross grain of any kind materially reduces the tensile strength of wood, since the tensile strength at right angles to the grain is only a small fraction of that parallel to the grain.

Source: Excerpt from *The Mechanical Properties of Wood* by Samuel J. Record

RATIO OF STRENGTH OF WOOD IN TENSION AND IN COMPRESSION
(BUL. 10, U.S. DIV. OF FORESTRY, p. 44)

Kind of Wood	Ratio: $R = \dfrac{\text{Tensile strength}}{\text{Compressive strength}}$	A stick 1 square inch in cross section. Weight required to—	
		Pull apart	Crush endwise
Hickory	3.7	32,000	8,500
Elm	3.8	29,000	7,500
Larch	2.3	19,400	8,600
Longleaf Pine	2.2	17,300	7,400

NOTE.—Moisture condition not given.

27. According to the passage, all of the following probably lacked considerable tensile strength EXCEPT
   a. sills.
   b. beams.
   c. rods in a truss bridge.
   d. joists.
   e. flooring.

28. Based on information in the passage and the table, which of the following woods is most likely to have cross grain?
   a. hickory
   b. elm
   c. larch
   d. balsa
   e. longleaf pine

29. Based on information in the passage and the table, which of the following is a factor that may affect the tensile strength of wood that is not indicated in the passage?
   a. grain direction
   b. fiber strength
   c. nature of the wood elements
   d. moisture condition
   e. dimensions of the wood elements

Use the following passage to answer question 30.

The humorous story is strictly a work of art—high and delicate art—and only an artist can tell it; but no art is necessary in telling the comic and the witty story; anybody can do it.
5   The art of telling a humorous story—understand, I mean by word of mouth, not print—was created in America, and has remained at home.

Source: Excerpt from "How to Tell a Story" by Mark Twain

30. Which statement, if it were true, most significantly weakens the argument in the passage?
   a. Native American storytellers had been telling humorous stories for hundreds of years.
   b. The plays of Aristophanes are among the earliest examples of humorous stories in writing.
   c. Mark Twain is widely regarded as one of the wittiest writers in American literature.
   d. The word *art* is most commonly applied to visual arts such as painting, sculpture, and drawing.
   e. It is important to understand certain rules before attempting to tell a comic story.

Use the following passage to answer questions 31 through 33.

Whenever we hear the name of Napoleon mentioned, or see it printed in a book, it is usually in connection with a hard-fought victory on the battlefield. He certainly spent most of his
5   life in the camp, and enjoyed the society of soldiers more than that of courtiers. The thunder of guns, the charge of cavalry, and the flash of bayonets as they glittered in the sun, appealed to him with much the same force as music to
10   more ordinary folk. . . .

We are apt to forget that this mighty conqueror, whom Carlyle calls "our last great man," had a childhood at all. He was born nearly a century and a half ago, on the 15th August 1769
15   to be exact, in the little town of Ajaccio, the capital of picturesque Corsica.

Source: Excerpt from *The Story of Napoleon* by Harold F.B. Wheeler

31. As it is used in the context of the sentence, which word best describes the meaning of *force* (line 9)?
   a. compel
   b. intensity
   c. shove
   d. pry
   e. weight

32. Which conclusion can be reached from the passage?
  a. The childhoods of people with intimidating reputations are often ignored.
  b. Nobody had ever considered Napoleon's childhood before this passage was written.
  c. Nothing is known about Napoleon's childhood at all.
  d. All details about Napoleon's childhood are based on speculation rather than concrete fact.
  e. Great conquerors never have noteworthy childhoods.

33. According to the passage, which of the following did Napoleon most likely prefer?
  a. leading soldiers on the battlefield
  b. listening to music
  c. plotting a battle
  d. camping on a battlefield
  e. visiting Corsica

Use the following passage to answer questions 34 through 38.

The color of animals is by no means a matter of chance; it depends on many considerations, but in the majority of cases tends to protect the animal from danger by rendering it less conspicu-
5 ous. Perhaps it may be said that if coloring is mainly protective, there ought to be but few brightly colored animals. There are, however, not a few cases in which vivid colors are themselves protective. The kingfisher itself, though
10 so brightly colored, is by no means easy to see. The blue harmonizes with the water, and the bird as it darts along the stream looks almost like a flash of sunlight; besides which, protection is not the only consideration. Let us now
15 consider the prevalent colors of animals and see how far they support the rule.

Desert animals are generally the color of the desert. Thus, for instance, the lion, the antelope, and the wild ass are all sand-colored.
20 "Indeed," says Canon Tristram, "in the desert, where neither trees, brushwood, nor even undulation of the surface afford the slightest protection to its foes, a modification of color which shall be assimilated to that of the sur-
25 rounding country is absolutely necessary. Hence, without exception, the upper plumage of every bird, whether lark, chat, sylvain, or sand grouse, and also the fur of all the smaller mammals and the skin of all the snakes and
30 lizards, is of one uniform sand color."

Source: Excerpt from "The Colors of Animals" by Sir John Lubbock

34. The author's use of the word *harmonizes* in line 11 emphasizes
  a. the sweet sound of the kingfisher's song.
  b. the musical sound of flowing water.
  c. the appealing glimmer of sunlight.
  d. how the kingfisher blends with its environment.
  e. how the sounds of a bird and water blend.

35. Which of the following alternate titles would be the most appropriate for this passage?
  a. "Colors of the Desert"
  b. "Camouflage in the Wild"
  c. "The Plumage of Birds"
  d. "Why Kingfishers Are Blue"
  e. "The Vivid Colors of Animals"

36. In the first sentence, *conspicuous* most closely means
  a. hidden.
  b. conspiratorial.
  c. obvious.
  d. conscious.
  e. attractive.

37. The author includes the quotation from Canon Tristram in order to
   a. show that authorities agree with the author's opinions.
   b. illustrate an idea that the author could not have explained himself.
   c. support an argument that is not very popular.
   d. prove that birds are unique creatures.
   e. develop upon an idea the author had already introduced.

38. Based on the information in the passage, desert animals might not need to be the color of sand if the desert
   a. did not have so many trees.
   b. had more colorful sand.
   c. was cooler.
   d. experienced more surface changes.
   e. had fewer animals.

Use the following passage to answer questions 39 and 40.

Although very much yet remains to be learned about this old earth, it is a remarkable fact that man, through the exercise of his highest faculty, has come to know so much concerning it.
5   The following words, by the late Professor Barrell, admirably summarize the significance of geological history. "The great lesson taught by the study of the outer crust is that the earth mother, like her children, has attained her
10 present form through ceaseless change, which marks the pulse of life and which shall cease only when her internal forces slumber and the cloudy air and surf-bound ocean no more are moving garments. The flowing landscapes of
15 geologic time may be likened to a kinetoscopic panorama. The scenes transform from age to

age, as from act to act; seas and plains and mountains of different types follow and replace each other through time, as the traveler sees
20 them succeed each other in space."

Source: Excerpt from *Geology: The Science of the Earth's Crust* by William J. Miller

39. As used in the passage, the word *space* most nearly means
   a. portion of area.
   b. atmosphere beyond Earth.
   c. room.
   d. surface.
   e. depth.

40. Which of the following best describes the point of view of the passage?
   a. first person
   b. second person
   c. third person
   d. fourth person
   e. fifth person

Use the following passage to answer questions 41 and 42.

Science is knowledge; it is what we know. But mere knowledge is not science. For a bit of knowledge to become a part of science, its relation to other bits of knowledge must be found.
5   In botany, for example, bits of knowledge about plants do not make a science of botany. To have a science of botany, we must not only know about leaves, roots, flowers, seeds, etc., but we must know the relations of these parts and of
10 all the parts of a plant to one another. In other words, in science, we must not only *know*, we must not only have *knowledge*, but we must

know the significance of the knowledge, must know its *meaning*. This is only another way of

15 saying that we must have knowledge and know its relation to other knowledge.

Source: Excerpt from *The Science of Human Nature* by William Henry Pyle

41. The author of this passage would most likely agree with which of the following statements?
 a. A real botanist focuses more attention on leaves than roots.
 b. A biologist cannot understand how the heart works without knowing how the hand works.
 c. Plants actually are not the main concern of the science of botany.
 d. True scientists are not interested in acquiring knowledge.
 e. Anyone who only studies only Earth's crust is not a real Earth scientist.

42. The passage is primarily concerned with
 a. defining the term *knowledge*.
 b. explaining how scientists must use knowledge.
 c. emphasizing the importance of the whole over the part.
 d. proving that most people who call themselves scientists are frauds.
 e. showing how one becomes a scientist.

Use the following passage to answer questions 43 and 44.

At the end of the nineteenth century the two masters of the stage were Ibsen and Wagner, and both of them were in the show business—Wagner more openly and more frequently than

5 Ibsen. Yet the stern Scandinavian did not disdain to employ an avalanche in *When We Dead Awaken*, and to introduce a highly pictorial

shawl dance for the heroine of his *Doll's House*. As for Wagner, he was incessant in his search

10 for the spectacular, insisting that the music-drama was the "art-work of the future," since the librettist-composer could call to his aid all the other arts, and could make these arts contribute to the total effect of the opera. He con-

15 formed his practise to his principles, and as a result there is scarcely any one of his music-dramas which is not enriched by a most elaborate scenic accompaniment. The forging of the sword, the ride of the Valkyries, the swimming

20 of the singing Rhinemaidens, are only a few of the novel and startling effects which he introduced into his operas; and in his last work, *Parsival*, the purely spectacular element is at least as ample and as varied as any that can be found

25 in a Parisian fairy-play or in a London Christmas pantomime.

Source: Excerpt from *A Book about the Theater* by Brander Matthews

43. Which sentence best summarizes the main point of the passage?
 a. Ibsen and Wagner may be considered great theater artists, but they were really nothing more than showmen.
 b. The most spectacular moment of Ibsen's play *When We Dead Awaken* involves an on-stage avalanche.
 c. Wagner considered music-drama to be the *art-work of the future* because it incorporated numerous other art forms.
 d. Every great theater artist knows that no one would enjoy their plays without spectacular stage effects.
 e. Ibsen and Wagner were both great theater artists but they also understood the value of putting on a spectacular show.

44. Which sentence from the passage represents an opinion rather than a fact?
   a. "At the end . . . Ibsen."
   b. "Yet the . . . *House.*"
   c. "As for Wagner . . . opera."
   d. "He conformed . . . accompaniment."
   e. "The forging . . . pantomime."

Use the following passage to answer questions 45 through 49.

Wendel Bollman's name survives today solely in association with the Bollman truss, and even in this respect is known only to a few older civil and railroad engineers. The Bollman system of
5   trussing, along with those of Whipple and Fink, may be said to have introduced the great age of the metal bridge, and thus, directly, the modern period of civil engineering.

Bollman's bridge truss, of which the first
10   example was built in 1850, has the very significant distinction of being the first bridging system in the world employing iron in all of its principal structural members that was used consistently on a railroad.

15   The importance of the transition from wood to iron as a structural and bridge building material is generally recognized, but it may be well to mention certain aspects of this change.

20   The tradition of masonry bridge construction never attained the great strength in this country which it held in Europe, despite a number of notable exceptions. There were several reasons for this. From the very beginning
25   of colonization, capital was scarce, a condition that prevailed until well into the 19th century and which prohibited the use of masonry because of the extremely high costs of labor and transport. An even more important eco-

30   nomic consideration was the rapidity with which it was necessary to extend the construction of railways during their pioneer years. Unlike the early English and European railways, which invariably traversed areas of dense popu-
35   lation and industrial activity, and were thus assured of a significant financial return almost from the moment that the first rail was down, the Baltimore and Ohio and its contemporaries were launched upon an entirely different com-
40   mercial prospect.

Source: Excerpt from *The Engineering Contributions of Wendel Bollman* by Robert M. Vogel

45. What will the writer of this passage most likely explain next?
   a. The commercial prospect upon which the Baltimore and Ohio railways were launched.
   b. The thing with which Wendel Bollman's name is most closely associated today.
   c. When capital for railway building in America ceased to be scarce.
   d. The kinds of areas that the early English and European railways traversed.
   e. Who the most famous engineers on the Baltimore and Ohio railways were.

46. What is the country to which the author refers in the first sentence of the fourth paragraph?
   a. England
   b. France
   c. Germany
   d. Mexico
   e. the United States

47. The passage indicates that railway bridges changed from
  a. a wood-based system to an iron-based system.
  b. a European system to an international system.
  c. being dominated by Whipple and Fink to being dominated by Bollman.
  d. being used to mainly transport materials to being used to mainly transport people.
  e. a system that uses bridges to a system that uses trusses.

48. The author compares the early English and European railways to
  a. the California and New York railways.
  b. Bollman's bridge truss.
  c. the Baltimore and Ohio railways.
  d. more recent English and European railways.
  e. the railway innovations of Whipple and Fink.

49. Information in this passage can be applied to
  a. a biography of Whipple and Fink.
  b. an advertisement for the Ohio railway system.
  c. a history of developments in railway systems.
  d. a railway engineering manual.
  e. an essay on the European railway system.

Use the following passage to answer questions 50 through 53.

Gettysburg is the market town—or borough, accurately speaking—of an exclusively farming population, planted in one of the most productive sections of the Keystone State. It is the seat
5 of justice of the county. It has a seminary and college of the German Lutheran Church, which give a certain tone and cast to its social life. In
short, Gettysburg seems in all things so entirely devoted to the pursuits of peace, there is so lit-
10 tle that is suggestive of war and bloodshed, even if time had not mostly effaced all traces of that gigantic struggle that, coming as we do with one absorbing idea in mind, we find it hard to reconcile the facts of history with the facts as
15 we find them.

There is another side to Gettysburg—a picturesque, a captivating side. One looks around upon the landscape with simple admiration. One's highest praise comes from the
20 feeling of quiet satisfaction with which the harmony of nature reveals the harmony of God. You are among the subsiding swells that the South Mountain has sent rippling off to the east. So completely is the village hid away
25 among these green swells that neither spire nor steeple is seen until, upon turning one of the numerous low ridges by which the face of the country is so cut up, you enter a valley, not deep, but well defined by two opposite ranges
30 of heights, and Gettysburg lies gleaming in the declining sun before you—a picture to be long remembered.

Source: Excerpt from *The Battle of Gettysburg 1863* by Samuel Adams Drake

50. According to the passage, Gettysburg is best described as a
  a. market town.
  b. farm.
  c. county.
  d. city.
  e. borough.

51. Which sentence from the passage contains both a fact and an opinion?
   a. It is the seat of justice of the county.
   b. In short, Gettysburg seems in all things so entirely devoted to the pursuits of peace, there is so little that is suggestive of war and bloodshed, even if time had not mostly effaced all traces of that gigantic struggle that, coming as we do with one absorbing idea in mind, we find it hard to reconcile the facts of history with the facts as we find them.
   c. There is another side to Gettysburg—a picturesque, a captivating side.
   d. One's highest praise comes from the feeling of quiet satisfaction with which the harmony of nature reveals the harmony of God.
   e. So completely is the village hid away among these green swells that neither spire nor steeple is seen until, upon turning one of the numerous low ridges by which the face of the country is so cut up, you enter a valley, not deep, but well defined by two opposite ranges of heights, and Gettysburg lies gleaming in the declining sun before you—a picture to be long remembered.

52. As it is used in the context of the sentence, which word best describes the meaning of *cast* (line 7)?
   a. distance
   b. players
   c. throw
   d. company
   e. radiate

53. What was the author's primary purpose in describing Gettysburg?
   a. to encourage people to visit Gettysburg
   b. to prove that people actually know very little about Gettysburg
   c. to establish the setting in a discussion of a battle that took place there
   d. to show that people in Gettysburg are very religious
   e. to imply that Gettysburg was a completely unnatural place for a battle

Use the following passage to answer questions 54 through 56.

Animals below the level of zoophytes and sponges are called Protozoa. The word obviously means "First Animals," but all that we can say is that the very simplest of them may give us
5 some hint of the simplicity of the original first animals. For it is quite certain that the vast majority of the Protozoa today are far too complicated to be thought of as primitive. Though most of them are microscopic, each is an ani-
10 mal complete in itself, with the same fundamental bodily attributes as are manifested in ourselves. They differ from animals of higher degree in not being built up of the unit areas or corpuscles called cells. They have no cells, no
15 tissues, no organs, in the ordinary acceptation of these words, but many of them show a great complexity of internal structure, far exceeding that of the ordinary cells that build up the tissues of higher animals. They are complete liv-
20 ing creatures which have not gone in for body-making.

Source: Excerpt from *The Outline of Science, Vol. 1* by J. Arthur Thomson

54. The passage deals mainly with which of the following characteristics of modern protozoa?
  a. their primitive nature
  b. their relative complexity
  c. their similarity to humans
  d. their role as the first animals
  e. their microscopic size

55. Which sentence from the passage best supports the author's argument that protozoa are "complete living creatures"?
  a. "Animals below the level of zoophytes and sponges are called Protozoa."
  b. "The word obviously means 'First Animals,' but all that we can say is that the very simplest of them may give us some hint of the simplicity of the original first animals."
  c. "For it is quite certain that the vast majority of the Protozoa today are far too complicated to be thought of as primitive."
  d. "They differ from animals of higher degree in not being built up of the unit areas or corpuscles called cells."
  e. "They have no cells, no tissues, no organs, in the ordinary acceptation of these words, but many of them show a great complexity of internal structure, far exceeding that of the ordinary cells that build up the tissues of higher animals."

56. Which inference about the complexity of living creatures can be made from the information provided within the passage?
  a. Large living things are more complex than smaller ones.
  b. A living thing must have cells, tissues, and organs to be complex.
  c. The size of a living creature has little bearing on its complexity.
  d. No animal without a traditional body can be called complex.
  e. Tiny living creatures tend to be more complex than larger ones.

Praxis® Core Academic Skills for Educators: Reading Practice Test 1 Answers and Explanations

1. d. Only choice **d** sums up all the most important details in the passage. Choice **a** only summarizes the passage's opening sentences. Choice **b** makes a statement about the individual brothers' popularity that the passage does not actually support. Choices **c** and **e** are just details in the passage and fail to summarize all of its most important details.

2. d. Since the author had described the kind of automobile Frank Duryea drove in the race, the author likely mentions the types of cars Duryea beat to suggest that it was their innate qualities that caused them to lose the race. The author is not likely making a general statement about the automobiles built in Springfield, Massachusetts (choice **a**) or the rest of the world (choice **c**). There is also no evidence to support the prediction in choice **b**, and there are not enough details about the mechanical properties of two-cylinder and electric vehicles to support the conclusion in choice **e**.

3. a. The author spends much of the passage explaining how difficult it is to identify rocks that have been weathered. This point would be stronger if the reader could actually see how significantly weathering alters the appearance of rocks. The author only mentions the granite and porphyry classes as examples of rocks that might be misclassified, so illustrations of them would not reinforce the author's ideas very much. Therefore, choice **b** is not the best answer. There is no mention of rocks that have been procured from the bottom of the ocean, so choice **c** does not make much sense. There is no discussion of rocks commonly found in the United States, so choice **e** is not a very strong answer either. Although the author mentions that destroying rocks may help them to be identified, this is not as important an idea in the passage as is the weathering of rocks, so choice **a** remains a better answer choice than choice **d**.

4. e. A strong title should reflect a selection's main idea, and this selection is mainly about the difficulties of identifying rocks. Choice **a** is not as specific to this particular topic as choice **e**, so it is not the best answer. The passage never indicates why a certain rock is called *granite*, so choice **b** is not a good title. Choice **c** makes the mistake of assuming the selection is mainly about rock classes when it is actually about rock names. Choice **d** just reflects a minor detail in the selection, but the best answer choice should reflect the entire main idea.

5. b. Although each answer choice can be used as a synonym for *fresh*, only choice **b** makes sense in this particular context. Choice **a** would be appropriate only if the rock was new and unusual. Choices **c** and **d** refer to the surface appearance of the rock when the sentence refers to its physical state beyond the surface. Choice **e** is not a meaning of *fresh* one would use to describe a rock in any context.

6. b. This short passage is about the distinctive food Pennsylvania Dutch people make and the qualities that make that food distinctive, so choice **b** is the statement with which the author is most likely to agree. Although the author refers to the fact that Pennsylvania Dutch people work hard, the author does not compare their work ethic to the work ethic of any other people, so choice **a** is not the best answer. The author never indicates how well known the Pennsylvania Dutch people are throughout the world, so choice **c** is not a strong answer either. Choice **d** makes another unsupported comparison, and choice **e** makes an unsupported assumption based on the fact that the author mentions only the cooking of Pennsylvania Dutch mothers and daughters.

7. b. Passage 1 introduces ways spider survive and Passage 2 expands on it by describing ways spiders protect themselves. Neither passage makes an argument (choice **a**); both accept the idea that spiders have unique ways of protecting themselves. Passage 2 does not explain anything about spiders that has not already been described in Passage 1, so choice **c** is incorrect. Both passages focus on facts without indulging in opinions, so choice **d** does not make sense. Passage 1 does not make a general claim about spiders that it does not support, so choice **e** is not the best answer choice.

8. c. The author of Passage 1 describes the spider as *pretty*, and since its appearance is a significant enough trait of the spider to mention, it is likely that the author would agree that the spider is uniquely attractive. While the author acknowledges that the spider is *undescribed*, there is no evidence to support the idea that the author believes the spider deserves to be named, so choice **a** is not the best answer. There also isn't any evidence to support the idea that the spider is generally unimportant (choice **b**); if this were true, the author probably would not discuss it in this passage at all. The author only says the spider is a parasite, not an enemy of other animals, so choice **d** is not a strong answer. And though the spider sometimes gets frightened and pretends it is dead, this is more of a survival technique than an indication that the spider is cowardly (choice **e**).

9. d. Only Passage 1 includes the author's personal opinions, as the author describes one spider as *pretty*, which is an opinion not everyone might share. Both passages describe behaviors of several kinds of spiders (choice **a**), and there is no reason to believe that the information in Passage 2 is not based on scientific research (choice **b**). Both passages use the first-person pronoun *I*, so choice **c** is incorrect. Both passages also discuss ways that spiders use their bodies to protect themselves, so choice **e** is wrong.

10. e. Passage 2 is mainly concerned with explaining two ways spiders use their bodies to protect themselves: their protective resemblance to vegetable and inorganic things in the first paragraph and their inedible bodies in the second paragraph. The passage never actually defines the term *protective modification*, so choice **a** cannot be true. Choices **b** and **c** are just supporting details in the passage. Choice **d** refers to Passage 1, not Passage 2, which does not mention the Epeira clavipes of Fabricius at all.

11. c. The details about how Douglass was famous for speaking and conveyed his information in a uniquely *picturesque* way is reason to infer that he had a uniquely engaging personality. While the author of this passage suggests that Douglass was loved by his fellow people, there is no evidence to support the inference that this was his main concern (choice **a**). The fact that Douglass played a *part on the world's stage* contradicts the inference in choice **b**. Choice **d** may be true, but there simply is not evidence to support this conclusion in this particular passage. While it is true that his speeches were among the things for which Douglass was famous, choice **e** makes a general assumption that details in the passage do not support strongly.

12. a. The word *salient* means outstanding. While *factual* (choice **b**) would make some sense if used in place of *salient* in the passage, it does not share a meaning with *salient*, so it is not the correct answer choice. Choice **e** can be eliminated because it basically has the same meaning as *factual*. Choice **c** is a word that sounds similar to *salient* but does not share its meaning. Choice **d** is the opposite of *salient*.

13. b. The passage references both Marco Polo's noteworthy explorations, which indicate that he was an extraordinary explorer, and the fact that he also wrote a *wonderful* book about his travels, which suggests that he also possessed extraordinary skills as a writer. So choice **b** is the best answer. Although Polo made a journey based on a rumor regarding the location of Noah's ark, that is not enough evidence to make the general inference in choice **a**. Although the passage also indicates that Polo was afraid to use the same kind of sailing vessels certain Arab sailors used, choice **c** is also an extreme inference to make based on this evidence. He may have only been more cautious than those Arab sailors. While Marco apparently spent a good deal of his life away from home, the passage presents no evidence to infer that he was necessarily homesick much of the time (choice **d**). Choice **e** also makes an extreme inference based on just one slight detail about how Marco once fell ill.

14. d. This passage primarily describes the travels of Marco Polo in a general way. Polo's written work is only briefly mentioned in the first sentence of the passage, so it could hardly be the passage's primary concern (choice **a**). Choices **b** and **c** refer to places to which Polo traveled in this passage, but neither place is significant enough to the overall passage to describe its primary concern accurately. Marco Polo is definitely the most important person in the passage, so choice **e** does not make much sense.

15. a. As it is used in this particular passage, *account* is used to mean a report, which is the only answer choice that would make sense if used in place of *account* in the passage. Choices **b** and **d** would make sense only if *account* had financial implications, such as a bank account. Choices **c** and **e** could also be used as synonyms of *account* in other contexts, but they make no sense in this particular one.

16. c. Franklin's misspelling of the word *soap* and his abbreviation of the word *though* as *tho'* are evidence for the conclusion in choice **c**. Franklin's father was in the candle and soap making business, and Franklin's dislike of working in that business contradicts the conclusion in choice **a**. The fact that Franklin did work in that business for a time also contradicts the conclusion in choice **b**, while choice **d** reaches a conclusion that information in the passage simply does not support. Although Franklin says he sometimes led other boys into *scrapes*, that is not enough evidence to support the too-general conclusion in choice **e**.

17. d. While Passage 1 moves through the early events of Benjamin Franklin's life rapidly, Passage 2 slows down to focus more on the specific details of a particular period, which supports choice **d** and contradicts choice **e**. Passage 1 is strictly informative and not at all humorous, so choice **a** is not the best answer. Both passages tell the story of only one person's life, so choice **b** does not make much sense. That person is an important American, so choice **c** does not make sense either.

18. a. While Passage 1 tells the story of Benjamin Franklin's early life from an outsider's perspective, Passage 2 finds Benjamin Franklin telling the story of his own life. Passage 1 does not introduce a question that only Passage 2 answers (choice **b**) or describe any kind of method (choice **c**). The passages support each other, so choice **d** is not accurate. The opposite of choice **e** is true.

19. b. This passage mainly just provides information about the early history of the steamboat. Only the first sentence of the passage compares the steamboat to the steam engine, so choice **a** does not capture the purpose of the passage as a whole. Fulton is only briefly mentioned in the passage, so explaining his importance (choice **c**) is not likely the purpose of the entire passage. Choice **d** explains the purpose of the timeline that follows the passage, not the passage itself. Choice **e** only describes a single detail in the passage, not the purpose of the passage as a whole.

20. e. According to the passage, the *Clermont* was a significant steamship that sailed the Hudson River near New York the same year that, according to the timeline, the steamboat emerged as a practical form of travel. Based on this information, choice **e** is a logical conclusion. According to the passage, the *Charlotte Dundas* was a steamboat on the Firth of Clyde Canal, not on the Mississippi, so choice **a** is not correct. According to the passage, the *Savannah* was the first steamship to cross the Atlantic Ocean, so choice **b** cannot be correct. The fact that the *Savannah* was an American ship also makes choice **c** unlikely. There is no evidence in the passage or timeline to support choice **d**.

21. d. According to the passage, their easily smashed paddles were major flaws in the steamboats described in this passage, so it is likely that later steamboats eliminated this flaw. This likelihood also eliminates choice **a** and choice **e**, since the easily smashed paddles were what made it difficult for steamboats to cross oceans. Choice **b** cannot be correct because the passage explains that the *Clermont* was the first steamboat with British-built engines. Some of the steamships the passage describes were made in America, so this would not be a difference and choice **c** cannot be correct.

22. e. The final sentence of the passage is the passage's only example of how a specific culture used recording techniques. It is directly related to the passage's main idea, so choice **a** is incorrect. It does not contrast the rest of the passage; it supports the passage, so choice **b** is incorrect too. The final sentence does not really describe how a process was performed, so choice **c** is not the best answer. Choice **d** is incorrect because the final sentence of the passage is not written from a personal point of view.

23. d. The passage states that brick had to be impressed with a stamp *when in a soft state*, so it is logical to conclude that the brick would then harden since brick is hard. Brick is often red, but the passage only describes the coloring of shells and tablets, so choice **a** is not the most logical answer. Choice **e** also refers to shells and tablets, not bricks. There is no evidence to support the conclusion in choice **b** either. Since the passage is not clear about what material was used to build the walls, palaces, and towers of Babylon, choice **c** is not the best answer.

24. b. A faulty generalization builds a conclusion on weak evidence, and there simply is not strong enough evidence in the passage to reach such a general conclusion as the idea that architecture is *the noblest of the useful arts* since the writer does not really explain what is particularly noble about architecture. Choices **b**, **c**, **d**, and **e** are not logical errors present in the final sentence of the passage.

25. d. The author refers to mere utilitarian works of engineering to contrast the more artful constructions the author believes qualify as architecture. Since these works of engineering are distinct from architecture, choices **a**, **b**, **c**, and **e** cannot be correct because they all imply that mere works of engineering are examples of architecture in the author's opinion.

26. a. The author of the passage suggests that the most popular opinion is that eating is more important than such artful or poetic things as pictures and music, so choice **a** is the best conclusion. There is no evidence in the passage to support the conclusion in choices **b** or **c**. A book called *Dinners and Dishes* is likely more concerned with eating than pictures and music, and there is not enough evidence to support choice **d** in any event. Based on evidence in the passage, the author likely believes the opposite of choice **e**.

27. c. According to the passage, metal is higher in tensile strength than wood, and the rods in a truss bridge are identified as structural elements that must be made of metal. The author states that sills (choice **a**), beams (choice **b**), joists (choice **d**), and flooring (choice **e**) may all be made of wood.

28. e. According to the passage, *Cross grain of any kind materially reduces the tensile strength of wood*, so it is likely that the wood in the chart with the lowest tensile strength is the likeliest to have cross grain. Since longleaf pine has the lowest tensile strength, choice **e** is the likeliest answer. Hickory (choice **a**), elm (choice **b**), and larch (choice **c**) all have higher tensile strength than longleaf pine according to the table. Balsa (choice **d**) is not mentioned in the passage or the chart.

29. d. The table indicates that *moisture condition* is not provided in the table. Since this is an important enough factor to warrant mentioning, it is likely that moisture condition might affect the tensile strength of wood, and this factor is indicated only in the table, not in the passage. Choices **a**, **b**, **c**, and **e** are all factors indicated in the passage.

30. e. Choice **e** indicates that there is an art to telling comic stories, which contradicts the author's statement that only an artist can tell a humorous story but anyone can tell a comic or witty story. Choice **a** supports the author's statement about the humorous oral story originating in America. Since the author makes this statement only about oral storytelling, choice **b** does not weaken his argument. Choice **c** would not really undermine the author's argument regarding humorous storytelling; he could be a great teller of both humorous and witty stories. Choice **d** may be true, but it does not really weaken the author's argument since it does not suggest that visual arts are the only arts.

31. b. The author uses *force* to modify the action of appealing, so the correct answer choice must be an adjective such as *intensity*. Choices **a**, **c**, and **d** are all verbs, so they can be eliminated even though they might be used as synonyms of *force* in a different context. Choice **e** is not as strong as choice **b** since *weight* would be better used to describe something with actual physical dimension.

32. a. The author suggests that Napoleon's fame for being an intimidating conqueror has caused people to ignore his childhood before he developed that reputation, so choice **a** is a logical conclusion to reach. The conclusions in choices **b** and **e** are too extreme and general, so they are not the likeliest answers. Choice **c** is clearly untrue since the author does provide some details about Napoleon's childhood. There is no evidence in the passage to support choice **d**.

33. a. With the examples he supplies, the author shows that Napoleon was happiest when actually engaging in battle, and choice **a** is the only answer that shows Napoleon in the middle of battle. Choices **c** and **d** are related to battle, but neither takes place in the middle of battle. Choice **b** is directly contradicted in the passage. There is no evidence to support the idea that Napoleon had particularly strong feelings about his hometown, so choice **e** is not the best answer either.

34. d. Although the word *harmonizes* is most often used in relation to music, the author of this passage uses it to explain how a kingfisher blends with its environment visually. So choices **a**, **b**, and **e**, which all take the word more literally as a way of describing sound, can be eliminated. Since the word applies to a kingfisher and its watery environment, not the glimmer of sunlight mentioned further on in the passage, choice **c** is incorrect.

35. b. The art of camouflage uses colors for purposes of protection, and this passage focuses on how the colors of animals help protect them in the wild. A strong title should reflect the main idea of a passage, and this passage is not mainly about the colors of the desert (choice **a**) or the plumage of birds (choice **c**). Choice **d** relates to a single supporting detail in the passage too specifically. Not all coloring described in the passage is vivid, so choice **e** would not be the best title for this particular passage.

36. c. The word *conspicuous* means *obvious*. Choice **a** is an antonym of *conspicuous*, not a synonym. Choices **b** and **d** are spelled similarly to *conspicuous* but they do not share a meaning with it. Choice **e** is not a synonym of *conspicuous* either.

37. e. The quotation develops upon the author's earlier statement that *Desert animals are generally the color of the desert*. While it is likely that Canon Tristram is an authority, there is no reason to believe this person speaks for all authorities, so choice **a** is not the best answer. It also is not likely that the author could not have explained the idea himself if he had to do so, so choice **b** is not the best answer either. There is no evidence that the author's statement about animal coloring is unpopular, so choice **c** is not the best answer. The quotation deals more with why certain birds are certain colors than their general uniqueness, so choice **d** is not the best answer either.

38. d. The author suggests that the *undulation of the surface* of deserts might offer desert animals more protection, so choice **d** is the best conclusion. The author also provides information that contradicts choice **a**. The particular color of the sand in deserts is not the issue, so choice **b** is not the most logical answer. The temperature of the desert is not a factor in this passage either, so choice **c** is wrong. The number of animals in the desert does not affect their color, so choice **e** is wrong, too.

39. a. Each answer choice could be used as a synonym for *space*, but only *portion of area* makes sense in this particular context.

40. c. Third person point of view is when a narrator of a story is not present in the story. Choice **a**, first person point of view, is when the narrator speaks as an *I* within the story. Choice **b**, second person point of view, is when the narrator addresses the reader with *you*. Choices **d** and **e** do not exist.

41. e. The author is concerned with how science involves the interaction of various elements, so any Earth scientist who is only concerned with a single element of Earth probably would not qualify as a "real" Earth scientist in the author's opinion. This fact also eliminates choice **a**, which basically expresses the opposite of the author's opinion. Choice **b**, however, is too specific, and it is possible that the author might believe that a biologist can understand how the heart works without knowing how the hand works. Choice **c** is simply incorrect. While the author emphasizes the importance of knowing the meaning of knowledge over simply acquiring knowledge, one must acquire knowledge before knowing its meaning, so choice **d** is not a logical conclusion.

42. b. The passage is mainly concerned with showing how scientists must use knowledge. The author is not merely concerned with defining a term, so choice **a** is not the best answer. Choice **c** refers to an example the author uses, not the main point of the passage. Choice **d** is an extreme interpretation of the passage that the passage does not really support. Such a brief passage could not possibly explain how to do something as complex as becoming a scientist, so choice **e** does not make sense.

43. e. This answer choice summarizes the main idea of the passage perfectly. Choice **a** implies a judgment about Ibsen and Wagner that the author of the passage does not express. Choices **b** and **c** focus on supporting details in the passage rather than summarize the main idea of the passage as a whole. Choice **d** makes a sweeping generalization about all theater artists when this passage deals with only Wagner and Ibsen.

44. e. The final sentence of the passage contains opinions with which not everyone may agree: the opinion that the effects in Wagner's operas were *startling* and the comparison between the *spectacular* nature of Wagner's opera and that of London Christmas pantomimes. Choices **a**, **b**, **c**, and **d** each provide irrefutable facts only.

45. a. In the last sentence of the passage excerpt, the author states that *the Baltimore and Ohio and its contemporaries were launched upon an entirely different commercial prospect* but does not explain what that prospect is. So it would make sense that the specific nature of that commercial prospect would be the next matter the author will explain. The author explained what Wendel Bollman's name is most closely associated with in the first sentence of the passage, so it is unlikely that will get discussed again, so choice **b** is not the most logical prediction. The matter in choice **c** was already discussed earlier in the fourth paragraph of this passage. Choice **d** is explained in the final sentence of this excerpt. Specific engineers are not discussed in this passage, so there is no reason to assume that the author will begin discussing engineers in depth at this point in the passage. Therefore, choice **e** is not a very logical prediction.

46. e. The author indicates that the country in question includes railways running through Ohio and Baltimore, which are both places in the United States (choice **e**). The author discusses the country in contrast to England and other European countries, so the European countries in choices **a**, **b**, and **c** can be eliminated. Ohio and Baltimore are not in Mexico, so choice **d** can be eliminated as well.

47. a. Wendel Bollman pioneered the use of iron rather than wood in railway bridge construction, which is stated in the third paragraph of the passage. Choice **b** implies that Europe was the only place that had railway bridges initially, but this is not supported by information in the passage. The author indicates that Whipple, Fink, and Bollman all developed railway innovations around the same time, so choice **c** does not make much sense. There is no support for choice **d** either. The truss Bollman developed was a kind of bridging system, so choice **e** does not make sense.

48. c. The author makes this comparison in the final sentence of the passage. The comparisons in choices **a**, **b**, **d**, and **e** are never made in this passage.

49. c. The passage is mainly about an important development in the railway system, so it would be best applied to a history of that topic. Whipple and Fink are only mentioned in passing in this passage, and much more detailed information would be needed for the passage to be an adequate source for a biography of those two people (choice **a**). The passage is too detailed and specific to apply to an advertisement (choice **b**), which is usually short on technical details. However, the passage is not technical enough to serve as an adequate source for a railway engineering manual (choice **d**). Although the author briefly refers to the European railway system, there is not enough information about that system for this passage to be an adequate source for an essay on that topic (choice **e**).

50. e. The author makes this distinction explicitly in the first sentence of the passage. Although the author initially describes Gettysburg as a *market town*, he immediately clarifies that *borough* is a more accurate designation, so choice **a** is not the best answer. The author briefly mentions that there are farms (choice **b**) in Gettysburg and that Gettysburg is located in a county (choice **c**) but does not use them as designations of Gettysburg. There is no mention of a city (choice **d**) in the passage.

51. e. This is the only sentence that includes both facts (what is seen of Gettysburg when turning along certain ridges) and an opinion (the personal opinion that the landscape of Gettysburg is *a picture to be long remembered*). Choice **a** only includes a fact. Choices **b**, **c**, and **d** only express opinions.

52. d. The author discusses how the German Lutheran Church in Gettysburg brings a certain cast to the community, and the only answer choice that makes sense in this context is choice **d**, which indicates a company of people. The author clearly uses cast as a noun, so although *throw* (choice **c**) and *radiate* (choice **e**) might be used as synonyms of *cast* in different contexts, these verbs make no sense in this particular context. Choices **a** and **b** are nouns, but they are not the right nouns for this context.

53. c. The author refers to *war and bloodshed* in the first paragraph of the passage, which is an excerpt from a larger work called *The Battle of Gettysburg 1863*, so choice **c** is the likeliest answer. Although the author makes Gettysburg sound like a very appealing place to visit, he is not mainly concerned with appealing to readers to visit it in this passage, so choice **a** is not the best answer. The author implies that people may often have misconceptions about picturesque Gettysburg because of its role in a well-known war, but he is not mainly concerned with proving that people know very little about the place (choice **b**) or making an extreme statement about how it was *a completely unnatural place for a battle* (choice **e**). The author makes a couple of references to the religious nature of the people in Gettysburg, but this is not his main purpose, so choice **d** is not the best answer.

54. b. The author of this passage is mostly concerned with explaining that protozoa are complex compared to their relatively simple predecessors. Choice **a** is incorrect because the author explicitly states that *Protozoa today are far too complicated to be thought of as primitive*. The author briefly compares protozoa to humans, but he then describes ways they are not similar to humans (*They have no cells, no tissues, no organs*) so choice **c** is not the best answer. The author does not really explain the protozoa's role as the first animals (choice **d**) and does not dwell on their microscopic size (choice **e**).

55. e. Although this sentence begins with information that implies that protozoa are not complete living creatures (*They have no cells, no tissues, no organs*), it finishes with details about what makes them complete living creatures (*many of them show a great complexity of internal structure, far exceeding that of the ordinary cells that build up the tissues of higher animals*). Choices **a** and **b** do not relate to how protozoa are or are not complete living creatures. Choice **c** merely implies that protozoa are complete living creatures but provides no specific details to support that implication. Taken on its own, choice **d** seems to contradict the idea that protozoa are not complete living creatures.

56. c. The author emphasizes that protozoa are complex despite being microscopic and not having traditional bodies composed of cells, tissues, and organs. This contradicts the inferences in choices **b** and **d**. Choices **a** and **e** indicate general comparisons that are not really supported by evidence in the passage.

Praxis® Core Academic Skills for Educators: Writing Practice Test 1

Part I: Multiple-Choice
Time: 40 Minutes

Directions: Choose the letter for the underlined portion that contains a grammatical error. If there is no error in the sentence, choose **e**.

1. The finest authors are experts at creating
        a   b
realistic characters, building palpable
                                c
atmosphere, and plot intriguing stories.
                          d
No error
    e

2. The cat moved stealthy across the top of the
                    a
fence until the sudden sound of the barking
                    b   c
dog caused the startled feline to tumble to the
                                d
ground. No error
        e

3. Before becoming President of the United States
                        a   b
in 1961, John F. Kennedy was a Senator from
                                    c
Massachusetts. No error
    d   e

4. We spent the morning watching a flock of wild
    a
geese wind their way across the cloud-dappled
        b   c   d
sky. No error
      e

5. The <u>well-known</u> mystery writer Ellery Queen is
   <u>a</u>

actually a <u>pseudonym</u> for two authors<u>;</u>
   <u>b</u>   <u>c</u>

Frederic Dannay and Manfred Bennington Lee<u>.</u>
   <u>d</u>

<u>No error</u>
   e

6. Simon <u>and</u> Garfunkel <u>was</u> arguably the most
   <u>a</u>   <u>b</u>

successful <u>musical duo</u> of <u>1960s</u> pop. <u>No error</u>
   <u>c</u>   <u>d</u>   e

7. The team <u>seemed</u> to have neither the experience
   <u>a</u>

<u>or</u> the training to win the game last Saturday,
   <u>b</u>

but <u>it</u> emerged victorious <u>nonetheless</u>. <u>No error</u>
   <u>c</u>   <u>d</u>   e

8. <u>Sprinkling</u> the <u>scrumptious</u> cake with bits of
   <u>a</u>   <u>b</u>

chocolate was a classic case of <u>gliding</u> the lily,
   <u>c</u>

but the cake was no less delicious because of
the unnecessary <u>additions</u>. <u>No error</u>
   <u>d</u>   e

9. The <u>mayor</u> <u>itself</u> will be visiting our school to
   <u>a</u>   <u>b</u>

promote <u>civic</u> activities this <u>Monday</u> morning.
   <u>c</u>   <u>d</u>

<u>No error</u>
   e

10. The passengers on the *Mayflower* <u>included</u>
   <u>a</u>

John Alden, Isaac<u>,</u> and Mary Allerton, Peter
   <u>b</u>

Browne, Humility Cooper, William Holbeck,
and Stephen and Elizabeth Hopkins<u>,</u> as well
   <u>c</u>

as their children Constance, Giles<u>,</u> and
   <u>d</u>

Damaris. <u>No error</u>
   e

11. The actor <u>failed</u> to notice his <u>queue</u> to walk on
   <u>a</u>   <u>b</u>

stage<u>,</u> bringing the play to a momentary but
   <u>c</u>

<u>highly awkward</u> halt. <u>No error</u>
   <u>d</u>   e

12. <u>Despite the assumption</u> that he was embarking
   <u>a</u>

<u>on a doomed mission</u>, Thor Heyerdahl
   <u>b</u>

<u>successfully navigated</u> a wooden raft to the
   <u>c</u>

Polynesian Islands from South America called
the <u>Kon Tiki</u>. <u>No error</u>
   <u>d</u>   e

13. The lion <u>stalked</u> <u>it's</u> <u>prey</u> through the high,
   <u>a</u>   <u>b</u> <u>c</u>

golden grasses of the <u>savannah</u>. <u>No error</u>
   <u>d</u>   e

14. <u>Because</u> of the negative reviews the novel
   <u>a</u>

<u>received</u>, I was prepared to dislike it, <u>and</u> I was
   <u>b</u>   <u>c</u>

<u>actually</u> impressed with the author's grasp of
   <u>d</u>

language and plot. <u>No error</u>
   e

15. While <u>popular</u> votes indicate how many people
   <u>a</u>

voted for a particular <u>presidential</u> candidate,
   <u>b</u>

the number of <u>electrical</u> votes <u>actually</u>
   <u>c</u>   <u>d</u>

determines the winner. <u>No error</u>
   e

16. The sweater looked so <u>luxuriously soft</u> hanging
   <u>a</u>

on the mannequin<u>,</u> but when I tried the sweater
   <u>b</u>

on, it was <u>terribly</u> coarse and <u>rough</u>. <u>No error</u>
   <u>c</u>   <u>d</u>   e

Directions: Choose the best replacement for the underlined portion of the sentence. If no revision is necessary, choose **a**, which always repeats the original phrasing.

17. Walter intended to call <u>Hector but he wasn't home.</u>
    a. Hector but he wasn't home.
    b. Hector but she wasn't home.
    c. Hector but that wasn't home.
    d. it but he wasn't home.
    e. Hector but Hector wasn't home.

18. The filmmaker had planned to make an adaptation of the novel *Don Quixote* <u>for years however circumstances beyond</u> his control prevented the film from ever being completed.
    a. for years however circumstances beyond
    b. for years, however; circumstances beyond
    c. for years; however, circumstances beyond
    d. for years however circumstances beyond;
    e. for years: however circumstances beyond

19. All five of the cats <u>became a pet to very appreciative children</u>.
    a. became a pet to very appreciative children
    b. become a pet to very appreciative children
    c. became a pet to very appreciative children
    d. became pet to very appreciative children
    e. became pets to very appreciative children

20. The new building was created <u>according to a truly state of the art design.</u>
    a. according to a truly state of the art design
    b. according to a truly state of the art-design
    c. according to a truly state of-the art design
    d. according to a truly state-of-the-art design
    e. according to a truly state-of the-art design

21. We ran out of space on the bookshelves <u>in the living room we started storing books</u> on the shelf at the top of the closet as well.
    a. in the living room we started storing books
    b. in the living room: we started storing books
    c. in the living room, so we started storing books
    d. in the living room we started. Storing books
    e. in the living room we started; storing books

22. <u>To who should I address</u> this package?
    a. To who should I address
    b. To she should I address
    c. To us should I address
    d. To you should I address
    e. To whom should I address

23. Having failed to see the <u>stop sign, nearly got into an accident at the corner of</u> Main and Acme.
    a. stop sign, nearly got into an accident at the corner of
    b. stop sign, at the corner of
    c. stop sign, Toni nearly got into an accident at the corner
    d. stop sign, Toni nearly got into an accident, at the corner of
    e. stop sign, Toni nearly into an accident at the corner of

24. After Ronette <u>performed in the production of *Our Town*, she receives</u> a bouquet of roses from her parents.
    a. performed in the production of *Our Town*, she receives
    b. performed in the production of *Our Town*, she received
    c. will perform in the production of *Our Town*, she is receiving
    d. performed in the production of *Our Town* she receives
    e. performed in the production of *Our Town*, she is receiving

25. You can order <u>a printout of any Bill from the Senate</u>.

    a. a printout of any Bill from the Senate
    b. a printout of any Bill from the senate
    c. a Printout of any Bill from the Senate
    d. a Printout of any bill from the senate
    e. a printout of any bill from the Senate

26. The weather could <u>effect the trip to the bazaar we planned, so take my advice</u> and check the weather report as soon as you wake up tomorrow morning.

    a. effect the trip to the bazaar we planned, so take my advice
    b. effect the trip to the bazaar we planned, so take my advise
    c. effect the trip to the bizarre we planned, so take my advice
    d. affect the trip to the bazaar we planned, so take my advice
    e. affect the trip to the bizarre we planned, so take my advice

27. Poet Maya Angelou was renowned for being a prominent civil rights <u>activist who also worked to help African Americans win the liberties other people enjoyed.</u>

    a. activist who also worked to help African Americans win the liberties other people enjoyed.
    b. activist.
    c. who also worked to help African Americans win the liberties other people enjoyed.
    d. activist who worked to help African Americans win the liberties other people enjoyed.
    e. activist who also worked to help African-Americans win the liberties other people enjoyed.

28. My cell phone has run out of <u>power, but I cannot find my charger, anywhere!</u>

    a. power, but I cannot find my charger, anywhere!
    b. power, but I cannot find my charger anywhere!
    c. power but I cannot find my charger, anywhere!
    d. power, but I cannot find my charger anywhere
    e. power but I cannot find my charger anywhere

29. Ricardo <u>ate a hot bowl of soup for dinner</u> this evening.

    a. ate a hot bowl of soup for dinner
    b. ate a bowl of soup hot for dinner
    c. ate a bowl of hot soup for dinner
    d. ate a bowl of soup for dinner hot
    e. hot ate a bowl of soup for dinner

30. Each <u>flower in the vase are roses I grew</u> in my backyard garden.

    a. flower in the vase are roses I grew
    b. flowers in the vase is a rose I grew
    c. flower in the vase are roses we grew
    d. flower in the vase is a rose I grew
    e. flower are roses I grew

Directions: Choose the letter for the underlined portion of the citations that contains an error. If there is no error in the citation, choose **e**.

31. Newspaper citation:

Johnson, Leopold. "7 Planets Discovered
      a   **b**

Orbiting Nearby Star." *The Daily Voice*
[Baltimore] 21 Feb. 2017: A4. Print. No error
  c   **d**   **e**

32. Book citation:

Candace L. Lechance. *The Human Body*.
        a   **b**

Chicago: New Press Publishing, 2014. Print.
           c   **d**

No error
 e

Directions: Some parts of the following passage need to be improved. Read the passage and then answer the questions about specific sentences. In choosing your answers, pay attention to development, organization, word choice, tone, and the standards of written English.

(1) Confusion regarding dinosaur skeletons has helped create some of history's most enduring mythical creatures. (2) The Griffin is one such example of this fascinating phenomenon. (3) According to Greek myth, this whacky creature had the wings and head of an eagle and the body of a lion. (4) Greek writer Aristeas first became aware of the Griffin while traveling through the Altai and Tien Shan mountains in 675 BCE. (5) There the Greek writer met nomads who told him stories of the strange Griffins who use their mighty claws to defend their vast treasures. (6) The Greek writer learned that the nomads insisted that there were skeletal remains to prove the existence of Griffins. (7) However, according to Keiron Pim in his book *Dinosaurs: The Grand Tour*, the skeletons the nomads had most likely belonged to protoceratops, a long-extinct variety of it with a beak, a neck-frill that could easily be mistaken for wings, and a clawed, hefty, four-legged frame that could pass for the body of a lion.

(8) The dragons of myth also likely resulted from the discovery of dinosaur fossils. (9) Imagine having no strong knowledge of Earth's past and discovering massive, reptile-like skulls full of huge teeth and tremendous skeletons with equally elongated tails. (10) You may be able to begin to understand how these myths came to be. (11) In fact these, myths persist even today. (12) In 2007, media sources such as *The Washington Post* and BBC News reported that villagers in China's Ruyang County had dug up bones they believed to be dragon remains. (13) As it turns out, the bones actually belonged to an herbivorous species of dinosaur.

33. In context, which revision to sentences 4 through 6 (sentences 4 through 6 follow) is most needed?

Greek writer Aristeas first became aware of the Griffin while traveling through the Altai and Tien Shan mountains in 675 BCE. There the Greek writer met nomads who told him stories of the strange Griffins who use their mighty claws to defend their vast treasures. The Greek writer learned that the nomads insisted that there were skeletal remains to prove the existence of Griffins.

a. As it is now.

b. Greek writer Aristeas first became aware of the Griffin while traveling through the Altai and Tien Shan mountains in 675 BCE. There he met nomads who told him stories of the strange Griffins who use their mighty claws to defend their vast treasures. The nomads insisted that there were skeletal remains to prove the existence of Griffins.

c. Aristeas first became aware of the Griffin while traveling through the Altai and Tien Shan mountains in 675 BCE. There the Greek writer met nomads who told him stories of the strange Griffins who use their mighty claws to defend their vast treasures. The Greek writer learned that the nomads insisted that there were skeletal remains to prove the existence of Griffins.

d. The Greek writer first became aware of the Griffin while traveling through the Altai and Tien Shan mountains in 675 BCE. There the Greek writer met nomads who told him stories of the strange Griffins who use their mighty claws to defend their vast treasures. The nomads insisted that there were skeletal remains to prove the existence of Griffins.

e. Greek writer Aristeas first became aware of the Griffin while traveling through the Altai and Tien Shan mountains in 675 BCE. There he met nomads who told him stories of the strange Griffins who use their mighty claws to defend their vast treasures. The Greek writer learned that the nomads insisted that there were skeletal remains to prove the existence of Griffins.

34. For which detail does the writer cite multiple resources?
   a. Villagers in China's Ruyang County dug up bones they believed to be dragon remains.
   b. The nomads in the Altai and Tien Shan mountains most likely found protoceratops skeletons.
   c. The griffin had the wings and head of an eagle and the body of a lion.
   d. Aristeas traveled through the Altai and Tien Shan mountains in 675 BCE.
   e. Some people have no strong knowledge of Earth's past.

35. In context, which revision to sentence 3 (sentence 3 follows) is most needed?
   According to Greek myth, this whacky creature had the wings and head of an eagle and the body of a lion.
   a. Replace *whacky* with *kooky*.
   b. Replace *whacky* with *crazy*.
   c. Replace *myth* with *stories*.
   d. Replace *creature* with *monster*.
   e. Replace *whacky* with *fantastical*.

36. In context, which revision to sentence 7 (sentence 7 follows) is most needed?
   However, according to Keiron Pim in his book *Dinosaurs: The Grand Tour*, the skeletons the nomads had most likely belonged to protoceratops, a long-extinct variety of it with a beak, a neck-frill that could easily be mistaken for wings, and a clawed, hefty, four-legged frame that could easily pass for the body of a lion.
   a. Change *had* to *has*.
   b. Replace *it* with *dinosaur*.
   c. Replace *book* with *it*.
   d. Change *his* to *him*.
   e. Change *mistaken* to *mistook*.

Use the following passage to answer questions 37 through 40.

(1) In 1965, the most popular pop band in the world was busy making their second feature film. (2) The movie *Help!* would not be remembered as the Beatles' finest achievement. (3) Therefore, something happened while making the film that would have a significant effect on the band and pop music in general.

(4) The Beatles were filming a scene set in an Indian Restaurant when the Beatles' guitarist, George Harrison, heard an instrument called the sitar. (5) The sitar is a classical stringed Indian instrument with as many as 21 strings. (6) The instrument creates a haunting, "twanging" sound. (7) Although it bears some similarities to the kinds of guitars musicians had been using to make pop music, the sitar was completely unheard of in pop music. (8) That changed when Harrison fell under the spell of the instrument while making *Help!*

(9) After purchasing a sitar of his own, George Harrison began studying the instrument. (10) By the end of 1965, he had enough rudimentary knowledge of the instrument to play a basic melody on it while recording a Beatles song. (11) The use of the sitar in that song so impressed other pop musicians of the day that artists scrambled to incorporate the instrument into their music, helping to introduce a wide audience of pop fans outside of India to a classical instrument they had likely never even heard of before.

37. In context, which revision to sentence 3 (sentence 3 follows) is most needed?

Therefore, something happened while making the film that would have a significant effect on the band and pop music in general.

a. Change *has* to "*have*."
b. Replace *Therefore* with *However*.
c. Change *making* to *make*.
d. Replace *the film* with *it*.
e. Change *the band* to *them*.

38. In context, which revision to sentence 7 (sentence 7 follows) is most needed?

Although it bears some similarities to the kinds of guitars musicians had been using to make pop music, the sitar was completely unheard of in pop music.

a. As it is now.
b. Although the sitar bears some similarities to the kinds of guitars musicians had been using to make pop music, the sitar was completely unheard of in pop music.
c. Although it bears some similarities to the kinds of guitars musicians had been using to make pop music the sitar was completely unheard of in pop music.
d. Although it bears some similarities to the kinds of guitars musicians had been using to make pop music, the sitar was completely unheard of.
e. Although it bears some similarities to the kinds of guitars musicians had been using to make pop music, it was completely unheard of in pop music.

39. In context, which revision to sentence 10 (sentence 10 follows) is most needed?

> By the end of 1965, he had enough rudimentary knowledge of the instrument to play a basic melody on it while recording a Beatles song.

a. As it is now.

b. By the end of 1965, he had enough rudimentary knowledge of the instrument to play "Norwegian Wood (This Bird Has Flown)."

c. By the end of 1965, he had enough rudimentary knowledge of the instrument to play a basic melody on it while recording the Beatles' song "Norwegian Wood (This Bird Has Flown)."

d. He had enough rudimentary knowledge of the instrument to play a basic melody on it while recording the Beatles' song "Norwegian Wood (This Bird Has Flown)."

e. By the end of 1965, he had enough rudimentary knowledge to record the Beatles' song "Norwegian Wood (This Bird Has Flown)."

40. In context, which revision to sentence 11 (sentence 11 follows) is most needed?

> The use of the sitar in that song so impressed other pop musicians of the day that artists scrambled to incorporate the instrument into their music, helping to introduce a wide audience of pop fans outside of India to a classical instrument they had likely never even heard of before.

a. As it is now.

b. The use of the sitar in that song so impressed other pop musicians of the day that many others scrambled to incorporate the instrument into their music, helping to introduce a wide audience of pop fans outside of India to a classical instrument they had likely never even heard of before.

c. The use of the sitar in that song so impressed other pop musicians of the day that artists such as the Rolling Stones scrambled to incorporate the instrument into their music, helping to introduce a wide audience of pop fans outside of India to a classical instrument they had likely never even heard of before.

d. The use of the sitar in that song so impressed other pop musicians of the day that artists such as the Rolling Stones, Donovan, Procol Harum, Traffic, and many others scrambled to incorporate the instrument into their music, helping to introduce a wide audience of pop fans outside of India to a classical instrument they had likely never even heard of before.

e. The use of the sitar in that song so impressed other pop musicians of the day that artists such as the Rolling Stones, Donovan, Procol Harum, Traffic, and many others scrambled.

Part IIa: Argumentative Essay
Time: 30 Minutes

Directions: Carefully read the essay-writing topic that follows. Plan and write an essay that addresses all points in the topic. Make sure that your essay is well organized and that you support your central argument with concrete examples. Allow 30 minutes for your essay.

More and more, newsreaders are turning to untraditional news sources such as blogs and online video opinion pieces rather than traditional newspapers and television news programs to get their information. Write an essay in which you explain how you think the widespread use of alternative news sources is affecting society.

Part IIb: Source-Based Essay
Time: 30 Minutes

Directions: The following assignment requires you to use information from two sources to discuss the most important concerns that relate to a specific issue. When paraphrasing or quoting from the source, cite each source by referring to the author's last name, the text's title, or any other clear identifier. Allow 30 minutes for your essay.

Assignment

Read the two passages carefully and then write an essay in which you identify the most important concerns regarding the debates concerning fracking. Your essay must draw on information from both of the sources. In addition, you may draw on your own experiences, observations, or reading. Be sure to cite the sources whether you are paraphrasing or directly quoting.

Source 1

The Argument against Fracking

Better known as "fracking," hydraulic fracturing is the process of extracting fossil fuels from the earth. The process involves using intense pressure to inject liquid such as water into wells to crack rock below the earth's surface. Sand included in the water keeps the cracks open after the injection process is complete. The resulting cracks allow oil and gas to flow freely so they can then be extracted. While proponents of fracking celebrate the process's effectiveness, they fail to acknowledge the multitudinous downsides to this rather destructive process.

First of all, there is the matter of methane leaks. Methane is a greenhouse gas that contributes tremendously to the greenhouse effect that is helping to warm our planet abnormally. Methane tends to leak from the earth during several stages of the fracking process, so it is reasonable to conclude that fracking can have a direct and very negative effect on climate change.

Fracking also affects the water we drink. During the process, methane not only leaks into the atmosphere above the earth's surface; it also leaks into water below that surface. Consequently, tap water is rendered undrinkable. Methane can even make water become flammable. Chemicals used in fracking can also cause contamination, and some fracking companies will not even disclose the kinds of chemicals they use.

Fracking doesn't just taint water; it also wastes it. A single well may use anywhere from two to twenty million gallons of water. This is a major drain on the earth's water resources, which are becoming increasingly scarce in parts of the country such as California.

These are just a few of the serious issues with fracking. Along with the negative effect the process has on the atmosphere and water supplies, there is also the fact that fracking may help stimulate earthquakes; it discourages the use of alternative energy sources, such as wind and solar power; and the basic quality of life of people who live near noisy, dirty fracking sites must suffer. America's continued reliance on fracking may seem like a good idea to those who will most profit from it, but such people are extremely shortsighted. More likely, fracking will have dire long-term consequences for Earth and its residents.

Source 2

Taking a Stand for Fracking

The question of whether to frack or not to frack is a controversial issue. Enemies of the fossil-fuel extraction process insist that fracking has a negative impact on the environment. However, these people cannot seem to grasp all the benefits of fracking, and yes, some of those benefits are environmental in nature.

As a popular alternative to fossil fuels, coal is an unwise energy source. Thousands of people die every year because of the toxins that rise from burned coal. The rise of fracking has displaced coal considerably. In 2008, 50% of the United States' energy was coal generated, while only 20% was natural gas generated. Four years later, use of coal energy had dropped to just 37% while natural gas energy had risen to 30%, and during that time, there has been a major reduction in the kinds of deadly nitrogen and sulfur dioxide emissions that result from coal burning. I'm sure you'll agree that is a major environmental advance that can be attributed to fracking.

Now some people complain that fracking causes the contamination of drinking water. However, the water we drink is not at the same level of the earth as fossil fuels are. Fuels are located much deeper in the earth than water is. When fracking companies do their work carefully, and are mindful of pipe leaks within 1,000 feet of the earth's surface, there is no risk of water contamination.

So, fracking really is not all that damaging to the earth and its environment. It is even beneficial to our planet in certain significant ways. Fracking ensures that America will continue to have clean and efficient energy sources for generations to come.

Praxis® Core Academic Skills for Educators: Writing Practice Test 1 Answers and Explanations

1. d. There are three items in a series in this sentence: *creating realistic characters, building palpable atmosphere*, and *plot intriguing stories*. To make these three items parallel, the word *plot* should be changed to *plotting*.

2. a. There is an error in modifier use in this sentence. The word *stealthy* is an adjective, but it is used to describe the verb *moved*, so it should be in its adverb form: *stealthily*. There are no errors in choices **b**, **c**, or **d**.

3. e. There is no error in this sentence. All of the underlined words are capitalized correctly.

4. c. There is an error in pronoun number in this sentence. The pronoun should agree with the singular word *flock*, not the plural word *geese*, but *their* is a plural pronoun.

5. c. There is a punctuation error in this sentence. A semicolon should not be used to offset descriptive details from what they describe. A colon is used for this purpose.

6. e. In this sentence, *Simon and Garfunkel* describes a single duo, so the use of the singular verb *was* is correct in this context. There are actually no errors in this sentence.

7. b. The correlative conjunction *neither* must be paired with *nor*, but this sentence mistakenly uses *or* instead.

8. c. This sentence contains an idiom error. There is no such idiom as *gliding the lily*. The proper idiom to indicate an unnecessary addition to something that is already excellent is *gilding the lily*.

9. b. There is an error in the use of an intensifying pronoun in this sentence. The pronoun *itself* should be used only in reference to a nonhuman subject, but a mayor is a human being so the correct pronoun would be *herself* or *himself*.

10. b. There are a number of commas in this sentence, and one is used incorrectly. There should not be a comma after *Isaac* because the name is part of a compound entry on the list: *Isaac and Mary Allerton*.

11. b. There is an error in word choice in this sentence. The word *queue* does not mean *a signal for action*; it means *a line of people*. The correct word for this context is *cue*.

12. d. This sentence contains a misplaced modifier. The phrase *called the Kon Tiki* should be placed directly after the term it modifies: *a wooden raft*. Placing it after *South America* makes it seem as though South America is called the *Kon Tiki*, which does not make sense.

13. b. The word *it's* is a contraction of *it is*, but this sentence requires the possessive form of the pronoun *it*, which is *its*. There should not be an apostrophe in the word.

14. c. The conjunction *and* is not the best one to use in this sentence. Since the first part of the sentence introduces an idea that is contradicted after the conjunction, *but* would be a better conjunction to show the contradictory relationship between the sentence's clauses.

15. c. *Electrical* is the wrong word to use in this sentence. It should be replaced with the word *electoral*, which is actually the kind of vote that determines the winner of a presidential election.

16. d. The words *coarse* and *rough* share the same meaning. Eliminating the word *rough* would correct this redundancy.

17. e. The original sentence suffers from a vague pronoun since it is not clear whether *he* is supposed to refer to *Walter* or *Hector*. Choice **e** clears up this error by changing the pronoun to the proper noun *Hector*. Choice **b** makes the same error as the original sentence and uses incorrect gender. Choices **c** and **d** fail to correct the original error and make the additional error of referring to a human as *that* or *it*.

18. c. The original sentence is missing two necessary pieces of punctuation. Choice **c** corrects this error by inserting a semicolon between the sentence's two clauses and following the conjunctive adverb *however* with a comma. Choices **b** and **d** recognize that a semicolon is needed but both answer choices misplace their respective semicolons. Choice **e** mistakenly uses a colon instead of a semicolon.

19. e. There is an error in noun-noun agreement in the original sentence. The plural noun *cats* does not agree with the singular *pet*. Changing that word to the plural *pets* corrects the error. The other answer choices fail to correct that original error.

20. d. When two or more words are used as a single modifier, they need to be hyphenated. In this sentence, *state of the art* modifies *design*, so the phrase should be hyphenated as *state-of-the-art*. Choices **b**, **c**, and **e** recognize that the original sentence was missing hyphens, but they either use too few hyphens or misplace them.

21. c. As originally written, the sentence is a run-on because it lacks a conjunction and punctuation to join its two clauses. Choice **c** corrects this error with the conjunction *so* and a comma. Choice **b** uses the wrong punctuation; a semicolon would correct the original mistake but a colon does not. Choices **d** and **e** place the punctuation in the wrong spots, which turns the clauses into fragments.

22. e. The pronoun in the original sentence is in the subjective case, but the objective case is needed since the pronoun is being used as the object of this sentence. Choice **e** corrects this error by changing *who* to *whom*. Choice **b** uses a subjective pronoun incorrectly. Choices **c** and **d** use objective pronouns, but the pronouns they use are not the kind needed in a question in which the recipient of the package is unknown.

23. d. The original sentence is a fragment because it lacks a subject. Choice **d** corrects this error by introducing the subject *Toni*. Choice **b** deletes information that fails to correct the original problem. Choice **c** includes the subject but it deletes the necessary preposition *of*. Choice **e** introduces a subject but deletes the necessary verb *got*.

24. b. The original sentence has an incorrect shift in verb tense, following the past-tense verb *performed* with the present-tense *receives*. Choice **b** corrects this error by placing both verbs in the past tense. Choice **c** places the verbs in different tenses that still shift tense. Choice **d** deletes a comma without correcting the original error. Choice **e** changes the tense of *receives*, but it does not change it to the same tense as *performed*.

25. e. As used in this sentence, *bill* is a common noun so it should not be capitalized. However, *Senate* is a proper noun, so it should be capitalized, making choice **b** incorrect. Choice **c** introduces another capitalization error by capitalizing the common noun *printout*. Choice **d** makes the same error while also failing to capitalize *Senate*.

26. d. The original sentence confuses the word *effect*, which is a noun meaning *result*, for *affect*, which is a verb meaning *to change*. Choice **d** corrects this error. Choice **b** not only retains the original error but introduces a new one by changing *advice*, which is a noun meaning *recommendation*, to *advise*, which is a verb meaning *to recommend*. Choice **c** retains the original error, mistakenly changes *advice* to *advise*, and introduces a new error by changing *bazaar*, which is a noun meaning *market*, to *bizarre*, which is an adjective meaning *very strange*. Choice **e** makes that error regarding *bizarre* as well.

27. b. The original sentence includes a redundancy since stating that Maya Angelou was a *civil rights activist* already implies that she *worked to help African Americans win the liberties other people enjoyed*. By deleting that final phrase, choice **b** corrects the redundancy. Choice **c** mistakenly deletes the word *activist*, making it seem as though Angelou, herself, was civil rights, which does not make sense. Choice **d** merely deletes the word *also*, which fails to correct the original redundancy. Choice **e** fails to delete the original redundancy and introduces a punctuation error by placing an unnecessary hyphen between *African* and *American*.

28. b. The original sentence contains an unnecessary comma before *anywhere*. Choice **b** corrects that error by deleting the comma. Choice **c** introduces a new error by deleting the necessary comma before *but* while failing to correct the original comma error. Choices **d** and **e** correct the original error but delete the necessary end marks, and choice **e** also deletes that necessary comma before *but*.

29. c. The original sentence misplaces the modifier *hot*, making it seem as though the actual bowl was hot when it is the soup inside the bowl that was hot. Choice **c** corrects this error by placing *hot* so that it modifies *soup*. Choices **b**, **d**, and **e** also misplace the modifier.

30. d. There is a lack of agreement between the nouns in the original sentence. *Flower* and *roses* refer to the same thing so they should agree in number. Choice **d** corrects this error by changing *roses* to the singular *a rose* so that it agrees with the singular *flower*. Choice **b** merely reverses the original agreement error while introducing a new error with the incorrect phrase *Each flowers*. Choice **c** merely changes the pronoun, which does not correct the original error. Choice **e** deletes the phrase *in the vase*, which does not correct the original error either.

31. e. This newspaper article is cited correctly as originally written. There are no errors in it.

32. a. In a book citation, the author's last name precedes his or her first name. This citation fails to do so. The rest of the citation is written correctly.

33. b. As originally written, sentences 4 through 6 lack variety; each sentence includes the term *Greek writer*. Choice **b** corrects this problem by eliminating two of the repetitious uses of the term. Choices **c** and **e** each eliminate one use of the phrase, but they are still too repetitious. Choice **d** deletes the Greek writer's name, making his identity unclear, and fails to correct the original problem of repetition.

34. a. To support this detail, the author cites two media sources. Choice **b** is supported with only a single source. Choices **c**, **d**, and **e** are not supported with any sources.

35. e. The language used in the majority of this passage indicates that it was written for an educated, adult audience. The word *whacky* is too informal for this passage. Changing that phrase to *fantastical* maintains the passage's sophisticated style. Choices **a** and **b** merely replace one informal word with another. Choice **c** changes *myth* to the less specific *stories* while failing to correct the original stylistic error. Choice **d** changes *creature* to *monster* while failing to correct the original stylistic error.

36. b. As originally written, this sentence is unclear because the pronoun *it* is too vague. Replacing *it* with the term that pronoun stands for (*dinosaur*) clarifies the sentence's meaning. Choices **a** and **e** each introduce verb-tense errors into the sentence. Choice **c** introduces another vague pronoun, making the sentence even less clear than it originally was. Choice **d** introduces a pronoun error.

37. b. As originally written, sentence 3 begins with the wrong transitional word because *Therefore* suggests a result, yet sentence 3 provides a contrast to sentence 4. A better transitional word is *However*. Choices **a** and **c** introduce grammatical errors to the sentence. Choices **d** and **e** replace specific nouns with vague pronouns.

38. a. Sentence 7 is perfectly clear and grammatically correct as it is originally written. None of the answer choices improve the sentence.

39. c. The original sentence could use some clarification regarding the song in question, and choice **c** provides that without introducing any new errors. Choices **b** and **e** clarify the song but make George Harrison's contribution to it less clear than it was in the original sentence. Choice **d** clarifies the song but makes the timeframe of the event less clear than it was in the original sentence.

40. d. Choice **d** improves on the original sentence by introducing some examples of the other pop artists who used the sitar in their music. Choices **b** and **c** do not support the original sentence as well as choice **d** does because they do not include sufficient examples. Choice **e** includes those supportive examples, but it also deletes information, making it unclear what these other pop musicians did.

Sample Responses for the Argumentative Essay

Following are sample criteria for scoring an argumentative essay.

A score 6 writer will

- create an exceptional composition with a clear thesis that appropriately addresses the audience and given task.
- organize ideas effectively and logically, include very strong supporting details, and use smooth transitions.
- present a definitive, focused thesis and clearly support it throughout the composition.
- include vivid details, clear examples, and strong details to support the key ideas.

- exhibit an exceptional level of skill in the usage of the English language and the capacity to employ an assortment of sentence structures.
- build essentially error-free and varied sentences that accurately convey intended meaning.

A score 5 writer will

- create a commendable composition that appropriately addresses the audience and given task.
- organize ideas, include supporting details, and use smooth transitions.
- present a thesis and support it throughout the composition.
- include details, examples, and supporting text to enhance the themes of the composition.
- generally exhibit a high level of skill in the usage of the English language and the capacity to employ an assortment of sentence structures.
- build mostly error-free sentences that accurately convey intended meaning.

A score 4 writer will

- create a composition that satisfactorily addresses the audience and given task.
- display satisfactory organization of ideas, include adequate supporting details, and generally use smooth transitions.
- present a thesis and mostly support it throughout the composition.
- include some details, examples, and supporting text that typically enhance most themes of the composition.
- exhibit a competent level of skill in the usage of the English language and the general capacity to employ an assortment of sentence structures.
- build sentences with several minor errors that generally do not confuse the intended meaning.

A score 3 writer will

- create an adequate composition that basically addresses the audience and given task.

- display some organization of ideas, include some supporting details, and use mostly logical transitions.
- present a somewhat underdeveloped thesis but attempt to support it throughout the composition.
- exhibit an adequate level of skill in the usage of the English language and a basic capacity to employ an assortment of sentence structures.
- build sentences with some minor and major errors that may obscure the intended meaning.

A score 2 writer will

- create a composition that restrictedly addresses the audience and given task.
- display little organization of ideas, have inconsistent supporting details, and use very few transitions.
- present an unclear or confusing thesis with little support throughout the composition.
- include very few details, examples, and supporting text.
- exhibit a less than adequate level of skill in the usage of the English language and a limited capacity to employ a basic assortment of sentence structures.
- build sentences with a few major errors that may confuse the intended meaning.

A score 1 writer will

- create a composition that has a limited sense of the audience and given task.
- display illogical organization of ideas, include confusing or no supporting details, and lack the ability to effectively use transitions.
- present a minimal or unclear thesis.
- include confusing or irrelevant details and examples, and little or no supporting text.
- exhibit a limited level of skill in the usage of the English language and little or no capacity to employ basic sentence structure.

- build sentences with many major errors that obscure or confuse the intended meaning.

Sample Score 6 Argumentative Essay

Throughout the twentieth century, humans largely relied on traditional news sources such as newspapers, magazines, and television news programs to stay on top of current events. This situation has drastically changed with the widespread use of the Internet in the twenty-first century. Now people regularly consult such less formal sources as blogs and online video opinion pieces to find out what is happening in the world. While some argue that this change in the nature of our news is either a good thing or a bad thing, I believe there is a more nuanced assessment as there are both pros and cons to the proliferation of these relatively new news sources.

On the pro side, personal blogs and the kinds of video pieces anyone with a smart phone can post on sites such as YouTube are giving a voice to members of the population who did not have one before. Now everyone can play the role of political commentator, voicing alternative opinions about the world that may not be presented in traditional media. This helps people to feel more involved in the world events that so often feel beyond our control. The high quality of many blogs and video pieces has also inspired many commentators to put the kind of polish on their presentations that used to be exclusive to national newspapers and network television programs.

However, there is a downside to the relative ease of posting an editorial piece on a blog or YouTube. There is generally no system of checks and balances on these kinds of information outlets, which has caused a rise in what is commonly called "fake news." These are news items with no basis in reality that could actually have national and global impacts when readers believe them to be true. The rise of fake news is a highly dangerous consequence of the news items that pop up on unregulated blogs and video sites.

Nevertheless, the American ideal of free speech ensures that we will probably continue to see news items

appear on blogs and video sites no matter how professional, amateurish, factual, or fictional they may be. The key to navigating this tricky environment is cross checking the news items that appear on these sources with items in other sources. Doing so will help us to figure out which sources are the most reliable, earning our repeat attention and consideration. That way we readers can remain well informed with "real" news amidst the twenty-first century's complex media environment and all people can continue to take advantage of the more prominent voices the current news environment affords them.

Comments on the Sample Argumentative Essay That Received a Score of 6

The author has created an informative essay with a clear thesis. It answers the question and has a smooth, logical organization. Stylistically, it uses smooth transitions and relevant and correct examples. The key ideas are readily apparent and explored throughout the essay through well-written and varied sentences.

Sample Score 4 Argumentative Essay

More and more, newsreaders are turning to untraditional news sources such as blogs and online video opinion pieces rather than traditional newspapers and television news programs to get their information. This is causing some major problems in the world.

Basically, when anyone can provide the news, they can say anything they want to. Old-fashioned newspapers and TV news programs have editors that can separate what is true from what is not true. If a reporter comes in with fake information, an editor can stop that information from ever going in print or on TV. There aren't any kinds of things when it comes to blogs and video sights. So anyone can publish anything they want to. Fake news is the result of this. Nowadays, it is getting harder and harder to know what is fake and what is real because of fake news. People are getting really confused because of all this.

Still we have free speech in America and that means anyone can say anything they want to say. So that's why there is still fake news. Free speech is floored but it is the American way. So who are we to say it should be stopped? We must deal with a world where there is fake news as well as good, old-fashioned newspapers that always tell the truth. This can make it difficult to stay well informed, but with a little bit of care and work, we can still do that.

Comments on the Sample Argumentative Essay That Received a Score of 4

The author has created a serviceable composition. The thesis is readily perceived and adequately, if not spectacularly, defended. Details are correct, if vague. Stylistically, it is rather rough and too informal and the decision to begin the essay by quoting the prompt word-for-word is weak. However, the author displays adequate knowledge of the subject and sufficient command of the English language. Aside from a few errors in word choice (for example: using *sights* instead of *sites* and *floored* instead of *flawed*), the essay is grammatically and orthographically correct, even if it is not scintillating.

Sample Score 1 Argumentative Essay

First of all blogs are awesome. Their . . . I said it. They are awesome! I love to use blogs to right all about what I'm doing. Like what music I'm listening to. And TV shows I like. I bet that people could not do that before blogs. I mean they could right about that kind of stuff but they could not right about it so that EVRYONE IN THE WORLD literally could read it! Literally!

You need to be careful what you say though. You cant say anything bad about people cause they might read it and knowing that the whole world is reading bad things about them will make them feel BAD. Never do that. Only say good things about people on your blogs. Hey . . . it's all good!

Comments on the Sample Argumentative Essay That Received a Score of 1

The author neither understands the subject nor expresses an opinion in a clear and coherent manner. The author furthermore focuses on his or her experience with blogging, not with the role blogs play in the current news environment. There are grammatical and spelling errors, and the essay neither develops in a clear way nor has very much to say.

Sample Responses for the Source-Based Essay

Following are sample criteria for scoring a source-based essay.

A score 6 writer will

- create an exceptional composition explaining why the topic is important and support the explanation with specific references to both sources.
- organize ideas effectively and logically, include well-chosen information from both sources, and link the two sources in the discussion.
- exhibit an exceptional level of skill in the usage of the English language and the capacity to employ an assortment of sentence structures.
- build essentially error-free and varied sentences that accurately convey intended meaning.
- cite both sources when quoting or paraphrasing.

A score 5 writer will

- create a commendable composition that explains why the concerns are important and support the explanation with specific references to both sources.
- organize ideas effectively and logically, include information from both sources, link the two sources, and use smooth transitions.
- generally exhibit skill in the usage of the English language and the capacity to employ variety in sentence structures.

- build mostly error-free sentences that accurately convey intended meaning.
- cite both sources when quoting or paraphrasing.

A score 4 writer will

- create a composition that satisfactorily explains why the concerns are important and support the explanation with specific references to both sources.
- use information from both sources to convey why the concerns discussed in the sources are important.
- display satisfactory organization of ideas, include adequate details, and link the two sources.
- exhibit a competent level of skill in the usage of the English language and the general capacity to employ an assortment of sentence structures.
- build sentences with several minor errors that generally do not confuse the intended meaning.
- cite both sources when quoting or paraphrasing.

A score 3 writer will

- create an adequate composition that basically addresses the audience and given task but conveys the importance of the concerns in only a limited way.
- use information from only one source or inadequately from both sources to convey why the concerns discussed in the sources are important.
- display some organization of ideas and include some supporting details.
- exhibit an adequate level of skill in the usage of the English language and a basic capacity to employ an assortment of sentence structures.
- build sentences with some minor and major errors that may obscure the intended meaning.
- cite sources when quoting or paraphrasing.

A score 2 writer will

- fail to explain why the concerns are important.
- use information from only one source poorly or fail to convey why the concerns discussed in the sources are important.

- display little organization of ideas, have inconsistent supporting details, and fail to link the two sources.
- demonstrate a less than adequate level of skill in the usage of the English language and a limited capacity to employ a basic assortment of sentence structures.
- build sentences with a few major errors that may confuse the intended meaning.
- fail to cite sources when quoting or paraphrasing.

A score 1 writer will

- display illogical organization of ideas, include confusing or no supporting details, and fail to adequately address the concerns raised by the sources.
- include confusing or irrelevant details and examples, and few or no supporting references.
- exhibit a limited level of skill in the usage of the English language and little or no capacity to employ basic sentence structure.
- build sentences with many major errors that obscure or confuse the intended meaning.

Sample Score 6 Source-Based Essay

Despite its enormity, the Earth is a fragile place. Humankind cannot abuse our planet without consequences, which is something we are learning in the age of fracking. Properly known as "hydraulic fracturing," fracking is a method of drawing fossil fuels from the Earth. While the process has its proponents, there are serious consequences to the process that pose a very real threat to world on which we all live.

Fracking can negatively affect our planet both by what it does to the physical Earth and what it may release into the atmosphere above the planet. Fracking can cause the leaking of methane, a harmful greenhouse gas that can exacerbate climate change when it escapes into the atmosphere. Toxic substances can contaminate water when it leaks into the ground below.

Proponents of fracking argue that there is actually no danger of water contamination because the ground water we drink and fossil fuels are located at different levels of the Earth's interior. However, pipe leaks can still cause leakage as the fuels are drawn to the Earth's surface. The article "Taking a Stand for Fracking" argues that this is not a threat when fracking companies work carefully, but what of the ones that do not perform this clearly complex work with care? Do the risks really justify the consequences? Considering that these companies are profit driven, and some lack so much consideration for the public that they "will not even disclose the kinds of chemicals they use," according to "The Argument against Fracking," they may not deserve the benefit of the doubt.

I personally think that the argument against fracking is much stronger than the argument in favor of it. Additionally, the dependence on fossil fuels that the fracking industry promotes is drawing away support for alternative energy sources such as wind and solar energy. By simply focusing on the admittedly problematic alternative energy source of coal, the author of "Taking a Stand for Fracking" fails to examine this issue completely. The article's refusal to acknowledge the fact that fracking may stimulate earthquakes is another flaw in a piece clearly intent on cherry-picking information to present an unwavering pro-fracking position.

Granted, this issue is obviously too complex to address in articles as brief as "Taking a Stand for Fracking" and "The Argument against Fracking," but even in its truncated format, "The Argument against Fracking" makes the more convincing argument, as it uses more varied and well-supported examples than "Taking a Stand for Fracking" does. If I'm ever able to take a stand, myself, by using my vote to support or prevent fracking, I know that I will be taking my stand against the dangerous, potentially disastrous process.

Comments on the Sample Source-Based Essay That Received a Score of 6

This is a superb essay. This response evaluates the arguments in the source texts, develops an effective position supported by the text, and fulfills the criteria to earn a top score. This response establishes its stance at the conclusion of the first paragraph (*While the*

process has its proponents, there are serious consequences to the process that pose a very real threat to world on which we all live.) and provides a summary of support for that stance in the second, third, and fourth paragraphs. In the third and fourth paragraphs, the writer also weighs the validity of the evidence in the "against" argument, for example: "'Taking a Stand for Fracking' argues that this is not a threat when fracking companies work carefully, but what of the ones that do not perform this clearly complex work with care? Do the risks really justify the consequences?"

The essay is well organized, opens with a definitive stance, offers a discussion of the pros and cons of fracking and the evidence provided, and then provides a summary in support of the chosen stance. The writer provides multiple, specific examples and then elaborates on them, using an appropriately formal tone throughout. In addition, the writer adheres to proper grammar and usage.

Sample Score 4 Source-Based Essay

Fracking is one of the most controversial contemporary issues. Some people are against it because they think it is bad for the environment. Other people are for it because they think the complaints against fracking are incomplete. After reading two articles on this subject, one for it and one against it, I think I probably agree with "Taking a Stand for Fracking."

The writer of this article says that "As a popular alternative to fossil fuels, coal is an unwise energy source. Thousands of people die every year because of the toxins that rise from burned coal. The rise of fracking has displaced coal considerably." This is a pretty convincing argument because nothing is more serious than death. The other article called "The Argument against Fracking" doesn't even talk about how bad coal is. That is a major problem with that article.

That article also says that fracking taints drinking water. But "Taking a Stand for Fracking" shoots that argument right down by proving that "the water we drink is not at the same level of the earth as fossil fuels are." This makes the argument against fracking because of tainted water seem downright foolish.

Basically, I think the author of "Taking a Stand for Fracking" makes a more convincing argument because of the details and the way the article is written. I got a sense that the author was talking right to me by using a less formal way of speaking. I felt like it was written by a real person. This makes the information seem more like it was provided by an actual human being instead of some sort of computer or something.

Comments on the Sample Source-Based Essay That Received a Score of 4

This response makes a simple argument, supports it with some evidence from the source text, and offers a partial analysis of the opposing argument.

The writer generates an argument in favor of fracking and makes a clear statement of his or her position in the first paragraph (*After reading two articles on this subject, one for it and one against it, I think I probably agree with "Taking a Stand for Fracking."*). The writer does cite some evidence from the source text to support his or her position, but overly relies on direct quotation with a minimum of true insight into the details quoted and a tendency to not question those details. Consequently, the analysis is simplistic and limited. In addition, the focus on the author's tone and style in the final a paragraph is a weak way to end the essay, revealing that the writer may have been more swayed by how the article was written rather than the quality of its details.

The writer adheres to proper grammar and usage.

Sample Score 1 Source-Based Essay

Fracking is breaking up the Earths surface to get gas. I get that. But it is not the right name for this thing. It is really called hydraulic fracking. That is just one of the facinating details I learned while reading the two articles.

These were the only articles about hydraulic fracking Ive ever read I think they really made me known of

an issue I didn't know anything about at all. I learned about a lot of terms like hydraulic fracking and I learned why some people are against it like the guy who wrote "The Arguing Against Fracking" and some people are for it like "Taking Stand for Fracking." I'm pretty sure I have an opinion about this subject now to. And I didn't even know anything about it! Before reading these articles!

Comments on the Sample Source-Based Essay That Received a Score of 1

In general, this response provides a minimal summary of the source texts and lacks insight and topic analysis. The writer fails to summarize source texts in a coherent and organized structure. Although this response addresses the source material, the writer fails to cite evidence to support any arguments and does not take a firm stance despite suggesting that he or she now has an opinion about it (*I'm pretty sure I have an opinion about this subject now to . . .*). The writer wastes too much space dwelling on how he or she did not know anything about fracking before reading the assignment.

Overall, the response is poorly developed, is disorganized, and lacks any clear progression of ideas. The writer uses informal, colloquial, and vague language (*Fracking is breaking up the Earths surface to get gas. I get that. But it is not the right name for this thing.*) and misquotes details in and even titles of the source material (*It is really called hydraulic fracking.*). The response lacks organizational structure and a clear progression of ideas.

Many sentences lack sense and fluency and are incorrect and awkward. The writer misuses and confuses words, punctuation, and usage as well as the conventions of English in general, making the response almost incomprehensible. This short response shows flawed sentence structure, including run-on sentences (*These were the only articles about hydraulic fracking Ive ever read I think they really made me known of an issue I didn't know anything about at all*) and fragments (*Before reading these articles!*).

Praxis® Core Academic Skills for Educators: Mathematics Practice Test 1

Time: 85 Minutes

Directions: Choose the best answer to each of the following questions.

1. Which of the following is equal to $\sqrt{500}$?
   a. 50
   b. $10\sqrt{50}$
   c. $10\sqrt{5}$
   d. $50\sqrt{10}$
   e. $5\sqrt{10}$

2. As of 2016, the yearly average birth rate in India is approximately 19.3 births for every 1,000 people. Determine the total number of births expected in one year if India's population is 1.327 billion.

3. What is the median of the data set represented by this boxplot?

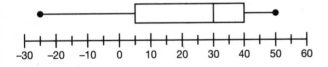

   a. 5
   b. 22.5
   c. 30
   d. 40
   e. 50

4. Solve the equation: $9 - x = -2(2x - 3)$
   a. –6
   b. –4
   c. –3
   d. –1
   e. 0

5. Brett can wash 2 full-length patio doors in 55 minutes. How many minutes would it take him to wash 17 full-length patio doors?

6. The radius of the base of circular cylindrical holding tank is 8 times the radius of the base of a circular cylindrical pipe that empties into it. If they have the same length, say L feet, the volume of the tank is how many times the volume of the pipe?
   a. 4
   b. 8
   c. 16
   d. 64
   e. 512

7. Which of the following is the solution set for the inequality $-4(3 - 2x) \geq 19 + 3(x - 2)$?
   a. $\{x \mid x \geq \frac{1}{11}\}$
   b. $\{x \mid x \geq 20\}$
   c. $\{x \mid x \geq -\frac{29}{5}\}$
   d. $\{x \mid x \geq -5\}$
   e. $\{x \mid x \geq 5\}$

8. Which of the following scatterplots indicates a positive trend?

a.

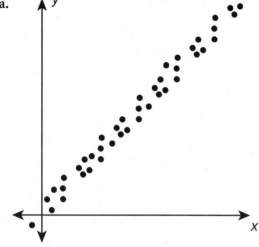

b.

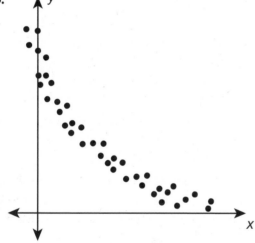

c.

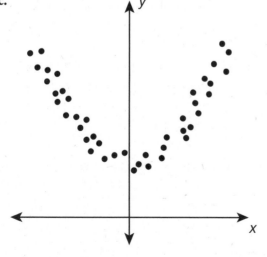

d.

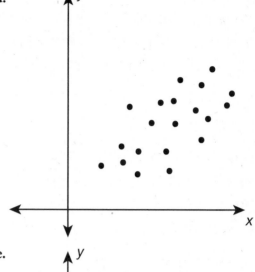

e.

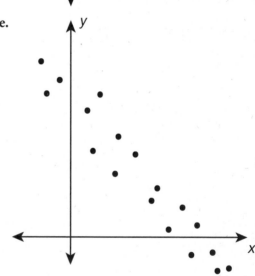

9. Which of the following is a reasonable estimate for the height of the first hill of a new extreme roller coaster?
   a. 2,000 mm
   b. 8 m
   c. 300 ft.
   d. 2.0 km
   e. 5 yards

10. Participants in a study concerned with the link between eating sugary foods and blood glucose levels are asked to measure their glucose levels every 4 hours during the day. One participant's readings for the first 24 hours of the study are as follows:

TIME	BLOOD GLUCOSE LEVEL (IN MILLIGRAMS PER DECILITER)
6 A.M.	50
10 A.M.	70
2 P.M.	50
6 P.M.	40
10 P.M.	60
2 A.M.	60

What is the mean blood glucose level for these readings?

11. What is the slope of the line graphed here?

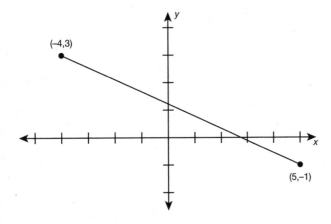

   a. 2

   b. $\frac{4}{9}$

   c. 0

   d. $-\frac{4}{9}$

   e. $-\frac{9}{4}$

12. Which of the following are factors of the number $2^3 \times 3^2 \times 5$? Select all that apply.

   a. 4

   b. 7

   c. 12

   d. 50

   e. 72

13. Pamela works a 40-hour week as a computer technician at a local library. She earns a base salary of $15 per hour, plus double this amount for any hour she works beyond 40 in a week. Her goal is to earn $960 each week prior to taxes. How many hours beyond the initial 40 must she work in a week to attain her goal?

14. An eighth-grade teacher needs to select a student representative to serve as an assistant crossing guard for after-school programs. To do this, she randomly selects a letter from the alphabet and then chooses the first student from the bottom of her class roster whose first name begins with that letter. Which of the following statements is true?

   a. The selection process is unfair because there may not be an equal number of students whose first names start with each letter of the alphabet.

   b. The selection process is unfair because she did a random selection of letters instead of numbers.

   c. The selection process is fair because each letter has an equal chance of being selected.

   d. The selection process is fair because students with an uncommon first name will not be singled out.

   e. This would be a fair method for making such a selection if the class size were 60, but not for a class size of 25.

15. If the triangle $\triangle ABC$ with vertices $A(3,-5)$, $B(-4,4)$, and $C(-6,3)$ is reflected over the line $y = -1$, what are the coordinates of the image of vertex C?
   a. $(3,-6)$
   b. $(4,-5)$
   c. $(4,3)$
   d. $(6,-3)$
   e. $(-6,-5)$

16. Consider the following relative frequency distribution:

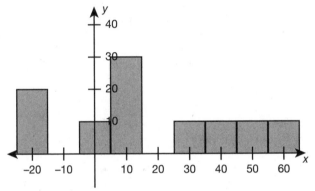

Select all statements that are true.
   a. The standard deviation is zero.
   b. The distribution is symmetric about the y-axis.
   c. The median of this distribution is positive.
   d. The distribution is skewed right.
   e. The distribution is bimodal.

17. Which of the following is equivalent to $24a^3b^5 - 8a^4b^2 + 36ab^3 - a^4b^2$?
   a. $55a^{12}b^{12}$
   b. $3ab^2(8a^2b^3 - 9a^4b^2 + 36ab^3)$
   c. $9ab^2(3a^2b^3 + 4b - 1)$
   d. $60a^3b^5 - 9a^4b^2$
   e. $3ab^2(8a^2b^3 - 3a^3 + 12b)$

18. Which of the following is equivalent to $\frac{30\sqrt{24}}{6\sqrt{3}}$?
   a. $5\sqrt{21}$
   b. $20\sqrt{3}$
   c. $5\sqrt{2}$
   d. $10\sqrt{2}$
   e. 20

19. Consider the following set of numbers: $\{6, 16, 26, 36, 46, 56, 66, 108\}$
If a number is selected at random from this set, what is the probability of selecting a number that is divisible by 6 and 9?
   a. 0.125
   b. 0.25
   c. 0.50
   d. 0.75
   e. 1.00

20. The group exercise classes at a local YMCA begin at 7 A.M. and the last class ends at 3:56 P.M. There are 10 classes offered with 4 minutes between classes. What is the duration of each class, in minutes?

21. Corn is being poured out of a silo into a pile in the form of a right circular cone. If the height of the final pile is 12 feet and the volume is 324π cubic feet, what is the radius of the circular base (in feet)?

22. Let $m(x) = -5x + 4x^3 - 3x^4$ and $n(x) = 6x^3 - 2x^4$. Which of the following is equivalent to $4m(x) - 3n(x)$?
   a. $-x(5x^3 + 14x^2 + 20)$
   b. $-2x(3x^3 + x^2 + 10)$
   c. $-2x(9x^3 + x^2 + 10)$
   d. $-2x(9x^3 - 17x^2 + 10)$
   e. $-x(x^3 + 2x^2 + 5)$

23. Two hundred parents and students in the audience of a high school freshmen orientation session were asked if they had ever heard of the concept of student-centered learning. The responses are tabulated as follows:

	PARENTS	STUDENTS
Yes	12	32
No	118	38

What is the probability that a randomly selected member of the audience answers Yes to this question given that the audience member is a parent?

a. $\frac{3}{50}$

b. $\frac{6}{65}$

c. $\frac{3}{11}$

d. $\frac{16}{35}$

e. 12

24. A dog boarding facility devotes $\frac{4}{5}$ of its time to dog grooming services. Of this time, $\frac{7}{24}$ is spent on bathing dogs. What fraction of its dog-grooming time does this facility NOT devote to bathing dogs?

25. Which of the following quadratic equations has imaginary solutions? Select all that apply.

a. $6x^2 - 42 = 0$

b. $3x^2 + x + 8 = 0$

c. $4x^2 + 20 = 0$

d. $-8x^2 + 40x = 0$

e. $x^2 + 11x + 4 = 0$

26. A family goes to an apple orchard to pick apples for autumn baking. The cost for the excursion is a $7.50 entrance fee plus $5.00 per pound of apples. If they want to spend no more than $50, which of the following inequalities can be used to determine the number of pounds of apples, x, they can purchase?

a. $5.00x + 7.50 \leq 50.00$

b. $5.00 + 7.50x \leq 50.00$

c. $5.00x + 7.50 \geq 50.00$

d. $5.00 + 7.50x \geq 50.00$

e. $12.50x \leq 50.00$

27. A zip line extends from peak to peak, as shown in the diagram.

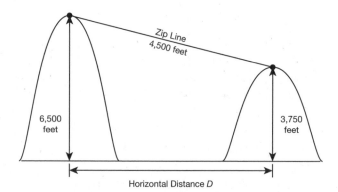

Horizontal Distance D

The length of the zip line is 4,500 feet. The height of the higher peak is 6,500 feet and the height of the lower one is 3,750 feet. What is the approximate horizontal distance between the two peaks?

a. 750 feet

b. 3,562 feet

c. 4,500 feet

d. 5,858 feet

e. 8,250 feet

28. Which of the following is equivalent to the expression $(3g^2h) \cdot (2j^3gh^5)$?

   a. $72g^3h^6j^3$

   b. $6g^2h^5j^3$

   c. $6(gh^6j)^3$

   d. $g^3h^6j^3$

   e. $6g^3h^6j^3$

29. The top of a giant gumball machine is a spherical glass globe with a diameter of 3 feet. What is the volume of the tank in cubic inches?

   a. $1,296\pi$ cubic inches

   b. $1,944\pi$ cubic inches

   c. $5,184\pi$ cubic inches

   d. $7,776\pi$ cubic inches

   e. $62,208\pi$ cubic inches

30. Which of the following is the solution of this system of equations?

$$\begin{cases} 2x - 3y = 21 \\ 3y + 2x = 27 \end{cases}$$

   a. $x = -\frac{3}{2}, y = -8$

   b. $x = 0, y = -7$

   c. $x = 12, y = 1$

   d. $x = 0, y = 9$

   e. no solution

31. Assume that the line passing through points A and C is tangent to the circle (centered at point B) at point A, as shown:

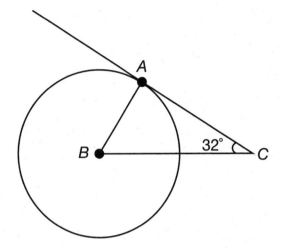

What is the measure of angle ABC in degrees?

32. Suppose that a random variable X has the following probability distribution:

x	−6	−2	0	3	5
$P(X = x)$	$\frac{3}{2}$	$\frac{2}{9}$	$\frac{1}{6}$	$\frac{7}{18}$	$\frac{1}{6}$

What is the expected value of X?

   a. −6

   b. 0

   c. .1

   d. $\frac{11}{9}$

   e. 3

33. On an amusement park map, 1 inch corresponds to 750 feet. If the length of the path from the Looper Dooper Coaster to the Over the Falls Flume Ride on the map is 3.8 inches, what is the actual distance between these amusement rides?

    a. 197.4 feet

    b. 753.8 feet

    c. 1,508 feet

    d. 2,850 feet

    e. cannot determine from the given information

34. Which of the following equations has solutions that correspond to the intersection points of the graph?

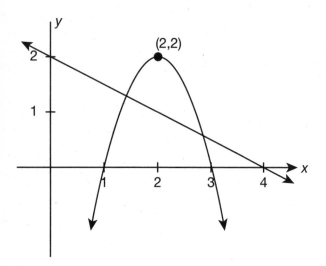

    a. $2(x-2)^2 = -\frac{1}{2}x$

    b. $-2(x-2)^2 = -\frac{1}{2}x$

    c. $-(x-2)^2 + 2 = -2x + 2$

    d. $(x-2)^2 = x$

    e. $-(x-2)^2 + 2 = -\frac{1}{2}x + 4$

35. Nathan spent $1,175 on equipment needed to start a power-washing business. For each deck or fence he power-washes, he earns $50, but it costs $6.50 in gas for each job. Determine the number of decks or fences he must power-wash to break even.

    a. 21

    b. 24

    c. 27

    d. 28

    e. 54

36. A professional racquetball player can return a ball at 70 miles per hour. Which numerical expression gives the speed of his return in feet per second?

    a. $\frac{70 \times 5,280}{60 \times 60}$ feet per second

    b. $\frac{70 \times 5,280}{60}$ feet per second

    c. $\frac{70 \times 60 \times 60}{5,280}$ feet per second

    d. $\frac{70}{60}$ feet per second

    e. $\frac{70}{60 \times 60}$ feet per second

37. Suppose that f is an invertible function with the following values:

x	−6	−5	−2	0	3	8
f(x)	3	8	6	4	−2	−6

What is the value of the expression $f^{-1}(f^{-1}(-6))$, where f^{-1} represents the inverse function of f?

38. Write the following product as a decimal: $(30.5 \times 10^4) \times (1.2 \times 10{-7})$

39. Consider the line graphed here:

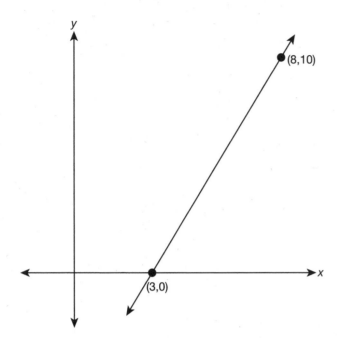

Which of the following is the equation of this line?
a. $2x - y = 3$
b. $x - 2y = 3$
c. $2x + 3y = 6$
d. $2x - y = 6$
e. $2x - y = -3$

40. The height of a scuba training pool in the shape of a right circular cylinder is three times the diameter of the base. If the diameter of the base of the cylinder is 60 feet, what is its volume?
a. $10,800\pi$ cubic feet
b. $54,000\pi$ cubic feet
c. $162,000\pi$ cubic feet
d. $648,000\pi$ cubic feet
e. $1,944,000\pi$ cubic feet

41. Assume the point $(-1,6)$ lies on the graph of the function $y = f(x)$. Consider the translation of this function given by $g(x) = f(x - 7) + 2$. To what point would the given point correspond on the graph of $g(x)$?

42. A tent is in the shape of a right triangular prism with dimensions shown:

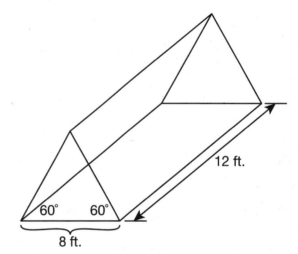

What is its total surface area?
a. $(288 + 32\sqrt{3})$ ft.^{2}
b. $192\sqrt{3}$ ft.^{2}
c. $(192 + 32\sqrt{3})$ ft.^{2}
d. $(96 + 32\sqrt{3})$ ft.^{2}
e. $(288 + 16\sqrt{3})$ ft.^{2}

43. If p and q are prime numbers, what is the greatest common factor of $18p^2q$, $30pq^2$, $12pq^3$?
a. $180p^2q^3$
b. $12pq^2$
c. $3pq$
d. $2,880p^4q^6$
e. $6pq$

44. Which of the following collections of data, if any, has/have a median and a mean of 26?

    I.   26, 26, 0, 26, 26

    II.   −22, 98, −22, 98, −22

    III. 26, 26, 26, 26

  a. I only

  b. II only

  c. III only

  d. I and II

  e. I, II, and III

45. Which of the following is equivalent to $\frac{32x - 8}{4x^2 - 1} \div \frac{16x^2 - 4x}{2x - 1}$?

  a. $\frac{2}{2x^2 + x}$

  b. $\frac{2}{2x^2 + 1}$

  c. $\frac{1}{x^2 + x}$

  d. $\frac{1}{x^2 + 1}$

  e. $\frac{2}{2x^2 - x}$

46. Which of the following distributions has a positive median? Select all that apply.

  a.

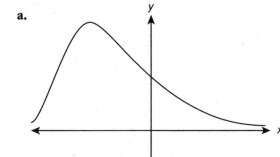

  b.

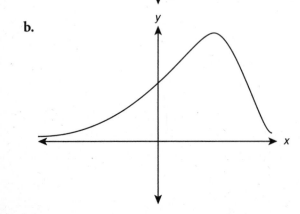

  c.

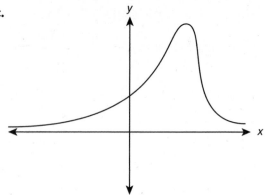

  d.

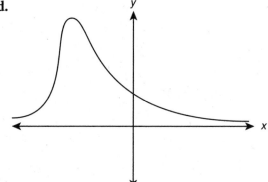

  e.

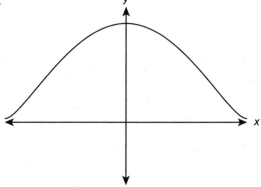

47. Assume that a and b are positive integers. Which of the following statements is/are always true?

    I. $\frac{a}{a + b} = \frac{1}{b}$

    II. $a \times b > a$

    III. $\frac{b}{a} + \frac{a}{b} = \frac{b^2 + a^2}{a \times b}$

  a. I and II only

  b. II and III only

  c. I only

  d. II only

  e. III only

48. Consider the two squares *ABCD* and *LMNP*:

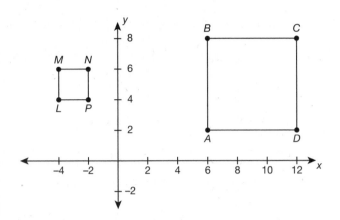

Assume that *ABCD* can be transformed into *LMNP* by first translating *ABCD* and then applying an appropriate dilation emanating from the lower left vertex of the square. Which of the following translation rule–dilation combinations will result in this transformation?

a. Translate using the rule $(x,y) \rightarrow (x + 10, y - 2)$ and then perform a dilation centered at the vertex *A* with a scale factor of 3.

b. Translate using the rule $(x,y) \rightarrow (x - 10, y - 2)$ and then perform a dilation centered at the vertex *A* with a scale factor of 3.

c. Translate using the rule $(x,y) \rightarrow (x - 10, y + 2)$ and then perform a dilation centered at the vertex *A* with a scale factor of $\frac{1}{3}$.

d. Translate using the rule $(x,y) \rightarrow (x - 4, y + 2)$ and then perform a dilation centered at the vertex *A* with a scale factor of 3.

e. Translate using the rule $(x,y) \rightarrow (x + 10, y - 2)$ and then perform a dilation centered at the vertex *A* with a scale factor of $\frac{1}{3}$.

49. A certain probability model suggests that when a standard 8-sided die is rolled, the probability of it landing with the 4 side up is $\frac{1}{8}$. Select all the following statements that are true.

a. In the long run, you expect to have the die land on a 4 one-eighth of the time.

b. If you roll ten consecutive 4s, the probability model must be invalid.

c. It is impossible to roll the die 100 times and get only five 4s.

d. It is possible to roll 20 consecutive 4s.

e. It is possible to roll the die 50 times and get one 4, and to roll it another 50 times and get thirty 4s without violating this model.

50. Jacob needs to build five identical, adjacent rectangular pens in the backyard in such a way that the backside of all five pens is against the barn, as shown.

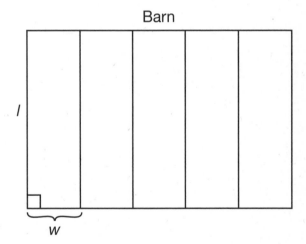

He has 1,200 feet of fence to use to construct the pens. Fence is not needed along the backside of the barn. If the combined area of all five pens must be 70,000 square feet, create a quadratic equation that can be used to find the width, *w*, of one of the five pens.

51. Which of the following statements is/are true? Select all that apply.
  a. The square root of a rational number must be irrational.
  b. The quotient of two nonzero rational numbers can be an irrational number.
  c. The product of two irrational numbers can be a rational number.
  d. The sum of an irrational number and a rational number must be an irrational number.
  e. The quotient of two irrational numbers can be irrational.

52. What is the value of x in the following diagram? Assume O is the center of the circle and that OP and OK are both radii of this circle.

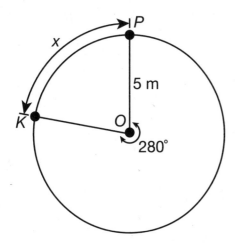

53. Which of the following is equivalent to $\frac{2}{(x+1)^2} \div \frac{x}{x+1}$?
  a. $\frac{1-x}{x+1}$
  b. $\frac{2-x}{(x+1)^2}$
  c. $\frac{-(x+2)}{x+1}$
  d. $\frac{1-x}{(x+1)^2}$
  e. $\frac{-(x-1)(x+2)}{(x+1)^2}$

54. Consider the set of whole numbers $\{6, 12, 18, 24, \ldots\}$. Select all of the following statements that are true about the members of this set.
  a. None of the numbers are prime.
  b. All the numbers are divisible by 4.
  c. None of the numbers are odd.
  d. All the numbers are multiples of 6.
  e. All the numbers are factors of 6.

55. A great room measures 18 feet by 22 feet and the ceiling is 10 feet high. One gallon of paint can be used to apply one coat of paint to 300 square feet of wall or ceiling space. How many gallons of paint will it take to paint all but the floor of the room if three coats of paint must be applied? Round your answer to the nearest tenth of a foot.

56. Which of the following statements is/are true? Select all that apply.
  a. $\sqrt{9} + \sqrt{16} = \sqrt{25}$
  b. $\sqrt{\frac{1}{5}} = \frac{\sqrt{5}}{5}$
  c. $e = 2.71828$
  d. $\pi = 314159$
  e. $\sqrt{\frac{1}{5}} > \sqrt{\frac{1}{7}}$

Praxis® Core Academic Skills for Educators: Mathematics Practice Test 1 Answers and Explanations

1. c. Observe that $\sqrt{500} = \sqrt{10 \times 10 \times 5} = 10\sqrt{5}$. Choice **a** is incorrect because 50 squared does not equal 500, so $\sqrt{500}$ cannot equal 50. Choice **b** is incorrect because $10\sqrt{50} = \sqrt{10 \times 10 \times 50} = \sqrt{5,000}$, not $\sqrt{500}$. Choice **d** is incorrect because $50\sqrt{10} = \sqrt{50 \times 50 \times 10} = \sqrt{25,000}$, not $\sqrt{500}$. Choice **e** is incorrect because the 5 and 10 are switched.

2. 25,611,100. Let x represent the expected number of births. Set up the following proportion:

$$\frac{19.3}{1,000} = \frac{x}{1,327,000,000}$$

Solving for x yields

$$1,000x = (19.3)(1,327,000,000)$$
$$x = \frac{(19.3)(1,327,000,000)}{1,000}$$
$$x = 25,611,100$$

3. c. The median is depicted in a boxplot as the vertical line segment occurring within the box portion of the plot itself. Here, that line occurs at the value 30. So, the median of the data set is 30. Choice **a** is incorrect because it represents the 25th percentile, not the median. Choice **b** is incorrect because although 22.5 is the midpoint between the outer boundaries of the box (which occur at 5 and 40), it is not the center of the *data set*. The vertical line contained within the box depicts the median of the data set. Choice **d** is incorrect because it represents the 75th percentile, not the median. Choice **e** is incorrect because this is the maximum value of any data point in the data set, not the middle (or median) of the data set.

4. d. Use the distributive property on the right side. Then, gather all x-terms on the left side and the constant terms on the right, combine like terms, and finally divide both sides by the coefficient of x, as follows:

$$9 - x = -2(2x - 3)$$
$$9 - x = -4x + 6$$
$$4x - x = 6 - 9$$
$$3x = -3$$
$$x = -1$$

Choice **a** is incorrect because when solving for x, you divide both sides by its coefficient, you do not subtract it from both sides. Choice **b** is incorrect because you did not distribute the -2 to both terms within the parentheses on the right side. Choice **c** is incorrect because you did not divide both sides by 3 in the last step. Choice **e** is incorrect because you added coefficient of x to both sides in the last step instead of dividing both sides by it.

5. 467.5 minutes. Let x represent the number of minutes needed to wash 17 full-length patio doors. Set up the following proportion:

$$\frac{2 \text{ patio doors}}{55 \text{ minutes}} = \frac{17 \text{ patio doors}}{x \text{ minutes}}$$

Cross multiply and solve for x:

$$2x = (17)(55)$$
$$2x = 935$$
$$x = 467.5$$

So, it would take Brett 467.5 minutes to wash 17 full-length patio doors.

6. d. Let R be the radius of the base of the pipe. Then, the radius of the base of the tank is $8R$. The volume of the pipe is $\pi R^2 L$, while the volume of the tank is $\pi(8R)^2 L = 64\pi R^2 L$. So, the volume of the tank is 64 times the volume of the pipe. Choice **a** is incorrect because you took one-half of the radius instead of squaring it when computing the volume of the tank. Choice **b** is incorrect because you forgot to square the 8 when computing the volumes of the pipe and tank. Choice **c** is incorrect because when squaring $8R$, you mistakenly multiplied 8 by 2 instead of raising 8 to the second power. Note that $8^2 = 64$, not 16. Choice **e** is incorrect because you cubed the radius when computing the volumes of the pipe and tank, but should have squared it.

7. e. To solve this inequality, use the distributive properties on both sides of the inequality. Then, combine like terms on each side. Take the x-terms to the left and the constants to the right and combine like terms again. Then, divide both sides by the coefficient of x:

$$-4(3 - 2x) \geq 19 + 3(x - 2)$$
$$-12 + 8x \geq 19 + 3x - 6$$
$$-12 + 8x \geq 13 + 3x$$
$$5x \geq 25$$
$$x \geq 5$$

So, the solution set is $\{x \mid x \geq 5\}$. Choice **a** is incorrect because when gathering the x-terms on one side and the constant on the other side of inequality, you add the opposite of a term to one side, not the term itself. Choice **b** is incorrect because in the last step, instead of dividing both sides by 5, you subtracted 5 from both sides. Choice **c** is incorrect because you did not apply the distributive property correctly. Choice **d** is incorrect because you made a sign error when balancing the equation.

8. a. The points rise from left to right in this scatterplot, which indicates a positive trend. Choice **b** is incorrect because the points follow a nonlinear graph on which the points fall from left to right, which indicates a negative trend. Choice **c** is incorrect because while the correlation is very strong (and nonlinear), part of the time the points fall from left to right, and part of the time they rise from left to right; so the trend is not positive. Choice **d** is incorrect because while the points are all above the x-axis, so that the y-values are all *positive*, there is no discernible trend, positive or negative, apparent in the scatterplot. Choice **e** is incorrect because this is a loose negative trend since the points tend to fall from left to right.

9. c. Of all the choices listed, this is by far the most reasonable. Choice **a** is incorrect because 2,000 mm is equivalent to 20 cm, which is less than 1 foot. Choice **b** is incorrect because 8 meters is about 24 feet, which may be fine for a kiddie coaster, but not an extreme roller coaster. Choice **d** is incorrect because this exceeds one mile, which is way too high. Choice **e** is incorrect because this is 15 feet, which may be fine for a kiddie coaster, but not an extreme roller coaster.

10. 55 milligrams per deciliter. Add the six measurements and divide the sum by 6 to get $\frac{330}{6} =$ 55 milligrams per deciliter.

11. d. Use the two labeled points (–4,3) and (5,–1) to compute the slope:
$$m = \frac{3-(-1)}{-4-5} = \frac{4}{-9} = -\frac{4}{9}$$
Choice **a** is incorrect because you added the y-values and the x-values when forming the numerator and denominator, respectively, of the slope, but you should compute the differences. Choice **b** is incorrect because the sign is wrong. Be certain to subtract the y-values and the x-values in the same order when computing the slope. Choice **c** is incorrect because the slope cannot be 0 since the line is not horizontal. Choice **e** is incorrect because this is the reciprocal of the slope; remember, the slope of a line is the change in y-values divided by the change in x-values.

12. a, c, and e. A factor of a whole number must divide it evenly. Observe that $4 = 2^2$, which divides 2^3 evenly; $12 = 2^2 \times 3$, which divides $2^3 \times 3^2$ evenly; and $72 = 2^3 \times 3^2$, which clearly divides $2^3 \times 3^2$ evenly. Choice **b** is not a correct selection because 7 is not a prime factor listed in the given product and so cannot divide it evenly. Choice **d** is not a correct selection because $50 = 2 \times 5^2$, which has one more factor of 5 than occurs in the given product, so it cannot divide it evenly.

13. 12 hours. Let x be the number of hours beyond 40 that Pamela must work to attain her goal. Her salary for the first 40 hours is $40(15) = 600$ dollars. Since she earns double per hour beyond 40 hours, her salary for working x hours beyond 40 is $30x$ dollars. The sum of these two dollar amounts must equal $960. This yields the equation $600 + 30x = 960$. Solve for x as follows:
$$600 + 30x = 960$$
$$30x = 360$$
$$x = 12$$
So, Pamela must work 12 hours beyond the initial 40 to reach her earning goal.

14. a. A fair selection would result in each student having an equal chance of being selected. However, if 6 students have first names starting with the letter M, while 14 have first names starting with the letter B, then students do not have an equal chance of being selected. Choice **b** is incorrect because random selection can be done with letters or numbers or without any assignment of either depending on the method used. Choice **c** is incorrect because while each *letter* has an equal chance of being selected, the goal is to select a student, and the number of first names beginning with each letter can be, and likely are, different. Choice **d** is incorrect because to be fair, each student should have an equal chance of being selected whether his or her name is common or not. Choice **e** is incorrect because the size of the class is not the deciding criterion on fairness of the method. This issue is that there may not be an equal number of students whose first names begin with each letter.

15. e. When reflecting a point across the line $y = -1$, the x-coordinate will stay the same, but the y-coordinate will change. You subtract $3 - (-1) = 4$ and *add* this to -1 to get the new y-coordinate. So, the image of vertex C is $(-6,-5)$. Choice **a** is incorrect because this is the image across the line $y = x$. Choice **b** is incorrect because while the y-coordinate is correct, the x-coordinate should not change when reflecting across the line $y = -1$. Choice **c** is incorrect because this is the image across the line $x = -1$, not $y = -1$. Choice **d** is incorrect because this is the image across the origin, meaning that it is reflected about the y-axis and then the x-axis.

16. c and d. Choice **a** is not a correct selection because the only way the standard deviation can be zero is if there is a single data value, which is not the case here. Choice **b** is not a correct selection because if you fold the distribution over the *y*-axis, the graph does not line up, so it is not symmetric. Choice **c** is a correct selection because the median is the data value that divides the data in half. In this distribution, the data value that does this occurs within the bar on the 10, which is positive. Choice **d** is a correct selection because the bulk of the data is to the right of the data value 10. Choice **e** is not a correct selection because there are 5 data values with the same relative frequency.

17. e. First, combine the second and fourth terms since they have the same variable part (and so are like terms): $24a^3b^5 - 9a^4b^2 + 36ab^3$. Now, factor out the greatest common factor $3ab^2$ from *all* terms to get: $3ab^2(8a^2b^3 - 3a^3 + 12b)$. Choice **a** is incorrect because you cannot add all four terms together like this. When monomials have the same variable part, you can add/subtract their coefficients. If they do not have the exact same variable part, you cannot combine them. Choice **b** is incorrect because when you factor out a greatest common factor, you must do so from all terms, not just the first one in an expression. Choice **c** is incorrect because 9 is not a common factor of *all* terms in the simplified expression $24a^3b^5 - 9a^4b^2 + 36ab^3$. Choice **d** is incorrect because you cannot combine the first and third terms of the given expression since their variable parts are different.

18. d. Use the properties of radicals, together with the way fractions are multiplied, to simplify the expression:

$$\frac{30\sqrt{24}}{6\sqrt{3}} = \frac{30}{6} \cdot \frac{\sqrt{24}}{\sqrt{3}}$$
$$= 5 \cdot \sqrt{\frac{24}{3}}$$
$$= 5\sqrt{8}$$
$$= 5\sqrt{4 \cdot 2}$$
$$= 5\sqrt{4} \cdot \sqrt{2}$$
$$= 5 \cdot 2 \cdot \sqrt{2}$$
$$= 10\sqrt{2}$$

Choice **a** is incorrect because you subtracted the radicands instead of dividing them. Remember, $\frac{\sqrt{a}}{\sqrt{b}} = \sqrt{\frac{a}{b}}$. Choice **b** is incorrect because you cannot cancel the 6 in the denominator with the 24 in the radicand in the numerator. Choice **c** is incorrect because you did not simplify $\sqrt{8}$ correctly. Choice **e** is incorrect because you cannot cancel the 3 in the denominator with the 30 in the radicand in the numerator, and you cannot cancel the 6 in the denominator with the 24 in the radicand in the numerator.

19. b. A number is divisible by 6 if it is even and its digit sum is divisible by 3. The numbers in the set for which this is true are 6, 36, 66, and 108. A number is divisible by 9 if its digit sum is divisible by 9. The numbers in the set for which this is true are 36 and 108. So, the probability that a number selected randomly from this set satisfies both conditions is $\frac{2}{8} = \frac{1}{4}$, or 0.25. Choice **a** is incorrect because it represents $\frac{1}{8}$. There are 2 numbers divisible by 6 and 9: 36 and 108. Choice **c** is incorrect because this is the probability that the number selected is divisible by 6; you did not account for the fact that it must also be divisible by 9. Choice **d** is incorrect because this is the probability of the complement of the event. Choice **e** is incorrect because this would mean all members of the set are divisible by 6 and 9. But 26 is divisible by neither of these, for instance.

20. 50 minutes. The amount of time between 7 A.M. and 3:56 P.M. is 8 hours 56 minutes, which equals $8(60) + 56 = 536$ minutes. Since there are 10 classes, we must subtract 4 minutes times 9 to account for the time *between* consecutive classes. This gives 36 minutes. Subtracting this from 536 gives 500 minutes, which is evenly divided among 10 classes. This means each class lasts 50 minutes.

21. 9 feet. The volume of a right circular cone with radius r and height h is given by the formula $V = \frac{1}{3}\pi r^2 h$. Substituting $h = 12$ and $V = 324\pi$ yields the equation $\frac{1}{3}\pi \cdot 12 \cdot r^2 = 324\pi$. Solving for r^2 yields $4\pi \times r^2 = 324\pi$, or $r^2 = 81$. So, $r = 9$ feet.

22. b. To compute $4m(x) - 3n(x)$, first distribute 4 through each term of $m(x)$ and distribute the 3 through each term of $n(x)$, and then add like terms. Finally, factor out the greatest common factor from all terms.

$$\begin{aligned} 4m(x) - 3n(x) &= 4(-5x + 4x^3 - 3x^4) - 3(6x^3 - 2x^4) \\ &= -20x + 16x^3 - 12x^4 - 18x^3 + 6x^4 \\ &= -6x^4 - 2x^3 - 20x \\ &= -2x(3x^3 + x^2 + 10) \end{aligned}$$

Choice **a** is incorrect because you did not apply the distributive property correctly when computing $4m(x)$ and $3n(x)$. Multiply each term of the expressions $m(x)$ and $n(x)$ by 4 and –3, respectively. Choice **c** is incorrect because you applied the negative 1 to only the first term of $n(x)$. You must distribute it to all terms. Choice **d** is incorrect because you added the polynomials instead of subtracting them. Choice **e** is incorrect because you ignored the constant multiples of $m(x)$ and $n(x)$.

23. b. This is a conditional probability question. Since we are given that the audience member is a parent, we reduce the sample space down from 200 members to 130. Of these, 12 answer Yes. So, the probability we seek is $\frac{12}{130} = \frac{6}{65}$. Choice **a** is incorrect because you divided 12 by 200, so you did not restrict the sample space down to only those who are parents. Choice **c** is incorrect because you used the wrong given information. Specifically, you are given that the audience member is a parent, not that the audience member answers Yes. Choice **d** is incorrect because this is the probability that an audience member answers Yes given that the audience member is a student, not a parent. Choice **e** is incorrect because this is the number of parents who answer Yes, but it is not a probability.

24. $\frac{23}{30}$. To determine the fraction of dog-grooming time that the facility devotes to bathing dogs, multiply as follows: $\frac{4}{5} \times \frac{7}{24} = \frac{7}{30}$. So, the facility spends $1 - \frac{7}{30} = \frac{23}{30}$ of its dog grooming on activities other than bathing dogs.

25. **b and c.** Choice **a** is not a correct selection. The solutions are $\pm\sqrt{7}$, which are real numbers. Choice **b** is a correct selection. The discriminant is $1^2 - 4(3)(8) = -95 < 0$, so the solutions are imaginary. Choice **c** is a correct selection. Since $4x^2 + 20$ is always positive, it can never equal zero. So, the equation $4x^2 + 20 = 0$ has no real solutions. Choice **d** is not a correct selection. The solutions are -5 and 0, which are real numbers. Choice **e** is not a correct selection. The discriminant is $11^2 - 4(1)(4) = 105 > 0$, so the equation has two distinct real solutions.

26. **a.** The cost for x pounds of apples is $5.00x$ dollars. This, plus the entrance fee of $7.50, cannot exceed $50. This yields the inequality $5.00x + 7.50 \le 50.00$. Choice **b** is incorrect because 5.00 and 7.50 should be interchanged. Choice **c** is incorrect because the inequality sign should be reversed. Choice **d** is incorrect because 5.00 and 7.50 should be interchanged, and the inequality sign should be reversed. Choice **e** is incorrect because the entrance fee plus the cost of a pound of apples should not be multiplied by the number of pounds of apples purchased.

27. **b.** First, construct a right triangle whose hypotenuse is the zip-line (4,500 feet), whose height is the difference between the heights of the two peaks (2,750 feet), and whose base is the horizontal distance we seek, D.

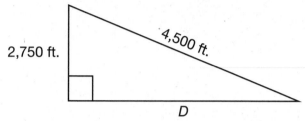

Use the Pythagorean theorem to determine the value of D: $2,750^2 + D^2 = 4,500^2$, which simplifies to $D^2 = 12,687,500$, so that $D = \sqrt{12,687,500} \approx 3,562$ feet. Choice **a** is wrong because when applying the Pythagorean theorem, you forgot to square the sides. Choice **c** is wrong because this is a right triangle, so the two longest sides cannot have the same length. Choice **d** is wrong because when applying the Pythagorean theorem, you treated the zip line as a leg when it is the hypotenuse. Choice **e** is wrong because when applying the Pythagorean theorem, you treated the zip line as a leg when it is actually the hypotenuse, and you forgot to square the sides.

28. **e.** Gather like variables in the product and add their exponents:
$$(3g^2h) \cdot (2j^3gh^5) = (3 \cdot 2)(g^2 \cdot g) \cdot (h \cdot h^5) \cdot (j^3)$$
$$= 6g^3h^6j^3$$
Choice **a** is wrong because you applied the exponents of the adjacent variable to each coefficient, but this would require there to be another set of parentheses. Specifically, $(3g)^2 = 3^2g^2$, but this does not equal $3g^2$. Choice **b** is wrong because you multiplied the exponents instead of adding them. Choice **c** is wrong because the power on h should be 2 in this form. Choice **d** is wrong because you ignored the coefficients.

29. d. The radius of the globe is 1.5 feet, which equals 18 inches (since 1 foot = 12 inches). The volume of a sphere with radius r is $\frac{4}{3}\pi r^3$. Substituting $r = 18$ inches into this formula gives a volume of $7{,}776\pi$ cubic inches. Choice **a** is wrong because this is the surface area, not the volume; the volume formula is $\frac{4}{3}\pi r^3$. Choice **b** is wrong because you need to multiply by 4; the volume formula is $\frac{4}{3}\pi r^3$. Choice **c** is wrong because this would be the surface area, not the volume, of a sphere with radius 3 feet (or 36 inches). You used the wrong formula and used the diameter in place of the radius. Choice **e** is wrong because you used the diameter in place of the radius when computing the volume.

30. c. The most expedient approach is to use the elimination method because simply adding the equations will result in the y-terms canceling. Doing so yields $4x = 48$, so that $x = 12$. Substituting this value into the first equation yields $2(12) - 3y = 21$. This is equivalent to $-3y = -3$, so that $y = 1$. Thus, the solution is $x = 12$, $y = 1$. Choice **a** is incorrect because you subtracted the left sides of the equations, but added the right sides. Choice **b** is incorrect because this pair satisfies the first equation, but not the second one; hence, it is not a solution of the system. Choice **d** is incorrect because this pair satisfies the second equation, but not the first one; hence, it is not a solution of the system. Choice **e** is incorrect because adding the equations yields an equation for which there is a value of x; substituting this value into either equation then yields the corresponding value of y.

31. 58 degrees. Since the line passing through A and C is tangent at point A, the radial segment connecting the center, B, to A is perpendicular to it. So, the triangle ABC is a right triangle. Since the sum of the three interior angles of a triangle is 180 degrees, the measure of angle ABC must be 58 degrees.

32. d. To compute the expected value of such a random variable, multiply x times $P(X = x)$ and sum all of them. Doing so yields:
$$(-6)\left(\frac{1}{18}\right) + (-2)\left(\frac{2}{9}\right) + 0\left(\frac{1}{6}\right) + 3\left(\frac{7}{18}\right) + 5\left(\frac{1}{6}\right)$$
$$= -\frac{1}{3} - \frac{4}{9} + \frac{7}{6} + \frac{5}{6} = \frac{22}{18} = \frac{11}{9}.$$
Choice **a** is wrong because this is the minimum value of the data set, not the expected value. Choice **b** is wrong because you added the x-values, but did not multiply each one by $P(X = x)$. Choice **c** is wrong because you summed the probabilities, which must add to 1, but you must multiply each one by its respective value of x. Choice **e** is wrong because even though this value of x has the highest probability associated with it, the expected value is not simply this value. Rather, you must multiply each value of X by its probability of occurring and sum those values.

33. d. Let x represent the actual distance between the two rides. Using the information provided, we have the following proportion:

$$\frac{1 \text{ inch}}{750 \text{ feet}} = \frac{3.8 \text{ inches}}{x \text{ feet}}$$

$$(1 \text{ inch})(x \text{ feet}) = (750 \text{ feet})(3.8 \text{ inches})$$

$$x = \frac{(750 \text{ feet})(3.8 \text{ inches})}{1 \text{ inch}}$$

$$= 2{,}850 \text{ feet}$$

Solving for x yields $x = 2{,}850$ feet. Choice **a** is wrong because you set up the proportion incorrectly; you should be multiplying 750 by 3.8, not dividing by it. Choice **b** is wrong because you simply added 750 feet to 3.8 inches, which is incorrect. You must set up a proportion consisting of two ratios, one corresponding to what 1 inch represents and one corresponding to what 3.8 inches represents. Choice **c** is wrong because you seem to have misunderstood how to work with proportions. Set up the proportion $\frac{1 \text{ inch}}{750 \text{ feet}} = \frac{3.8 \text{ inches}}{x \text{ feet}}$ and solve for x. Choice **e** is wrong because you can set up the following proportion, where x represents the actual length of the path:

$$\frac{1 \text{ inch}}{750 \text{ feet}} = \frac{3.8 \text{ inches}}{x \text{ feet}}$$

34. b. You must determine the equation of the parabola and the line and equate them. The equation of the parabola has the form $y = a(x - h)^2 + k$. The vertex is (2,2), so this becomes $y = a(x - 2)^2 + 2$. To find a, use one of the labeled x-intercepts, say (1,0). Substitute this into the equation to obtain $0 = a(1 - 2)^2 + 2$. Solving for a yields $a = -2$. So, the equation of the parabola is $y = -2(x - 2)^2 + 2$. To find the equation of the line in slope-intercept form $y = mx + b$, use the two labeled points to find the slope: $m = \frac{2-0}{0-4} = -\frac{1}{2}$. Since the y-intercept is 2, the equation of the line is $y = -\frac{1}{2}x + 2$. Equating these the equation $-2(x - 2)^2 + 2 = -\frac{1}{2}x + 2$. The solutions of this equation would yield the x-coordinates of the points of intersection of the two graphs shown. Canceling the constant 2 on each side yields the simplified equation $-2(x - 2)^2 = -\frac{1}{2}x$. Choice **a** is wrong because the coefficient on the left side should be -2 since the parabola opens downward. Otherwise, the equation is correct. Choice **c** is wrong because there are errors in the equation of the parabola and the line. The coefficient on the left side should be -2 and the slope of the line is $-\frac{1}{2}$, not -2. Choice **d** is wrong because this is the result of getting the slope wrong for the line; it is $-\frac{1}{2}$, not -2. Choice **e** is wrong because there are errors in the equation of the parabola and the line. The coefficient on the left side should be -2 and the y-intercept of the line is 2, not 4.

35. d. You must express profit as an expression involving the number of decks or fences power-washed. The $1,175 spent on materials is *negative profit*, so it will appear as –1,175 in the expression. Next, since Nathan earns $50 per deck or fence power-washed and it costs $6.50 per job, his net gain per job is $50 – $6.50 = $43.50. This is constant, so the profit gained from power-washing x fences or decks is 43.50x dollars. The expression describing his profit is thus 43.50x – 1,175. Now, to compute the break-even point, we need to determine the number of decks or fences power-washed that will yield a profit of 0 dollars. This requires that we solve the equation 0 = 43.50x – 1,175:

$$0 = 43.50x - 1,175$$
$$1.175 = 43.50x$$
$$27.01 \approx x$$

You must round up and conclude that Nathan will break even after power-washing 28 decks or fences. Choice **a** is wrong because you mistakenly included the cost of gas, $6.50 per job, as *profit* rather than as *debt*. For each deck or fence power-washed, he earns $50 – $6.50, not $50 + $6.50. Choice **b** is wrong because you did not account for the cost in gas for each job. Choice **c** is wrong because you must round *up*, not down, to ensure he has earned enough cash to break even. Choice **e** is wrong because this is the number of driveways Nathan must clear to earn $1,175 *in profit*, not just break even.

36. a. There are 60 minutes in one hour and 60 seconds in one minute. So, there are 60×60 seconds in one hour. There are 5,280 feet in a mile. Using these enables us to convert from miles per hour to feet per second as follows:

$$\frac{70 \text{ miles}}{1 \text{ hour}} = \frac{70 \text{ miles}}{1 \text{ hour}} \times \frac{1 \text{ hour}}{60 \times 60 \text{ seconds}} \times \frac{5,280 \text{ feet}}{1 \text{ mile}}$$

$$= \frac{70 \times 5,280}{60 \times 60} \text{ feet per second}$$

Choice **b** is wrong because there are 60×60 seconds in one hour, not just 60. Choice **c** is wrong because when setting up the conversion, you inverted both fractions. Choice **d** is wrong because you did not account for the fact that there are 5,280 feet in one mile. Also, there are 60×60 seconds in one hour. Choice **e** is wrong because you did not account for the fact that there are 5,280 feet in one mile.

37. –5. Use the fact that $y = f(x)$ if and only if $x = f^{-1}(y)$. Using this with the table shows that $f^{-1}(-6) = 8$ and $f^{-1}(8) = -5$. Thus, $f^{-1}(f^{-1}(-6)) = f^{-1}(8) = -5$.

38. 0.0366. The most efficient approach is to group the powers of 10 together and the two decimals together. Simplify each, and then convert the resulting expression to a decimal.

$$(30.5 \times 10^4) \times (1.2 \times 10^{-7}) = (30.5 \times 1.2)$$
$$\times (10^4 \times 10^{-7})$$
$$= 36.6 \times 10^{-3}$$
$$= 0.0366$$

39. d. Use the two labeled points on the line—(3,0) and (8,10)—to compute the slope: $m = \frac{10-0}{8-3} = \frac{10}{5} = 2$. Using point-slope form with the point (3,0) yields $y - (0) = 2(x - 3)$. This simplifies to $y = 2x - 6$, which is equivalent to $2x - y = 6$. Choice **a** is wrong because when converting the equation from point-slope formula (namely $y = 2(x - 3)$) to standard form, you did not distribute the 2 to both terms in parentheses on the right side. Choice **b** is wrong because you calculated the slope incorrectly; it should be the change in y-coordinates divided by the change in x-coordinates, not the reciprocal. Choice **c** is wrong because you computed the slope by subtracting the x-coordinates from the y-coordinates of each point, but the slope is computed as the change in y-coordinates divided by the change in x-coordinates. Choice **e** is wrong because you mistakenly treated the point (3,0) as the y-intercept and used $b = 3$ in the slope-intercept form $y = mx + b$. But it is the x-intercept.

40. c. The height is 3(60 feet) = 180 feet and the radius is $\frac{1}{2}$(60 feet) = 30 feet. So, the volume of the cylinder is

$$V = \pi r^2 h = \pi (30 \text{ feet})^2 (180 \text{ feet})$$
$$= 162{,}000\pi \text{ cubic feet}$$

Choice **a** is wrong because you used the diameter in place of the radius, and forgot to square the radius when computing the volume. Choice **b** is wrong because you used the formula for the volume of a right circular cone $V = \frac{1}{3}\pi r^2 h$, but the volume of a cylinder does not include a multiple of $\frac{1}{3}$. Choice **d** is wrong because you used the diameter in place of the radius when computing the volume. Choice **e** is wrong because you misinterpreted the relationship between the radius and the height. Specifically, the given information means that the height is 3(60 feet), not that the radius is 3(60 feet).

41. (6,8). You need to translate the given point 7 units to the right and 2 units upward. Consequently, the point (−1,6) translates to the point $(−1 + 7, 6 + 2) = (6,8)$.

42. a. The tent is made up of five faces. The front and the back of the tent are congruent equilateral triangles. Dropping an altitude from the top vertex to the opposite side gives the height of the triangle. This creates a 30-60-90 triangle, so the height is $4\sqrt{3}$ feet. Thus, the area of the front and back is $(4\sqrt{3} \text{ ft.})(8 \text{ ft.}) = 16\sqrt{3} \text{ ft.}^2$; so their combined area is $32\sqrt{3} \text{ ft.}^2$. The other three faces of the tent are congruent rectangles with width 8 feet and length 12 feet, so each has an area of $(8 \text{ ft.})(12 \text{ ft.}) = 96 \text{ ft.}^2$. Their combined area is $3(96) = 288 \text{ ft.}^2$. Therefore, the surface area is $(288 + 32\sqrt{3}) \text{ ft.}^2$. Choice **b** is the volume, not the surface area. Choice **c** did not include the bottom of the tent. Choice **d** did not include the two top side portions of the tent. Choice **e** included only one of the two triangular sides of the tent (that is, you forgot either the front or the back).

43. e. The largest whole number that goes into all of 18, 30, and 12 is 6. The largest power of p that goes into all of $18p^2q$, $30pq^2$, $12pq^3$ is p, and the largest power of q that goes into all of these terms is q. So, the greatest common factor is $6pq$. Choice **a** is the least common multiple. Choice **b** is wrong because 12 is not a factor of 18 or 30, and the power of q is not correct. Choice **c** is a common factor of all three terms, but is not the *greatest* common factor. Choice **d** is the product of all three terms; this is a common multiple, but not a common factor.

44. c. First, arrange the members of each data set in increasing order. Then, compute each of their means and medians.

　　I.　　0, 26, 26, 26, 26

　　II.　　−22, −22, −22, 98, 98

　　III.　　26, 26, 26, 26

The median for I is 26, but the mean is $\frac{26(4)}{5} = 20.8$. So, the mean is not 26. The median for II is −22, which is not 26. The median for III is $\frac{26 + 26}{2} = 26$. The mean is $\frac{26(4)}{4} = 26$.

45. a. Transform the division problem into a multiplication problem. Then, factor all numerators and denominators and cancel factors common to the numerator and denominator, as follows:

$$\frac{32x - 8}{4x^2 - 1} \div \frac{16x^2 - 4x}{2x - 1} = \frac{32x - 8}{4x^2 - 1} \cdot \frac{2x - 1}{16x^2 - 4x}$$

$$= \frac{{}^2\!8(4x - 1)}{(2x - 1)(2x + 1)} \cdot \frac{2x - 1}{4x(4x - 1)}$$

$$= \frac{2}{x(2x + 1)}$$

$$= \frac{2}{2x^2 + x}$$

Choice **b** is incorrect because you did not distribute the x through both terms in the denominator when simplifying $\frac{2}{x(2x + 1)}$. Choice **c** is incorrect because you incorrectly canceled the 2's in numerator and denominator of $\frac{2}{2x^2 + x}$; these are terms, not factors, and cannot be canceled in this manner. Choice **d** is incorrect because you did not distribute the x through both terms in the denominator when simplifying $\frac{2}{x(2x + 1)}$, and you incorrectly canceled the 2's in numerator and denominator of $\frac{2}{2x^2 + x}$; these are terms, not factors, and cannot be canceled in this manner. Choice **e** is incorrect because you canceled the wrong factor in the denominator with $2x - 1$ in the numerator.

46. b and c. Choices **a** and **d** are not correct selections because the bulk of the data (more than 50%) are to the left of the y-axis, so the median is negative. Choices **b** and **c** are correct selections because more than 50% of the data are to the right of the y-axis, so the median is positive. Choice **c** is not a correct selection because the median is 0.

47. e. Statement I is false because it is the result of incorrectly canceling common terms, not factors, in the numerator and denominator. This is never true when a and b are positive integers. In fact, the only way it can be true is if either a or b is zero. Statement II is false because if $b = 1$, then $a \cdot b = a$. Statement III is true because this is the way fractions are added. The common denominator is ab. Multiplying the top and bottom of first fraction by b and the top and bottom of the second fraction by b and then adding the fractions yields this statement.

48. c. First, observe that to move A to A', we must move the point left 10 units and then up 2 units. The translation rule $(x,y) \rightarrow (x - 10, y + 2)$ describes this action. Applying this to all points of the square $ABCD$ moves it to a new location in the plane. Now, observe that this square is larger than $LMNP$ so that the scale factor must be less than 1. Observe that $A'B'$ is three times the length of AB; the same is true of the other three pairs of sides since it is a square. So, the scale factor should be $\frac{1}{3}$. Choice **a** would be used to transform square $LMNP$ into $ABCD$. Choice **b** used the wrong scale factor; this would create a square three times larger than $ABCD$. Choice **d** is wrong because you did not pay attention to the value of the hash marks when forming the translation rule. Choice **e** is wrong because while the scale factor is correct, the translation rule moves $ABCD$ to the right and down rather than left and up.

49. a, d, and e. Choice **a** is a correct selection because this is the very definition of probability. Choice **b** is not a correct selection because the model suggests a *long-run* likelihood of getting a 4. No definitive conclusion can be drawn from just ten rolls of the die, though if you were to continue to roll the die and repeatedly get a 4 and no other number, then the validity of the model could be called into question. Choice **c** is not a correct selection because the model suggests a *long-run* likelihood of getting a 4. No definitive conclusion can be drawn from 100 rolls of the die, though it does suggest that the model *may* be incorrect. Choice **d** is a correct selection because the model suggests a *long-run* likelihood of getting a 4. No definitive conclusion can be drawn from just 20 rolls of the die. Choice **e** is a correct selection because the model suggests a *long-run* likelihood of getting a 4. Such rolls are independent of each other and certainly can come out this way and not contradict the model.

50. $\frac{25}{6}w^2 + -1,000w + -70,000 = 0.$ Since the five pens are identical and no fence is needed along the backside by the barn, there are five sides of length w and six sides of length l that need fencing. Since Jacob has 1,200 feet of fence to use to construct all five pens, the sum of the lengths of all sides of the five pens must be 1,200. This leads to the following equation relating w and l: $5w + 6l = 1,200$. Next, the combined area of the five pens is $(5w) \cdot l$. To get an expression in terms of only w, solve the perimeter equation for l and substitute it in:

$$5w + 6l = 1,200 \Rightarrow l = \frac{1,200 - 5w}{6}$$

The combined area of the pens is

$$(5w) \cdot l = (5w) \cdot \frac{1,200 - 5w}{6} = 1,000w - \frac{25}{6}w^2$$

We are given that the combined area is to be 70,000 square feet. To find the width of each pen, we equate the expression for the area to 70,000: $1,000w - \frac{25}{6}w^2 = 70,000$. Take all terms to the right side to get the equivalent equation $\frac{25}{6}w^2 - 1,000w - 70,000 = 0$.

51. c, d, and e. Choice **a** is not a correct selection because the square root of any perfect square is rational; for instance, $\sqrt{9} = 3$. Choice **b** is not a correct selection because the set of rational numbers is closed under division, so the quotient must be rational. Choice **c** is a correct selection because $\sqrt{2} \cdot \sqrt{2} = 2$, for instance. Choice **d** is a correct selection by the very nature of how rational and irrational numbers behave. Choice **e** is a correct selection because $\frac{\sqrt{2}}{\sqrt{3}} = \frac{1}{3}\sqrt{6}$, which is irrational.

52. $\frac{20}{9}\pi$ **meters.** Since the radius of the circle is 5 meters, the circumference of the entire circle is $2\pi r = 10\pi$ meters. The central angle opposite the arc whose length we seek, labeled x, is 80°. So, the portion of the circle to which this arc corresponds is $\frac{80}{360} = \frac{2}{9}$. So, the length, x, of this arc is $\frac{2}{9} \cdot 10\pi$ meters $= \frac{20}{9}\pi$ meters.

53. e. First, write each fraction with the least common denominator $(x + 1)^2$. Then, subtract the numerators by simplifying each expression and then combining like terms, as follows:

$$\frac{2}{(x+1)^2} - \frac{x}{x+1} = \frac{2}{(x+1)^2} - \frac{x(x+1)}{(x+1)^2}$$
$$= \frac{2 - x(x+1)}{(x+1)^2}$$
$$= \frac{2 - x^2 - x}{(x+1)^2}$$
$$= \frac{-(x^2 + x - 2)}{(x+1)^2}$$
$$= \frac{-(x-1)(x+2)}{(x+1)^2}$$

Choice **a** is wrong because you did not distribute x to both terms when simplifying the product $x(x + 1)$. Choice **b** is wrong because you subtracted the numerators without first converting the second fraction to an equivalent one whose denominator is $(x + 1)^2$. Choice **c** is wrong likely because of factoring $x^2 + x - 2$ incorrectly. Choice **d** is wrong because you did not distribute x to both terms when simplifying the product $x(x + 1)$ and you used $(x + 1)^3$ as the least common denominator instead of $(x + 1)^2$, but in so doing did not multiply the numerator and denominator of the first fraction by $x + 1$ to convert it to an equivalent fraction with this denominator.

54. a, c, and d. Choice **a** is a correct selection because each number in this set has 2, 3, and 6 as factors and so cannot be prime. Choice **b** is not a correct selection because 6, for instance, is not divisible by 4. Choice **c** is a correct selection because every number in this set is divisible by 2 and hence is even, not odd. Choice **d** is a correct selection because every number in this set is of the form $6n$ for some whole number n, which means each number is a multiple of 6. Choice **e** is not a correct selection because you are confusing the term *factor* with *multiple*. For the members of this set to be factors of 6, they must all divide *into* 6 evenly. The only one for which this is true is 6 itself, because all the other members are larger than 6.

55. 12 gallons. Two of the walls have dimensions 18 feet by 10 feet; the combined area of these two walls is $2 \cdot (18 \cdot 10)$ feet^2 = 360 feet^2. The other two walls have dimensions 22 feet by 10 feet; the combined area of these two walls is $2 \cdot (22 \cdot 10)$ feet^2 = 440 feet^2. The ceiling has dimensions 18 feet by 22 feet, so its area is 396 feet^2. The total square footage that must be painted is $360 + 440 + 396 = 1{,}196$ square feet. This must be multiplied by 3 to apply three coats, giving the total square footage to be 3,588 square feet. Finally, divide this by 300 to obtain 11.96 gallons of paint, which we round to 12.

56. b and e. Choice **a** is not a correct selection because the left side equals 7, but the right side equals 5. Choice **b** is a correct selection because using the properties of radicals yields $\sqrt{\frac{1}{5}} = \frac{\sqrt{1}}{\sqrt{5}} = \frac{\sqrt{1} \cdot \sqrt{5}}{\sqrt{5} \cdot \sqrt{5}} = \frac{\sqrt{5}}{5}$. Choices **c** and **d** are both not correct selections because e and π are irrational and so cannot be *equal to* finite decimals; these are only approximations. Choice **e** is a correct selection because $\frac{1}{5} > \frac{1}{7}$ and taking the square root of both sides retains the inequality.

4 ▶ PRAXIS® CORE ACADEMIC SKILLS FOR EDUCATORS: PRACTICE TEST 2

CHAPTER SUMMARY

Here is your second full-length test for each Praxis® Core Academic Skills for Educators test: Reading, Writing, and Mathematics. Now that you have completed the first practice test, take these tests to see how much your score has improved.

Like Chapter 3, this chapter contains three full-length tests that mirror the Reading, Writing, and Mathematics Core tests. Although the actual exam you will take is computer-based, the question types for each exam are replicated here for you in the book.

This time, as you take these practice tests, you should simulate the actual test-taking experience as closely as you can. Find a quiet place to work where you won't be disturbed. Follow the time constraints noted at the beginning of each test.

After you finish taking your tests, review the answer explanations. (Each individual test is followed by its own answer explanations.) See **A Note on Scoring** on page 375 to find information on how to score your exam.

Good luck!

Praxis® Core Academic Skills for Educators: Reading Practice Test 2

Time: 85 Minutes

Directions: Read the following passages and answer the questions that follow.

Use the following passage to answer questions 1 through 4.

Commuting to an office was once the work-force norm, but communication technologies such as e-mail and Skype have made working from home a desirable and common option for
5 an increasingly large number of today's work-ers. Working from home—or telecommuting—has a number of benefits that working in an office simply does not offer. The time clock does not rule telecommuters, forcing them to
10 complete their duties between nine and five.
    Telecommuters can perform their duties according to their own schedules. Plus, they don't have to work with managers breathing down their necks or with potentially distracting
15 coworkers. It's no surprise that 47% of telecom-muters are "very satisfied" with their work situ-ations, as opposed to the paltry 27% of traditional commuters who are "very satisfied" with theirs. Job satisfaction is not just a boon to
20 the worker; it also benefits the employer, because when workers are happier with their jobs, they are more productive. Furthermore, when they do not have to punch out at 5:00 P.M., Monday through Friday, employees are
25 more likely to work late nights or weekends until their projects are completed.

1. Which of the following statements best describes the relationship between telecom-muting and job satisfaction?
   a. Telecommuting is a problem and job satisfaction is a solution.
   b. Telecommuting is a cause and job satisfaction is an effect.
   c. Telecommuting is an idea and job satisfaction is supporting evidence.
   d. Telecommuting is an idea and job satisfaction is an explanation.
   e. Telecommuting is a view and job satisfaction is a contrasting view.

2. In order to evaluate the validity of the author's claim regarding the percentage of telecommut-ers who are "very satisfied" with their jobs, it would be most helpful to know which of the following?
   a. the companies that employ these telecommuters
   b. the names of the people polled
   c. how many people are "somewhat satisfied"
   d. the source of the statistic
   e. the definition of "very satisfied"

3. Which off the following is an unstated assump-tion the author of the passage makes?
   a. Skype is a more useful communication technology than e-mail is.
   b. Working from home did not exist before communication technologies such as Skype and e-mail.
   c. Companies should ban traditional commuting altogether.
   d. Traditional commuters will go home at 5:00 even if they have work to complete.
   e. There are no benefits to spending one's day with coworkers.

4. Which of the following conclusions can be made from the passage?
   a. Companies that make telecommuting an option for their employees are likelier to be successful than ones that don't.
   b. Traditional commuting will likely cease to exist sometime in the near future.
   c. Companies that rely on traditional commuters will have to make the work day longer to compete with ones that allow telecommuting.
   d. Telecommuting has a negative impact on the economy, because it means the sale of fewer cars and less gasoline.
   e. Office managers at companies that do not allow telecommuting are incapable of increasing office productivity.

Use the following passage pair to answer questions 5 through 8.

Passage 1

Many studies make it clear that sleep deprivation is dangerous. Sleep-deprived people who are tested by using a driving simulator or by performing a hand-eye coordination task per-
5 form as badly as or worse than those who are intoxicated. Sleep deprivation also magnifies alcohol's effects on the body, so a fatigued person who drinks will become much more impaired than someone who is well rested.
10 Since drowsiness is the brain's last step before falling asleep, driving while drowsy can—and often does—lead to disaster. Caffeine and other stimulants cannot overcome the effects of severe sleep deprivation.

Passage 2

I used to have terrible trouble sleeping—or more accurately—staying asleep. The cause was not psychological but physical. I would wake up in the middle of the night with severe lower
5 back pains and be unable to fall back to sleep for as much as four hours. I initially thought the cause of this pain was my daytime activities. Perhaps I was exercising improperly or I was lugging around too much weight in my back-
10 pack during my morning and evening commutes. Ultimately, I realized the problem was my mattress. The pillow-top mattress on my bed seemed so comfortable in the showroom, but it does not provide uniform body support.
15 Not long after purchasing a new, medium-firm mattress, I enjoyed my first night of uninterrupted sleep in years.

5. For which of the following situations would information in both Passage 1 and Passage 2 be useful?
   a. improving one's health
   b. selecting the best mattress
   c. understanding the effects of caffeine
   d. writing an essay on hand-eye coordination
   e. evaluating the effectiveness of sleeping pills

6. Which of the following statements best describes the relationship between the two passages?
   a. Passage 1 describes a cause and Passage 2 describes an effect.
   b. Passage 1 describes the first step in a process, and Passage 2 describes the next step.
   c. Passage 1 describes a problem, and Passage 2 describes a possible solution.
   d. Passage 1 describes a general principle, and Passage 2 describes a specific detail.
   e. Passage 1 describes a condition, and Passage 2 contrasts it by describing the opposite condition.

7. The author of Passage 2 explains that he thought his daytime activities caused his back pains to
   a. imply that his conclusions may not be entirely reliable.
   b. indicate that understanding the cause of back pains can be difficult.
   c. explain all the possible causes of back pains.
   d. prove that the source of back pains can never be explained definitively.
   e. show that he was putting too much strain on his back during the daytime.

8. In Passage 1, the term *impaired* most nearly means
   a. sentient.
   b. apprehensive.
   c. disturbed.
   d. blemished.
   e. hampered.

Use the following passage to answer questions 9 through 12.

Necessity is the first lawgiver; all the wants that had to be met by this constitution were originally of a commercial nature. Thus, the whole constitution was founded on commerce, and
5   the laws of the nation were adapted to its pursuits. The last clause, which excluded foreigners from all offices of trust, was a natural consequence of the preceding articles. So complicated and artificial a relation between the
10   sovereign and his people, which in many provinces was further modified according to the peculiar wants of each, and frequently of some single city, required for its maintenance the liveliest zeal for the liberties of the country,

15   combined with an intimate acquaintance with them. From a foreigner, neither could well be expected. This law, besides, was enforced reciprocally in each particular province; so that in Brabant no Fleming, and in Zealand no Hol-
20   lander could hold office; and it continued in force even after all these provinces were united under one government.

Above all others, Brabant enjoyed the highest degree of freedom. Its privileges were
25   esteemed so valuable that many mothers from the adjacent provinces removed thither about the time of their accouchement, in order to entitle their children to participate, by birth, in all the immunities of that favored country; just
30   as, says Strada, one improves the plants of a rude climate by removing them to the soil of a milder.

Source: Excerpt from *History of the Revolt of the Netherlands* by Friedrich von Schiller

9. The author of this passage would most likely agree with which of the following assumptions?
   a. Foreigners are generally not to be trusted.
   b. Crossing borders to give birth is morally suspect.
   c. Laws, as a rule, develop in response to a need for laws.
   d. Unification is a natural tendency for smaller provinces.
   e. No person should be immune to legal restrictions.

10. Which statement, if true, would most weaken the position that foreigners are not able to hold a position of trust?
   a. People are able to study the laws of other countries through comprehensive programs designed to immerse them in the intricacies of the laws.
   b. Even after many years living in a foreign land, politicians have generally shown favoritism toward their native land.
   c. Research shows that the age of a candidate holding an office of trust has a greater influence than his or her country of origin on his or her ability to succeed.
   d. The level of distrust a population feels for a foreign-born leader or politician can rarely be eradicated.
   e. Many successful nations, such as the United States, were built on a population that mostly originated from other locations.

11. This passage can best be summarized as a
   a. defense of a thesis that increased freedom leads to more vigorous commerce.
   b. reconciliation of opposing views of constitutional development.
   c. contrasting and comparison of vagaries of preunification provincial law.
   d. review of similarities and contrasts among preunification provincial laws.
   e. polemic advocating the desirability of legal reciprocity among neighboring provinces.

12. Which justification does the text provide as support for the exclusion of foreigners from all offices of trust?
   a. The laws were extremely complex, necessitating extensive familiarity with their nuances.
   b. Stringent enforcement of the laws would be impossible.
   c. Mutual distrust prevailed at this time among the various provinces.
   d. The election of foreigners to offices of trust would necessitate an unnatural unification.
   e. Opening up positions to foreigners that were previously limited to citizens could take away local job opportunities.

Use the following passage to answer questions 13 through 16.

The night and the day are not generally equal. There is, however, one occasion in spring, and another in autumn about half a year later, on which the day and the night are each twelve
5   hours at all places on Earth. When the night and day are equal, the point which the Sun occupies on the heavens is termed the equinox; an equinox occurs in March and then again in September. In any investigation of the celestial
10   movements, the positions of these two equinoxes on the heavens are of primary importance. The discovery of this remarkable celestial movement known as the precession of the equinoxes is attributed to the mastermind
15   Hipparchus. The inquiry that led to his discovery involved a most profound investigation, especially when it is remembered that in the days of Hipparchus, the means of observation of the heavenly bodies were only of the crudest
20   description. We can but look with astonishment on the genius of the man who, in spite of such

difficulties, was able to detect such a phenomenon as the precession, and to exhibit its actual
magnitude. The ingenuity of Hipparchus
25 enabled him to determine the positions of each
of the two equinoxes relative to the stars that lie
in its immediate vicinity. After examination of
the celestial places of these points at different
periods, he was led to the conclusion that each
30 equinox was moving relatively to the stars,
though that movement was so slow that 25,000
years would necessarily elapse before a complete circuit of the heavens was accomplished.
It can be said of his discovery that this was the
35 first instance in the history of science in which
we find that combination of accurate observation with skillful interpretation, of which, in
the subsequent development of astronomy, we
have so many splendid examples.

Source: Excerpt from *Great Astronomers* by
Robert S. Ball

13. It can be inferred from the passage that the way
in which Hipparchus contributed most impor-
tantly to science was which of the following?
   a. He was the first to observe the heavens.
   b. He was first to perceive the equinoxes.
   c. He was the first to combine observation with
   skillful interpretation.
   d. He worked primarily with crude
   instruments of observation.
   e. He was the first to realize that Earth rotates
   with a tilted axis around the Sun.

14. According to the passage, which is NOT a true
statement about the earth's equinoxes?
   a. Day and night are equivalent in length on
   the equinoxes.
   b. The equinoxes fall on the same day for both
   the northern and southern hemispheres.
   c. It takes 25,000 years for a complete
   precession to occur.
   d. The distance from Earth to the Sun is the
   same on the equinoxes.
   e. One equinox follows about six months after
   another.

15. Which best describes the general organization
of the passage?
   a. Two opposing scientific theories are
   introduced, and then those theories are
   dissected.
   b. The problem of balanced sunlight is
   presented, and then the solution is
   determined.
   c. An inequality is established, and then the
   causes of the inequality are investigated.
   d. A scientific breakthrough is portrayed, and
   then the resulting effects are illustrated.
   e. A natural phenomenon is described, and
   then its definition and discovery are detailed.

16. In the context of the text, the word *immediate*
in line 27 could be replaced with which of the
following words to have the least impact on
what the sentence means?
   a. swift
   b. neighboring
   c. firsthand
   d. current
   e. remote

Use the following passage to answer questions 17 through 19.

The information on a standard compact disc (CD) is contained in a single spiral track of pits, starting at the inside of the disc and circling its way to the outside. This information is read by
5 shining light from a 780 nm wavelength semiconductor laser. Information is read as the laser moves over the bumps (where no light will be reflected) and the areas that have no bumps, also known as land (where the laser light will be
10 reflected off the aluminum). The changes in reflectivity are interpreted by a part of the compact disc player known as the detector. It is the job of the detector to convert the information collected by the laser into the music that was
15 originally recorded onto the disc.

LASER DISC MEDIA			
MEDIA	THICKNESS	LASER WAVELENGTH	INFORMATION CAPACITY
CD	1.2 mm	780 nm	700 MB
DVD	0.6 mm	650 nm	4.7 GB
Blu-ray Disc	1.1 mm	405 nm	25 GB

17. According to the table, if a disc's capacity depends on the size of the laser's wavelength, and 1 gigabyte (GB) equals 1,000 megabytes (MB), then
   a. the longer the wavelength, the smaller the capacity.
   b. the shorter the wavelength, the smaller the capacity.
   c. the longer the wavelength, the larger the capacity.
   d. the shorter the wavelength, the larger the capacity.
   e. the wavelength and the capacity are unrelated.

18. Which information is included in both the passage and the table?
   a. The wavelength of the laser that reads a CD.
   b. How a laser reads a CD.
   c. A comparison between the DVD and the CD.
   d. The capacity of a CD.
   e. The length of the laser that reads a DVD.

19. Based on the information in the passage, what would most likely happen if the detector on a CD player malfunctioned?
   a. The spiral track would not be read properly.
   b. The pits and land would look like one unit.
   c. The changes in reflectivity would be absorbed back into the laser.
   d. The music would play backward.
   e. The information read by the laser would not be converted into music.

Use the following passage to answer questions 20 and 21.

Astronauts expose themselves to a wide range of dangers and hardships as a result of their profession. Space travel is itself, of course, a risky endeavor. But one of the most imperceptible
5 sources of distress for astronauts is the constant exposure to microgravity, a gravitational force in space that is one millionth as strong as the force on Earth. In prolonged space flight, aside from the obvious hazards of meteors, rocky

10   debris, and radiation, astronauts have to deal with muscle atrophy brought on by weightlessness caused by this microgravity. To try to counteract this deleterious effect, astronauts engage in a daily exercise regimen while in
15   space. Effective workouts while in space include riding a stationary bike, treadmill running while harnessed, and working against a resistive force, such as a bungee cord. When they return to Earth, astronauts face a protracted period of
20   weight training to rebuild their strength.

20. Which sentence in the passage best presents readers with a major point rather than a minor point of the passage?
    a. "Astronauts expose . . . profession."
    b. "Space travel . . . endeavor."
    c. "But one . . . Earth."
    d. "To try . . . space."
    e. "Effective workouts . . . cord."

21. As it appears in the passage, the word *atrophy* (line 11) most closely means
    a. pain.
    b. deterioration.
    c. weakening.
    d. cramping.
    e. augmentation.

Use the following passage to answer questions 22 through 24.

    Geometry sets out from certain conceptions such as "plane," "point," and "straight line," with which we are able to associate definite ideas, and from certain simple propositions (axioms)
5   which, in virtue of these ideas, we are inclined to accept as "true." Then, on the basis of a logical process, the justification of which we feel ourselves compelled to admit, all remaining propositions are shown to follow from those
10   axioms, i.e., they are proven. A proposition is then correct ("true") when it has been derived in the recognized manner from the axioms. The

question of "truth" of the individual geometrical propositions is thus reduced to one of the
15   "truth" of the axioms. Now it has long been known that the last question is not only unanswerable by the methods of geometry, but that it is in itself entirely without meaning. We cannot ask whether it is true that only one straight
20   line goes through two points. We can only say that Euclidean geometry deals with things called "straight lines," to each of which is ascribed the property of being uniquely determined by two points situated on it.

Source: Excerpt from *The Special Theory of Relativity* by Albert Einstein

22. The author's assertion in line 18 that *it is in itself entirely without meaning* refers to
    a. geometrical propositions.
    b. the nature of straight lines.
    c. the truth of the axioms of geometry.
    d. the methods of geometry.
    e. any question of the truth of geometry.

23. It can be inferred from the passage that the truth of a geometrical proposition depends on which of the following?
    a. the concept of straight lines
    b. the validity of Euclidean geometry
    c. the logical connection of the ideas of geometry
    d. our inclination to accept it as true
    e. the truth of the axioms

24. In this passage, the author is chiefly concerned with which of the following topics?
    a. a definition of geometric axioms
    b. the truth, or lack thereof, of geometrical propositions
    c. the logical process of defining straight lines
    d. the ability to use geometrical propositions to draw conclusions
    e. the precise conceptions of objects such as planes or points

Use the following passage to answer questions 25 through 30.

What Will the New Procedures Do?

Memo
To: Employees of IMPEL
From: Management
Re: New Security Procedures
Date: June 15

As a result of some incidents that have occurred with unauthorized persons in secure parts of Building A, as of June 30, new procedures will go into effect for security in that building. From

5   now on, all employees reporting to work should enter through the employee entrance at the side of the building on Murray Street. No employee is to enter through the main entrance. In order to be admitted, each employee must have a

10   valid photo ID. The ID needs to be swiped to unlock the door. Make sure not to allow another person to enter with you even if you know the person. Each employee needs to swipe his or her own ID in order to be regis-

15   tered as being on the job.

The main entrance will be for visitors only. The receptionist there will call the party that the visitor is coming to meet so that he or she can come to the main desk to escort the guest to his

20   or her office. Visitors will be given temporary passes, but they cannot have full run of the office.

In addition, all employees will also be required to log in on their computer when they begin

25   work and log out when they take a break. Make sure to log out and in when taking lunch breaks.

If an employee sees someone whom he or she believes is unauthorized to be in Building A,

30   that employee should take immediate action and report the event to Mr. Shields, our head of

security. Do not approach the person, but simply call Mr. Shields's office. His extension is 890. If there is no answer, make a written report and

35   e-mail it to cshields@impel.com.

If employees have any questions regarding these regulations, please contact the Human Resources department at extension 550. Ms. Hardy will be able to respond to your queries.

40   Thank you for your cooperation in this matter. We feel that with these additional procedures, our workplace will be made more secure for everyone concerned. Ideally, this will result in improved work output, since any possibility of

45   a security breach will be prevented.

25. Which of the following best restates the phrase "security breach" (line 45)?
  a. a compromise in the safety of the office
  b. a blow to the confidence of employees
  c. a distraction because of an employee's personal problems
  d. a defense against employees not doing their jobs
  e. an overstepping of boundaries by an employee

26. Based on the excerpt, which of the following can be inferred about management?
  a. They are concerned about the safety of employees.
  b. They believe that the office is completely secure.
  c. They want employees to fill out time sheets.
  d. They want to track employee work habits.
  e. They are suspicious of specific employees.

27. Which of the following could be prevented by the new security procedures?
   a. visitors entering through the main entrance
   b. employees swiping IDs to open doors
   c. employees entering through the side entrance
   d. unauthorized persons wandering around Building A
   e. any complaints about company procedures

28. Imagine an employee sees a person in Building A without an ID badge. According to the memo, which of these actions should the employee take?
   a. Call Mr. Shields's office to make a report.
   b. Tell the person to leave the building.
   c. Call the receptionist in the main entrance.
   d. Report the event to Ms. Hardy.
   e. Send a company-wide alert email.

29. Which of the following best describes the style in which this memo is written?
   a. complicated and unclear
   b. academic and dry
   c. straightforward and direct
   d. detailed and technical
   e. friendly and warm

30. Which of the following best describes the way in which the memo is organized?
   a. by listing information in the order of importance
   b. by sequence of events
   c. by presenting a problem and then a solution
   d. by comparing and contrasting issues
   e. by offering anecdotes to illustrate points made

Use the following passage pair to answer questions 31 through 34.

Passage 1
The demotion of Pluto's status in our solar system from planet to dwarf planet in 2006 was an upsetting development for many fans. After all, Pluto is shaped like the other planets—and Pluto even has its own moon! However, the recent discovery of additional celestial bodies similar to Pluto's shape and size forced scientists to agree on the definition of a planet; planets must now be round, orbit the sun, and dominate the neighborhood along their orbit through their gravitational pull.

5

10

Passage 2
A dwarf planet has the mass of a standard planet, but it does not orbit the sun. The term came into use in 2006 as part of a recategorization of our Sun's natural satellites. It became a household word when Pluto—formerly categorized as one of our solar system's nine planets—became a dwarf planet officially. Surely, it is the best-known dwarf planet, yet it is only one of four in our solar system. Closer to Earth than Pluto is Ceres, which was also formerly classified as a planet. Further out are Haumea, Makemake, and Eris. Eris is informally known as "the tenth planet."

5

10

31. Which of the following best describes the relationship between Passage 1 and Passage 2?
   a. Passage 1 introduces an idea and Passage 2 expands upon it.
   b. Passage 1 makes an argument and Passage 2 contradicts it.
   c. Passage 1 introduces a difficult concept and Passage 2 explains it.
   d. Passage 1 states facts and Passage 2 states opinions.
   e. Passage 1 makes a claim and Passage 2 supports that claim.

32. Which of the following phrases from Passage 2 is an example of figurative language?
  a. standard planet
  b. household word
  c. best-known
  d. formerly classified
  e. the tenth planet

33. In what way is the attitude of the author of Passage 1 different from that of the author of Passage 2?
  a. The author of Passage 1 is more serious than the author of Passage 2.
  b. The author of Passage 1 is more skeptical than the author of Passage 2.
  c. The author of Passage 1 is more cynical than the author of Passage 2.
  d. The author of Passage 1 is more technical than the author of Passage 2.
  e. The author of Passage 1 is more playful than the author of Passage 2.

34. Which statement, if true, would best help to explain why Pluto lost its official designation as a planet?
  a. Its size was significantly smaller than any other designated planet.
  b. Its general orbit contains a greater amount of debris in its path than the other planets.
  c. Its moon was discovered to be merely an asteroid that was captured by Pluto's gravity.
  d. Its orbit around the sun had a greater elliptical shape than the orbits of the other planets.
  e. Its mass is responsible for hydrostatic equilibrium, creating a nearly round shape.

Use the following passage to answer questions 35 through 37.

Jessie Street is sometimes called the Australian Eleanor Roosevelt. Like Roosevelt, Street lived a life of privilege, while at the same time devoting her efforts to working for the rights of the dis-
5 enfranchised, including workers, women, refugees, and Aborigines. In addition, she gained international fame when she was the only woman on the Australian delegation to the conference that founded the United Nations—just
10 as Eleanor Roosevelt was for the United States.

JESSIE STREET TIMELINE	
DATE	EVENT
April 18, 1889	Born
June 17, 1911	Joins suffragettes to fight for women's right to vote
February 10, 1916	Marries Kenneth Whistler Street
December 18, 1929	Establishes the United Associations of Women
March 12, 1932	Proposes the General Social Insurance Scheme
April 1945	Appointed to Australia's delegation to found the United Nations
November 1945	Helps found the Women's International Democratic Federation
February 1947	Becomes the deputy chair of the Status of Women Commission
March 14, 1967	Publishes her autobiography, *Truth or Repose*
July 2, 1970	Dies

35. Based on information in the passage and the chart, when did Jessie Street gain international fame?
   a. April 1889
   b. June 1911
   c. December 1929
   d. April 1945
   e. March 1967

36. Which of the following can be learned only by reading the chart?
   a. Jessie Street worked for women's rights.
   b. Jessie Street was interested in the plight of Aborigines.
   c. Jessie Street lived a life of privilege.
   d. Jessie Street was very similar to Eleanor Roosevelt.
   e. Jessie Street wrote an autobiography.

37. Which of the following inferences may be drawn from the information presented in the passage?
   a. Eleanor Roosevelt and Jessie Street worked together to include women in the United Nations Charter.
   b. Usually, people who live lives of privilege do not spend much time participating in political activities.
   c. Discrimination in Australia is much worse than it ever was in the United States.
   d. At the time of the formation of the United Nations, few women were involved in international affairs.
   e. The United Nations has been ineffective in helping the disenfranchised all over the world.

Use the following passage to answer questions 38 through 41.

Mental and physical health professionals may consider referring clients and patients to a music therapist for a number of reasons. It seems a particularly good choice for the social
5   worker who is coordinating a client's case. Music therapists use music to establish a relationship with the patient and to improve the patient's health, using highly structured musical interactions. Patients and therapists may sing,
10   play instruments, compose music, dance, or simply listen to music.

The course of training for music therapists is comprehensive. In addition to their formal musical and therapy training, music
15   therapists are taught to discern what kinds of interventions will be most beneficial for each individual patient. Because each patient is different and has different goals, the music therapist must be able to understand the patient's
20   situation and choose the music and activities that will do the most toward helping the patient achieve his or her goals. The referring social worker can help this process by clearly articulating each client's history.
25   Although patients may develop their musical skills, that is not the main goal of music therapy. Any client who needs particular work on communication or on academic, emotional, and social skills, and who would benefit
30   from music therapy, is an excellent candidate for music therapy.

38. Which of the following would be the most appropriate title for this passage?
a. "The Use of Music in the Treatment of Autism"
b. "How to Use Music to Combat Depression"
c. "Music Therapy: A Role in Social Work?"
d. "Training for a Career in Music Therapy"
e. "The Social Worker as Music Therapist"

39. Which of the following inferences can be drawn from the passage?
a. Music therapy can succeed where traditional therapies have failed.
b. Music therapy is a relatively new field.
c. Music therapy is particularly beneficial for young children.
d. Music therapy probably will not work well for psychotic people.
e. Music therapy is appropriate in only a limited number of circumstances.

40. Which of the following best organizes the main topics addressed in this passage?
a. I. the role of music therapy in social work
II. locating a music therapist
III. how to complete a music therapist referral
b. I. using music in therapy
II. a typical music therapy intervention
III. when to prescribe music therapy for sociopaths
c. I. music therapy and social work
II. training for music therapists
III. skills addressed by music therapy
d. I. how to choose a music therapist
II. when to refer to a music therapist
III. who benefits the most from music therapy
e. I. music therapy as a cost-effective treatment
II. curriculum of a music therapy program
III. music therapy and physical illness

41. Which of the following lines from the passage contains an error in logic?
a. Mental and physical health professionals may consider referring clients and patients to a music therapist for a number of reasons.
b. Music therapists use music to establish a relationship with the patient and to improve the patient's health, using highly structured musical interactions.
c. The course of training for music therapists is comprehensive.
d. Because each patient is different and has different goals, the music therapist must be able to understand the patient's situation and choose the music and activities that will do the most toward helping the patient achieve his or her goals.
e. Any client who needs particular work on communication or on academic, emotional, and social skills, and who would benefit from music therapy, is an excellent candidate for music therapy.

Use the following passage to answer question 42.

According to a recent poll, the number of students in the high school environmental club has increased by 40% over the past three years. This increase is the reason why more students
5 have begun recycling their paper and cans during this period.

42. Which of the following, if true, most significantly weakens the preceding argument?
a. The school installed recycling bins in all classrooms five years ago.
b. Most students join the environmental club in order to add one more activity to their college applications.
c. Not all students participated in the poll.
d. Two years ago, the school began giving detention to any student caught throwing recyclable materials in the regular trash.
e. The environmental club has begun hanging up more posters about recycling.

Use the following passage to answer questions 43 through 45.

Businesses today routinely keep track of large amounts of both financial and nonfinancial information. Sales departments keep track of current and potential customers; marketing
5 departments keep track of product details and regional demographics; accounting departments keep track of financial data and issue reports. To be useful, all this data must be organized into a meaningful and useful system.
10 Such a system is called a *management information system*, abbreviated MIS. The financial hub of the MIS is accounting.

43. This passage is most likely taken from
a. a newspaper column.
b. an essay about modern business.
c. a legal brief.
d. a business textbook.
e. a business machine catalog.

44. According to the information in the passage, which of the following is least likely to be a function of accounting?
a. helping businesspeople make sound judgments
b. producing reports of many different kinds of transactions
c. assisting with the marketing of products
d. assisting companies in important planning activities
e. providing information to potential investors

45. According to the information in the passage, all of the following would be included in a company's MIS EXCEPT
a. potential customers.
b. financial data.
c. regional demographics.
d. employee birthdates.
e. product details.

Use the following passage to answer question 46.

The salesperson of the month at Smith's Used Cars sold 26 cars in February. Diana sold 22 cars in February.

46. Based only on the information provided, which of the following must be true?
a. Diana is not salesperson of the month at Smith's Used Cars.
b. The salesperson of the month is the person who sold the most cars that month.
c. Diana does not work at Smith's Used Cars.
d. The salesperson of the month made more money in February than Diana did.
e. The salesperson of the month is better at selling cars than Diana is.

Use the following passage to answer question 47.

Thomas Nast (1840–1902), the preeminent political cartoonist of the second half of the nineteenth century, demonstrated the power of his medium when he used his art to end the
5   corrupt Boss Tweed Ring in New York City. His images, first drawn for *Harper's Weekly,* are still in currency today: Nast created the tiger as the symbol of Tammany Hall, the elephant for the Republican Party, and the donkey for the
10 Democratic Party.

47. The author cites Thomas Nast's depiction of an elephant for the Republican Party as an example of
   a. an image that is no longer recognized by the public.
   b. the saying, "the pen is mightier than the sword."
   c. art contributing to political reform.
   d. a graphic image that became an enduring symbol.
   e. the ephemeral nature of political cartooning.

Use the following passage to answer questions 48 and 49.

Typically people think of genius, whether it manifests in Mozart's composing symphonies at age five or Einstein's discovery of relativity, as having a quality not just of the supernatural,
5   but also of the eccentric. People see genius as a "good" abnormality; moreover, they think of genius as a completely unpredictable abnormality. Until recently, psychologists regarded the quirks of genius as too erratic to describe
10 intelligibly; however, Anna Findley's groundbreaking study uncovers predictable patterns in the biographies of geniuses. These patterns do not dispel the common belief that there is a kind of supernatural intervention in the lives of

15 unusually talented men and women, however, even though they occur with regularity. For example, Findley shows that all geniuses experience three intensely productive periods in their lives, one of which always occurs shortly before
20 their deaths; this is true whether the genius lives to 19 or 90.

48. Which of the following would be the best title for this passage?
   a. "Understanding Mozarts and Einsteins"
   b. "Predicting the Life of a Genius"
   c. "The Uncanny Patterns in the Lives of Geniuses"
   d. "Pattern and Disorder in the Lives of Geniuses"
   e. "Supernatural Intervention in the Life of the Genius"

49. Given the information in the passage, which of the following statements is true?
   a. Anna Findley is a biographer.
   b. All geniuses are eccentric and unpredictable.
   c. A genius has three prolific periods in his or her life.
   d. Mozart discovered relativity.
   e. Geniuses experience three fallow periods in their lives.

Use the following passage to answer question 50.

Sushi, the thousand-year-old Japanese delicacy, was once thought of in this country as unpalatable and too exotic. But tastes have changed, for a number of reasons.

50. In the passage, *unpalatable* most nearly means
   a. not visually appealing.
   b. not tasting good.
   c. bad smelling.
   d. too expensive.
   e. rough to the touch.

Use the following passage to answer questions 51 through 54.

The Caribbean island of Saint Martin is a favorite vacation spot, one that is popular with tourists from various countries. The French and Dutch settled on the island in the 1600s. Today,
5   the island is divided between the two. The French capital is Marigot; the Dutch capital is Philipsburg.

Tourists on vacation soon discovered that Saint Martin has an intriguing history. Twelve
10 hundred years ago, the Arawak Indians inhabited all the islands of the West Indies, and were a peaceful people living under the guidance of their chiefs. In the 1300s, three hundred years after the Arawaks first arrived on Saint Martin,
15 they were defeated and forced to abandon the island by a more hostile tribe of Indians that originated in South America. This new tribe was called the Carib. The Caribbean Sea was named after them. Unlike the Arawaks, they
20 had no permanent chiefs or leaders, except in times of strife. They were also extremely warlike. Worse, they were cannibalistic, eating the enemy warriors they captured. In fact, the very word *cannibal* comes from the Spanish name
25 for the Carib Indians. The Spanish arrived in the fifteenth century and, unfortunately, they carried diseases to which the Indians had no immunity. Many Indians succumbed to common European illnesses. Others died from the
30 hard labor forced upon them.

51. According to the passage, all the following are true about the Carib Indians EXCEPT
   a. a sea was named after them.
   b. they were peaceful fishermen, hunters, and farmers.
   c. they ate human flesh.
   d. they settled after defeating the Arawak Indians.
   e. during times of war, they had temporary leaders.

52. According to the passage, the Carib Indians were finally defeated by
   a. sickness and forced labor.
   b. the more aggressive Arawak tribe.
   c. the Dutch West India Company.
   d. the French explorers.
   e. a cannibalistic tribe.

53. One can infer from the passage that the word *strife* (line 21) means
   a. cannibalistic.
   b. war.
   c. labor.
   d. chief.
   e. Carib.

54. According to the article, present-day Saint Martin
   a. belongs to the Spanish.
   b. is independent.
   c. belongs to the Carib.
   d. is part of the U.S. Virgin Islands.
   e. is shared by the French and the Dutch.

Use the following passage to answer questions 55 and 56.

Although protected by the Australian government, the Great Barrier Reef faces environmental threats. Crown-of-thorns starfish feed on coral and can destroy large portions of reef.
5   Pollution and rising water temperatures also threaten the delicate coral. But the most preventable hazard to the reef is tourists. Tourists have contributed to the destruction of the reef ecosystem by breaking off and removing pieces
10 of coral to bring home as souvenirs. The government hopes that by informing tourists of the dangers of this seemingly harmless activity they will quash this creeping menace to the fragile reef.

55. Which key word from the passage helps the transition from the natural threats the Great Barrier Reef faces to the human-caused threats it faces?
 a. Although
 b. also
 c. But
 d. and
 e. creeping

56. The primary purpose of this passage is to
 a. inform the reader that coral reefs are a threatened, yet broadly functioning, ecosystem.
 b. alert the reader to a premier vacation destination in the tropics.
 c. explain in detail how the Great Barrier Reef is constructed.
 d. recommend that tourists stop stealing coral off the Great Barrier Reef.
 e. dispel the argument that coral is a plant, not an animal.

Praxis® Core Academic Skills for Educators: Reading Practice Test 2 Answers and Explanations

1. b. In this passage, telecommuting and job satisfaction share a cause-and-effect relationship, because job satisfaction is the result of telecommuting. That means telecommuting is the opposite of a problem (choice **b**). Since telecommuting and job satisfaction share a complementary, not contrasting, relationship, choice **e** can be eliminated.

2. d. Statistics are hard to trust if the reader does not know from where the statistics were taken. For all the reader of this passage knows, the author could have taken these statistics from an unreliable blog or even made them up himself. Including the source of the statistics would help the reader to evaluate their validity. Knowing the names of the people polled (choice **b**), the companies for which they work (choice **a**), or how many people were "somewhat satisfied" (choice **c**) would have little bearing on the validity of these statistics. The term "very satisfied" is fairly self-explanatory, so **e** is not the best answer choice.

3. d. The author makes the point that telecommuters who do not have to punch a time clock at 5:00 are likely to work past that time, with the implication that this is different from how traditional commuters approach their work. So, you can conclude that the author probably assumes traditional commuters will go home at 5:00 even if they have work to complete. However, the author never implies a comparison between Skype and e-mail (choice **a**) or suggests that working from home did not exist before communication technologies such as these (choice **b**), which is untrue anyway. Although the author clearly favors telecommuting over traditional commuting, choice **c** is an extreme assumption. The same can be said of choice **e**, even though the author mentions one downside of sharing an office with coworkers.

4. a. The author explains that telecommuters are more satisfied with their jobs and more productive than traditional commuters, which should result in a company with less employee turnover and greater output than those that do not allow telecommuting. So, it is fairly logical to conclude that companies that make telecommuting an option for their employees are likelier to be successful than ones that don't, even though the author does not cite any explicit evidence to support this conclusion. However, it is extreme to conclude that traditional commuting is likely to cease to exist altogether (choice **b**), since many jobs simply cannot be done from home. The author does not suggest that companies with employees who do not telecommute will have to make the work day longer (choice **c**), nor is there any discussion of the impact of telecommuting on the economy at all (choice **d**). Although the author mentions a downside of office managers, choice **e** is still an extreme conclusion to draw.

5. a. A good night of rest is essential to good health, and both of these passages suggest ways to achieve better rest. Passage 1 suggests drinking less alcohol and Passage 2 suggests sleeping on a mattress that provides uniform body support. Choice **b** is too specific; only Passage 2 refers to mattress selection, so this choice does not make use of information in both passages. Only Passage 1 refers to caffeine, and it only explains that caffeine does not help one to stay awake; it does not explain the effects of caffeine (choice **c**). Only Passage 1 refers to hand-eye coordination, and the passage does not provide very much information about it, so the passage would not be a very good source for an essay on hand-eye coordination (choice **d**). Neither passage mentions sleeping pills (choice **e**).

6. c. Passage 1 describes the problem of sleep deprivation, and for those suffering sleep deprivation because they sleep on an inadequate mattress, Passage 2 provides a possible solution to that problem. Passage 1 neither describes a cause (choice **a**) nor a first step in a process (choice **b**) nor a general principle (choice **d**). Although Passage 1 does describe the condition of sleep deprivation, Passage 2 does not contrast it by describing the opposite condition (choice **e**); the conditions in both passages are very similar.

7. b. If understanding the cause of back pains was not difficult, the author would have known his mattress was causing his pains right away. This information helps the reader understand that back pains can have a number of causes, and figuring out the exact cause might not be easy. Making a wrong guess is not enough to prove that someone's ultimate findings should be questioned, so **a** is not the best answer choice. The author's daytime activities explain only a couple of possible causes of back pains, so choice **c** is too extreme. The author's back pains reduce dramatically, so that he can enjoy his *first night of uninterrupted sleep in years* after getting a new mattress, which indicates that the source of back pains can be explained definitively and contradicts choice **d**. Since the author's daytime activities were not the cause of his back pains, choice **e** does not make sense.

8. e. The passage claims that lack of sleep *magnifies alcohol's effects on the body*, implying that it *hampers* a person's ability to function. The other choices (**a**, **b**, **c**, and **d**) aren't accurate definitions of *impaired*.

9. c. The assertion that laws develop in response to a need for laws is contained in the first sentence of the passage and further supported in the second sentence. Choice **a** is incorrect; while the author explicitly argues that foreigners should not hold a position of offices of trust, the reason is not simply because they are not to be trusted. The author provides the example of children being born in a different province *to entitle their children to participate*, but he gives no clear indication as to whether such a practice is or is not morally suspect, so choice **b** is incorrect. The author gives no indication that unification is a natural tendency for smaller provinces, making choice **d** incorrect. The statement in choice **e** may seem like something the author might agree with, given that the author supports foreigners' exclusion from holding offices of trust. However, it is a leap to assume that he would necessarily agree that just because foreigners should not hold an office of trust, no person should be immune to legal restrictions. It is beyond the scope of the passage.

10. a. One reason the author provides as to why foreigners cannot hold offices of trust is because they cannot be as familiar with the laws as natural-born citizens. However, a program such as the one described in this choice might eliminate this unfamiliarity, thus weakening the author's argument. Choices **b** and **d** are incorrect because either would *strengthen* the author's position; they would provide further evidence that foreigners should not hold offices of trust. The fact in choice **c** might weaken the author's argument slightly—by suggesting that age is an even greater factor in a person's ability to hold an office of trust—but it does not say that being born abroad is not still a factor. A better choice more significantly weakens the argument. The overly general statement in choice **e** does not address the specific issues that the author raises in regard to a foreigner's ability to hold an office of trust. While this point may help weaken the argument somewhat, there is a more specific statement that weakens the argument more significantly.

11. d. The author discusses the laws of preunified Netherlands provinces, specifically pointing out similarities and differences, such as that certain laws were enforced in each province but that other provinces were so free that mothers moved there before giving birth to earn the immunities of that land. The passage does not defend the argument that increased freedom leads to increased commerce, so choice **a** is incorrect. Choice **b** is incorrect: This passage discusses the origins of provincial law in the preunified Netherlands, but the only mention of a constitution is to suggest that it was founded on commerce. Choice **c** is incorrect. To know that this choice is incorrect requires you to know the meaning of the word *vagaries*, which connotes capriciousness and does not apply to the author's discussion of legal development in the provinces. Choice **e** is incorrect; reciprocity in neighboring provinces is mentioned in this passage in regard to the rights of foreigners holding office. However, this specific attribute of the law—or the advocacy of its desirability—is *not* the main point of the passage.

12. a. The first three sentences set up and support the discussion of the exclusion of foreigners from office. In that section of the passage, it is mentioned that a foreigner could not be expected to be acquainted with these unnecessarily complicated laws, meaning that choice **a** is correct. The end of the first paragraph refers to the reciprocity of the laws across provinces, suggesting that the laws would need to be enforced. But that did not say that enforcement would be *impossible*, making choice **b** incorrect. Even though foreigners were excluded from holding office, the passage does not provide *distrust*, choice **c**, as a cause of the exclusion. Neither a necessary unification nor a potential job loss is given as support for the main idea, so choices **d** and **e** are both incorrect.

13. c. This passage discusses Hipparchus's discovery of the equinoxes. The final sentence in the passage sums up the importance in terms of the discovery's contribution to science, saying that it was the "first instance in the history of science" in which observation was combined with such skillful interpretation. Hipparchus observed the heavens as part of his investigation, but the passage does not suggest that he was the *first* to do this, making choice **a** incorrect. The statement in choice **b** is not supported by the passage; Hipparchus may have discovered the equinoxes and determined the magnitude of their precession, but he was not the first to perceive them. The passage states that Hipparchus used crude instruments, but this statement is not given to describe his most important contribution to the sciences, so choice **d** is incorrect. The statement in choice **e** is not a contribution made by Hipparchus, at least not as mentioned in the given passage. Earth's tilt may cause the seasons, but that is not mentioned in the passage, nor is Hipparchus given the credit for the contribution.

14. d. The passage makes no statement about the distance from the Sun to Earth on the equinoxes, so there is no support for the statement in choice **d**. The passage begins with the statement that day and night are not generally equal. However, it then states that day and night *are* equal on the equinoxes, making choice **a** an incorrect selection. By suggesting that this occurs "at all places on Earth," the passage indicates that the equinoxes fall on the same day for both hemispheres. While the spring equinox occurs in the northern hemisphere in March and the southern hemisphere in September, the two general equinoxes both share the same day on Earth. Therefore, choice **b** is also an incorrect selection. Hipparchus discovered that the equinox was moving in relation to the stars, but that it would take 25,000 years to complete a precession, making choice **c** an incorrect selection. Because the equinoxes are separated by "half a year" in the passage, choice **e** must be an incorrect selection as well.

15. e. The passage begins with a description of the phenomenon of the equinoxes, and then goes on to define the term *equinox* and explain its discovery by Hipparchus. The passage does not begin with an introduction of opposing scientific theories or a problem, so choices **a** and **b** are incorrect. Likewise, the passage does not begin with a scientific breakthrough, so choice **d** cannot be correct. Choice **c** mentions an inequality, which could describe the unequal day and night, but it is not the inequality but the equality— the equivalent day and night on the equinoxes—that the passage focuses on, making choice **c** incorrect.

16. b. The word *immediate* in the sentence is being used to describe the nearby stars that are adjacent to the area of the equinoxes. The words in choices **a**, **c**, and **d** could each be used to replace the word *immediate* in different sentences, but they would have an impact on the meaning of the sentence from this passage. Therefore, each is incorrect. *Remote*, choice **e**, nearly means the opposite of the word *immediate* as it appears in this passage, so it is not correct either.

17. d. According to the table, the Blu-ray disc is the disc that uses the laser with the shortest wavelength (405 nm), and it also has the largest capacity (25 GB); therefore, it is reasonable to conclude that the shorter the wavelength, the larger the capacity. Choices **a**, **b**, and **c** are incorrect. Choice **e** contradicts the question.

18. a. The wavelength of the laser that reads a CD (780 nm) is the only information included in both the passage and the table. There is no mention of the DVD in the passage, so choices **c** and **e** do not make sense. How a laser reads a CD is discussed only in the passage (choice **b**), and a CD's capacity (choice **d**) is included only in the chart.

19. e. The last sentence in the passage states that the detector's function is to convert the information collected by the laser into music, which wouldn't happen if the detector malfunctioned. The other choices (**a**, **b**, **c**, and **d**) aren't the most accurate or likely occurrences of a detector malfunction.

20. c. The main point of the passage is the effect of microgravity on astronauts. This third sentence of the passage both introduces microgravity to the reader and describes it as an imperceptible source of distress for astronauts. The initial sentence of the passage, choice **a**, makes a general claim about the difficulties of life as an astronaut. However, the passage is not merely about these difficulties, but it is specifically about one particular danger: microgravity and its effects. The fact that space travel is a risky endeavor, choice **b**, is not the main point of the passage. This sentence serves to point out the obvious, but it is the following sentence— which serves to contrast this apparent fact— that better sums up the main point of the passage. The main point of the passage is not the astronauts' attempts to counteract the negative effects of microgravity or a list of astronauts' workouts, so choices **d** and **e** are incorrect.

21. b. Atrophy represents *deterioration*, frequently in response to underuse. When in space, muscles adapt to the lack of gravity and lose their strength through deterioration. There is no indication in the passage that atrophied muscles cause the astronauts any amount of pain, so choice **a** is incorrect. Although a muscle that atrophies may be weakened, the primary meaning of the phrase *to atrophy* is *to waste away* or *deteriorate*, making choice **c** incorrect. The passage does not suggest that astronauts' muscles cramp during space flight, so choice **d** is not correct. An augmentation means an increase or an expansion. This is opposite to the effect that microgravity has on astronauts' muscles, so choice **e** is not correct either.

22. c. To answer this question, you have to find the antecedent of *it*. First, you discover that *it* refers to *the last question*. Then you must trace back to realize that *the last question* itself refers to *the "truth" of the axioms* in the previous sentence. By determining how the parts of the text relate to one another, you can determine the meaning of the assertion. Choice **a** is incorrect; the *it* in this line does not refer to geometrical propositions. While the question of the "truth" of the individual geometrical propositions is thus reduced to one of the "truth" of the axioms, it is therefore the *truths* that are being referred to as without meaning, not the propositions themselves. The passage does not delve into the nature of straight lines until after the line referred to in this question, so choice **b** is not correct. Choice **d** is incorrect; the passage states that *the last question is not only unanswerable by the methods of geometry*, meaning that the *it* is referring to the *last question* and not the subject of the prepositional phrase that follows: *by the methods of geometry*. Choice **e** is a bit tricky, but it can help to identify the subject. The *it* from this line refers to *the last question*, which can be traced back to mean *the "truth" of the axioms* in the previous sentence. It is not, therefore, the *question* of the truth, but the truth itself.

23. e. Lines 12 through 15 contain the statement that argues that the truth of the propositions depends on the truth of the axioms, making choice **e** correct. The concept of straight lines is not addressed until late in the passage, and it is not introduced as the basis for the truth of geometrical propositions, so **a** is not correct. It is the truth of the axioms, not the validity of Euclidean geometry or a connection of geometric ideas, choices **b** and **c**, that plays the role of determining the truth of a geometrical proposition. Choice **d** is incorrect; there is no indication that suggests that it is merely our inclination to accept the truth that determines whether a geometrical proposition is indeed true.

24. b. The author repeatedly refers to *truth* in relation to geometrical propositions. See, for example, lines 12 through 15. The author (Albert Einstein) is laying the groundwork for an argument that the principles of geometry are only *apparently* true. Choices **a** and **c** are incorrect. While the author presents a definition for axioms and straight lines, they are not the topic, which presents his chief concern. While geometrical propositions are a key aspect of the passage and the subject of the author's chief concern, it is not the ability to use them to draw conclusions that is his primary focus, so choice **d** is incorrect. The author introduces planes and points as a starting point to show how geometry is built on certain conceptions. However, these conceptions are not the author's primary concern, so choice **e** is not the best answer.

25. a. This phrase means that the security was somehow broken, so choice **a** is correct. This can be seen in the very first section of the memo: "As a result of some incidents that have occurred with unauthorized persons in secure parts. . . ." The other choices are not suggested by these words. They have nothing to do with security being compromised.

26. a. The point of the memo is that there were some security incidents that needed to be addressed. Based on the memo, you cannot infer any of the other choices. The only clear inference is choice **a**.

27. d. If you read the memo carefully, you will see that choice **d** is the one option the new regulations will definitely help prevent. It is mentioned in the first paragraph. The other options are not mentioned in the memo.

28. a. Again, a close reading of the text will reveal an employee should call Mr. Shields if a stranger is seen in Building A. This information can be found in the fourth paragraph. This is the only correct option.

29. c. The memo is direct and to the point. It is not technical. It's quite clear and not at all academic. The tone is professional, not warm.

30. c. The memo states a problem at the beginning and then describes the new regulations that will solve it—a way to keep unauthorized people out of secure parts of Building A. The memo does not rank events in any order (choices **a** or **b**), and does not offer a comparison or contrast of any points.

31. a. Passage 1 introduces the ideas of dwarf planets and Pluto's status as a dwarf planet; Passage 2 expands upon those ideas by discussing other, less well-known dwarf planets. Neither passage makes an argument (choice **b**); both accept the idea of dwarf planets and Pluto's status as one. Passage 2 does not explain anything about dwarf planets that has not already been described in Passage 1, so choice **c** is incorrect. Both passages focus on facts without indulging in opinions, so choice **d** does not make sense. Passage 1 makes a claim that Pluto is a dwarf planet, but it also supports that claim with its own details; the details in Passage 2 are not needed to support Passage 1, so choice **e** is not the best answer choice.

32. b. The phrase *household word* is an idiom meaning a familiar name or phrase. Choices **a**, **c**, and **d** are not examples of figurative language. You may have been confused by choice **e** because it is a nickname, but a nickname is not a form of figurative language.

33. e. The author of Passage 1's playful attitude is evident in the description of Pluto's changed status as a "demotion" (planets cannot be demoted; only people can), the reference to the planet's "fans," and the exclamation that "Pluto even has its own moon!" There are no such playful touches in Passage 2. The first author's playfulness contradicts the idea that he or she is more serious than the author of Passage 2, so choice **a** is incorrect. The author of Passage 1 is nether skeptical (choice **b**) nor cynical (choice **c**). One cannot have a technical (choice **d**) attitude.

34. b. The final stipulation of a planet's attributes, according to the new definition of a planet, is that it must dominate the neighborhood along its orbit through its gravitational pull. The statement in choice **b**, referring to the debris in its path, suggests that Pluto does *not* dominate its neighborhood in the same way that the other planets do. It is true that Pluto is much smaller than the other planets, choice **a**, but the size of an object is not listed among the new criteria for a planet. Pluto had always been much smaller than any other planet. Passage 1 mentions that Pluto has a moon as evidence for its status as a planet. However, the absence or presence of a moon is not cited as justification for the classification of a planet, making choice **c** incorrect. According to the new definition of a planet, a planet must orbit the sun. But neither passage mentions the specific orbit of the sun—or its shape—so the statement in choice **d** cannot be a possible explanation. The statement in choice **e** describes why Pluto is round, as are the eight planets in our solar system. This actually meets the first definition of a planet and would therefore *not* be a reason why Pluto lost its status as an official planet.

35. d. According to the passage, Jessie Street "gained international fame when she was the only woman on the Australian delegation to the conference that founded the United Nations." The chart indicates this happened in April 1945. Choice **a** is very unlikely because few people gain international fame in the month in which they are born. Choices **b**, **c**, and **e** also are incorrect.

36. e. Only the chart mentions Jessie Street's autobiography, *Truth or Repose*. The fact that she worked to secure women's rights (choice **a**) is mentioned in both the passage and the chart. The information in choices **b**, **c**, and **d** is only mentioned in the passage.

37. d. Because the author mentions that two women attending an international conference is an accomplishment (for which at least one gained international fame), the reader can surmise that it was a rare occurrence. Choices **b**, **c**, and **e** are far beyond the scope of Passage 1; choice **a** might be true, but would require information not contained in the passage.

38. c. This passage provides information to social workers about music therapy, and makes the claim that it can have a positive role, which the title in choice **c** indicates. Choice **e** is incorrect because the first sentence speaks of mental and physical health professionals referring their clients and patients to music therapists, not actually serving as music therapists. Choice **d** is possible, but does not summarize the passage as well as choice **c**. Choices **a** and **b** refer to topics not covered in the passage.

39. a. Based on the information provided in the passage, particularly in the last sentence, choice **a** is the best inference. The other choices (choices **b**, **c**, **d**, and **e**) are beyond the scope of the passage.

40. c. Choice **c** provides the best outline of the passage. The other choices (**a**, **b**, **d**, and **e**) all contain points that are not covered by the passage.

41. e. The sentence in choice **e** makes the error of circular reasoning by stating that a client "who would benefit from music therapy . . . is an excellent candidate for music therapy." Circular reasoning is when someone makes a claim that is the same as its own conclusion. The statements in the other answer choices (**a**, **b**, **c**, and **d**) are perfectly logical.

42. d. If students have a strong motivation to recycle other than membership in the environmental club (i.e., detention), then this weakens the author's assertion that recycling has gone up because of increased membership in the club. Choice **a** is incorrect because it refers to a change made prior to the increase in the number of students recycling. Choice **b** is wrong because the students' motivation for joining the club is unrelated to whether they recycle. Choice **c** is incorrect because not all students need to participate in order for the poll to be valid. Choice **e** is incorrect because it would strengthen the author's argument, not weaken it.

43. d. The passage contains objective language and straightforward information about accounting, such as one might find in a business textbook. While the information could theoretically appear in any of the other answer choices (**a**, **b**, **c**, and **e**), a business textbook is the most likely spot.

44. c. The second sentence of the passage speaks of a marketing department separate from the accounting department, so it is least likely that assisting with the marketing of products would be a function of accounting. The other choices (**a**, **b**, **d**, and **e**) are much more likely to be handled by the accounting department.

45. d. All the other choices (**a**, **b**, **c**, and **e**) are listed in the passage; employee birthdates (choice **d**) would not be included.

46. a. While all the other choices (**b**, **c**, **d**, and **e**) may be true, the fact that Diana sold 22 cars in February and the salesperson of the month sold 26 means that they are not the same person. None of the other choices can be proven based only on the information given.

47. d. The author cites Thomas Nast's symbols for Tammany Hall and the Democratic and Republican Parties as examples of images that have entered the public consciousness and are "still in currency today"; thus they are enduring. Choices **a** and **c** are inaccurate, and choices **b** and **e** are unrelated to Nast's depiction.

48. c. This title expresses the main point of the passage—that while there are predictable patterns in the life of a genius, the pattern increases the sense of something supernatural touching his or her life. Choices **a** and **b** are too general. Choice **d** is inaccurate because the passage does not talk about disorder in the life of a genius. Choice **e** covers only one of the two main ideas in the passage.

49. c. Based on the information provided in the passage, it's true that a genius has three prolific periods in his or her life. All the other statements (choices **a**, **b**, **d**, and **e**) are not supported by information provided in the passage.

50. b. *Unpalatable* may be defined as not agreeable to taste (from the Latin *palatum*, which refers to the roof of the mouth). The other choices (**a**, **c**, **d**, and **e**) aren't accurate definitions of the word.

51. b. The Carib were not in any way described as peaceful, but rather as hostile people. All the other choices (**a**, **c**, **d**, and **e**) are accurate descriptions of the Caribs and are explicitly mentioned in the passage.

52. a. The last two lines of the passage explicitly state that the Caribs were defeated by sickness and the ravages of forced labor. Choice **b** is incorrect because the Arawaks were defeated by the Carib. Neither the Dutch (choice **c**) nor the French (choice **d**) nor another cannibalistic tribe (choice **e**) was mentioned in the role of conquerors.

53. b. *Strife* means war, which can be inferred by the information provided in the passage. Choice **a** is mentioned as a characteristic that the Carib exhibited toward their enemies in times of strife; it is not the meaning of *strife*. Choices **c** and **e** are not mentioned in conjunction with being warlike or with strife. Choice **d** makes no sense because the times of strife were when the tribe allowed a chief to be chosen.

54. e. Present-day Saint Martin belongs to the French and the Dutch. Choices **b** and **d** have no support in the passage. Choices **a** and **c** are incorrect. The Spanish are mentioned in the passage only in conjunction with the Carib Indians.

55. c. The sentence that introduces the idea of human-caused threats to the Great Barrier Reef is, "But the most preventable hazard to the reef is tourists." *But* is the transitional word that begins this sentence. *Although* (choice **a**), *also* (choice **b**), and *and* (choice **d**) can all be used as transitional words, but they are not used in this passage to transition from the natural threats the Great Barrier Reef faces to the human-caused threats it faces. You may have been confused by choice **e** since *creeping* seems like a threatening word. However, *creeping* cannot function as a transitional word.

56. a. This statement encapsulates the primary purpose of the entire passage, not just a part of it. Choices **c** and **e** are too specific to be correct. Choices **b** and **d** are not supported by the passage.

Praxis® Core Academic Skills for Educators: Writing Practice Test 2

Part I: Multiple-Choice
Time: 40 Minutes

Directions: Choose the letter for the underlined portion that contains a grammatical error. If there is no error in the sentence, choose **e**.

1. <u>Even as</u> the music industry pushes <u>further into</u>
   a   b
the realm of the digital world, <u>there are</u> still a
                             c
large number of people who collect vinyl
records and old-style <u>amplifiers and</u> speakers.
                      d
<u>No error</u>
 e

2. <u>Today's</u> ski jackets are made with synthetic
   a
fabrics <u>that are</u> very light <u>but yet</u> provide
      b   c
exceptional <u>warmth and</u> comfort. <u>No error</u>
          d   e

3. After the <u>director and assistant</u> director both
            a
<u>resigned, we</u> could only guess <u>who would be</u>
   b   c
hired to take <u>their</u> positions. <u>No error</u>
        d   e

4. In <u>Homers</u> <u>painting,</u> a man in a storm at sea
      a   b
is <u>realistically</u> portrayed. <u>No error</u>
 c   d   e

5. My favorite <u>part though,</u> <u>is</u> the vegetable chips
         a   b
my <u>mom</u> buys from the health food <u>store; they</u>
   c   d
are delicious. <u>No error</u>
         e

6. *Kwanzaa*, a <u>S</u>wahili word meaning

               a

<u>a harvest's first fruits</u>, is a nonreligious holiday

         b

<u>that honors</u> African-American <u>heritage and</u>

    c   d

culture. <u>No error</u>

        e

7. The record time for solving a Rubik's cube

   <u>is</u> held by a <u>14-year-old</u> male named Feliks

   a   b

Zemdegs, who <u>affectively</u> completed the puzzle

               c

in 6.77 seconds on <u>November 13, 2010</u>. <u>No error</u>

                   d   e

8. There are many types of extreme sports, <u>such like</u>

                                 a

slacklining, a sport of <u>daredevil</u> proportions

               b

<u>in which</u> athletes walk and tumble across nylon

 c

webbing that has been stretched across <u>a cavern</u>

                          d

and anchored on each end. <u>No error</u>

                    e

9. Either the <u>physicians or</u> the hospital

           a

administrator <u>are</u> going to have to make a

          b

decision to <u>ensure</u> the <u>fair</u> treatment of

       c   d

patients. <u>No error</u>

       e

10. Because they <u>close</u> resemble each <u>other, many</u>

           a   b

people think that Sara and Heather <u>are</u>

                       c

identical twins <u>instead of</u> fraternal. <u>No error</u>

         d   e

11. The Department of State <u>has</u> foreign policy

                     a

<u>responsibilities</u> that include the promotion of

     b

peace, <u>must protect</u> U.S. citizens abroad, <u>and</u>

      c   d

the assistance of U.S. businesses in the foreign
marketplace. <u>No error</u>

              e

12. Contestants in the Scripps <u>national spelling bee</u>

                           a

watched <u>eighth-grader</u> Sukanya Roy from

          b

Pennsylvania win the spelling <u>bee's</u> coveted

                        c

trophy and $40,000 in <u>college scholarship funds</u>.

                            d

<u>No error</u>

  e

13. Here <u>are</u> one of the three <u>scarves</u> you <u>left</u> at

     a   b   c

my house <u>yesterday</u> morning. <u>No error</u>

         d   e

14. I think I will do <u>good</u> on my final exam

               a

because I am <u>confident</u> that I am <u>well prepared</u>,

          b   c

rested, and relaxed <u>going into</u> the classroom.

                 d

<u>No error</u>

  e

15. I thought <u>Johan's</u> dish of gumbo was

         a

<u>more spicier</u> than <u>Harold's</u>, but the <u>judges</u>

   b   c   d

disagreed. <u>No error</u>

         e

16. Last <u>Thursday</u>, as the <u>president of the university</u>
          a   b

addressed the <u>student body, she</u> made an
                   c

<u>illusion to</u> the construction of a new stadium
  d

for the football team. <u>No error</u>
                    e

Directions: For questions 17–28, choose the best replacement for the underlined portion of the sentence. If no revision is necessary, choose **a**, which always repeats the original phrasing.

17. The <u>principle objective of the documentary is to show you how global warming will effect</u> climates around the world.
  a. principle objective of the documentary is to show you how global warming will effect
  b. principle objective of the documentary is to show you how global warming will affect
  c. principal objective of the documentary is to show you how global warming will affect
  d. principal objective of the documentary is to show you how global warming will effect
  e. principle objective of the documentary is to show you how global warming will have effected

18. <u>This was the third of the three assignments the professor gave during this the month of October.</u>
  a. This was the third of the three assignments the professor gave during this the month of October.
  b. Of the three assignments the professor gave during October, this was the third one.
  c. Thus far during the month of October, the professor had given three assignments and this was the third.
  d. This third assignment of the professor's given during the month of October was one of three assignments.
  e. This was the third assignment the professor had given during the month of October.

19. <u>I don't have no math homework this weekend, but I have to work on my paper for social studies.</u>
  a. I don't have no math homework this weekend, but I have to work on my paper for social studies.
  b. I dont have any math homework this weekend, but I have to work on my paper for social studies
  c. I don't have any math homework this weekend, but I have to work on my paper for social studies.
  d. I don't have any math homework this weekend, but I have too work on my paper for social studies.
  e. I don't have any math homework this weekend, but I has to work on my paper for social studies.

20. Built in Boston, the *U.S.S. Constitution* was given the nickname "Old Ironsides" because her thick oak planks had deflected many deadly cannonballs in battle.
   a. Built in Boston, the *U.S.S. Constitution* was given the nickname "Old Ironsides" because her thick oak planks had deflected
   b. Built in Boston, the *U.S.S. Constitution* was given the nickname "Old Ironsides" because her thick oak planks deflect
   c. The *U.S.S. Constitution*, being built in Boston, is nicknamed "Old Ironsides" because her thick oak planks had deflected
   d. Built in Boston, the *U.S.S. Constitution* will be given the nickname "Old Ironsides" because her thick oak planks had deflected
   e. The *U.S.S. Constitution*, to be built in Boston, was given the nickname "Old Ironsides" because her thick oak planks had deflected

21. Any passenger who is getting off at the next stop should move to the front.
   a. passenger who is getting off at the next stop
   b. passenger, who is getting off at the next stop
   c. passenger who is getting off at the next stop,
   d. passenger, who is getting off at the next stop,
   e. passenger, whom is getting off at the next stop,

22. The Gulf Stream is a warm current on the Atlantic's surface, it originates in the Gulf of Mexico and flows northeast.
   a. Atlantic's surface, it originates
   b. Atlantics' surface; it originates
   c. Atlantic's surface. Originating
   d. Atlantics' surface, and originating
   e. Atlantic's surface; it originates

23. My sister is mowing the lawn; my cousins and I is washing the windows.
   a. mowing the lawn; my cousins and I is washing the windows.
   b. mowing the lawn; my cousins and I are washing the windows.
   c. mowing the lawn, my cousins and I are washing the windows.
   d. mowing the lawn: my cousins and I are washing the windows.
   e. mowing the lawn my cousins and I are washing the windows.

24. Thomas has various study strategies; he takes notes, an outline, and answering practice questions.
   a. takes notes, an outline, and answering practice questions.
   b. took notes, outlining, and practicing questions.
   c. takes notes, makes outlines, and answers practice questions.
   d. taking notes, outlines and practiced questions.
   e. took notes, making outlines, and answer practice questions.

25. Prometheus and epimetheus, his brother, created life on earth, Epimetheus began with animals.
   a. Prometheus and epimetheus, his brother, created life on earth, Epimetheus began with animals.
   b. Prometheus and Epimetheus, his brother, created life on Earth; Epimetheus began with animals.
   c. Prometheus and epimetheus his brother, created life on earth, Epimetheus began with animals.
   d. Prometheus and Epimetheus: his brother created life on earth; Epimetheus began with animals.
   e. Prometheus and Epimetheus, his brother, created life on earth Epimetheus began with animals.

26. We loved our trip to the top of the Empire State Building where you could see the Statue of Liberty, all of New York's bridges, and the tiny people on the streets below.
   a. Empire State Building where you could see
   b. Empire State Building; you could see
   c. Empire State Building; where we saw
   d. Empire State Building; we saw
   e. Empire State Building in that you saw

27. When my father was young, him chopped firewood with axes.
   a. When my father was young, him chopped firewood with axes.
   b. When my father was young, he chopped firewood with axes.
   c. When my father was young, his chopped firewood with axes.
   d. When my father was young, they chopped firewood with axes.
   e. When my father was young, it chopped firewood with axes.

28. I have, an author of thrilling books for children, always admired Virginia Hamilton.
   a. I have, an author of thrilling books for children, always admired Virginia Hamilton.
   b. I have, an author, always admired Virginia Hamilton, of thrilling books for children.
   c. I have always admired Virginia, an author of thrilling books for children, Hamilton.
   d. I have always admired Virginia Hamilton an author of thrilling books for children.
   e. I have always admired Virginia Hamilton, an author of thrilling books for children.

Directions: Select the best answer for the following questions.

29. Which of the following pieces of information would be *least* relevant in an essay about the causes of World War II?
   a. The causes of World War II have been the topic of many books.
   b. World War II officially began when Germany invaded Poland.
   c. World War II began on September 1, 1939.
   d. The treaty that ended World War I caused unrest that led to World War II.
   e. World War II finally ended on September 2, 1945.

30. Which of the following pieces of information would be *least* relevant in an essay about the silent film era?
  a. Buster Keaton, Lillian Gish, and Charlie Chaplin were some of the biggest stars of the silent film era.
  b. The silent film era saw the rise of all the most important film genres, including drama, historical epic, comedy, horror, and science fiction.
  c. Released in 1927, *The Jazz Singer* was the first film to include spoken dialogue.
  d. Title cards with printed words conveyed dialogue and narration in silent films.
  e. Many contemporary films include long stretches of silent footage.

Directions: Choose the letter for the underlined portion of the citations that contains an error. If there is no error in the citation, choose **e**.

31. Ebook citation:
Brueton, Diana. <u>Many Moons: The Myth and Magic, Fact and Fantasy of Our Nearest Heavenly Body.</u> New York: <u>Prentice Hall Press,</u> 1991.
       a   b
Google Books. Web. <u>July 17, 2015.</u> <u>No error.</u>
    c   d   e

32. Magazine citation:
<u>Bhob, Stewart.</u> <u>"Who Was William M. Gaines?"</u>
     a   b
Comics Buyers Guide. <u>February 28, 1997.</u>
          c   d
<u>No error.</u>
  e

Use the following passage to answer questions 33 through 36.

(**1**) According to the U.S. Centers for Disease Control (CDC), almost 50% of American teens are not vigorously active on a regular basis, contributing to a trend of sluggishness among Americans of all ages. (**2**) Adolescent female students are particularly inactive: 29% are inactive compared with 15% of male students. (**3**) Unfortunately, the sedentary habits of young "couch potatoes" often continues into adulthood. (**4**) According to both the CDC and the Surgeon General's 1996 Report on Physical Activity and Health, Americans become increasingly less active with each year of age. (**5**) Inactivity can be a serious health risk factor, setting the stage for obesity and associated chronic illnesses like heart disease or diabetes. (**6**) Exercise sets the stage for building bone, muscle, and joints, controlling weight, and preventing the development of high blood pressure.

(**7**) Some studies suggest that physical activity may have other benefits for you. (**8**) One CDC study found that high school students who take part in team sports or are physically active outside of school are less likely to engage in risky behaviors, like using drugs or smoking. (**9**) Physical activity does not need to be strenuous to be beneficial. (**10**) The CDC recommends moderate, daily physical activity for people of all ages, such as brisk walking for 30 minutes or 15 to 20 minutes of more intense exercise. (**11**) A survey conducted by the National Association for Sport and Physical Education questioned teens about their attitudes toward exercise and what it would take to get them moving. (**12**) Teens chose friends (56%) as their most likely motivators for becoming more active, followed by parents (18%) and professional athletes (11%).

33. Which conclusion does the writer support with evidence from multiple resources?

  a. Americans become increasingly less active with each year of age.

  b. Exercise sets the stage for building bone, muscle, and joints, controlling weight, and preventing the development of high blood pressure.

  c. Physical activity needs to be strenuous to be beneficial.

  d. Inactivity can be a serious health risk factor, setting the stage for obesity and associated chronic illnesses like heart disease or diabetes.

  e. "Couch potatoes" are people who spend most of their time watching television and eating unhealthy snacks.

34. In context, which revision to sentence 3 (sentence 3 follows) is most needed?

> Unfortunately, the sedentary habits of young "couch potatoes" often continues into adulthood.

  a. As it is now.

  b. Unfortunately, the sedentary habits of young "couch potatoes" often continuing into adulthood.

  c. Unfortunately, the sedentary habits of young "couch potatoes" often continue into adulthood.

  d. Unfortunately, the sedentary habit of young "couch potatoes" often continues into adulthood.

  e. The sedentary habits of young "couch potatoes" often continues into adulthood.

35. In context, which revision to sentences 5 and 6 (sentences 5 and 6 follow) is most needed?

> Inactivity can be a serious health risk factor, setting the stage for obesity and associated chronic illnesses like heart disease or diabetes. Exercise sets the stage for building bone, muscle, and joints, controlling weight, and preventing the development of high blood pressure.

  a. As it is now.

  b. Inactivity can be a serious health risk factor, setting the stage for obesity and associated chronic illnesses like heart disease or diabetes. Building bone, muscle, and joints, controlling weight, and preventing the development of high blood pressure.

  c. Inactivity can be a serious health risk factor, setting the stage for obesity and associated chronic illnesses like heart disease or diabetes. Exercise sets the stages for building bone, muscle, and joints, controlling weight, and preventing the development of high blood pressure.

  d. Inactivity can be a serious health risk factor, setting the stage for obesity and associated chronic illnesses like heart disease or diabetes. Exercise sets the stage for building bone, muscle, and joints, and preventing the development of high blood pressure.

  e. Inactivity can be a serious health risk factor, setting the stage for obesity and associated chronic illnesses like heart disease or diabetes. The benefits of exercise include building bone, muscle, and joints, controlling weight, and preventing the development of high blood pressure.

36. In context, which revision to sentence 7 (sentence 7 follows) is most needed?

> Some studies suggest that physical activity may have other benefits for you.

a. Change *studies* to *study*.
b. Replace *for you* with *as well*.
c. Replace *suggest* with *suggests*.
d. Replace *other* with *the same*.
e. Replace *benefits* with *advantages*.

Use the following passage to answer questions 37 through 40.

(**1**) Toni Morrison is one of the most renowned and respected writers of our generation. (**2**) Morrison's visions are as epic and vivid as her social conscience is formidable. (**3**) She is perhaps best known for her 1977 novel *Song of Solomon* and the 1987 novel *Beloved*, which director Jonathan Demme adapted into a major feature film starring Oprah Winfrey. (**4**) Then, I personally find her most powerful work to be the 1973 novel *Sula*.

(**5**) The fictional setting of *Sula*—the African-American section of Medallion, Ohio, a community called "the Bottom"—is a place where people, and even natural things, are apt to go awry, to break from their prescribed boundaries, a place where bizarre and unnatural happenings and strange reversals of the ordinary are commonplace. (**6**) The very name of the setting of *Sula* is significant; the Bottom is located high up in the hills. (**7**) The novel is furthermore filled with images of bad stuff, both psychological and physical. (**8**) A great part of the lives of the characters, therefore, is taken up with making sense of the world, setting boundaries, and devising methods to control what is essentially uncontrollable. (**9**) One of the major devices used by the people of the Bottom is the seemingly universal one of creating a scapegoat—in this case, the title character Sula—upon which to project both the evil they perceive outside themselves and the evil in their own hearts. (**10**) Essentially, Morrison uses the small community of Sula to convey good insights about our global society.

37. In context, which revision to sentences 3 and 4 (sentences 3 and 4 follow) is most needed?

> She is perhaps best known for her 1977 novel *Song of Solomon* and the 1987 novel *Beloved*, which director Jonathan Demme adapted into a major feature film starring Oprah Winfrey. Then, I personally find her most powerful work to be the 1973 novel *Sula*.

a. Replace *Then* with *However*.
b. Replace *She* with *Morrison*.
c. Replace *best* with *greatest*.
d. Replace *director* with *filmmaker*.
e. Change *I* to *me*.

38. In context, which revision to sentence 5 (sentence 5 follows) is most needed?

> The fictional setting of *Sula*—the African-American section of Medallion, Ohio, a community called "the Bottom"—is a place where people, and even natural things, are apt to go awry, to break from their prescribed boundaries, a place where bizarre and unnatural happenings and strange reversals of the ordinary are commonplace.

a. As it is now.

b. The fictional setting of *Sula* is the African-American section of Medallion, Ohio, a community called "the Bottom." It is a place where people, and even natural things, are apt to go awry, to break from their prescribed boundaries, a place where bizarre and unnatural happenings and strange reversals of the ordinary are commonplace.

c. The fictional setting of *Sula*—the African-American section of Medallion, Ohio, a community called "the Bottom"—is a place where people, and even natural things, are apt to go awry. They break from their prescribed boundaries.

d. The fictional setting of *Sula*—the African-American section of Medallion, Ohio, a community called "the Bottom"—is a place where people, and even natural things, are apt to go awry.

e. The fictional setting of *Sula* is a place where people, and even natural things, are apt to go awry, to break from their prescribed boundaries, a place where bizarre and unnatural happenings and strange reversals of the ordinary are commonplace.

39. In context, which revision to sentence 7 (sentence 7 follows) is most needed?

> The novel is furthermore filled with images of bad stuff, both psychological and physical.

a. Replace *novel* with *book*.

b. Change *bad stuff* to *mutilation*.

c. Replace *furthermore* with *not*.

d. Change *physical* to *philosophical*.

e. Replace *is* with *are*.

40. In context, which revision to sentence 10 (sentence 10 follows) is most needed?

> Essentially, Morrison uses the small community of Sula to convey good insights about our global society.

a. Replace *Essentially* with *Incidentally*.

b. Change *small* to *pathetic*.

c. Replace *good* with *profound*.

d. Change *Sula* to *novel*.

e. Replace *global* with *worldwide*.

Part IIa: Argumentative Essay
Time: 30 Minutes

Directions: Carefully read the essay topic that follows. Plan and write an essay that addresses all points in the topic. Make sure that your essay is well organized and that you support your central argument with concrete examples. Allow 30 minutes for your essay.

There are more vegetarians in this country than ever before. Should school and workplace cafeterias accommodate this dietary preference by offering vegetarian selections? Use specific reasons and examples to support your argument.

Part IIb: Source-Based Essay
Time: 30 Minutes

Directions: The following assignment requires you to use information from two sources to discuss the most important concerns that relate to a specific issue. When paraphrasing or quoting from the source, cite each source used by referring to the author's last name, the text's title, or any other clear identifier. Allow 30 minutes for your essay.

Assignment

Read the two passages carefully and then write an essay in which you identify the most important concerns regarding the debates concerning the adoption of the Bill of Rights to the United States Constitution. Your essay must draw on information from both of the sources. In addition, you may draw on your own experiences, observations, or reading. Be sure to cite the sources whether you are paraphrasing or directly quoting.

Source 1

"John DeWitt" (pseudonym), Anti-Federalist Paper #2, Massachusetts, October 27, 1787

That the want of a Bill of Rights to accompany this proposed System, is a solid objection to it, provided there is nothing exceptionable in the System itself, I do not assert. . . . A people, entering into society, surrender such a part of their natural rights, as shall be necessary for the existence of that society. They are so precious in themselves, that they would never be parted with, did not the preservation of the remainder require it. They are entrusted in the hands of those, who are very willing to receive them, who are naturally fond of exercising of them, and whose passions are always striving to make a bad use of them. They are conveyed by a written compact, expressing those which are given up, and the mode in which those reserved shall be secured. Language is so easy of explanation, and so difficult is it by words to convey exact ideas, that the party to be governed cannot be too explicit. The line cannot be drawn with too much precision and accuracy. The necessity of this accuracy and this precision increases in proportion to the greatness of the sacrifice and the numbers who make it. That a Constitution for the United States does not require a Bill of Rights, when it is considered, that a Constitution for an individual State would, I cannot conceive. The difference between them is only in the numbers of the parties concerned[;] they are both a compact between the Governors and Governed the letter of which must be adhered to in discussing their powers. That which is not expressly granted, is of course retained.

The Compact itself is a recital upon paper of that proportion of the subject's natural rights, intended to be parted with, for the benefit of adverting to it in case of dispute. Miserable indeed would be the situation of those individual States who have not prefixed to their Constitutions a Bill of Rights . . . those powers which the people by their Constitutions expressly give them; they enjoy by positive grant, and those remaining ones, which they never meant to give them, and which the Constitutions say nothing about, they enjoy by tacit implication, so that by one means and by the other, they became possessed of the whole. . . . That insatiable thirst for unconditional control over our fellow-creatures, and the facility of sounds to convey essentially different ideas, produced the first Bill of Rights ever prefixed to a Frame of Government. The people, although fully sensible that they reserved every title of power they did not expressly grant away, yet afraid that the words made use of, to express those rights so granted might convey more than they originally intended,

(continues)

they chose at the same moment to express in different language those rights which the agreement did not include, and which they never designed to part with, endeavoring thereby to prevent any cause for future altercation and the intrusion into society of that doctrine of tacit implication which has been the favorite theme of every tyrant from the origin of all governments to the present day.

Source 2

Alexander Hamilton writing as "Publius," Federalist Paper #84, "Certain General and Miscellaneous Objections to the Constitution Considered and Answered" (1788)

It has been several times truly remarked that bills of rights are, in their origin, stipulations between kings and their subjects, abridgements of prerogative in favor of privilege, reservations of rights not surrendered to the prince. . . . It is evident, therefore, that, according to their primitive signification, they have no application to constitutions professedly founded upon the power of the people, and executed by their immediate representatives and servants. Here, in strictness, the people surrender nothing; and as they retain every thing they have no need of particular reservations. . . .

But a minute detail of particular rights is certainly far less applicable to a Constitution like that under consideration, which is merely intended to regulate the general political interests of the nation, than to a constitution which has the regulation of every species of personal and private concerns. If, therefore, the loud clamors against the plan of the convention, on this score, are well founded, no epithets of reprobation will be too strong for the constitution of this State. But the truth is, that both of them contain all which, in relation to their objects, is reasonably to be desired.

I go further, and affirm that bills of rights, in the sense and to the extent in which they are contended for, are not only unnecessary in the proposed Constitution, but would even be dangerous. They would contain various exceptions to powers not granted; and, on this very account, would afford a colorable pretext to claim more than were granted. For why declare that things shall not be done which there is no power to do? Why, for instance, should it be said that the liberty of the press shall not be restrained, when no power is given by which restrictions may be imposed? I will not contend that such a provision would confer a regulating power; but it is evident that it would furnish, to men disposed to usurp, a plausible pretense for claiming that power. They might urge with a semblance of reason, that the Constitution ought not to be charged with the absurdity of providing against the abuse of an authority which was not given, and that the provision against restraining the liberty of the press afforded a clear implication, that a power to prescribe proper regulations concerning it was intended to be vested in the national government. This may serve as a specimen of the numerous handles which would be given to the doctrine of constructive powers, by the indulgence of an injudicious zeal for bills of rights.

Praxis® Core Academic Skills for Educators: Writing Practice Test 2 Answers and Explanations

1. e. Because there are no grammatical, idiomatic, logical, or structural errors in this sentence, choice **e** is the best answer.

2. c. Because the words *but* and *yet* mean the same thing, this sentence contains a redundancy. Either one of these words should be deleted.

3. e. Because there are no grammatical, idiomatic, logical, or structural errors in this sentence, choice **e** is the best answer.

4. a. *Homer's* requires an apostrophe "s" to show possession.

5. a. A comma is needed in this sentence to indicate or set off parenthetical elements. A parenthetical element is segment that can be removed without changing the essential meaning of that sentence.

6. e. Because there are no grammatical, idiomatic, logical, or structural errors in this sentence, choice **e** is the best answer.

7. c. The correct word choice would be *effectively*, meaning "to cause a result." *Affective* refers to "the ability to influence or alter someone's mental state."

8. a. In this comparison, the word *as* should be used instead of *like*. The use of *as* completes the idiom *such as*.

9. b. When two subjects are connected with the conjunction *or*, the subject that is closer to the verb will determine whether the verb is singular or plural. The verb in this sentence should be *is* because *administrator*—the closer subject—is singular.

10. a. This is a grammatical error. Because the word modifies the verb *resemble*, the adverb *closely* should be used instead of the adjective *close*.

11. c. This is an error in sentence construction. For proper parallel construction in the sentence, *must protect* should be changed to *the protection of* to match *the promotion of* and *the assistance of*.

12. a. *Scripps National Spelling Bee* is a proper noun. It is the specific name used to identify a contest, so it must be capitalized.

13. a. This is an error in agreement. The singular noun *one* requires the singular verb *is*. When the subject (in this case *one*) follows the verb, as in a sentence beginning with *here* or *there*, be careful to determine the subject. In this sentence, the subject is not the plural noun *scarves* but the singular *one of the three scarves*.

14. a. In this sentence, the word *good* is being used as an adverb telling how the student thinks he or she will do on the test. Therefore, *good* should be replaced with *well*. This is a word-choice error.

15. b. Using *more* or *most* before a comparative adjective or adverb is an example of a redundancy. In this sentence, just using the word *spicier* is enough to establish the proper comparison between the two dishes of gumbo.

16. d. This is an error of commonly confused homonyms (words that sound alike). The use of the word *illusion* makes this sentence illogical. An illusion is something that is not what it seems. The correct word choice would be *allusion*, which means a reference or hint.

17. c. The word *principle*, meaning rule, can only be used as a noun. *Principal*, meaning leading or main, can be used as a noun or as an adjective. In this sentence, it is clearly an adjective, which rules out choices **a**, **b**, and **e**. Choice **d** incorrectly uses the word *effect*. The verb *affect* means to produce an *effect* (noun) on something.

18. e. This is the only choice that does not contain excessive wordiness and matches the tenses of *was* and *had given*. In choice **a**, the phrase *the third of the three* is a redundancy. Choice **b** is also repetitive in using both *three* and *third*. Choices **c** and **d**, although constructed differently, make the same error.

19. c. This is the only choice that is grammatically correct in every way. Choice **a** is a double negative using the word *no*. Choice **b** needs an apostrophe in the word *don't*. Choice **d** uses the word *too* when it should be *to*. Choice **e** uses the word *has*, which is the wrong subject-verb agreement.

20. a. When constructing sentences, unnecessary shifts in verb tenses should be avoided. Choice **a** is best because all three verbs in the sentence indicate that the action occurred in the past (*built*, *was given*, and *had deflected*). In choice **b**, there is a shift to the present (*deflect*). Choice **c** begins in the present (*being built*, *is nicknamed*), and then shifts to the past (*had deflected*). Choice **d** starts in the past tense (*built*), shifts to the future (*will be given*), and then reverts back to the past (*had deflected*). Finally, choice **e** shifts from the future (*to be built*) to past tense (*was given*, *had deflected*).

21. a. The clause *who is getting off at the next stop* is a restrictive (essential) clause and should not be set off by commas. Choices **b**, **c**, **d**, and **e** are all punctuated incorrectly. In addition, choice **e** uses the pronoun *whom*, which is the wrong case.

22. e. There are two potential problems in this sentence. One is the possessive form of the word *Atlantic*, and the other is the punctuation between the two clauses. Choice **e** uses the correct possessive form (there is only one Atlantic Ocean), and the correct punctuation (a semicolon should be used between two independent clauses). Choice **a** is incorrect because it creates a comma splice. Choice **b** uses the incorrect possessive form. Choice **c** creates a sentence fragment. Choice **d** creates faulty subordination.

23. b. This sentence requires a semicolon to separate the independent clauses and subject-verb agreement between *my cousins and I* and *are*.

24. c. The second clause of this sentence requires a parallel construction. Choice **c** is the only one in which all three elements are parallel.

25. b. Choice **b** is correct, as it correctly punctuates this sentence with commas around the parenthetical *his brother*, inserts a semicolon between the independent clauses, and capitalizes *Earth* and *Epimetheus* (as the latter is a person's name and therefore a proper noun).

26. d. Choice **d** is correctly punctuated with a semicolon between two independent clauses, and there is no shift in person (i.e., everything is in the first person). Choices **a**, **b**, and **e** are incorrect because the sentence shifts from the first person (*we*) to the second person (*you*). Choice **c** uses a semicolon when no punctuation is necessary.

27. b. The original sentence has an error in pronoun case; it requires the nominative pronoun *he* instead of the objective pronoun *him*. Choice **c** requires *he* instead of the possessive pronoun *his*. Choices **d** and **e** would not be grammatically incorrect if the pronoun did not refer to *my father*, but because the pronoun does refer to *my father*, they are wrong.

28. e. The original sentence contains a misplaced modifier. The phrase *an author of thrilling books for children* modifies *Virginia Hamilton*, so it should be placed directly before or after that name and offset with a comma. Only choice **e** places the modifier correctly. Choice **b** is particularly confusing because it splits up the modifier. Choice **c** mistakenly places the modifier in the middle of the name it modifies. Choice **d** fails to offset the modifier with a comma.

29. a. Books about the causes of World War II might be relevant resources for an essay on that topic, but the fact that such books exist is irrelevant. Choices **b** and **d** pertain directly to the causes of World War II. The date the war began (choice **c**) would certainly be relevant information to include in an essay about the causes of World War II. While the date the war ended (choice **e**) might seem off topic for an essay about the causes of the war, it would likely be more relevant than the fact that World War II has been the topic of many books.

30. e. The fact that many contemporary films include long stretches of silent footage is not particularly relevant to a discussion of the silent film era. The information in choices **a**, **b**, **c**, and **d** are all more relevant to the topic.

31. a. The title of a book should always be italicized, but this citation fails to italicize the title. The other elements of the citation are all written and formatted correctly.

32. d. When citing a magazine article, it is important to include the page number/numbers on which the article originally appeared immediately after the date of publication. This citation fails to include the page number/numbers. The other elements of the citation are all written and formatted correctly.

33. a. In sentence 4, the writer cites both the CDC and the Surgeon General's 1996 Report on Physical Activity and Health as sources of this information. Although the information in choices **b** and **d** may have come from resources, the writer does not cite them in the passage, so they are not the best answer choices. In sentence 9, the writer states the *opposite* of the conclusion in choice **c**. The writer never explicitly defines the term *couch potato* in the passage, so choice **e** cannot be correct.

34. c. Sentence 3 contains a subject-verb agreement error. The plural subject *habits* needs the plural verb *continue*. Choice **c** corrects this error with the plural verb *continue*. Choice **b** uses the wrong verb tense. While choice **d** uses the singular verb *continues* with the singular subject *habit*, the subject refers to the plural *couch potatoes*, so it needs to be plural, as well. Choice **e** merely removes the transitional word *Unfortunately* without correcting the subject-verb agreement error.

35. e. As originally written, sentence 6 repeats the phrase *set the stage* from sentence 5. Removing that phrase from sentence 6 makes the sentences less repetitious and monotonous. Choice **e** removes that phrase while remaining grammatically correct. Choice **b** removes the phrase, but it is a fragment because it also removes the subject *exercise*. Choice **c** changes the singular *stage* to the plural *stages*, which makes the sentence awkward and fails to correct the original problem of monotony. Choice **d** removes information arbitrarily (*controlling weight*) and fails to correct the original problem of monotony.

36. b. As it is originally written, sentence 7 is not consistent with the style of the rest of the passage. The majority of the passage is written in the third-person point of view. Sentence 7 switches to the second person by referring to the reader as *you*. Choice **b** corrects this shift in style by removing the phrase *for you*. Choice **c** fails to correct that shift in style and introduces a subject-verb agreement error by changing *suggest* to *suggests*. Choice **d** changes the meaning of the sentence. Choice **e** merely replaces the word *benefits* with the synonym *advantages* without correcting the style-shift error.

37. a. Sentence 4 introduces an idea (*Sula* is Toni Morrison's most powerful novel) that is somewhat contrary to the ideas in sentence 3 (*Song of Solomon* and the 1987 novel *Beloved* are Toni Morrison's best-known novels). Therefore, *However* would be the best transitional word to begin sentence 4, since it indicates a contrary idea. *Then* indicates an idea that follows the previous one without contradicting it. Choice **b** changes a pronoun to a proper name unnecessarily. Choice **c** replaces a word with a synonym that creates an idiom error (*greatest known*). Choice **d** replaces *director* with the synonym *filmmaker* without improving the sentence. Choice **e** makes the sentence grammatically incorrect.

38. a. Although sentence 5 is long and complex, it is grammatically correct, and its length and complexity provide the variety necessary to maintain the reader's interest and prevent the passage from becoming monotonous. Although the other answer choices are all grammatically correct, none of them improves upon sentence 5 as it is now. Choices **c**, **d**, and **e** make cuts that deprive the passage of information.

39. b. The majority of this passage is written for an educated, adult audience. Using the euphemism *bad stuff* does not respect that audience's intelligence. The word *mutilation* is much more precise. Choice **a** replaces *novel* with the synonym *book* without improving the sentence. Choices **c** and **d** change the meaning of the sentence. Choice **e** creates a grammatical error.

40. c. The word *good* is not used incorrectly in this sentence, but it is not a very strong word choice. Replacing it with the stronger word *profound* makes the sentence more effective. Choice **a** changes the sentence's meaning since *Incidentally* has the opposite meaning of *Essentially*. Choice **b** also makes the meaning of the sentence inaccurate. Choice **d** is incorrect because the writer is not using the word *Sula* to mean the novel's title in this sentence; she is referring to the community in the novel. Choice **e** replaces the word *global* with a synonym (*worldwide*) that does not make the sentence incorrect, but does not improve it either.

Sample Responses for the Argumentative Essay

Following are sample criteria for scoring an argumentative essay.

A score 6 writer will

- create an exceptional composition with a clear thesis that appropriately addresses the audience and given task.
- organize ideas effectively and logically, include very strong supporting details, and use smooth transitions.
- present a definitive, focused thesis and clearly support it throughout the composition.

- include vivid, strong details, clear examples, and supporting text to support the key ideas.
- exhibit an exceptional level of skill in the usage of the English language and the capacity to employ an assortment of sentence structures.
- build essentially error-free and varied sentences that accurately convey intended meaning.

A score 5 writer will

- create a commendable composition that appropriately addresses the audience and given task.
- organize ideas, include supporting details, and use smooth transitions.
- present a thesis and support it throughout the composition.
- include details, examples, and supporting text to enhance the themes of the composition.
- generally exhibit a high level of skill in the usage of the English language and the capacity to employ an assortment of sentence structures.
- build mostly error-free sentences that accurately convey intended meaning.

A score 4 writer will

- create a composition that satisfactorily addresses the audience and given task.
- display satisfactory organization of ideas, include adequate supporting details, and generally use smooth transitions.
- present a thesis and mostly support it throughout the composition.
- include some details, examples, and supporting text that typically enhance most themes of the composition.
- exhibit a competent level of skill in the usage of the English language and the general capacity to employ an assortment of sentence structures.
- build sentences with several minor errors that generally do not confuse the intended meaning.

A score 3 writer will

- create an adequate composition that basically addresses the audience and given task.
- display some organization of ideas, include some supporting details, and use mostly logical transitions.
- present a somewhat underdeveloped thesis but attempt to support it throughout the composition.
- exhibit an adequate level of skill in the usage of the English language and a basic capacity to employ an assortment of sentence structures.
- build sentences with some minor and major errors that may obscure the intended meaning.

A score 2 writer will

- create a composition that restrictedly addresses the audience and given task.
- display little organization of ideas, have inconsistent supporting details, and use very few transitions.
- present an unclear or confusing thesis with little support throughout the composition.
- include very few details, examples, and supporting text.
- exhibit a less than adequate level of skill in the usage of the English language and a limited capacity to employ a basic assortment of sentence structures.
- build sentences with a few major errors that may confuse the intended meaning.

A score 1 writer will

- create a composition that has a limited sense of the audience and given task.
- display illogical organization of ideas, include confusing or no supporting details, and lack the ability to effectively use transitions.
- present a minimal or unclear thesis.
- include confusing or irrelevant details and examples, and little or no supporting text.

- exhibit a limited level of skill in the usage of the English language and little or no capacity to employ basic sentence structure.
- build sentences with many major errors that obscure or confuse the intended meaning.

Sample Score 6 Argumentative Essay

It's a fact: more and more people across the United States are vegetarian, and school and workplace cafeterias should be required to provide vegetarian lunch options for them. There are many reasons why vegetarians choose this diet: health concerns, moral issues, and religion among them. Schools and workplaces should honor these reasons by making it easier for vegetarians to purchase healthful, meat-free lunches.

Some vegetarians are responding to the generally unhealthy American diet, which often includes plenty of fast food and processed meats. They prefer salads, vegetables, and protein sources such as beans, soy-based products, and dairy products. However, cafeterias, both in schools and in businesses, tend to resemble fast food restaurants, offering such items as hamburgers, fried chicken, pizza, French fries, and sodas. If they also stocked healthier, meat-free choices, not only would the vegetarians be accommodated, but others would have the opportunity to enjoy healthier options.

It would not be difficult to transform the typical school or workplace cafeteria into a vegetarian-friendly one. Many of the lunch selections currently offered could be made vegetarian with a few simple and inexpensive substitutions. Veggie burgers offered alongside beef burgers, for example, would give vegetarians a satisfactory option. Tacos, burritos, and other Mexican entrees could be made with beans rather than ground beef. A salad bar would serve the dual purpose of providing both vegetarians and others concerned about their health and weight the opportunity for a satisfying meal. These changes, while relatively simple for cafeterias to incorporate, would provide vegetarians with acceptable lunch selections, and in the process, provide all the students or employees they serve with more healthful alternatives.

Comments on the Sample Argumentative Essay That Received a Score of 6

The author has created a solid, good argument with a clear thesis that is both definitive and focused. This essay successfully addresses the issue at hand with an effective organization. The supporting details are correct, logical, and relevant. It uses smooth transitions, clear examples, and specific details. The key ideas are readily apparent and explored throughout the essay through varied sentence structures. The author displays a clear mastery of the subject and of the English language.

Sample Score 4 Argumentative Essay

In the United States there are many people who are vegetarian. Many of these people are students or workers who eat lunch at their cafeterias on a daily basis. Surprisingly though, school and workplace cafeterias are not required to provide vegetarian options. That means that most often they don't. That means that vegetarians may be limited to lunches comprised of French fries, or pizza loaded with cheese. While these are vegetarian (non-meat), they are not healthy, especially if they are eaten every day.

Schools and businesses should have a wider variety of vegetarian options. Such as a salad bar, or perhaps even something with tofu. Entrees that use beans or soy-based products instead of meat would also be good. It wouldn't cost cafeterias more money to provide vegetarian lunches. In fact, the ingredients used to make them (like beans) are typically much cheaper than their carnivorous counterparts (like ground beef). Salads require little preparation in comparison with French fries, which could save money on payroll. Also, cafeterias could buy premade vegetarian selections in bulk, just as they do non-vegetarian dishes. These premade foods are becoming more and more popular, and are not more expensive.

While cafeterias can't meet all the demands of those they serve, it is important to offer those committed to a vegetarian lifestyle the choice to eat healthfully and meat-free. Schools should create a menu that offers these options for all students.

Comments on the Sample Argumentative Essay That Received a Score of 4

The author has done a workmanlike job. The essay accomplishes what it sets out to do, addressing the issue at hand. It is fairly well organized and gives reasonable details and arguments. It wants somewhat for style, but displays adequate rhetorical skills and mastery of the English language. For the most part, it is grammatically and orthographically correct.

Sample Score 1 Argumentative Essay

Many people are vegetarian and don't eat meat. This may be because they are afraid of diseases found in meat, such as mad cow disease, salmanella, or avian influenza. Or, they may not eat meat because of their religion. Some care about animal rites, and others are vegetarian because they are concerned about their health. They believe a vegetarian diet will help them lose weight and in general improve their health. But this is not necessarily the case. You could just eat French fries, cold cereal, and pizza every day and be a vegetarian. Vegetarians need to learn about how to eat this diet and make it healthy too. School and workplace cafeterias could help by offering them good selections at lunch.

Comments on the Sample Argumentative Essay That Received a Score of 1

The essay is short, poorly organized, and does not fulfill the requirements. There are a number of grammatical and spelling mistakes, as well as poor transitions and weak sentence structure. The argument is not convincing, and the author does not give the appearance of caring much about the subject.

Sample Responses for the Source-Based Essay

Following are sample criteria for scoring a source-based essay.

A score 6 writer will

- create an exceptional composition explaining why the concerns are important and support the explanation with specific references to both sources.
- organize ideas effectively and logically, include well-chosen information from both sources, link the two sources in the discussion, and use smooth transitions.
- exhibit an exceptional level of skill in the usage of the English language and the capacity to employ an assortment of sentence structures.
- build essentially error-free and varied sentences that accurately convey intended meaning.
- cite both sources when quoting or paraphrasing.

A score 5 writer will

- create a commendable composition that explains why the concerns are important and supports the explanation with specific references to both sources..
- organize ideas effectively and logically, include information from both sources, link the two sources, and use smooth transitions.
- generally exhibit skill in the usage of the English language and the capacity to employ variety in sentence structures.
- build mostly error-free sentences that accurately convey intended meaning.
- cite both sources when quoting or paraphrasing.

A score 4 writer will

- create a composition that satisfactorily explains why the concerns are important and supports the explanation with specific references to both sources.

- use information from both sources to convey why the concerns discussed in the sources are important.
- display satisfactory organization of ideas, include adequate details, and link the two sources.
- exhibit a competent level of skill in the usage of the English language and the general capacity to employ an assortment of sentence structures.
- build sentences with several minor errors that generally do not confuse the intended meaning.
- cite both sources when quoting or paraphrasing.

A score 3 writer will

- create an adequate composition that basically addresses the audience and given task but conveys the importance of the concerns in only a limited way.
- use information from only one source or inadequately from both sources to convey why the concerns discussed in the sources are important.
- display some organization of ideas and include some supporting details.
- exhibit an adequate level of skill in the usage of the English language and a basic capacity to employ an assortment of sentence structures.
- build sentences with some minor and major errors that may obscure the intended meaning.
- cite sources when quoting or paraphrasing.

A score 2 writer will

- fail to explain why the concerns are important.
- use information from only one source poorly or fail to convey why the concerns discussed in the sources are important.
- display little organization of ideas, have inconsistent supporting details, and fail to link the two sources.
- exhibit a less than adequate level of skill in the usage of the English language and a limited capacity to employ a basic assortment of sentence structures.

- build sentences with a few major errors that may confuse the intended meaning.
- fail to cite sources when quoting or paraphrasing.

A score 1 writer will

- display illogical organization of ideas, include confusing or no supporting details, and fail to adequately address the concerns raised by the sources.
- include confusing or irrelevant details and examples, and few or no supporting references.
- exhibit a limited level of skill in the usage of the English language and little or no capacity to employ basic sentence structure.
- build sentences with many major errors that obscure or confuse the intended meaning.

Sample Score 6 Essay

The Bill of Rights—the first ten amendments to the U.S. Constitution—is a part of American jurisprudence that is today often taken for granted. The Bill of Rights grants such fundamental liberties as the freedom of speech, freedom of religion, and protection against unreasonable search and seizure. However, there was a vigorous debate in the early Republic over whether a Bill of Rights should be adopted. Ironically, it was Alexander Hamilton, author of many of the Federalist Papers and proponent of a strong central government— the side eventually victorious—that would argue against the adoption of such a bill.

"John DeWitt," speaking for the anti-Federalists, raises sound arguments in favor of a bill of rights. Entering into a form of government, by its nature, entails giving up some of one's natural rights. (This train of thought was in keeping with Enlightenment figures such as John Locke.) These rights are so important and fundamental, that one must carefully delineate what powers are allotted to the government, and which retained, or, as he writes, "The line cannot be drawn with too much precision and accuracy." Furthermore, such legislation would prevent any confusion. Anticipating modern debates over the "original intent" of the

Founding Fathers, "DeWitt" points out that "Language is so easy of explanation, and so difficult is it by words to convey exact ideas, that the party to be governed cannot be too explicit." Thus, the new nation needed a bill of rights to eliminate any ambiguity.

One Federalist argument claimed that a constitutional bill of rights was unnecessary owing to the fact that states already had such verbiage affixed to their own constitutions. DeWitt counters this by saying that if states had Bills of Rights, why not the Federal government? To do so would be a check on governmental overreach, and reassure people that they retained all rights not specifically allocated to the Federal government.

In rebutting this, Hamilton, writing for the Federalists, deploys two arguments. First, he makes an appeal to the dignity of the new nation: bills of rights were made between rulers and subjects, and are not suited to a free country of free citizens. This, however, is mere rhetoric, and Hamilton proceeds to the meat of the matter. He points out that the central government was intended to be weak, and thus a Bill of Rights is superfluous: "a minute detail of particular rights is certainly far less applicable to a Constitution like that under consideration . . . than to a constitution which has the regulation of every species of personal and private concerns." Worse, by explicitly mentioning exceptions to powers not even mentioned, they would "afford a colorable pretext to claim more than were granted." Thus, a bill of rights, Hamilton feared, could lead to emboldened citizens seeking to overstep their granted rights.

The debates over the American Bill of Rights are one of the ironies of history. The very statutes that today ensure our liberties—and which have been expanded by judicial opinion to include contingencies that would have been completely foreign to the Founding Fathers like immigration rights and interracial marriage—were once seen as superfluous and even detrimental to a democratic way of life. Ultimately—in this matter, at least—the Anti-Federalists would prevail, and the first ten amendments to the U.S. Constitution stand as one of the foundational documents of the Western concept of freedom and liberty.

Comments on the Sample Source-Based Essay That Received a Score of 6

This is an outstanding essay. The author has clearly explained why the topic is important, making reference to both sources, and clearly, effectively, and logically organized the ideas under discussion. The author has linked these ideas together into a thematic and impartial essay on the subject of the debate over the Bill of Rights. She or he clearly understands the issue, and has additionally brought in a great deal of outside information. The use of the English language is exemplary, with a wide variety of error-free sentences that clearly convey the intended meaning. Both sources are extensively and accurately cited. The author furthermore correctly understands the use of advanced rhetorical techniques like irony and logical fallacies.

Sample Score 4 Essay

From the very beginning, the Bill of Rights, which gives Americans freedom of speech, the freedom of religion, and freedom to own guns has been the subject of the controversy. The two sides of the debate were the Federalists and Anti-Federalists. The Federalists did not want a Bill of Rights, while the Anti-Federalists did.

John de Witt says that when people form governments, they give up some rights. It is therefore important to say which rights are given up, for as he says, "The line cannot be drawn with too much precision and accuracy." He also says that people might be confused as to which rights were given up. A Bill of Rights would help to prevent this confusion. Also, if states had Bills of Rights, why shouldn't the Federal government? This would prevent people from taking too much power, since people naturally want to gain power over other people.

Alexander Hamilton disagrees with this opinion. First, he says that Bills of Rights were made between rulers and subjects. Since Americans are not subjects, they do not need a Bill of Rights. He also says that since the government would not have any powers the Constitution did not grant it, a Bill of Rights is not needed.

He is even afraid that giving a Bill of Rights might make the government think it had more power than it really did.

Obviously, the Anti-Federalists won this debate. Still, I feel that that people should listen to Alexander Hamilton today. The government has taken too much power. The Bill of Rights is there to stop the government from over-reaching.

Comments on the Sample Source-Based Essay That Received a Score of 4

This composition satisfactorily explains why the concerns in the topic are important and supports the explanation with specific information and references to both sources. However, though the author is able to deploy information from both sources to discuss the source, he or she does not have a deep historical background. The essay is satisfactorily organized and uses adequate details. The use of English is competent, with some variety in sentence structures. Errors are minor, and do not interfere with general understanding. Finally, the essay writer fails to be completely objective.

Sample Score 1 Essay

Today, the government does a lot of things it shouldn't. The government wants to take away guns (2 Amendment) and make us buy health care even if we like the health care we have right now (1 Amendment). Also the CIA and NSA are spying on us and violating our rights against searching and seizing.

The Founding Fathers came up with the best system of government anywhere. They knew what they were ding. In the Bill of Rights to the Constitution, they insured that we would not have our rights taken away. The problem with America today is that people are not listening to what the Founding Fathers said.

I think that we should go back to the original intent of the Founding Fathers. The USA should be One Nation Under God, Indivisible, With Liberty and Justice.

Comments on the Sample Source-Based Essay That Received a Score of 1

This essay displays an illogical organization of ideas and badly mismanages supporting details. The author shows no understanding of the issues. What details the essay does bring in are completely irrelevant. It also fails to adequately address the concerns raised by the sources. The level of English usage is poor at best and confuses the intended meaning. Finally, it fails to deal with the sources objectively.

Praxis® Core Academic Skills for Educators: Mathematics Practice Test 2

Time: 85 Minutes

Directions: Choose the best answer to each of the following questions.

1. Alec needs 432 inches of molding to put along the ceiling of his dining room. How many yards of molding should he buy?
   a. 12
   b. 43.2
   c. 15,552
   d. 36
   e. 440

2. John, Mike, and Dillon are painting a fence. John paints $\frac{1}{4}$ of the fence and Mike paints $\frac{2}{5}$ of the fence. How much of the fence is left to paint for Dillon?

3. The Andersons went out to dinner Saturday night and had a bill of $190.00. They gave the server a 25% tip. How much money did the Andersons tip their server?
   a. $19
   b. $47.50
   c. $38
   d. $38.50
   e. $47

4. Tanya can pack 4 boxes of fragile dishware in 25 minutes. How many minutes would it take her to pack 28 boxes of fragile dishware?

5. Consider the line in the graph that follows:

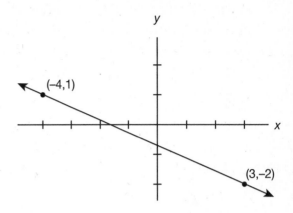

   Which of the following is the equation of this line?
   a. $7x + 3y = 15$
   b. $3x + 7y = -5$
   c. $7x + 3y = 15$
   d. $y + 2 = -(x - 3)$
   e. $y + 4 = -\frac{3}{7}(x - 1)$

6. John must rent vans to take the children from his summer camp on a field trip. There are 34 children, 6 counselors, and 11 assistants who will be going on the trip. If each van can accommodate 9 people, how many vans must John rent?
   a. 9
   b. 51
   c. 6
   d. 5
   e. 7

7. Which of the following is equivalent to $6 \times 7 + 6 \times 9$?
   a. $6(7 + 9)$
   b. $6 + 7 \times 6 + 9$
   c. $(6 \times 7) + 9$
   d. $(6 \times 7) \times (6 \times 9)$
   e. $6(7 \times 9)$

8. Out of 100 workers polled at a local factory, 75 said they would favor being offered a course in management. If there are 25,000 workers, how many would you expect to favor being offered such a course?
- **a.** 1,875
- **b.** 18,750
- **c.** 15,000
- **d.** 16,000
- **e.** 19,000

9. Which of the following is equivalent to the expression $xy \cdot yzx^5$?
- **a.** $5x^2y^2z$
- **b.** x^5y^2z
- **c.** $12xyz$
- **d.** x^6y^2z
- **e.** $x^6y^6z^5$

10. Jake rents a car for $200 each month, which includes 1,000 miles for the month. He is charged an additional $0.55 for each mile driven over 1,000. If x represents the total mileage Jake drives each month, and if he always drives over 1,000 miles per month, which of the following expressions can be used to calculate his total monthly car rental bill?
- **a.** $200 + 0.55x$
- **b.** $200 + 0.55(x - 1{,}000)$
- **c.** $200x + 0.55$
- **d.** $200 \times 0.55x$
- **e.** $200x + 0.55(x - 1{,}000)$

11. Suppose $a = -5$, $b = -2$, and $c = -3$. Evaluate $2ac - abc$.

12. Given the equation $y = 7 + 3(2x - 2)$, what is the value of y when $x = 6$?
- **a.** 14
- **b.** 21
- **c.** 25
- **d.** 35
- **e.** 37

Use the following chart to answer question 13.

How People Get to Work

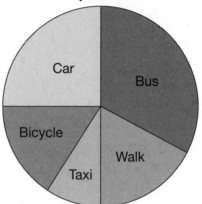

13. What is the total percentage of people who use a car or bicycle to get to work?
- **a.** 50%
- **b.** 25%
- **c.** 80%
- **d.** 40%
- **e.** 55%

14. Which of the following fractions is/are between $\frac{1}{5}$ and $\frac{1}{8}$? Indicate all that apply.
- **a.** $\frac{1}{4}$
- **b.** $\frac{1}{3}$
- **c.** $\frac{1}{7}$
- **d.** $\frac{2}{7}$
- **e.** $\frac{3}{16}$

15. Jessica received grades of 85, 90, 70, 85, and 100 on her math tests this semester. What grade will she receive in math for the semester?

a. 70

b. 85

c. 86

d. 90

e. 100

Use the following figure to answer questions 16 and 17.

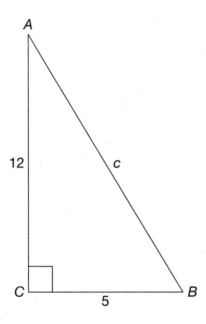

(Numbers indicate miles)

16. Paul drives to work each day using the route *A* to *C* to *B*, which is a total of 17 miles. Recently, a new road was finished that went directly from *A* to *B*. How many fewer miles will Paul be driving each day to work if he uses the new route?

a. 2 miles

b. 3 miles

c. 4 miles

d. 5 miles

e. 6 miles

17. If Paul drives to work five days a week using route *A* to *B*, how many fewer miles will he drive than if he used route *A* to *C* to *B* over a period of 3 weeks?

a. 15 miles

b. 20 miles

c. 35 miles

d. 45 miles

e. 60 miles

18. Which of the following is the solution of this system of equations?

$$\begin{cases} x - 4y = 18 \\ 4y + x = 26 \end{cases}$$

a. $x = 10, y = -2$

b. $x = 2, y = 6$

c. $x = 0, y = 0$

d. $x = 22, y = 1$

e. no solution

19. Aidan and James sell a total of 48 magazines. If Aidan sells 3 times more magazines than James, how many magazines does James sell?

20. Nella wants to buy wood chips to cover the play area in her backyard. The area is 12 feet long and 6 feet wide. She wants the wood chips to be 3 inches deep. How many cubic inches of wood chips does Nella need to buy?

a. 216 cubic inches

b. 500 cubic inches

c. 2,160 cubic inches

d. 21,160 cubic inches

e. 31,104 cubic inches

Use the following dot plot to answer questions 21 and 22.

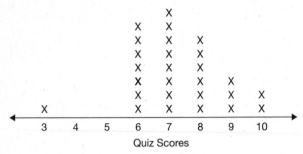

Quiz Scores

KEY: X = 1 Student

21. According to the dot plot, how many students scored at least an 8 on the quiz?

a. 5

b. 8

c. 11

d. 16

e. 27

22. What fraction of students earned a 7 or 8 on the quiz?

a. $\frac{8}{10}$

b. $\frac{6}{10}$

c. $\frac{8}{27}$

d. $\frac{6}{27}$

e. $\frac{14}{27}$

23. Alexa is making costumes for the school play. She needs 15 yards of fabric to make 3 costumes. How many yards of fabric would she need to make 8 costumes?

a. 30 yards

b. 40 yards

c. 45 yards

d. 50 yards

e. 60 yards

24. Mary has exactly 1,560 hours until her vacation begins. How many days are there before her vacation begins?

a. 30

b. 50

c. 65

d. 75

e. 37,440

25. A rose garden on a square plot of land has an open wooden fence that is 320 feet long around its perimeter. What is the approximate length of the diagonal of this plot of ground to the nearest foot?

a. 80 feet

b. 226 feet

c. 6,400 feet

d. 139 feet

e. 113 feet

Use the following graph to answer questions 26 and 27.

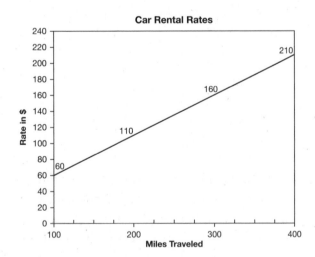

26. Which equation best represents the graph?

a. $y = 2x$

b. $y = x - 40$

c. $y = 2x - 40$

d. $y = \frac{1}{2}x + 40$

e. $y = \frac{1}{2}x + 10$

27. If the *x*-axis is extended, what will *y* be when *x* = 700?
   a. 260
   b. 300
   c. 310
   d. 360
   e. 400

28. A factory operates 15 machines that each make between 90 and 120 tennis balls per minute. Which of the following could be the number of tennis balls produced in an hour if all 15 machines are working at the same time?
   a. 900
   b. 1,200
   c. 9,000
   d. 28,000
   e. 90,000

29. The area of Melissa's rectangular garden is 330 square feet. The width of the garden is 15 feet. How many feet of fence does Melissa need to buy to surround the entire garden?
   a. 20 feet
   b. 34 feet
   c. 74 feet
   d. 85 feet
   e. 94 feet

30. Which of the following numerical expressions is an *irrational* number?
   a. $\sqrt{8} \times \sqrt{2}$
   b. $\frac{\sqrt{125}}{\sqrt{5}}$
   c. $(\sqrt{21})^2$
   d. $2 - \sqrt{81}$
   e. $\sqrt{169 - 49}$

31. Let $s(x) = \frac{3}{2} - 2x^2 + \frac{1}{3}x^4$ and $r(x) = 5x^2 - 10x^4$. Which of the following is equivalent to $6s(x) - \frac{1}{5}r(x)$?
   a. $-11x^2 + 9$
   b. $\frac{31}{3}x^4 - 3x^2 + 9$
   c. $4x^4 - 13x^2 + 9$
   d. $4x^4 - 13x^2$
   e. $4x^4 + 13x^2 - 9$

32. Write the following expression as a single decimal: $(2.7 \times 10^{-3}) \div (3.6 \times 10^{-3})$.

33. For which of the following values of *a* does the trinomial $x^2 + ax + 24$ factor? Select all that apply.
   a. 25
   b. −10
   c. −11
   d. 11
   e. 2

34. Patrick has $1,860 saved up from his past five birthdays. He wants to allot himself $75 per week for social activities and $40 per week for gas and food, and wants to keep $400 in the account to avoid monthly maintenance fees. Which of the following inequalities can be used to determine *x* as the number of weeks he can continue to withdraw from the account?
   a. $115x + 1,860 \geq 400$
   b. $115 + 1,860x \geq 400$
   c. $75x + 1,860 \leq 400$
   d. $-115x + 1,860 \geq 400$
   e. $1,860 \leq 400 + 115x$

Use the following table to answer questions 35 and 36.

SNOWMOBILE RENTAL RATES	
HOURS OVER 1	RATE
1	$17
2	$24
3	$31
4	$38

35. It costs $250 to rent a snowmobile for the first hour. The chart shows the rates for additional hours. What would be the total cost for Tom and Mary if Tom rented a snowmobile for 4 hours, and Mary rented one for 3 hours?
  a. $281
  b. $288
  c. $560
  d. $569
  e. $622

36. Letting r = rate, and x = number of hours, which equation best represents the data in the chart?
  a. $r = 7x + 10$
  b. $r = 10 + 7$
  c. $r = 5x + 12$
  d. $r = 16x + 1$
  e. $r = 5x + 10$

Use the following bar graph to answer questions 37 and 38.

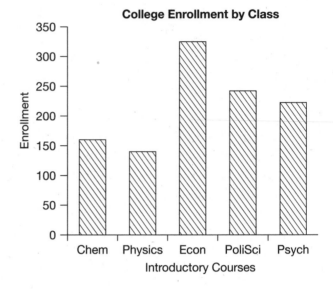

37. According to the chart, what was the approximate total enrollment for the classes shown?
  a. 900
  b. 1,000
  c. 1,025
  d. 1,050
  e. 1,100

38. What is the approximate proportion of students who took PoliSci?
  a. $\frac{1}{2}$
  b. $\frac{1}{4}$
  c. $\frac{1}{3}$
  d. $\frac{2}{3}$
  e. $\frac{3}{4}$

39. The formula for the surface area of a right circular cylinder (including the areas of the two bases) is given by $SA = 2\pi r^2 + 2\pi rh$, where r is the radius of the base and h is the height of the cylinder. If the height equals 3 times the radius and the surface area is 200π square feet, which of the following is the radius?

a. 5 feet
b. $\sqrt{50}$ feet
c. 25 feet
d. 15 feet
e. 5π feet

40. Let $y = f(x)$ be a given function and suppose the point (2,–3) lies on its graph. Consider the translation of this function given by $g(x) = f(x + 4) - 1$. To what point would the given point correspond on the graph of $g(x)$?

41. Jackie's bank balances were $20 on Monday, $0 on Tuesday, $45 on Wednesday, and $25 on Thursday. What was Jackie's mean balance for the week?

a. $20.00
b. $22.50
c. $25.00
d. $25.50
e. $30.00

Use the dot plot to answer questions 42 through 44.

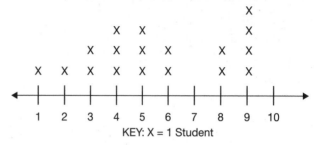

Number of Pencils Each Student Has

KEY: X = 1 Student

42. How many students are surveyed on this dot plot?

a. 9
b. 10
c. 18
d. 38
e. 40

43. What is the approximate average number of pencils owned by the students surveyed?

a. 5.6
b. 4.5
c. 10
d. 6.6
c. 10.2

44. What is the mode of the data indicated by the dot plot?

a. 2
b. 5
c. 6
d. 9
e. 10

45. Neil digitally records birthday parties and charges $120 for the recording. His weekly overhead expenses amount to $390, and he spends $30 on supplies for each recording. How many birthday parties must Neil record each week before he breaks even?

   a. 3
   b. 4
   c. 5
   d. 10
   e. 50

46. Jan and her sister entered a raffle at the football game. Jan put her name on 3 tickets, and her sister put her name on 5 tickets. If there are 100 total tickets and only one winner, what are the chances that Jan or her sister will win the raffle?

   a. 5.0
   b. 0.50
   c. 0.005
   d. 0.8
   e. 0.08

47. Which of the following statements is/are true? Select all that apply.

   a. All rectangles are rhombi.
   b. There is a rectangle that is not a parallelogram.
   c. Some rhombi are not squares.
   d. A parallelogram is a square.
   e. All squares are rectangles.

Use the chart to answer question 48.

x	y
2	4
4	7
6	10
8	13

48. Which of the following equations best describes the relationship shown in the chart?

   a. $2x = y$
   b. $y = x + 3$
   c. $2x + 3 = y$
   d. $\frac{3x + 2}{2} = y$
   e. $\frac{2x + 3}{2} = y$

49. The ages of the starting lineup for the New York Yankees are as follows:

   26, 29, 35, 29, 22, 31, 35, 21, 27

   What is the median age of the Yankees' starting lineup?

   a. 21
   b. 35
   c. 14
   d. 28.5
   e. 29

50. Ellen's square kitchen has a perimeter of 48 feet. What is the area of the kitchen?

   a. 12 square feet
   b. 12 feet
   c. 24 square feet
   d. 560 square feet
   e. 144 square feet

51. Jessica has 3 skirts, 4 shirts, and 2 hats. How many different combinations of skirts, shirts, and hats can she wear?
   a. 7
   b. 14
   c. 24
   d. 28
   e. 32

52. If p and q are prime numbers, what is the least common multiple of $18p^2$, $30pq^2$, $42pq^3$?
   a. $6p$
   b. $6p^2q^3$
   c. $2p$
   d. $630p^2q^3$
   e. $22{,}680p^4q^5$

53. Tom needs to buy paint so that he can paint the emblem on the basketball court. The circular emblem has a diameter of 12 feet. If paint cans come in quarts, and it takes 1 quart to paint 50 square feet, how many quarts of paint will Tom have to buy? Use 3.14 for π.
   a. 1
   b. 2
   c. 3
   d. 4
   e. 5

54. Consider the two triangles $\triangle ABC$ and $\triangle A'B'C'$:

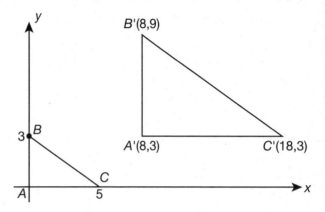

Assume that $\triangle ABC$ can be transformed into $\triangle A'B'C'$ by first translating $\triangle ABC$ and then applying an appropriate dilation centered at the origin. Which of the following translation rule–dilation combinations will result in this transformation?
   a. Translate using the rule $(x,y) \rightarrow (x - 8, y - 3)$ and then perform a dilation centered at the origin with a scale factor of 2.
   b. Translate using the rule $(x,y) \rightarrow (x + 8, y - 3)$ and then perform a dilation centered at the origin with a scale factor of $\frac{1}{2}$.
   c. Translate using the rule $(x,y) \rightarrow (x + 8, y + 3)$ and then perform a dilation centered at the origin with a scale factor of $\frac{1}{2}$.
   d. Translate using the rule $(x,y) \rightarrow (x + 8, y + 3)$ and then perform a dilation centered at the origin with a scale factor of 3.
   e. Translate using the rule $(x,y) \rightarrow (x + 8, y + 3)$ and then perform a dilation centered at the origin with a scale factor of 2.

55. Six students are running for class president. John has a $\frac{1}{8}$ chance of winning and is half as likely to win as Mike. Kelly has the same chance of winning as Mike. Julie, Kelvin, and Roger all have the same chance of winning. What chance does Kelvin have of winning?

a. $\frac{1}{2}$

b. $\frac{1}{3}$

c. $\frac{1}{4}$

d. $\frac{3}{8}$

e. $\frac{1}{8}$

56. Jason was asked to choose a marble from a bag. If he chose a red marble, he would win a prize. The bag contained 20 blue marbles, 20 black marbles, 20 green marbles, 18 yellow marbles, and 2 red marbles. Which of the following decimals shows Jason's chances of choosing a red marble?

a. 0.025

b. 0.25

c. 0.08

d. 0.8

e. 2.5

Praxis® Core Academic Skills for Educators: Mathematics Practice Test 2 Answers and Explanations

1. a. This is a conversion problem. There are 36 inches in 1 yard. Converting from a smaller unit to a larger unit requires division: $432 \div 36 = 12$. You can also check division with multiplication: $36 \times 12 = 432$.

2. $\frac{7}{20}$. The first step is to rewrite all fractions with a common denominator. The lowest common denominator for $\frac{1}{4}$ and $\frac{2}{5}$ is 20: $\frac{1}{4} \times \frac{5}{5} = \frac{5}{20}$, and $\frac{2}{5} \times \frac{4}{4} = \frac{8}{20}$. These fractions represent portions of the fence that have been painted, so $\frac{5}{20} + \frac{8}{20} = \frac{13}{20}$ of the fence has been painted. Therefore, $1 - \frac{13}{20} = \frac{20}{20} - \frac{13}{20} = \frac{7}{20}$ of the fence is left for Dillon to paint.

3. b. To compute a percent of a number, multiply by the decimal of the percent. The decimal for 25% is 0.25: $0.25 \times \$190 = \$47.50$.

4. **175 minutes.** Let x represent the number of minutes needed to pack 28 boxes of fragile dishware. Set up the following proportion:

$$\frac{4 \text{ boxes}}{25 \text{ minutes}} = \frac{28 \text{ boxes}}{x \text{ minutes}}$$

Cross multiply and solve for x:

$4x = (25)(28)$

$x = 25(7)$

$x = 175$

So, Tanya can pack 28 boxes in 175 minutes.

5. b. We can identify two points on the graph: $(-4,1)$ and $(3,-2)$. The slope of the line containing these two points is $m = \frac{1-(-2)}{-4-3} = -\frac{3}{7}$. Using point-slope form with this slope and the point $(3,-2)$ yields $y - (-2) = -\frac{3}{7}(x-3)$. Now, we simplify as follows:

$$y - (-2) = -\frac{3}{7}(x-3)$$
$$y + 2 = -\frac{3}{7}(x-3)$$
$$7y + 14 = -3(x-3)$$
$$7y + 14 = -3x + 9$$
$$3x + 7y = -5$$

6. c. For this problem, you must first determine how many people will be going on the trip by adding: $34 + 6 + 11 = 51$. Since these people will be splitting into groups of 9, you should divide: 51 total people divided by 9 in each van equals 5 remainder 6. However, the remainder here represents people, so there will be 5 vans with 9 people, and one van with 6 people, for a total of 6 vans.

7. a. This is an example of the distributive property of multiplication over addition. Factor out 6 to get the equivalent expression $6(7 + 9)$.

8. b. 75 out of 100 is 75%. To compute 75% of 25,000, multiply $25,000 \times 0.75 = 18,750$.

9. d. Gather like variables in the product and add their exponents:
$$xy \cdot x^5yz = (x \cdot x^5) \cdot (y \cdot y) \cdot z = x^6y^2z$$

10. b. His rental fee will include the $200 plus $0.55 \times$ the number of miles he drives over 1,000 miles. If $x =$ total miles, then $x - 1,000$ = the total miles driven over 1,000. Therefore, the expression becomes $200 + 0.55(x - 1,000)$.

11. 60. Substitute the values of a, b, and c into the expression and use the order of operations to simplify:
$$
\begin{aligned}
2ac - abc &= 2(-5)(-3) - (-5)(-2)(-3) \\
&= 30 - (-30) \\
&= 30 + 30 \\
&= 60
\end{aligned}
$$

12. e. Substitute $x = 6$ and follow the order of operations (PEMDAS). Multiply inside the parentheses first, and then subtract: $y = 7 + 3(2 \times 6 - 2)$; $y = 7 + 3(12 - 2)$; $y = 7 + 3(10)$. Then, multiply: $y = 7 + 3(10)$; $y = 7 + 30$. Finally, add: $y = 37$.

13. d. Since there are no values given, you must approximate the percentages based on the size of the areas for car and bicycle. It could not be 50%, 55%, or 80% because that would be half the chart or bigger. 25% is $\frac{1}{4}$ of the chart, but this only describes the percentage who take a car to work. 40% is the best choice because it accurately describes how the percentage of people who take a car or bicycle to work is slightly less than half of the graph.

14. c and e. To solve this problem, convert each fraction to a decimal. You are looking for fractions with decimals between $\frac{1}{8} = 0.125$ and $\frac{1}{5} = 0.2$. Of the fractions given, only $\frac{1}{7} \approx 0.1429$ and $\frac{3}{16} = 0.1875$ fall between these two values.

15. c. Jessica's overall grade for the semester will be the average of the grades on her tests. To find the average of a group of numbers, first add the numbers; then divide by the number of numbers: $\frac{70 + 85 + 86 + 90 + 100}{5} = \frac{430}{5} = 86$.

16. c. The new route from A to B represents the hypotenuse of the right triangle. You can find the hypotenuse using the Pythagorean theorem, $a^2 + b^2 = c^2$: $12^2 + 5^2 = c^2$; $144 + 25 = 169$. The square root of $169 = 13$. Subtract the length of the new route from the length of his old route: $17 - 13 = 4$ miles.

17. e. Using the 4 fewer miles that Paul drives each day using this new route, multiply that value by 5 to get 20 fewer miles driven each week. Over a period of 3 weeks, this would be $20 \times 3 = 60$ fewer miles driven.

18. d. The method of elimination is the most efficient one to use here. Add the two equations to cancel the y terms:

$$x - 4y = 18$$
$$+ (x + 4y = 26)$$
$$2x = 44$$
$$x = 22$$

Now, substitute $x = 22$ into the first equation $x - 4y = 18$ to obtain $22 - 4y = 18$. Solving for y then yields $y = 1$. So, the solution of the system is $x = 22, y = 1$.

19. 12. For this problem, use an algebraic equation. Let James be J, and since Aidan sells 3 times more than James, Aidan will be $3J$. The equation becomes $3J + J = 48$. Combine like terms:
$4J = 48$. Finally, divide each side by 4: $J = 12$. James sells 12 magazines.

20. e. To correctly solve this problem, it is important to first change the feet to inches. Remember, there are 12 inches in 1 foot: 12 feet is equal to 144 inches, and 6 feet is equal to 72 inches. To find the volume of this rectangular area, multiply length times width times height: $144 \times 72 \times 3 = 31{,}104$ cubic inches.

21. c. On this dot plot, one X is equal to one student who earned a particular score on the quiz. Looking only at the X's for 8, 9, and 10, add to see that there are 11 students represented.

22. e. Add all the X's on the dot plot to find the total number of students who took the quiz. There are 27 X's, so this is the denominator of the fraction. The question asks for the fraction of students who scored a 7 or 8, so add the X's for those two scores. There are 14 students who scored either a 7 or 8, so the fraction is $\frac{14}{27}$.

23. b. To solve this problem, set up a proportion and cross multiply: $\frac{15}{3} = \frac{x}{8}$. Cross multiply: $15 \times 8 = 3x$; $120 = 3x$. Finally, divide both sides by 3: $x = 40$ yards.

24. c. This problem requires you to convert a smaller unit to a larger unit. To go from a smaller unit to a larger unit, you must divide. Divide 1,560 hours by 24 hours per day to get 65 days.

25. e. Since the garden is a square, each of its four sides has the same length. Since the perimeter is 320 feet, each side has length 80 feet. The diagonal of the garden can be viewed as the hypotenuse h of a right triangle whose legs both have length 80 feet. Using the Pythagorean theorem yields $80^2 + 80^2 = h^2$, which simplifies to $h^2 = 12{,}800$. So, $h = \sqrt{12{,}800} \approx 113$ feet.

26. e. Because there are points labeled on the graph, you can use them to find the slope of the line: $m = \frac{160 - 110}{300 - 200} = \frac{50}{100} = \frac{1}{2}$. This eliminates all but two of the equations given. To determine which of the two equations is correct, plug an x-value into the equations. The one that produces the correct y-value is the correct equation: $y = \frac{1}{2}(200) + 10$; $y = 100 + 10$; $y = 110$. The point $(200,100)$ is labeled on the line, so $y = \frac{1}{2}x + 10$ is the correct equation.

27. d. To find the y-value, plug $x = 700$ into the equation of the line: $y = \frac{1}{2}(700) + 10$; $y = 350 + 10$; $y = 360$.

28. e. First, calculate the minimum number of tennis balls that could be produced in an hour by 15 machines: 90 balls per minute $\times$ 60 minutes in an hour $\times$ 15 machines $= 81{,}000$. Do the same for the maximum number: $120 \times 60 \times 15 = 108{,}000$. Of the given possible numbers of balls produced, only 90,000 falls within this range.

29. c. To determine how much fencing is needed to go around the entire garden, you need to calculate the perimeter. The perimeter of a rectangle is found by adding twice the length and twice the width. So, you must first find the length of the garden. You are given the area and width of the garden, and remember that the area of a rectangle is found by multiplying length times width. Find the length by dividing: $330 \div 15 = 22$ feet. Now, the perimeter of the garden is $2(22) + 2(15) = 44 + 30 = 74$ feet.

30. e. Observe that $\sqrt{169 - 49} = \sqrt{120}$. Since 120 is not the square of a rational number, this quantity is irrational.

31. c. To compute $6s(x) - \frac{1}{5}r(x)$, first distribute 6 through each term of $s(x)$ and distribute the $-\frac{1}{5}$ through each term of $r(x)$, and then add like terms:

$$6s(x) - \frac{1}{5}r(x) = 6(\frac{3}{2} - 2x^2 + \frac{1}{3}x^4) - \frac{1}{5}(5x^2 - 10x^4)$$
$$= (9 - 12x^2 + 2x^4) - (x^2 - 2x^4)$$
$$= 9 - 12x^2 + 2x^4 - x^2 + 2x^4$$
$$= 4x^4 - 13x^2 + 9$$

32. **0.75.** Simplify each of the two quantities enclosed within parentheses. Then, divide resulting decimals, as follows:

$$(2.7 \times 10^{-3}) \div (3.6 \times 10^{-3})$$
$$= 0.0027 \div 0.0036 = 27 \div 36 = 0.75$$

33. **a, b, c, and d.** For **a**, the trinomial would factor as $(x + 1)(x + 24)$. For **b**, the trinomial would factor as $(x - 4)(x - 6)$. For **c**, the trinomial would factor as $(x - 3)(x - 8)$. For **d**, the trinomial would factor as $(x + 3)(x + 8)$.

34. d. Let x represent the number of weeks he can make withdrawls from the account. Since he withdraws \$115 per week (for social activities, gas, and food), the total he withdraws in x weeks is \$115x. So, after x weeks, there is $1,860 - 115x$ dollars left in the account. This amount must be greater than or equal to 400 dollars in order to avoid fees. So, the inequality used to model this situation is $-115x + 1,860 \geq 400$.

35. d. Use the table to determine the cost of each person's rental, and then add the values. Tom's first hour was \$250, and then his 4 additional hours were \$38 more: \$250 + \$38 = \$288. Mary's first hour was also \$250, and then her 3 additional hours were \$31 more: \$250 + \$31 = \$281. Therefore, the total cost is \$288 + \$281 = \$569.

36. a. Use trial and error to find which equation best represents the data in the chart. By plugging the hours in the chart in for x, you see that $r = 7x + 10$ is the equation that shows all the correct values for r.

37. e. The question asks for the approximate total enrollment, so you must round the numbers represented by the bars on the graph. By rounding, represent Chem as 150, Physics as 150, Econ as 325, PoliSci as 250, and Psych as 225: $150 + 150 + 325 + 250 + 225 = 1,100$.

38. b. There are approximately 1,100 total students enrolled, and 250 of them are enrolled in PoliSci. This represented as a fraction would be $\frac{250}{1,100}$. Because the question asks for the approximate fraction, round 1,100 to 1,000 and then reduce: $\frac{250}{1,000} = \frac{1}{4}$.

39. a. Let r represent the radius of the base. Then, the height $h = 3r$. Using the surface area formula for a right circular cylinder yields the following equation that we must solve for r:

$$200\pi = 2\pi r^2 + 2\pi r(3r)$$
$$200\pi = 2\pi r^2 + 6\pi r$$
$$200\pi = 8\pi r^2$$
$$25 = r^2$$
$$5 = r$$

So, the radius is 5 feet.

40. **(–2,–4).** You need to translate the given point 4 units to the left and 1 unit down. In such case, (2,–3) would become (2 – 4, –3 – 1) = (–2,–4).

41. **b.** The mean is the same as the average. To find the average, add all the values and divide by the total number of values: $\frac{\$20 + \$0 + \$45 + \$25}{4} = \frac{\$90}{4} = \$22.50$.

42. **c.** On this particular dot plot, one X represents one student. There are a total of 18 X's on the line plot, so there were 18 students surveyed.

43. **a.** To find the average, add all the values and divide by the total number of values. However, in this situation, the values are the numbers of pencils, not the numbers of students. You must add the amount of each number indicated by the X's, not just the number of X's. For example, 4 students had 9 pencils, so this value in the average would be 4 × 9. Do this for each column where there are X's, and since there are 18 students, divide this all by 18:

$$\frac{(1 \times 1) + (2 \times 1) + (3 \times 2) + (4 \times 3) + (5 \times 3) + (6 \times 2) + (7 \times 0) + (8 \times 2) + (9 \times 4) + (10 \times 0)}{18}$$
$$= \frac{1 + 2 + 6 + 12 + 15 + 12 + 0 + 16 + 36 + 0}{18} = \frac{100}{18} = 5.555555\ldots$$
$$\approx 5.6.$$

44. **d.** The mode is the number that occurs most often. In this case, that would be 9 pencils, which occurs 4 times.

45. **c.** Neil reaches the break-even point when his sales for a week equal his costs for the week. We know that Neil's weekly overhead expenses are fixed at $390. He also spends $30 on materials for each recording. He then charges $120 for the recording. Use the following equation to find this point:

$$\$390 + \$30x = \$120(x)$$

Solve for x:

$$390 + 30x = 120x$$
$$390 = 90x$$
$$x = 4.3$$

So, Neil must record 5 parties to break even (4 would not be enough).

46. **e.** Since either Jan *or* her sister is being picked, we must add 3 and 5. There are 100 total tickets, so the chances that Jan or her sister will win are $\frac{8}{100}$. Since the probabilities are written in decimal form, change $\frac{8}{100}$ to the decimal 0.08.

47. **c and e.** For **c**, any quadrilateral whose opposite sides are parallel and for which all four sides have the same length is a rhombus. If there is no right angle, then it cannot be a square. For **e**, a rectangle must have opposite sides parallel and contain a right angle. Squares satisfy these conditions, as well as having all four sides congruent.

48. **d.** The easiest way to solve problems like these is to use substitution and the process of elimination. By substituting each x-value into the equations, you find that the only equation that works for every value of x is $y = \frac{3x + 2}{2}$.

49. **e.** The median is the middle number of a set of data when arranged in increasing order. The given ages in increasing order are 21, 22, 26, 27, 29, 29, 31, 35, 35. The number 29 is in the middle, so it is the median age for the Yankees' starting lineup.

50. **e.** The kitchen is a square, so its four sides are of equal length. You can find the length of the sides by dividing the perimeter by 4: 48 ÷ 4 = 12 feet. Area is then calculated by multiplying length × width: 12 × 12 = 144 square feet.

51. **c.** Each skirt, shirt, and hat can be paired together in any combination, and order doesn't matter. This can be solved using the counting principle and multiplication: 4 × 3 × 2 = 24 combinations.

52. d. The smallest whole number into which all of 18, 30, and 42 divides evenly is 630. Also, the smallest power of p into which each of $18p^2$, $30pq^2$, $42pq^3$ divides is p^2, and the smallest power of q into which each divides is q^3. Hence, the least common multiple of $18p^2$, $30pq^2$, $42pq^3$ is $630p^2q^3$.

53. c. The equation for the area of a circle is $A = \pi r^2$. The diameter of the circle is given as 12 feet, so the radius is 6 feet: $A = \pi(6)^2 = 36\pi \approx 113.04$ square feet. If each quart of paint will cover 50 square feet, then Tom needs to buy 3 cans of paint.

54. e. First, observe that in order to move A to A', we must move the point right 8 units and then up 3 units. This is described by the translation rule $(x,y) \rightarrow (x + 8, y + 3)$. Applying this to all points of the triangle ΔABC moves it to a new location in the plane. Now, observe that this triangle is smaller than $\Delta A'B'C'$, so that the scale factor must be greater than 1. Observe that $A'B'$ is twice the length of AB, and $A'C'$ is twice the length of AC. So, the scale factor should be 2.

55. e. The chance of someone winning the election is 1. If John has a $\frac{1}{8}$ chance of winning, and if he is half as likely to win as Mike, that means that Mike has a $\frac{1}{4}$ chance of winning. Since Kelly has the same chance of winning as Mike, she also has a $\frac{1}{4}$ chance. If you add the chances for John, Mike, and Kelly, you get $\frac{5}{8}$, leaving a $\frac{3}{8}$ chance that Julie, Kelvin, or Roger will win. Since they all have the same chance, each has a $\frac{1}{8}$ chance to win. Therefore, Kelvin has a $\frac{1}{8}$ chance of winning.

56. a. First, determine the total number of marbles in the bag by adding the numbers given: $20 + 20 + 20 + 18 + 2 = 80$. Since there are only 2 red marbles, Jason's chances of choosing a red marble are $\frac{2}{80}$. To find the decimal, divide 2 by 80, which is 0.025.

5 ▶ PRAXIS® CORE ACADEMIC SKILLS FOR EDUCATORS: PRACTICE TEST 3

CHAPTER SUMMARY

Here is your third set of full-length tests in this book for each Praxis® Core Academic Skills for Educators test: Reading, Writing, and Mathematics. Now that you have taken two full sets of practice exams, take these exams to see how much your score has improved.

T his time, as you take these practice tests, you should simulate the actual test-taking experience as closely as you can. Find a quiet place to work where you won't be disturbed. Follow the time constraints noted at the beginning of each test.

After you finish taking your tests, review the answer explanations. (Each individual test is followed by its own answer explanations.) See **A Note on Scoring** on page 375 to find information on how to score your test.

Good luck!

Praxis® Core Academic Skills for Educators: Reading Practice Test 3

Time: 85 Minutes

Directions: Read the following passages and answer the questions that follow.

Refer to the following passage for questions 1 through 7.

For reasons scientists have yet to fully understand, reasons that might be related to warming
water temperatures or overfishing, jellyfish
populations are swelling across the planet's
5   oceans. This gives rise to a number of concerns.
For swimmers and recreational divers, this is a
problem, as jellyfish are not only a nuisance but
also a potential danger. Unfortunately, jellyfish
offer almost no nutritional value and serve little
10   function in the seas—meaning that their
unpleasant population growth might be difficult to curtail. However, one animal that can
help address this problem is the ocean sunfish.
One of the most unusual-looking creatures
15   found in the oceans, the mammoth and oddly
shaped ocean sunfish is the heaviest bony fish
ever discovered. This giant fish averages more
than a ton in weight, and its diet consists
almost entirely of jellyfish. Because jellyfish
20   contain so few nutrients, the sunfish must eat
the jellyfish in large quantities. Though sunfish
are a delicacy in some countries, such as Japan,
the world would be better served to adopt the
European Union's ban on the sale of sunfish.

1. Which is most similar to the sunfish, based on
   the way in which its diet results in a clear benefit to human beings?
   a. the spider, which eats mosquitoes and other
      insects
   b. the tuna, which eats squid and shellfish
   c. the rhinoceros, which eats grass and fruits
   d. the grizzly bear, which eats fish
   e. the tick, which eats mammalian blood

2. Which description of a sunfish best represents
   a statement of opinion, rather than a statement
   of fact?
   a. It is the largest bony fish.
   b. It eats primarily jellyfish.
   c. It has an unusual appearance.
   d. Its sale is banned in Europe.
   e. It is eaten by people.

3. Which best describes how the passage is
   structured?
   a. Two ocean creatures are compared and
      contrasted.
   b. Events related to a sea creature are provided
      in chronological order.
   c. A sea creature is described, and then its
      attributes are detailed.
   d. The dietary constraints of one creature are
      listed, and then a solution is given.
   e. A distressing trend related to a sea creature is
      described, and then a potential solution is
      offered.

4. In the context of the passage, the word *curtail*
   in line 12 most nearly means
   a. reverse.
   b. increase.
   c. withstand.
   d. curb.
   e. liberate.

5. Which key word from the passage helps transition the passage from the negative characteristics of jellyfish to the positive attributes of
   ocean sunfish?
   a. unfortunately
   b. difficult
   c. however
   d. entirely
   e. though

6. Which statement best describes the author's position regarding ocean sunfish?

a. There are creatures larger than the sunfish in the ocean.

b. Population change of the sunfish remains a mystery to scientists.

c. The sunfish should expand its diet to other creatures besides the jellyfish to better adapt.

d. Protections for sunfish should be set in place to help limit the jellyfish population.

e. The sunfish fails to serve a valuable or important purpose in the ocean.

7. Which idea provides the best support for the statement in the last sentence of the passage?

a. Waters are warming throughout the United States and the remainder of the world.

b. The increase in jellyfish populations might be related to warming waters or overfishing.

c. Due to the limited nutritional value of jellyfish, sunfish must eat great quantities of them.

d. The ocean sunfish is a large creature and has been described as having an odd appearance.

e. Japan is one country where jellyfish are located.

Refer to the following passage for questions 8 through 10.

Arguably the most famous feature on the most famous mountain on Earth, the Hillary Step is a narrow, nearly vertical 40-foot rock wall near the peak of Mount Everest. Covered in snow
5   and ice at 28,750 feet, the Hillary Step presents the last great danger for climbers trying to reach the summit. Once the Hillary Step has been conquered, climbers have only a few hundred feet of moderate climbing to reach the
10   mountain's top at 29,028 feet—the planet's highest point. Named for Sir Edmund Hillary, one of the two climbers to first ascend it, the step now features a fixed rope for modern-day climbers to use; such an advantage was unavail-
15   able during Hillary's initial 1953 ascent, making his achievement all the more venerable.

8. For which reason is the Hillary Step most likely the most famous feature on Mount Everest?

a. The Hillary Step was named after the great climber Sir Edmund Hillary.

b. The Hillary Step acts as the final significant obstacle to the mountain's summit.

c. The Hillary Step is one of the most difficult technical climbs in mountain climbing.

d. The Hillary Step had not been successfully ascended until 1953.

e. The highest point of the world is located where the Hillary Step ends.

9. In the passage, the word *venerable* in line 16 most nearly means

a. hazardous.

b. technical.

c. advantageous.

d. serious.

e. admirable.

10. According to the information in the passage, it can reasonably be concluded that the Hillary Step

a. is easier to ascend now than it was in 1953.

b. is responsible for countless casualties on the mountain.

c. requires several hours of climbing to traverse.

d. is located at the highest point on the planet.

e. has been traversed by a total of two climbers since the early 1950s.

Refer to the following graph for questions 11 and 12.

This graph provides data regarding average precipitation in the town of Springfield during the months of December, January, February, and March.

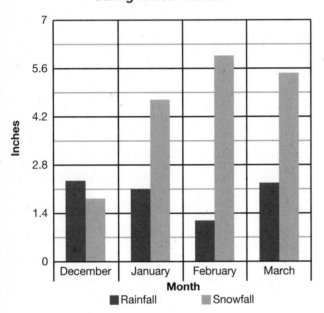

Average Precipitation in Springfield during Winter Months

11. Which conclusion about the precipitation in Springfield is supported by the information in the bar graph?
  a. The only months of the year when snowfall occurred were December, January, February, and March.
  b. There was more combined precipitation, in inches, in February than in March.
  c. Each month depicts a decreasing amount of rainfall, in inches.
  d. There was less snowfall, in inches, in December and January combined than in February.
  e. The only month depicted in which rainfall exceeded snowfall was December.

12. Based on the information provided in the graph, which of the following statements is true on average?
  a. There is more hail than snow in February.
  b. There is more snowfall in January than in March.
  c. There is less sleet than snow during the month of December.
  d. There is slightly higher rainfall in December than in March.
  e. Snowfall and rainfall amounts are equal during the month of February.

Refer to the following passage for questions 13 through 16.

The success of the immune system in defending the human body relies on a dynamic regulatory communications network consisting of millions and millions of cells. Organized into sets
5   and subsets, these cells pass information back and forth like clouds of bees swarming around a hive. The result is a sensitive system of checks and balances that produces a prompt, appropriate, effective, and self-limiting immune
10 response.
        At the heart of the immune system is the ability to distinguish between self and nonself molecules. When immune defenders encounter cells or organisms carrying nonself molecules,
15 the immune troops move quickly to eliminate the intruders. The body's immune defenses do not normally attack its own tissues because of the presence of self-markers, which are unique to the DNA and indicate that the cells belong to
20 the host body. Rather, immune cells and other body cells coexist peaceably in a state known as self-tolerance.
        When a normally functioning immune system attacks a nonself molecule, the system

25   can remember the specifics of the foreign body. Upon subsequent encounters with the same species of molecules, the immune system reacts accordingly. With the possible exception of antibodies passed during lactation, this so-

30   called immune system memory is not inherited: An immune system must learn from experience with the many millions of distinctive nonself molecules in the sea of microbes we live in.

13. When a person gets the chicken pox virus for the first time, the person's immune system will most likely
  a. prevent the person's offspring from future infection with the chicken pox virus.
  b. distinguish between its body cells and the cells of the chicken pox virus.
  c. remember previous experiences with the chicken pox virus.
  d. attack its own tissues.
  e. recall the specifics of the foreign body from ancestors' experiences.

14. Which statement represents the main idea rather than a supporting detail from the passage?
  a. The effectiveness of the human body's immune system lies in its complex organizational structure.
  b. The basic function of the immune system is to distinguish between self and nonself.
  c. Immune cells and body cells can coexist due to self-tolerance.
  d. The human body is an extraordinary and complicated mechanism.
  e. The human body presents an opportune habitat for microbes.

15. Based on the information in the passage, why might tissue transplanted from father to daughter have a greater risk of being detected as foreign than tissue transplanted between twins who share the same DNA?
  a. The twins' tissue would carry the same self-markers and therefore would be less likely to be rejected.
  b. The age of the twins' tissue would be the same and, therefore, less likely to be rejected.
  c. The daughter's immune system would reject tissue from a male donor.
  d. The twins' immune systems would remember the same encounters with childhood illnesses.
  e. The immune systems of twins contain more self-markers than the immune systems of nontwins.

16. As it appears in the passage, the word *sensitive* in line 7 most nearly means
  a. able to react.
  b. delicate.
  c. indifferent.
  d. nervous.
  e. sensible.

Refer to the following passage for question 17.

It might be difficult to envision with today's technologies and comforts, but the early European expeditions to the Americas were incredibly arduous. The journeys took several months, during which time the travelers faced extreme isolation, limited supplies due to space constraints, and great uncertainty about what to expect upon arrival.

17. Which journey would be most similar to the early European expeditions to the Americas?
a. luxury cruise across the Atlantic
b. solo skydive
c. robotic probe sent to Venus
d. jet flight to Asia
e. trip by astronauts to another planet

Refer to the following passage for questions 18 through 22.

One of Benjamin Franklin's most useful and important inventions was a stove called, appropriately, the Franklin stove. This invention improved the lives of countless homeowners in
5   the eighteenth century and beyond. Compared to the stoves that were used at the time of his invention, Franklin's stove allowed a fire to be maintained inside a home in a much less dangerous way. Franklin's stove could burn less
10 wood and generate more heat than its predecessors. This feature saved its users considerable amounts of money that would have been needed to buy wood.

As its inventor, Benjamin Franklin was
15 offered the right to patent his stove. A patent would have meant that only Franklin could make and sell the useful stoves, resulting in his

becoming one of the richest people in the country. However, Franklin declined the oppor-
20 tunity for the patent, believing instead that the stove's design should be available to anyone who wanted to use it. In his autobiography, Franklin wrote, "As we enjoy great advantages from the inventions of others, we should be
25 glad of an opportunity to serve others by any invention of ours; and this we should do freely and generously."

18. The primary purpose of the first paragraph of the passage is to
a. discuss a particularly useful invention by Franklin.
b. provide details for materials needed to build a Franklin stove.
c. explain the scientific process through which a Franklin stove works.
d. tell the ways in which Franklin made money from his stoves.
e. compare different types of stoves.

19. Which best describes the function of the word *however* in the second paragraph?
a. to compare important physical descriptions of a critical development
b. to compare several benefits of a lifesaving invention
c. to contrast the advantages of an invention with its drawbacks
d. to compare the usefulness of an invention with its extreme costs
e. to contrast an inventor's altruistic motives with the potential for great wealth

20. Considering the context of the passage and the sentence in which it appears, the word *right* in line 15 most likely means
   a. correct.
   b. good health.
   c. turn.
   d. legal permission.
   e. exact.

21. Based on information provided in the passage, it can reasonably be concluded that Benjamin Franklin was
   a. afraid of financial setbacks due to starting a fire inside his home.
   b. interested primarily in inventing items that would be good investments.
   c. about to become one of the wealthiest people in the country.
   d. less concerned with acquiring money than with helping his fellow humans.
   e. limited to stoves as an invention because they were inexpensive.

22. Based on information in the passage, it can reasonably be inferred that the Franklin stove was
   a. expensive.
   b. dangerous.
   c. efficient.
   d. small.
   e. stylish.

Refer to the following passage for questions 23 through 25.

The U.S. government has spent more than $10 billion each year since 1989 on the National Aeronautics and Space Administration (NASA). Furthermore, the government agency's budget

5 is expected to increase every year, with its annual spending estimated to surpass $20 billion for the first time during the mid-2010s. A hefty fraction of this budget is spent on space operations, including the construction
10 and maintenance of the International Space Station (ISS). At a time when the country is facing domestic crises with unemployment, energy, and healthcare, it can be difficult to justify the exorbitant costs of space exploration.
15 Nevertheless, the indirect benefits of space exploration are impossible to ignore; the valuable research and development associated with NASA's space program have resulted in an incredibly wide variety of important everyday
20 technological advancements, ranging from water filters to improved highway safety.

23. How is the key word *nevertheless* used in the last sentence of the passage?
   a. to accentuate the financial concerns of space exploration
   b. to list additional domestic concerns that should be granted a higher priority
   c. to suggest that too great a portion of NASA's budget is spent on space operations
   d. to show that the financial expenditures of the agency have been changing
   e. to provide a contrast with the monetary costs of a government agency

24. As it is used in the context of the sentence, which word best describes the meaning of *exorbitant* in line 14?
   a. excessive
   b. external
   c. extra
   d. excellent
   e. exciting

25. Which sentence best describes the author's attitude toward the financial costs of the National Aeronautics and Space Administration?
   a. The costs must be curtailed to allow for increased funding for domestic crises.
   b. The costs are very high, but the rewards make the agency a worthwhile expense.
   c. The costs should decrease at a time when the government operates with a financial deficit.
   d. The increasing costs of running the government agency are simply indefensible.
   e. The high costs should be validated during periods of planetary exploration, such as a trip to Mars.

Refer to the following passage for questions 26 through 32.

Sharks have layers of sharp teeth in their jaws that allow them to cut through a fish's bones or a shellfish's hard shell. The shark will eat almost all creatures found in the ocean—from crabs
5 and turtles to seals and penguins. If an animal is too big, a shark will simply tear it into smaller chunks before eating it. This ancient fish has been patrolling Earth's waters for longer than 400 million years and can now be found in all
10 the planet's seas, from the surface to a depth of below a mile. Species of sharks can be massive, with a length of up to 46 feet, and some can be swift, with bursts of speed of up to 30 miles per hour.
15   Despite all the impressive physical characteristics of the shark that would make it seem especially treacherous to humans, an average of fewer than five people in the world are killed each year by sharks—fewer than are killed by
20 wasps or lightning. By contrast, an estimated 100 million sharks are killed each year as a result of fishing. In addition to the negative results of overfishing, sharks suffer from habitat loss due to coastal development and the impact

25 of water pollution; some species are facing severe population decline as a result. Many people share a groundless fear of shark attacks; perhaps they should instead be fearful of losing one of the planet's most remarkable creatures
30 to extinction.

26. Which statement, if it were true, would most significantly strengthen the author's argument?
   a. The smallest shark in the world reaches a length of only about 8 inches when fully grown.
   b. Of the nearly 400 species of sharks in the world, only four have been known to be dangerous to humans.
   c. Swimming in a group is safer than swimming alone because sharks are less likely to attack an individual in a group.
   d. Other than humans, sharks have very few natural predators.
   e. The bull shark, known for its aggressive and often unpredictable nature, can often be found in shallow waters near beaches.

27. In the context of the passage, the word *groundless* in line 27 can be replaced by which word to incur the least alteration in meaning?
   a. sound
   b. aquatic
   c. terrifying
   d. justifiable
   e. unwarranted

28. The author's attitude toward sharks could best be described as
   a. reverential.
   b. frightened.
   c. ambivalent.
   d. quarrelsome.
   e. cautionary.

29. Which sentence best describes the organization of the two paragraphs of the passage?

    a. A detailed description of the creature is provided, and then common perceptions of it are supported.

    b. The evolution and history of an animal are offered, and then its present-day status is detailed.

    c. The intimidating physical characteristics are listed, and then a defense of the creature is given.

    d. A series of harmless attributes is discussed, and then a list of hazardous characteristics is described.

    e. The distinguishing features of an organism are provided, and then those features are described in further detail.

30. Which creature shares a relationship with humans that is similar to the relationship between sharks and humans?

    a. ladybugs, because they are often purchased to rid a garden of pests

    b. frogs, because, despite their attractive appearance, most species are toxic

    c. caterpillars, because they go through a series of life stages during complete metamorphosis

    d. deer, because they generally have a fear of humans and frequently will run when approached

    e. snakes, because many people fear them, despite the fact that very few types of snakes are venomous

31. Which detail from the passage would best support the idea that Congress should pass a bill to protect sharks?

    a. More people are killed each year by wasps or lightning than by shark attacks.

    b. The shark will eat almost every creature found in the ocean.

    c. The shark can be found in all the planet's seas.

    d. Some shark species are facing severe population loss.

    e. Many people share a groundless fear of shark attacks.

32. Which sentence from the passage contains an opinion from the author?

    a. Sharks have layers of sharp teeth in their jaws that allow them to cut through a fish's bones or a shellfish's hard shell.

    b. The shark will eat almost all creatures found in the ocean—from crabs and turtles to seals and penguins.

    c. This ancient fish has been patrolling Earth's waters for longer than 400 million years and can now be found in all the planet's seas, from the surface to a depth of below a mile.

    d. By contrast, an estimated 100 million sharks are killed each year as a result of fishing.

    e. Many people share a groundless fear of shark attacks; perhaps they should instead be fearful of losing one of the planet's most remarkable creatures to extinction.

Refer to the following passage for questions 33 and 34.

Jane Austen died in 1817, leaving behind six novels that have since become English classics. Most Austen biographers accept the image of Jane Austen as a sheltered spinster who knew
5   little of life beyond the drawing rooms of her Hampshire village. They accept the claim of

Austen's brother, Henry: "My dear sister's life was not a life of events."

10   Biographer Claire Tomalin takes this view to task. She shows that Jane's short life was indeed tumultuous. Not only did Austen experience romantic love (briefly, with an Irishman), but her many visits to London and her relationships with her brothers (who served in

15   the Napoleonic wars) widened her knowledge beyond her rural county, and even beyond England. Tomalin also argues that Austen's unmarried status benefited her ability to focus on her writing. I believe that Jane herself may have

20   viewed it that way. Although her family destroyed most of her letters, one relative recalled that "some of her [Jane's] letters, triumphing over married women of her acquaintance, and rejoicing in her freedom, were most

25   amusing."

33. In order to evaluate the validity of the author's claim that Austen's marital status helped her writing, it would be helpful to know which of the following?
   a. why the author mentions the biographer Claire Tomalin
   b. how single women were regarded in Austen's time period
   c. whether marriage would actually prevent a woman from writing during Austen's era
   d. the reliability of the source of the quotation at the end of the passage
   e. more details about Austen's tumultuous life

34. What word best describes the tone of the passage?
   a. somber
   b. critical
   c. apathetic
   d. appreciative
   e. playful

Refer to the following graph for questions 35 and 36.

The local zoo provided this graph to offer data regarding the animals known as "big cats."

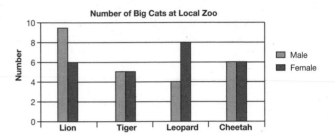

35. Based on the information in the chart, which statement can accurately be made?
   a. Lions are the most popular big cats at the local zoo.
   b. The zoo has an equal number of female cheetahs and female lions.
   c. Tigers are more difficult than other animals to contain in captivity.
   d. The zoo has more male leopards than female leopards.
   e. The cheetah is the fastest animal on the planet.

36. Based on the graph, it is clear that
   a. lions are the largest of the cats.
   b. only lions and tigers are considered big cats.
   c. not all zoos identify lions, tigers, and leopards as big cats.
   d. the local zoo identifies lions, tigers, leopards, and cheetahs as big cats.
   e. the only animals considered big cats are lions, tigers, leopards, and cheetahs.

Refer to the following passage for questions 37 through 40.

Experts generally assert that Guiana, located north of the Pará river district, and Brazil, located south of the Pará river district, form two distinct provinces in terms of animal and
5   vegetation species. This is due to the fact that Guiana and Brazil each support a large number of ecologically distinct habitats. Many species are indigenous to each region, meaning that these species originated in the region naturally.
10 As a result, experts consider Guiana and Brazil to be centers of distribution in the dissemination of their indigenous species across tropical America.

        The Pará river district is located midway
15 between Guiana and Brazil. Guiana and Brazil each have a nucleus of tableland—a broad, elevated area. The Pará river district, the valley between them, forms an expanse of low-lying land. Due to the geography of the area, it is
20 necessary to examine whether the river valley received its population of animal and vegetation species from Guiana and Brazil or it has a sufficient number of endemic species, meaning that, like Guiana and Brazil, it is a center of dis-
25 tribution of species rather than merely a recipient of these species. To make this determination, it is necessary to closely compare the species found in the river valley with the species in the other regions. Based on the
30 comparisons, it is necessary to determine whether species are identical, only slightly modified, or quite specific to the river valley.

37. Which sentence best summarizes the main point of the passage?
  a. The animals and vegetation of the Pará river district are distinct from those of Guiana and Brazil.
  b. The Pará river district supports a substantial quantity of ecologically distinct habitats.
  c. Ecological considerations override most other considerations with respect to the Pará river district.
  d. It has yet to be determined whether the Pará river district is an ecologically distinct area.
  e. The government of the Pará river district has historically failed to support biological expeditions.

38. Based on passage details, Guiana and Brazil form two distinct provinces due to the
  a. distribution center.
  b. nucleus of tableland.
  c. valleys and expanses.
  d. recipients and comparisons.
  e. animal and vegetation species.

39. The location of the Pará river valley is important to information in the passage, as this river valley is located
  a. north of Guiana and Brazil.
  b. between Guiana and Brazil.
  c. south of Guiana and Brazil.
  d. east of Guiana and Brazil.
  e. far from Guiana and Brazil.

40. Based on statements in the passage, which of the following actions would the author most likely support?
a. additional research regarding species in the Pará river valley and in nearby areas
b. relocation of endemic species from Guiana and Brazil to the Pará river valley
c. blocking comparison of species found in Guiana and Brazil
d. removal of indigenous species from Guiana and Brazil
e. introduction of new species to the Pará river valley

Refer to the following passage for questions 41 through 43.

One of the most unusual creatures on Earth, the sloth of Central and South America is famous for its sluggish speed. In fact, its name is actually a form of a word frequently used to
5   describe it: "slow." However, don't mistake the sloth's lack of speed for simple laziness. The creature's languid motion developed out of a necessity to avoid predators. For example, by moving so slowly in the trees they call home,
10 sloths have adapted a self-defense against harpy eagles that might be attracted to obvious movements. As seen from above or below a tree, a sloth can easily be mistaken for vegetation. In fact, its fur is specialized to grow algae, adding
15 to the creature's camouflage. Combined with its renowned slow pace, the sloth appears much more like hanging foliage than an appetizing snack.

41. Based on information in the passage, which conclusion can reasonably be drawn?
a. The sloth is the slowest creature on Earth.
b. The sloth's fur is dangerous to other animals.
c. The sloth refuses to leave the protection of the trees.
d. Deforestation of the Americas is endangering the sloth.
e. Sloths find unusual ways to protect themselves from other animals.

42. Based on the content of the passage, the author would most likely agree with which of the following statements?
a. Algae is important to the sloth's diet.
b. Many animals are similar to the sloth.
c. There is a great deal to be learned from observing sloths.
d. Harpy eagles should be eliminated from the sloth's environment.
e. Sloths' trees should be groomed by humans to provide a safer habitat.

43. Which statement is supported by the discussion of the sloth's sluggish speed?
a. Sloths are lazy.
b. Sloths have developed in such a way as to be able to avoid predators.
c. Sloths lack intelligence.
d. Sloths exemplify curious creatures that can be viewed from above or below a tree.
e. Sloths need new habitats.

Refer to the following passages for questions 44 and 45.

Passage 1

Wolfgang Amadeus Mozart's remarkable musical talent was apparent even before the age most children are able to sing a simple nursery rhyme. His father Leopold recognized his
5   unique gifts and devoted himself to his son's musical education. By age 5, Wolfgang had composed his first original work. By age 6, when Wolfgang was not only a virtuoso harpsichord player but also a master violin player, he
10 gave his first public concert. The audience was stunned, and word of his genius traveled.

Passage 2

After Wolfgang Mozart's first public concert, his father was quickly inundated with invitations for the boy to play. Leopold seized the opportu-
15 nity and booked as many concerts as possible at courts throughout Europe. A concert could last up to three hours, and Wolfgang played at least two of these concerts per day. Today, Leopold might be considered the worst kind of stage
20 parent, but at the time it was not uncommon for prodigies to make extensive concert tours. Even so, it was an exhausting schedule for a child who was just past the age of needing an afternoon nap.

44. Which is the best summary of the information in *both* passages?
a. Wolfgang Mozart was a popular musical artist and is still popular today. His father assumed a big role in beginning Wolfgang's lengthy and exhausting career.
b. Wolfgang Mozart performed at least two three-hour concerts daily. This exhausting schedule began when Wolfgang gave his first concert and people learned that he was a genius who could do amazing musical work.
c. Wolfgang Mozart created many musical compositions, and he was spurred on by his father. His music is now used in schools around the world, including elementary schools, middle schools, high schools, and colleges.
d. Wolfgang Mozart wrote his first composition at the age of 5, and by the age of 6 he could play the harpsichord and the violin. People were amazed when Wolfgang gave his first concert. His musical talent was clear.
e. Wolfgang Mozart began composing music at a young age. His father set up many concerts for the boy to perform. While Wolfgang's father might be considered too demanding today, this was not the case long ago.

45. Based on the passages, which claim would the author most likely make?
a. Children should take long naps much more frequently.
b. People should be judged within the context of the historical framework in which they live.
c. Parents should make certain their children play musical instruments during the school day.
d. Musical artists should refrain from playing multiple concerts in a single day.
e. Family members should mind their own business and refrain from meddling in the business of others.

Refer to the following passage for questions 46 through 49.

The skyline of St. Louis, Missouri, is fairly unremarkable, with one prodigious excep-tion—the Gateway Arch, located on the banks of the Mississippi River. Part of the Jefferson
5   National Expansion Memorial, the arch is an amazing structure built to honor St. Louis's role as the gateway to the west. In 1947, a group of citizens, the Jefferson National Expansion Memorial Association, held a nationwide com-
10 petition to select a design for a new monument to celebrate the growth of the United States. Other U.S. monuments at the time featured spires, statues, or imposing buildings, but the winning plan for this contest was a completely
15 different type of structure. The man who won, Eero Saarinen, later became a famous architect. In designing the arch, Saarinen wanted to "cre-ate a monument that would have lasting signifi-cance and would be a landmark of our time."
20   The Gateway Arch is a masterpiece of engineering, a monument even taller than the Great Pyramid in Egypt. In its own way, the arch is at least as majestic as the Great Pyramid. The Gateway Arch is shaped as an inverted cat-
25 enary curve, the same shape that a heavy chain will form if suspended between two points. Covered with a sleek skin of stainless steel, the arch often reflects dazzling bursts of sunlight.

46. Which statement from the passage includes both a fact and an opinion?
   a. In its own way, the arch is at least as majestic as the Great Pyramid.
   b. The Gateway Arch is part of the St. Louis skyline.
   c. The Gateway Arch is located on the banks of the Mississippi River.
   d. The Gateway Arch is a masterpiece of engineering, a monument even taller than the Great Pyramid in Egypt.
   e. The Gateway Arch is shaped as an inverted catenary curve, the same shape that a heavy chain will form if suspended between two points.

47. According to the passage, Saarinen's winning design was
   a. sanctioned by the U.S. government.
   b. unlike any other existing monument.
   c. part of a series of monuments.
   d. less expensive to construct than other monuments.
   e. shaped like the Great Pyramid.

48. The role that the Jefferson National Expansion Memorial Association played in relation to the Gateway Arch was to
   a. build a tall structure.
   b. hold a design competition.
   c. create spires and statues.
   d. provide clear blueprints.
   e. develop a stainless steel skin.

49. Which best describes the author's attitude toward the Gateway Arch?
   a. impressed
   b. curious
   c. agitated
   d. surprised
   e. humorous

Refer to the following graph for questions 50 and 51.

Significant wolf populations exist in Idaho and Wyoming. The graph depicts the wolf populations in these two states during a six-year period.

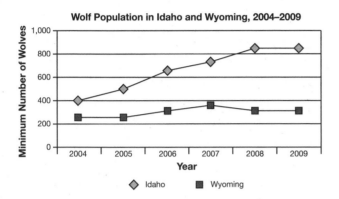

Wolf Population in Idaho and Wyoming, 2004–2009

Idaho ◆   Wyoming ■

50. Which statement is supported by data in the graph?
   a. The minimum wolf population in Idaho in 2002 was greater than 200.
   b. The combined minimum wolf population in Idaho and Wyoming in 2007 was greater than 1,000.
   c. By 2010, there were more than 1,000 wolves in Idaho.
   d. The wolf population decline in Wyoming in 2008 was a result of low temperatures.
   e. In 2004, there were large numbers of wolf subspecies in Wyoming and Idaho.

51. Based on data in the graph, which statement about wolves is accurate?
   a. Food sources were more readily available for wolves in Wyoming than those in Idaho during the years shown in the graph.
   b. From 2005 to 2006, the minimum wolf population in Idaho declined.
   c. From 2008 to 2009, the minimum wolf population remained about the same in Idaho.
   d. There are fewer predators of wolves in Idaho than in Wyoming.
   e. From 2006 to 2007, wolves were better cared for in Idaho than in Wyoming.

Refer to the following passage for questions 52 through 56.

With more than 22,000 miles behind her on her 29,000-mile journey around the world, Amelia Earhart piloted her plane through overcast skies, far above ocean waves. The time was
5   8:40 A.M., July 2, 1937: 39 years after Earhart's birth, 15 years after Earhart had become the first woman to make a solo U.S. round-trip flight, one month after Earhart had begun the current journey, one day after Earhart had
10 taken off on the current leg of the trip, and scant minutes before Earhart would make her final radio transmission—and then disappear.

  Earhart accumulated vast accolades prior to her disappearance; her passion for flying was
15 clear. When Earhart was 23, she convinced her father to pay the $10 fee for her to ride skyward as a passenger at an air show. Her father's investment paid off in myriad ways. She would later say, "By the time I had got two or three
20 hundred feet off the ground, I knew I had to fly." To pay for flying lessons and her first small

plane, Earhart drove a sand and gravel truck and organized mail at a telephone company. These endeavors became additional invest-
25 ments in her future.

Earhart's disappearance has been the source of great speculation; however, no definitive evidence has ever been uncovered to show what happened on that fateful day. And only
30 speculation can detail the additional impact Earhart's investments might have had on history if she and her plane had not disappeared in 1937.

52. Within the context of the passage, the word *leg* in line 10 could be replaced with which of the following words to have the least impact on the meaning of the sentence?
   a. limb
   b. joke
   c. segment
   d. appendage
   e. dilapidation

53. Which is a thread woven by the author throughout the passage?
   a. Earhart's disappearance remains a mystery.
   b. Earhart's father was instrumental in her career.
   c. Earhart's experiences emphasize the dangers of flying.
   d. The final journey of Earhart's flying career was clearly difficult.
   e. The investments in Earhart's life resulted in major achievements.

54. Which event included in the passage was the earliest event to spark Earhart's interest in flight?
   a. driving a sand and gravel truck
   b. ending an important radio transmission
   c. heading skyward as a passenger at an air show
   d. soaring above ocean waves in overcast weather
   e. becoming the first woman to make a historical solo flight

55. Based on information in the passage, which statement is a logical conclusion?
   a. Evidence regarding Earhart's final flight has been hidden from officials.
   b. Earhart's radio was the major cause of the fate that befell her aircraft in 1937.
   c. Efforts were not made to locate Earhart and her plane after the disappearance.
   d. Earhart would have continued to garner accolades if she had continued to fly beyond 1937.
   e. Earhart would not have begun to fly if she had not earned funds through sorting mail.

56. If Amelia Earhart were alive today, which would most likely and most accurately describe her attitude toward space travel?
   a. bored and irritated
   b. interested and content
   c. startled and belligerent
   d. trepidatious and scornful
   e. captivated and exhilarated

Praxis® Core Academic Skills for Educators: Reading Practice Test 3 Answers and Explanations

1. a. The ocean sunfish eats jellyfish, which is beneficial to human beings, as this aids in limiting the population of jellyfish. The spider's diet of mosquitoes is beneficial to human beings, as it helps to minimize the number of mosquitoes and other insects in the environment. The diet in choices **b** and **d** might be similar to the diet of sunfish, as both eat water-dwelling creatures, but this is not the information addressed by the question; the question relates to diets that are beneficial to human beings. In choices **c** and **e**, the diet is neither similar to the diet of the sunfish nor beneficial to human beings.

2. c. Whether an item looks unusual is a matter of opinion, not a matter of fact that can be proven or disproven. Choices **a**, **b**, **d**, and **e** can be proven.

3. e. The beginning of the passage references the rapidly expanding population of jellyfish and the problems presented by the jellyfish. The remainder of the passage references a specific type of fish that eats jellyfish in large quantities, thus providing a potential solution for overpopulation. While two creatures are described in the passage, the passage does not focus on comparing and contrasting these creatures, so choice **a** is incorrect. Choices **c** and **d** describe things not in the passage. Because events are not provided in chronological order, choice **b** is incorrect.

4. d. The word *curtail* in the passage is describing the difficulty of limiting the population growth of jellyfish. The word *curtail*, therefore, must have a meaning similar to that of *limit*, such as *curb*. If growth were curtailed, it might not reverse. It could simply be limited in the future, so choice **a** is incorrect. Choices **b** and **e** are incorrect because they are antonyms of *curtail*. Context makes it clear that *curtail* does not refer to withstanding continuing population growth (choice **c**).

5. c. The beginning of the passage includes information about negative aspects of the jellyfish population. The key word *however* suggests a shift from negative to positive within the passage. The words in choices **a** and **b** do not help to provide a transition from negative to positive. The word *entirely* in choice **d** does not help to provide a transition from one direction to an opposite direction within the passage. The word *though* in choice **e** does provide a transition at the end of the passage, but it does not help to transition from content about jellyfish to content regarding sunfish.

6. d. The author makes the case throughout the passage that unpleasant jellyfish are increasing in numbers, but the sunfish might be able to curtail this population growth. Therefore, the author would most likely agree that sunfish should be protected. Choices **a**, **b**, and **c** are not supported by any evidence in the passage. Choice **e** is negated by the information in the passage.

7. c. The final sentence of the passage states that the ocean sunfish should be protected across the world, as it is in the European Union. This answer choice provides the best support for the statement. Choices **d** and **e** do not provide support for the final sentence in the passage. Choice **a** does not provide a reason that ocean sunfish should be protected, while choice **b** does not relate to a ban on fishing for sunfish.

8. b. The passage states that once the difficult Hillary Step is conquered, it is only a few hundred feet of moderate climbing to the mountain's top. Therefore, the step is the final significant obstacle to the summit, and this is the reason it is most likely the mountain's most famous feature. Choices **a** and **d** do not explain why the step is such a well-known feature; instead, they provide history regarding the mountain. Although the Hillary Step is difficult, the passage does not say that is the reason it is most likely the mountain's most famous feature, so choice **c** is not the best answer choice. Choice **e** is incorrect because several hundred feet remain to be ascended after the Hillary Step.

9. e. The end of the passage accentuates the difficulties that Sir Edmund Hillary faced in his initial ascent of Mount Everest; consequently, his climb must be respected. Therefore, the best synonym for *venerable* is *admirable*. The climb itself might have been hazardous (choice **a**) or technical (choice **b**); however, *venerable* describes the achievement. The rope is *advantageous* (choice **c**); however, this word cannot correctly be used to replace *venerable* in the passage. The passage context shows that *serious* (choice **d**) is not correct in meaning to replace *venerable*.

10. a. The passage mentions the advantage of the fixed rope on the Hillary Step, a climbing advantage that has not always been available. Therefore, although it is still difficult to ascend, it is now easier to ascend than it once was. There is no mention in the passage that the step is responsible for many casualties (choice **b**) or requires several hours to traverse (choice **c**). Choice **d** is incorrect because the passage states that there are several hundred feet to travel above the step. It is also not reasonable to conclude that only two climbers have traversed the Hillary Step since the early 1950s (choice **e**).

11. e. In December the total rainfall was 2.4 in., whereas the total snowfall was 1.8 in. Although the graph depicts only the four months of December, January, February, and March, it is possible that snowfall occurred during other months, so choice **a** is incorrect. Choice **b** is incorrect because in February the total was 7.2 in., whereas in March the total was 7.8 in. The amount of rainfall rose in March, so choice **c** is incorrect. Choice **d** is incorrect because the total was 6.5 in. in December and January but 6 in. in February.

12. d. The average amount of rainfall during December is 2.4 inches, and the average amount during March is 2.3 inches. The graph provides the average snowfall and rainfall but not the amount of hail, so it is not possible to determine the amount of hail referred to in choice **a**. Choice **b** is incorrect because the graph shows that snowfall is greater during March than during January. The graph depicts snowfall and rainfall but not the amount of sleet, so it is not possible to determine the amount of sleet referred to in choice **c**. Choice **e** is incorrect because the bars depict a much greater quantity of snowfall than rainfall during February.

13. b. The passage mentions that the immune system is capable of distinguishing between body cells and nonbody cells. Every person's immune system must learn to recognize and deal with nonself molecules through experience; therefore, people's immune systems are not able to prevent their offspring from contracting an infection (choice **a**), nor can the immune system remember ancestors' experiences with a virus (choice **e**). Choice **c** is incorrect because this is the person's first encounter with the virus; the immune system has not had previous experiences with it. A normally functioning immune system will not attack its own tissues, so choice **d** is incorrect.

14. b. According to the passage, the ability to distinguish between self and nonself is at the heart of the immune system. This is evident in the first half of the passage and further emphasized throughout the passage. Choice **a** is an incorrect selection because, although the passage begins with a description of the complexity of the immune system, the passage as a whole does not focus specifically on the structure of the immune system. While the point expressed in choice **c** is made in the passage, it represents only a minor point about the balance between self cells and nonself cells; it does not represent the main point of the passage. The statement in choice **d** is too general to be considered the main idea of the passage. A major point could be that the human body's immune system is an extraordinary and complicated mechanism, but the passage does not focus on the human body's capabilities in general. The final sentence of the passage suggests that the human body is exposed to a sea of microbes (choice **e**), but this is not the focus of the passage. The passage is about the immune system as a whole.

15. a. The passage states that self-markers are unique to DNA, meaning that identical twins would have the same self-markers; because self-markers are responsible for preventing the body's immune system from attacking its own tissues, this explanation makes the most sense. There is no indication in the passage that the age of tissue would have any relevance to whether a body identifies the tissue as self or nonself; therefore, there is no support for answer choice **b**. Choice **c** is incorrect because the passage does not suggest that gender of the host body plays any role in an immune system identifying a cell or tissue as self or nonself. Choice **d** is incorrect because previous illnesses, even if they were shared by the twins during childhood, would not set precedent for tissues being shared between them. Choice **e** is incorrect because the passage does not provide information about the number of self-markers in twins versus nontwins.

16. a. The word *sensitive* has several definitions. In the context of this passage, it is being used to describe the immune system—specifically, the ability of the immune system to react quickly and effectively. The meaning *able to react* is accurate. The word *sensitive* can also mean delicate (choice **b**), but this meaning does not make sense within the context of the passage. The meaning of *indifferent* in choice **c** does not make sense within the context of the passage. The word *sensitive* can mean nervous (choice **d**), but this meaning does not make sense within the context of the passage. Although the word *sensible* in choice **e** has the same base as *sensitive*, these words have different meanings.

17. e. Because a trip by astronauts would be lengthy, it would expose astronauts to extreme isolation. The size of the spacecraft would also limit the available supplies. Additionally, the astronauts would be uncertain about what to expect when they arrived. These factors are similar to the early European expeditions to the Americas. A luxury cruise (choice **a**) and a jet flight (choice **d**) would provide passengers with comfort and expediency, both of which the early European expeditions to the Americas lacked. A solo skydive (choice **b**) might be similarly frightening, but it would not require a considerable amount of time, so this is not the best answer choice. During a robotic probe (choice **c**), there would be no explorer who would undergo the stress and difficulties of the journey.

18. a. The first paragraph of the passage discusses one specific invention created by Benjamin Franklin: a stove called the Franklin stove. Choice **b** is incorrect because details for these materials are not included. The passage does not provide much information about the scientific process through which a Franklin stove works (choice **c**). Choice **d** is incorrect because, although the passage mentions the fact that Franklin *could have* made a great deal of money from his stoves, it also states that he declined to patent the stove. The first paragraph offers only a general comparison of the Franklin stove to other stoves; that is not the primary purpose of the paragraph, so choice **e** is incorrect.

19. e. The word *however* separates ideas about the riches Franklin could have received from his invention from ideas about his decision to share the stove's design. Choice **a** is incorrect because the word *however* is not being used to compare important physical descriptions. Nor is the word *however* being used to compare benefits (choice **b**), to contrast advantages and drawbacks (choice **c**), or to compare usefulness with costs (choice **d**).

20. d. Benjamin Franklin was the inventor of the Franklin stove. Therefore, according to the passage, he was offered the right, or legal permission, to patent his stove. The other choices (**a**, **b**, **c**, and **e**) are incorrect. Those meanings of *right* do not make sense within the context of the passage and the sentence in which the word *right* appears.

21. d. Based on the fact that Franklin declined the opportunity to patent his stove, it can be inferred that he was less concerned with making money than with helping others. This is reinforced by the quote from Franklin at the end of the passage. There is no evidence in the passage to support the statement in choice **a**. The passage states that Franklin could have become one of the richest people in the country if he had patented his stove; the fact that he did not patent the stove indicates that he was not primarily motivated by potential income or becoming wealthy, so choices **b** and **c** are incorrect. There is no evidence in the passage to support the inference in choice **e**.

22. c. The passage mentions that the Franklin stove burned less wood and generated more heat than its predecessors, which means it was very efficient. Since neither the price, the size, nor the style of the stove is mentioned in the passage, it cannot reasonably be inferred that the Franklin stove was expensive (choice **a**), small (choice **d**), or stylish (choice **e**). Choice **b** is incorrect because the Franklin stove was designed to be much safer than other stoves.

23. e. The word *nevertheless* is generally used to provide a contrasting transition. In this passage, it is used to contrast the high costs of NASA with its important technological advancements. The use of the word *nevertheless* to provide a contrasting transition is not shown by answer choices **a** and **b**. Choice **c** is incorrect because the word *nevertheless* does not suggest that space operations specifically make up too great a fraction of NASA's budget. Contrary to choice **d**, the passage states that the financial expenditures of the agency have not changed a great deal throughout the past decade, but are steadily increasing.

24. a. The passage focuses on the high costs of NASA. Therefore, the meaning of *exorbitant* must reflect these high costs. Choices **b**, **c**, and **d** are incorrect, as they are not supported by context in the sentence. Choice **e** is incorrect because although space travel might be exciting, that is not the meaning of *exorbitant*.

25. b. The author mentions the high costs of operating NASA but ends the passage with a declaration of support for the agency's valuable research and development. Choice **a** is incorrect because after acknowledging that it might be difficult to justify the expense during times of domestic crises, the author states: *Nevertheless, the indirect benefits of space exploration are impossible to ignore.* There is no specific support in the passage to suggest that the author would want the costs to decrease during a time of deficit (choice **c**) or to be validated during periods of planetary exploration (choice **e**). Choice **d** is not supported by evidence in the passage.

26. b. The author's chief argument is that, despite the public perception, sharks are not especially dangerous to humans; if only 1% of shark species were dangerous to humans, this would strengthen the argument. The statements in choices **a** and **d** are not relevant to the author's argument. The statement in choice **c** provides a potential method for avoiding a shark attack; however, it does nothing to weaken or strengthen the author's argument. The statement in choice **e** would make sharks seem more dangerous to people, which would weaken the author's argument.

27. e. The author explains that fatal shark attacks are exceedingly rare, and then refers to the fear of sharks as *groundless*, which means *without support* or *unwarranted*. Choices **a** and **d** are not supported by the context of the passage. It is true that sharks are aquatic (choice **b**), but this is not the meaning of the word *groundless* as it appears in the passage. While some might describe sharks as terrifying (choice **c**), this is not the meaning of the word *groundless* as it appears in the passage.

28. a. The author describes the shark as massive, swift, and impressive, and refers to it as *one of the planet's most remarkable creatures*. This shows that the author is treating the shark with reverence. Choice **b** is incorrect since the author explains that fear of sharks is largely unwarranted. The author has a strong positive opinion about sharks, so the attitude would not be best described as ambivalent (choice **c**). The author has not made statements to reasonably lead to the conclusion in choice **d**. The author's attitude toward sharks would not be best described as cautionary (choice **e**).

29. c. The first paragraph of the passage describes the physical characteristics of the shark, such as its size, speed, and jaws. The passage initially describes the shark in ways that are intimidating, but the second paragraph defends the shark as causing few human deaths and in turn suffering from population decline. Choice **a** is incorrect, as common perceptions of the shark are not supported in the second paragraph. Choice **b** is incorrect because, although the passage briefly mentions the history of the animal, its evolution and present-day status are not the focus of the organization of the passage. Choice **d** is incorrect; the attributes discussed are not harmless. Choice **e** is incorrect; features of the shark are not described in further detail in the second paragraph.

30. e. The author points out that many people fear shark attacks, even though they do not happen often. Similarly, many people fear snakes, even though most snakes are not dangerous. Choices **a**, **b**, and **c** are incorrect; people do not generally fear ladybugs, frogs, or caterpillars. Choice **d** is incorrect; deer may fear people, but people do not generally fear deer as they do sharks.

31. d. The detail that the shark's population numbers are declining would best support the idea of a conservation bill. The details in choices **a** and **e** might provide reasons to refrain from killing sharks, but they do not necessarily indicate that sharks need protection through legislation. The details in choices **b** and **c** do not directly support the protection of the shark.

32. e. This answer is an opinion; it cannot be supported by concrete evidence. When the author suggests that people should be fearful of losing one of the planet's most remarkable creatures, the author is providing a statement of personal beliefs. The other choices (**a**, **b**, **c**, and **d**) are statements of fact. They can be proven through concrete evidence.

33. d. This evaluation question asks you to consider the evidence used to support the author's claim that Jane Austen viewed her unmarried status as a benefit to her writing. Because the author employs a quotation from one of Austen's relatives to back up her claim, it would be helpful to know more about the source. A greater degree of detail and description (which relative? can the relative be considered reliable?) would strengthen the author's argument.

34. b. To determine the tone of the passage, you need to look at the author's point of view, style, and word choice. Because the author's style and word choice are not formal, you can eliminate choice **a**, somber. Her style and word choice are not overly casual, either, so you can strike choice **e**, playful. The author uses the third-person point of view for most of the passage, signaling that the passage is attempting to be objective. Because the author uses the first-person point of view to make a claim, you can infer that the author is not apathetic (choice **c**) about her subject. Although the author may indeed be appreciative (choice **d**) about her subject, her word choice does not support this.

35. b. According to the graph, the zoo has six female lions and six female cheetahs. Choice **a** is incorrect because the graph does not provide data regarding the popularity of the cats at the zoo. The graph does not provide data regarding the difficulty of containing animals in captivity (choice **c**). The graph shows that the zoo has eight female leopards and only four male leopards, not more male leopards than female leopards as stated in choice **d**. Choice **e** is incorrect because the graph does not provide data regarding the speed of animals.

36. d. The graph title is "Number of Big Cats at Local Zoo." This makes it clear that the zoo identifies all of the animals included in the graph as big cats. Although the zoo has more lions than other big cats, the chart does not indicate that lions are the largest of the cats as stated by choice **a**. The graph title is "Number of Big Cats at Local Zoo," which makes it clear that the zoo identifies all of the animals included in the graph as big cats, not just lions and tigers as stated in choice **b**. Choices **c** and **e** are incorrect. The graph does not provide any details that support these claims.

37. d. The author's main point in this passage is to set forth the need to investigate the ecological status of Pará. Choice **a** is incorrect because the animals and vegetation of Pará are not necessarily distinct; the passage asks whether the species in the Pará district are identical, only slightly modified, or quite specific to the species of the other regions. The passage states that Guiana and Brazil support a large number of ecologically distinct habitats, but it does not make this claim definitively about Pará, so choice **b** is incorrect. The passage does not focus on the overriding importance of Pará's ecological considerations (choice **c**). There is no evidence in the passage to support the claim that Pará's government has failed to be supportive of expeditions as stated in choice **e**.

38. e. The passage states that Guiana and Brazil form two distinct provinces in terms of their animal and vegetation species. The passage references the fact that Guiana and Brazil are considered distribution centers (choice **a**), but this is not the major reason Guiana and Brazil form two distinct provinces. Choice **b** is incorrect because, although the passage references the nucleus of tableland that exists in Guiana and in Brazil, these tablelands are not the major reason Guiana and Brazil form two distinct provinces. The passage references valleys and expanses (choice **c**), but these are not major reasons Guiana and Brazil form two distinct provinces. These terms in choice **d** are referenced in the passage, but they do not identify the major reason Guiana and Brazil form two distinct provinces.

39. b. The fact that the Pará river valley is located between Guiana and Brazil is important to the information in the passage, which relates to the species in Guiana, Brazil, and the Pará river valley. The other choices (**a**, **c**, **d**, and **e**) are incorrect. Passage details show that they are not the location of the river valley.

40. a. In the passage, the author suggests that comparing species found in the Pará river valley with those found in contiguous regions should be pursued. There is no evidence in the passage to suggest that the author would advise relocation of species (choice **b**), blocking comparison of species (choice **c**), removal of indigenous species from Guiana and Brazil (choice **d**), or introduction of new species (choice **e**).

41. e. Disguising itself as vegetation in a tree is an unusual method of protection. It is true that the passage references the slow speed of the sloth; however, based on information in the passage, it is not logical to draw the conclusion in choice **a** that the sloth is the slowest creature on Earth. There is no evidence in the passage to support the conclusions in choices **b**, **c**, and **d**.

42. c. The passage focuses on the observation of the sloth and the information gleaned from such observation. It makes sense that the author would agree that there is a great deal to be learned from observing sloths. Algae is mentioned only in conjunction with the sloth's fur growing algae; there is no evidence to support choice **a**'s statement that algae is important to the sloth's diet. The author states that the sloth is *one of the most unusual creatures on Earth*, so likely would not agree with choice **b**'s statement that many animals are similar to the sloth. While the author mentions harpy eagles as predators, there is no evidence in the passage to support the idea that they should be removed from the sloth's habitat (choice **d**). There is no evidence in the passage to support choice **e**.

43. b. The information in the passage makes it clear that the languid motion is a factor in the sloth's ability to avoid predators. Choice **a** is incorrect because the author states that the sloth's speed should *not* be mistaken for laziness. There is no evidence in the passage to support the argument that sloths lack intelligence (choice **c**) or need new habitats (choice **e**). While the passage mentions the fact that sloths may be viewed from above or below a tree, this is not related to the sloth's speed or curiosity, so choice **d** is incorrect.

44. e. This answer includes information from the first passage, which details the early years of Wolfgang's musical career. It also includes information from the second passage about the many concerts Wolfgang performed and the attitudes in the past and present regarding his father's demands. Choice **a** is incorrect because there is no information in either passage about Mozart's popularity today. Choice **b** summarizes only information from Passage 2. The details in the passages do not support the summary in choice **c** that Wolfgang's music is now used in schools around the world. Choice **d** summarizes only information from Passage 1.

45. b. In Passage 2, the author states that whereas Leopold would be considered the worst kind of stage parent today, this would not have been the case in the historical period during which Wolfgang and Leopold lived. While naps are mentioned in one of the passages, there is no evidence in either of the passages to support the statement in choice **a**. Although the author mentions musical instruments, there is no evidence in either passage to support the statement in choice **c**. Although the author mentions Wolfgang playing at least two concerts a day when he was a child, there is no evidence in either passage to support the statement in choice **d**. Although the author references the many concerts played by Wolfgang at the demand of his father, the statement in choice **e** is not supported by evidence in the passages.

46. d. *The Gateway Arch is a masterpiece* is an opinion because it cannot be verified through facts or statistics, and the fact that the monument is *even taller than the Great Pyramid* can be verified through measurements. Choice **a** contains an opinion but not a fact. Choices **b**, **c**, and **e** each contain a fact but not an opinion; the buildings that compose the skyline, the location of the arch, and the arch's shape can all be verified.

47. b. The passage states that the plan was a completely different type of structure. The details in choices **a**, **c**, **d**, and **e** are not included in the passage.

48. b. The passage indicates that the association held a design competition. The passage does not indicate that the task of the association was to build a tall structure (choice **a**). The passage does not indicate that the task of the association was to create spires and statues (choice **c**). The passage does not indicate that the task of the association was to provide blueprints (choice **d**). The passage does not indicate that the task of the association was to develop a stainless steel skin (choice **e**).

49. a. The author describes the Great Arch as a *masterpiece* and as being *as majestic as the Great Pyramid*. This makes it clear that the author is impressed by the Great Arch. Although the author might be curious about the Great Arch and want to learn more about it, choice **b** is not directly supported by information in the passage. There is no evidence in the passage to indicate that the author feels agitated about the Great Arch (choice **c**). Choice **d** is not directly supported by information in the passage. Choice **e** is incorrect because there is no evidence in the passage to suggest that the author's attitude is humorous.

50. b. This response is supported by data in the graph. Choice **a** is incorrect because the graph does not provide data for 2002. Choice **c** is incorrect because the graph does not provide data for 2010. The graph does not provide data regarding temperatures (choice **d**), nor does it provide data regarding wolf subspecies (choice **e**).

51. c. The graph shows that the minimum wolf population was higher than 800 during both 2008 and 2009. Choice **a** is incorrect because the graph does not provide information about food sources. The graph does not show that the minimum wolf population decreased during this time span (choice **b**). Choice **d** is incorrect because, although there were fewer wolves in Wyoming than in Idaho during the years depicted in the graph, the graph does not indicate why; this could have been due to predators, but there are no data in the graph to support this assumption. Choice **e** is incorrect because, although the depicted population was greater in Idaho than in Wyoming during this time, there is insufficient information in the graph to determine the reason for this disparity.

52. c. A leg of a trip is a segment of a trip. Choice **a** is incorrect because the definition of *limb* that relates to *leg* would reference a part of the anatomy, and this meaning does not make sense within the context of the passage. Although there is an idiom that refers to "pulling someone's leg," this meaning of a joke (choice **b**) does not make sense within the context of the passage. The definition of *appendage* (choice **d**) that relates to *leg* would reference a part of the anatomy; this meaning does not make sense within the context of the passage. There is an idiom that refers to "being on its last legs" in reference to an item that is dilapidated (choice **e**) or falling apart, but this meaning does not make sense within the context of the passage.

53. e. The passage references the investment Earhart's father made and the investments Earhart made herself. Choice **a** is incorrect. It is true that Earhart's disappearance remains a mystery, but this is not a thread woven throughout the passage; this information is introduced only at the end of the passage. Choice **b** is incorrect. It is true that Earhart's father provided the funds for her first flight, but his influence is not a thread woven throughout the passage; information related to Earhart's father appears only in the middle of the passage. Choice **c** is incorrect. Earhart's disappearance is addressed in the passage, but there is not a general emphasis placed on the dangers of flying. Choice **d** is incorrect. It is clear that the final journey of Earhart's flying career must have been difficult—since she disappeared—but the final journey is not a thread woven throughout the passage.

54. c. Earhart's flight as a passenger at an air show sparked her interest. Choice **a** is incorrect. Earhart drove a sand and gravel truck to earn funds for her endeavors; however, driving the truck did not spark her interest in flight. Choice **b** is incorrect because Earhart's interest in flight was sparked long before she ended the radio transmission referenced in the passage; this radio transmission occurred just before she disappeared. Earhart's interest in flight was sparked long before the event in choice **d**; as the passage states, this event occurred just before she disappeared. The solo flight referenced in the passage (choice **e**) occurred *after* Earhart's interest in flight was initially sparked through a ride in a plane at an air show.

55. d. Passage details show that Earhart had received many accolades, and based on her dedication and accomplishments, it is logical to infer that she would have continued to garner accolades. Choice **a** is incorrect because there are no details in the text to support the inference that evidence has been hidden. Although the radio transmission occurred just before the disappearance, there are no details in the text to support the inference that the radio transmission caused the disappearance (choice **b**). Choice **c** is incorrect. Based on Earhart's accomplishments as detailed in the passage, and based on the fact that officials would make efforts to locate any missing pilot and flight, it would be logical to infer that great effort would have been made to locate Earhart and her aircraft after the disappearance. Choice **e** is incorrect because, based on passage details, it is clear that Earhart was dedicated to flight; if the job of sorting mail had not been available, it is logical to infer that she would have found another job to help her earn the funds she needed.

56. e. Text evidence shows that Earhart was captivated and exhilarated by flying airplanes. It is logical to assume that she would have the same feelings about space travel. Text evidence does not support choice **a**, as evidence in the text shows Earhart's enthusiasm for air travel. Choice **b** is incorrect because whereas Earhart would certainly be interested in space travel, text evidence shows that her interest would be much more passionate than mere contentment. While Earhart might be startled by the great advances in air travel, text evidence does not support answer choice **c**; it is not logical to assume that she would be belligerent about travel into space. Choice **d** is incorrect because text evidence shows that Earhart was at the forefront of air travel, so it does not indicate that she would feel trepidatious. Additionally, text evidence points to her support of air travel, so it does not make sense that she would be scornful of space travel.

Praxis® Core Academic Skills for Educators: Writing Practice Test 3

Part I: Multiple-Choice
Time: 40 Minutes

Directions: Each of the following 15 questions consists of a sentence that contains four underlined portions. Read each sentence, and decide whether any of the underlined parts contains an element that would be considered incorrect or inappropriate in carefully written English. The error or concern may be in grammatical construction, word use, punctuation, or capitalization. Select the underlined portion that must be revised to produce a correct sentence. If a sentence contains no errors, select "No error." **No sentence contains more than one error.**

1. They <u>had</u> already <u>clearly lied</u> to him, but he
       a   b
   was <u>very foolish enough</u> <u>to trust</u> them again.
           c   d
   <u>No error</u>
     e

2. Many locales have <u>statewide</u> laws <u>that</u>
                 a   b
   prohibit dog owners <u>from</u> allowing their dogs
                 c
   to run <u>lose</u> in specific types of public areas.
         d
   <u>No error</u>
     e

3. When Rosa <u>visited</u> <u>Japan</u> last summer
            a   b
   <u>for her graduate program</u>, she <u>sees</u> many
           c   d
   Shinto temples. <u>No error</u>
              e

4. <u>In reference to teaching children</u>, we would
         a
   agree that all <u>childrens</u> strengths <u>and challenges</u>
             b   c
   <u>should be considered</u>. <u>No error</u>
       d   e

5. Earthquakes are extremely difficult to
   <u>predict, that</u> is why <u>most scientific investigations</u>
      a   b
   take place <u>after occurrences</u> <u>of earthquakes</u>.
             c   d
   <u>No error</u>
     e

6. Midori <u>and Pat</u> disagreed regarding every
          a
   aspect of the <u>project; it</u> was clear that <u>they</u>
             b   c
   <u>saw eye to eye</u> on the preparations that needed
         d
   to be made. <u>No error</u>
           e

7. Some people believe <u>it's</u> <u>more important</u> to
                a   b
   enjoy working at a job than <u>large sums</u>
                         c
   <u>of money</u>. <u>No error</u>
    d   e

8. Contestants in the <u>international palms resort</u>
                        a
   <u>youth spelling bee</u> watched as <u>an eighth-grade</u>
                           b
   student from Pennsylvania <u>won</u> the spelling
                       c
   bee's trophy. <u>No error</u>
    d   e

9. The event brings in spectators from across
   the <u>globe, and</u> <u>they showcase</u> the <u>surfing</u> skills
        a   b   c
   of all the <u>local</u> surfers. <u>No error</u>
           d   e

10. He <u>knew</u> perfectly <u>good</u> that it was time for
       a   b

    him to do the <u>dishes; however,</u> immediately
                         c

    after dinner, he <u>thought</u> of an excuse for
                          d

    leaving the house. <u>No error</u>
                              e

11. The audience applauded <u>politely</u> for the
                                 a

    <u>sick</u> <u>actor, he</u> hadn't performed to the best of
     b   c

    <u>his</u> ability. <u>No error</u>
     d   e

12. Several <u>landscape designers</u> submitted bids
                    a

    for the shopping mall <u>project, and</u> the property
                                 b

    owner awarded the contract to the designer

    <u>whose</u> proposal was <u>the least expensive.</u>
     c   d

    <u>No error</u>
     e

13. The <u>first-year teachers</u> in <u>King Central</u>
              a   b

    <u>School District are;</u> <u>Kamal, Dana, Keisha, and</u>
              c   d

    <u>Julieta.</u> <u>No error</u>
                    e

14. The <u>customer</u> called the store <u>many times</u>
              a   b

    that <u>day, but</u> <u>they</u> never answered. <u>No error</u>
          c   d   e

15. Either the board president <u>or</u> the accounts
                                 a

    administrator will need to act <u>to insure</u> the fair
                                        b

    treatment <u>of all employees</u> in the <u>company.</u>
                     c   d

    <u>No error</u>
     e

Directions: In each of the following questions, part of the sentence or the entire sentence has been underlined. Beneath each sentence, the underlined words are written in five ways. The first option repeats the original underlined content, but the other four differ. If the original sentence is the best option, select the first choice; otherwise, select one of the other choices.

This part of the test measures correctness and effectiveness of expression. Pay particular attention to usage in grammar, word choice, sentence construction, capitalization, and punctuation. Select the option that best expresses information presented in the original sentence. Your answer should be free of awkwardness, ambiguity, and redundancy.

16. To improve his results, <u>the experiment was repeated</u> by exercising greater control of the variables.
    a. the experiment was repeated
    b. he repeated the experiment
    c. the experiment repeated
    d. he and me repeated the experiment
    e. their experiments was repeated

17. Alternative <u>medicine which includes massage and yoga, has</u> become increasingly appealing to Americans.
    a. medicine which includes massage and yoga, has
    b. medicine, which includes massage and yoga has
    c. medicine which include massage and yoga, has
    d. medicine, which include massage and yoga, has
    e. medicine, which includes massage and yoga, has

18. <u>Nobody could believe</u> the luck they had that day.
- **a.** Nobody could believe
- **b.** Nobody could hardly believe
- **c.** Nobody would never believe
- **d.** Nobody would not believe
- **e.** Nobody would always not believe

19. <u>Although the car hit the roadblock, it wasn't damaged.</u>
- **a.** Although the car hit the roadblock, it wasn't damaged.
- **b.** The car hit the roadblock but did not damage it.
- **c.** The car hit the roadblock, it wasn't damaged.
- **d.** Although the car hit the roadblock, it was damaged.
- **e.** Even though the car hit the roadblock, it wasn't damaged.

20. It is the general consensus that the principal <u>is kind and has intelligence.</u>
- **a.** is kind and has intelligence.
- **b.** is kinder and has intelligence.
- **c.** is kind and intelligent.
- **d.** has kind intelligence.
- **e.** has kindness and intelligent.

21. He asked if <u>my Aunt and Grandfather</u> would organize the family reunion.
- **a.** my Aunt and Grandfather
- **b.** My aunt and grandfather
- **c.** my Aunt and grandfather
- **d.** my aunt and Grandfather
- **e.** my aunt and grandfather

22. The committee threw a huge end-of-the-year party for <u>them and I</u>.
- **a.** them and I
- **b.** they and I
- **c.** their and me
- **d.** their and I
- **e.** them and me

23. <u>The dog, sleeping in its bed, not noticing the cat in the room.</u>
- **a.** The dog, sleeping in its bed, not noticing the cat in the room.
- **b.** The dog, asleep in its bed. Not noticing the cat in the room.
- **c.** The dog, sleeping in its bed; not noticing the cat in the room.
- **d.** The dog was sleeping in its bed, not noticing the cat in the room.
- **e.** The dog. Was sleeping. In its bed and not noticing the cat in the room.

24. <u>As past history has illustrated,</u> we should learn from our mistakes.
- **a.** As past history has illustrated,
- **b.** As past history has illustrated
- **c.** As history has illustrated,
- **d.** As history has illustrated
- **e.** As passed history has illustrated,

25. <u>The swimmer explained how to do the back-stroke on the train.</u>
- **a.** The swimmer explained how to do the backstroke on the train.
- **b.** The swimmer explain how to do the backstroke on the train.
- **c.** The swimmers explains how to do the backstroke on the train.
- **d.** The swimmer on the train explained how to do the backstroke.
- **e.** The swimmer on the train explain how to do the backstroke.

26. The therapist <u>massaged gently</u> along the patient's spine.
  a. massaged gently
  b. massaged gentle
  c. massage gentle
  d. massage gently
  e. messaged gently

27. Not only did we inadvertently write the wrong address on the invitations, <u>but</u> we also forgot to include a telephone number.
  a. but
  b. nor
  c. or
  d. and
  e. neither

28. After the solution splattered, <u>scientists took off their lab coat</u> right away.
  a. scientists took off their lab coat
  b. scientists took off their lab coats
  c. scientists take off their lab coat's
  d. scientists takes off their lab coats
  e. scientists' took off their lab coat

29. <u>They wouldn't have required such difficult instructions if they hadn't</u> developed such a complicated process.
  a. They wouldn't have required such difficult instructions if they hadn't
  b. They wouldnt have required such difficult instructions if they hadn't
  c. They wouldn't have required such difficult instructions if they, hadnt
  d. They wouldn't have, required such difficult instructions if they hadn't
  e. They wouldnt have required such, difficult instructions if they hadnt

Directions: Some parts of the following passage need to be improved. Read the passage and then answer the questions about specific sentences. In choosing your answers, pay attention to development, organization, word choice, tone, and the standards of written English.

(**1**) Creating a lush garden requires a great deal of care and time. (**2**) The flower bed should consist of appropriate proportions of soil, rice hulls, and mulch. (**3**) If flower beds have been properly covered with flowers, they will flourish.

(**4**) The Floral society of America publishes a number of annual pamphlets regarding the optimal shapes and layouts for flower beds. (**5**) Those who follow the advice will have good gardens. (**6**) Other than initial planting, there are many considerations in creating and maintaining a healthy garden. (**7**) For example, sufficient water is essential, sufficient sunlight is also a basic requirement.

(**8**) After flowers have bloomed, it is necessary to "deadhead" the blooms of some types of flowers. (**9**) Deadheading consists of pinching back the blooms that are beginning to die. (**10**) This practice results in fuller, lovelier blooms. (**11**) For flowers with multiple blooms, some gardeners like to begin the deadheading process at the top of the flower, descending down to the lowest blooms to complete the process. (**12**) Be certain to select flowers that will grow well in your region. (**13**) Pinching blooms is one of the steps that must be carefully considered by gardeners.

30. Which is the most effective way to write sentence 3 (reproduced below)?

> If flower beds have been properly covered with flowers, they will flourish.

a. As it is now.

b. Flower beds have been properly covered with flowers, they will flourish.

c. If flower beds have been properly covered with flowers, it will flourish.

d. If flower beds have been properly covered with flowers, the flowers will flourish.

e. Flower beds has been properly covered with flowers; properties will flourish.

31. What is the correct and most effective way to write sentence 4 (reproduced below)?

> The Floral society of America publishes a number of annual pamphlets regarding the optimal shapes and layouts for flower beds.

a. As it is now.

b. the Floral Society of america publishes a number of annual pamphlets regarding the optimal shapes and layouts for flower beds.

c. The Floral Society of America publishes a number of annual pamphlets regarding the optimal shapes and layouts for flower beds.

d. The floral society of america publishes a number of annual pamphlets regarding the optimal shapes and layouts for flower beds.

e. The Floral Society Of America publishes a number of annual pamphlets regarding the optimal shapes and layouts for flower beds.

32. Which is the most effective way to write sentence 5 (reproduced below)?

> Those who follow the advice will have good gardens.

a. As it is now.

b. Those who follow the advice will have gorgeous gardens.

c. Those who follow the advice will have giant gardens.

d. Those who follow the advice will have nice gardens.

e. Those who follow the advice will have gregarious gardens.

33. What is the most effective way to write sentence 7 (reproduced below)?

> For example, sufficient water is essential, sufficient sunlight is also a basic requirement.

a. As it is now.

b. For example, sufficient water is essential, sufficient sunlight is also. A basic requirement.

c. For example, sufficient water is essential sufficient sunlight is also a basic requirement.

d. For example sufficient water is essential, sufficient sunlight is also a basic requirement.

e. For example, sufficient water is essential; sufficient sunlight is also a basic requirement.

34. What is the most effective way to write sentence 11 (reproduced below)?

For flowers with multiple blooms, some gardeners like to begin the deadheading process at the top of the flower, descending down to the lowest blooms to complete the process.

a. As it is.

b. For flowers with multiple blooms, some gardeners like to begin the deadheading process at the top of the flower, descending to the lowest blooms to complete the process.

c. For flours with multiple blooms, some gardeners like to begin the deadheading process at the top of the flower, descending down to the lowest blooms to complete the process.

d. For flowers with multiple blooms, some gardeners likes to begin the deadheading process at the top of the flour, descending down to the lowest blooms to complete the process.

e. For flowers with multiple blooms, some Gardeners like to begin the deadheading process at the top of the flower, descending to the lowest blooms to complete the process.

35. Which sentence should be removed from the final paragraph to eliminate a sentence that fails to be relevant to the paragraph's main idea?

a. After flowers have bloomed, it is necessary to "deadhead" the blooms of some types of flowers.

b. Deadheading consists of pinching back the blooms that are beginning to die.

c. This practice results in fuller, lovelier blooms.

d. Be certain to select flowers that will grow well in your region.

e. Pinching blooms is one of the steps that must be carefully considered by gardeners.

36. Which sentence would be the most effective concluding sentence to add to the passage?

a. Guidance is available as you work to determine which flowers to plant in your garden.

b. The layout of your garden should be your first consideration as you tackle the many issues related to creating your dream garden.

c. Always remember the importance of planting in a sunny location as you prepare the soil and mulch for your garden.

d. Carefully planning and meticulously maintaining your garden will lead to the fine results desired by proficient gardeners.

e. Gardeners would be wise to have ample water for taking care of the many flowers they will purchase.

Directions: The questions that follow will measure your basic research skills. Read each question and then select the best option.

37. Read the following citation.

> Drummond, Analise M., and Johann Small, eds. *Assessing Education in Georgia and California.* Mahwah, NJ: Publishing Interest Associates, 2013. Print.

Based on the citation, which of the following is accurate?

a. Georgia, Analise, and Johann developed content for this book.

b. The edition of the book in the citation is the second edition.

c. The author of the book is N. J. Mahwah.

d. The book was published on the Web.

e. There are two editors of this book.

38. Which information would be most relevant to support a text expressing the following opinion?

> Opinion:
> Our city's sales tax should be increased by 1 cent.

a. Additional income is needed to repair the city's roads and bridges.

b. Some stores have opened in the city, while others have closed.

c. A major magazine recently declared the city to be one of the nicest in the nation.

d. The city is trying to attract shoppers from nearby areas to shop in the city's stores.

e. Home sales have increased near the city's lake, but sales have dropped in other areas.

39. Of these sources, which would be the most credible and relevant for a school project focused on consuming a balanced diet?

a. nutrition statements from a food manufacturer regarding a specific product

b. statistics and other data based on a university's nutrition studies

c. farming details from a vegetable farmer's nutritious crops

d. students' opinions regarding nutritious favorite foods

e. online nutrition articles about junk food

40. Of the listed strategies, which answer choice shows the most effective order to follow for writing a research paper?

a. revise, narrow, outline, brainstorm, draft

b. narrow, draft, revise, brainstorm, outline

c. draft, outline, narrow, revision, brainstorm

d. outline, draft, revise, brainstorm, narrow

e. brainstorm, narrow, outline, draft, revise

Part IIa: Argumentative Essay
Time: 30 Minutes

Directions: Read the opinion stated below. To what extent do you agree or disagree with this opinion? Support your views with specific reasons and examples from your own experiences, observations, or reading. Allow 30 minutes for your essay.

A football team should immediately and permanently remove a player accused of assault. If the team fails to do so, people should refuse to attend the team's games. Assault is a serious crime and is not to be tolerated. Football is glorified in our country, and after a player steps onto the field, the player's morals, ethics, and common sense go out the window.

Part IIb: Source-Based Essay
Time: 30 Minutes

Directions: The following essay assignment asks that you to use information from two different sources to discuss the most important concerns that relate to a specific issue. Allow 30 minutes to write your essay.

Assignment
Fossil fuels have come under fire due to their unsustainability and the pollution they cause when burned. As a result, alternative energy sources have been explored and implemented. There are many types of alternative energy sources, including solar and wind. Both of the following resources focus on the use of solar power. The benefits and detriments of each are explored. Each piece clearly reflects the viewpoint of its author.

Read the two passages carefully and then write an essay in which you identify the most important concerns regarding the issue and explain why they are important. Your essay must draw on information from *both* of the sources. In addition, you may draw on your own experiences, observations, or reading. Be sure to *cite* the sources whether you are paraphrasing or directly quoting.

Source 1

Solar energy is the wave of the future. Individuals and businesses should be moving forward to implement solar energy solutions for their energy needs. In an age when the practice of burning fossil fuels belches tremendous quantities of pollution into the atmosphere, solar power can provide for energy needs in a clean, environmentally friendly way. Of course, this is not the only advantage of solar power.

Unlike power that comes from the burning of fossil fuels, solar power is a renewable resource; it is a sustainable resource. There can be no life on Earth without the sun; as long as there is sunlight, the sun provides thermal energy. . . . Fossil fuels are not renewable. They can be depleted. Once this happens, they are no longer available to provide energy. The renewable, sustainable nature of solar energy is a major boon in supplying energy needs.

Some alternative methods of energy production, such as use of wind turbines, result in a great deal of noise, which is disturbing to those who live and work near the turbines. Noise is not an issue with solar energy. The thermal energy is collected from the sun's heat through solar panels; this process does not create noise.

A major positive factor in use of solar energy is the cost. Use of solar energy does not result in bills that must be paid to an electricity provider. This means astounding savings! Additionally, living off of the grid, meaning "away from electricity sources," means that energy can be obtained in places where the infrastructure to provide electricity has not been developed. . . . In addition to the savings from living off of the grid, rebates and other economic incentives are often available from state and local governments when consumers choose to use solar energy.

Utilizing solar energy is a positive experience in so many ways. It should definitely be the top contender for satisfying energy needs.

Adapted from: Ling, Andrea. *Energy: Crisis, Solutions, and Counterpoints.* Philadelphia: Pencil, Quill, and Scroll, 2014. 289–305. Web. Aug. 10, 2014.

Source 2

Solar energy has been touted as the energy source that everyone should pursue; however, while it is not without some merit, solar energy has serious drawbacks. Proponents speak volumes regarding the tremendous savings of solar energy. The major fact they tend to omit, however, is the astronomical expense of installing solar panels, also known as "solar cells."

A single solar cell can cost in excess of $1,500, and a single cell is generally not sufficient to serve the needs of an entire household or business. The price per cell rises for specific types of thin-film solar cells. . . . Installation fees must be added to these costs. And the idea that people can live "off of the grid" with solar panels is often a misnomer. Solar cells generally supply only a portion of the needs for a household or business, so there are still electricity bills to pay, albeit generally lower bills when solar cells are being used in addition to the electricity provided.

While it is true that local and federal governments often offer incentives for use of solar energy, they also often offer incentives for use of other energy types, some alternative and some traditional. . . . So, while there might be incentives when solar energy is used, there are also incentives with other types of energy sources.

Another major drawback of solar energy is its intermittent nature. Clearly, sunlight is required to catalyze solar energy. After the sun sets, there is no thermal energy being produced. It is impossible to accurately predict the number of cloudy days versus sunny days during a year. Of course, most consumers utilize the vast majority of energy during peak times of a hot day, so the corresponding nature of availability of solar energy is valuable. . . . Additionally, pollution can have a negative impact on productive use of solar energy, which adds to the intermittent nature of availability.

Proponents of solar energy often wax poetic about its pollution-free nature. Stating that solar energy is a completely pollution-free source is erroneous, however. Greenhouse gases might be emitted during production of some types of solar cells. Additionally, it is important to remember that the cells must be transported to locations of installation, and this transportation causes pollution. Granted, this might be considered less serious than the pollution caused by the burning of fossil fuels; however, it is important to provide a balanced outlook on the subject. . . .

Adapted from: Salazar, Oscar. "The Truth about Solar Energy." *Energy Forecasting for Our Times*. 15.1 (2013): 98–104. Web. Aug. 10, 2014.

Praxis® Core Academic Skills for Educators: Writing Practice Test 3 Answers and Explanations

1. c. The phrase *very foolish enough* is redundant. The adverb *very* could be used, or the adverb *enough* could be used, but not both. In choice **a**, the verb *had* agrees in person and number with the subject *they*. The word *clearly* in choice **b** is an adverb, the correct part of speech to modify the verb *lied*. There are no errors in the infinitive *to trust* in choice **d**.

2. d. The word *lose* has been mistaken for the word *loose*. The word *lose* means being unable to find, while the word *loose* means without restraint. In choice **a**, *statewide* is a correctly spelled adjective that modifies the word *laws*. The relative pronoun in choice **b**, *that*, is correct. The preposition *from* in choice **c** is correct.

3. d. The verb *sees* represents a shift in tense. The verb *visited* (in the dependent clause) is in the correct tense, the past tense, as indicated by the phrase *last summer*. To avoid a shift in tense, the verb in the independent clause must also be in the past tense, so the correct verb would be *saw*, rather than *sees*. The phrase *last summer* indicates that the verbs in the sentence must be in past tense. The verb *visited* in choice **a** is in past tense. In choice **b**, the word *Japan* identifies a country, so it must be capitalized. The preposition, modifiers, and object of the preposition in choice **c** have no errors.

4. b. The word *children's* is possessive in the sentence, so it requires an apostrophe between the letter *n* and the letter *s*. The introductory clause in choice **a** is correctly punctuated by a comma. The words in choice **c** are spelled correctly, and no comma is required preceding the word *and*, as it is not used to join two independent clauses. In choice **d** the word *should* does not create a shift from the word *would*.

5. a. This sentence contains two independent clauses, so a semicolon, not a comma, is required at the end of the first independent clause. There are no errors in the modifiers and the noun in choice **b**. The preposition and its object are correct, and the word *occurrences* is spelled correctly in choice **c**. In choice **d**, the preposition and its object are used correctly.

6. d. The meaning of the idiom *saw eye to eye* is "agreed with one another." This idiom does not make sense in the sentence, as the sentence begins by stating that Midori and Pat *disagreed* regarding every aspect of the project. No comma is required between *Midori* and *Pat* in choice **a**. The semicolon in choice **b** correctly punctuates two independent clauses. In choice **c** the pronoun *they* agrees with *Midori and Pat*.

7. c. As originally written, the sentence lacks parallel structure. The phrase *large sums* must be revised so it is parallel with the phrase *to enjoy your job* (e.g., *to have large sums*). In choice **a**, the apostrophe in the word *it's* is correct. *It's* is a contraction that means *it is*. The modifiers are correct in choice **b** and there are no errors in the preposition and its object in the prepositional phrase used in choice **d**.

8. a. *International Palms Resort Youth Spelling Bee* is a proper noun; all words in the proper noun must be capitalized. In choice **b**, the hyphenation for *eighth-grade* is correct, as *eighth-grade* precedes the noun. The past-tense verb *won* in choice **c** is parallel to the past-tense verb *watched*. An apostrophe is required to form the possessive in choice **d**. The name of the spelling bee is not included within this phrase, so capitalization of *bee's* is not required.

9. b. The pronoun *they* does not agree with the antecedent, which is *event*. The noun *event* is singular, so the correct pronoun would be *it* (singular), rather than *they* (plural), requiring *it showcases*. The comma in choice **a** is required, as it appears between two independent clauses joined by *and*. The word *surfing* is an adjective that is spelled and used correctly in choice **c**. The same is true for the word *local* in choice **d**.

10. b. This modifier modifies the verb *knew*, so it must be an adverb (*well*), not an adjective (*good*). The verb in choice **a** agrees with the subject and is in the correct tense. In choice **c**, the semicolon that appears before the conjunction (*however*) and the comma that appears after the conjunction are both correct punctuation. The verb *thought* (choice **d**) has been correctly written in the past tense. It is in the same tense as the verb *knew*, which appears in the other independent clause within the sentence.

11. c. As originally written, the sentence is a run-on. It contains two independent clauses. A semicolon would be required to replace the comma; alternatively, the original sentence could be split into two separate sentences. The word *politely* modifies the verb *applauded* in choice **a**, telling how the audience applauded, so the adverb *politely* is correct. The word *sick* modifies the noun *actor*, so the adjective *sick* is correct in choice **b**. The use of the possessive pronoun *his* in choice **d** is correct.

12. e. The sentence is free of errors. The noun *designers* is spelled correctly, and the plural form is correct in choice **a**. The comma in choice **b** is correctly placed, as the word *and* joins two independent clauses. The relative pronoun *whose* used in choice **c** is correct. The comparative adjective in choice **d**, *least*, is correct, as several designers are being compared.

13. c. The semicolon should be deleted. *The first-year teachers in King Central School District are* is not a complete sentence. The adjective *first-year* must by hyphenated in choice **a**, as it precedes the noun it modifies. In choice **b** the name of the school district is a proper noun, so all words must be capitalized. The capitalization and commas in choice **d** are correct.

14. d. In this sentence, *they* is a vague pronoun. The pronoun *they* does not have a clear antecedent. Who never answered? A store cannot answer. Employees at a store can answer, though, so the sentence could be corrected in this way: *The customer called the store many times that day, but the employees never answered.* In choice **a**, the word *customer* is spelled and used correctly. The adjective *many* correctly modifies the noun *times* in choice **b**. A comma is the correct punctuation to separate two independent clauses joined by the conjunction *but*, as shown in choice **c**.

15. b. The word *insure* means "to make arrangements for compensation." The phrase *insure against* means "to protect someone from something." The word *ensure* means "to make certain an event or condition will occur or be met." The word *ensure* would be correct in this sentence. The word *or* is the correct correlative conjunction to match the word *either* in choice **a**. The preposition, modifier, and object in choice **c** are all correct. The word *company* in choice **d** is spelled and used correctly.

16. b. As originally written, the sentence contains a dangling modifier. When the underlined part of the sentence is replaced by *he repeated the experiment,* the pronoun *he* cures the issue. With the revision offered in choice **c**, the sentence still contains a dangling modifier. If answer choice **d** included only the pronoun *he*, but not the pronoun *me*, it would be correct. The pronoun *me* is in the objective case, not the subjective case. Choice **e** is incorrect because the phrase *their experiments* does not comport to the pronoun *he* in the preceding clause.

17. e. The clause *which includes massage and yoga* is a nonessential clause, so it must be set off from the rest of the sentence by commas. The information in this clause is not essential to an understanding of the sentence. If the information in the clause were essential to the understanding of the sentence, then commas would not be required. In addition, the verb *includes* agrees with the subject *medicine*, so this answer choice is correct. The clauses presented in choices **a**, **b**, and **c** are nonessential clauses, so they must be set off from the rest of the sentence by commas. The information in these clauses is not essential to the understanding of the sentence. If the information in the clauses were essential to the understanding of the sentence, then commas would not be required. Choice **d** is incorrect because while the answer choice correctly includes commas to set off the nonessential clause, the verb *include* does not agree with the subject *medicine*, so this answer choice is incorrect.

18. a. Grammar and usage in the sentence are correct. Choices **b**, **c**, **d**, and **e** are incorrect because they all contain double negatives.

19. b. This sentence makes it clear that the car hit the roadblock but did not damage the roadblock. Choice **a** is incorrect because the antecedent of the pronoun *it* is unclear. Is it the car that was not damaged? Is the roadblock that was not damaged? Based on the construction of the sentence, it is not possible to make this determination. Choices **c**, **d**, and **e** are incorrect for the same reasons as **a**. Additionally, answer choice **c** includes a comma to separate two independent clauses, which creates a run-on, and the use of *although* in answer choice **d** and *even though* in choice **e** make the sentence even more confusing.

20. c. The words *kind* and *intelligent* are both adjectives, so use of the two adjectives provides parallel structure. Choices **a**, **b**, and **e** are incorrect because they all lack parallel structure, and choice **d** changes the meaning of the original sentence.

21. e. The words *aunt* and *grandfather* are common nouns; these words do not name a specific aunt and a specific grandfather, so the words *aunt* and *grandfather* should not be capitalized. Choices **a**, **c**, and **d** contain errors in capitalization. The words *aunt* and *grandfather* are common nouns; these words do not name a specific aunt and a specific grandfather, so neither of these words should be capitalized. Choice **b** contains a different error in capitalization. The word *my* does not begin the sentence, so it should not be capitalized.

22. e. The pronouns *them* and *me* are both in the objective case, as required for the object of a pronoun. The direct object *them* in choice **a** is in the correct case, the objective case, but the pronoun *I* is in the subjective case, rather than the objective case (*me*). Choice **b** is incorrect because the pronouns are in the subjective case (*they* and *I*), rather than the objective case (*them* and *me*). While the pronoun *me* is in the correct case for the object of a preposition, the word *their* is a possessive pronoun, making choice **c** incorrect. As in choice **c**, the word *their* in choice **d** is a possessive pronoun, and the pronoun *I* is in the subjective case, not the objective case, as required for the object of a preposition.

23. d. This is a complete sentence. Choices **a**, **b**, **c**, and **e** are incorrect because none of them are complete sentences.

24. c. The phrase *past history* is redundant, as the word *history* indicates a time in the past. The word *past* has been deleted in this answer choice, which cures the problem. Choices **a** and **b** both contain the redundant phrase *past history*, making them incorrect. Additionally, a comma is required after the introductory clause in choice **b**. This is also the reason why choice **d** is incorrect. Choice **e** mistakes the word *passed* for *past*, and even if the word *past* (rather than *passed*) had been included, the answer choice would still be incorrect, as the phrase *past history* is redundant.

25. d. The modifier *on the train* has been moved, so it is no longer misplaced. This sentence makes it clear that the swimmer on the train was explaining how to do the backstroke. Choices **a**, **b**, and **c** all contain a misplaced modifier (*on the train*). The swimmer is on the train while explaining the backstroke; the swimmer is not explaining a swimming style to be used while on the train. Additionally, in choices **b** and c, as well as choice **e**, the verb does not agree with the subject.

26. a. The word *gently* is an adverb that tells how the therapist massaged the spine. The word *gentle* in choice **b** is an adjective, so it would be correct to describe the noun *massage*—a gentle massage—but not the action of massaging the spine. In choices **c** and **d** the verb does not agree with the subject. While an adverb (*gently*), rather than an adjective (*gentle*) is included in choice **e**, the word *messaged* is mistaken for the word *massaged*.

27. a. The phrase *not only* appears in the first clause, so *but* is the correct correlative pronoun in the second clause. Due to use of *not only* and *also*, the correlative conjunctions *nor*, *or*, and *neither* are incorrect in choices **b**, **c**, and **e**. Choice **d** is incorrect because the use of the phrase *not only* in the first clause and the word *also* in the second clause requires a different correlative conjunction.

28. b. The noun in the subject, *scientists*, is plural. The noun in the predicate must agree with the plural subject. The noun in the predicate, *coats*, is plural, so it agrees with the plural subject. Choices **a** and **c** are incorrect because the noun in the subject is plural. The noun in the predicate must agree with the plural subject. The noun in the predicate does not agree with the plural subject. The singular verb, *takes*, in choice **d** does not agree with the plural subject, *scientists*. Choice **e** is incorrect because the word *scientists* in the sentence is not possessive, so the apostrophe in the word is incorrect. Additionally, the noun in the predicate does not agree with the noun in the subject.

29. a. The apostrophe in *wouldn't* and the apostrophe in *hadn't* replace the letter *o* in the word *not*. Apostrophes are required in the words *wouldn't* and *hadn't*, making choices **b**, **c**, and **e** incorrect. Additionally, the comma should not have been inserted in choice **d** as well as choice **e**.

30. d. This revision clarifies the sentence, as the vague pronoun *they* has been removed; the vague pronoun *they* is replaced by *the flowers*. This revision makes it clear that the flowers will flourish. There is a more effective way to write the sentence, as the original sentence contains the vague pronoun *they*. It is not possible to tell whether *they* refers to *flower beds* or to *flowers*. For this reason, choices **a**, **b**, and **c** are incorrect. Additionally, choice **b** creates a run-on sentence, and choice **c** uses the pronoun *it*, which is incorrect in number, as it is singular; the two nouns in the sentence, *beds* and *flowers*, are plural. Choice **e** is incorrect. The verb *has been* does not agree with the noun *beds*. Additionally, addition of the word *properties* changes the meaning of the sentence.

31. c. This is the correct answer. All of the words in the organization's name—other than the minor word *of*—must be capitalized, making choices **a**, **b**, **d**, and **e** incorrect. Additionally, the first word of the sentence must always be capitalized.

32. b. The adjectives *good* and *nice* (choice **d**) are vague and overused, but the adjective *gorgeous* is much stronger. Choice **c** is incorrect because the passage does not reference large flower beds or gardens, so the adjective *giant* does not make sense within the context of the passage. The word *gregarious* (choice **e**) means sociable; a garden would not be described in this way.

33. e. A semicolon has been inserted to replace the comma. This cures the run-on issue and creates two complete sentences. Answer choices **b**, **c**, and **d** all contain run-on sentences. A comma must follow the introductory phrase *for example*, and removing the comma between *essential* and *sufficient* does not cure the problem.

34. b. This is the correct answer. The phrase *descending down* is redundant, making choices **c** and **d** incorrect. The word *descending* means "proceeding in a downward direction." Additionally, in choice **c** the word *flour* has been mistaken for the word *flower* and in choice **d** the verb *likes* does not agree with the subject *gardeners*. The word *gardeners* is also a common noun, so capitalizing it as in choice **e** is incorrect.

35. d. Selecting flowers that grow well in a region is not relevant to the paragraph's main idea. The paragraph focuses on information about the deadheading process, and choices **a**, **b**, **c**, and **e** all relate to that process.

36. d. The entire passage relates to planning and maintaining a garden, so this sentence summarizes the information in the passage and provides a strong conclusion. While the passage does reference the importance of guidance, layout, sunlight, and water choices, **a**, **b**, **c**, and **e** fail to summarize the ideas in the passage and would not provide a strong conclusion.

37. e. The abbreviation *eds.* and the location of the text *Drummond, Analise M., and Johann Small, eds.* within the citation show that there are two editors of the book. Choice **a** is incorrect because the names *Analise* and *Johann* are the first names of the editors and *Georgia* is part of the title of the book. There is no indication within the citation that this is a second edition, making choice **b** incorrect. The publishing house is located in Mahwah, NJ, so choice **c** is incorrect. Choice **d** is incorrect because if the text had been published on the Web, the final word in the citation would be *Web*, not *Print*.

38. a. The city needs additional income to repair roads and bridges, and this additional income could come from an increase in the city's sales tax. Choices **b**, **c**, and **e** are not clearly relevant to the opinion. This statement in choice **d** undermines the opinion, rather than supporting it.

39. b. A university's nutrition studies are likely to be balanced and unbiased. A food manufacturer's statements might be biased in an effort to increase sales. The food manufacturer would have a vested interest in the framing and dissemination of information; therefore choice **a** is incorrect. The information from a vegetable farmer (choice **c**) would likely be narrow and would not be the most relevant. Students' opinions (choice **d**) might not be based on fact and might not be strongly supported. Such opinions could easily be based simply on personal preference, in which case the opinions would lack credibility for the purpose of the project. Choice **e** is incorrect because online articles might provide information about the problems with junk food, but they would not necessarily provide information about consuming a balanced diet.

40. e. The writing process generally proceeds in this order: brainstorming ideas, narrowing ideas, creating an outline, writing a draft, and writing at least one revision. Choices **a**, **b**, **c**, and **d** are incorrect.

Sample Responses for the Argumentative Essay

Sample Score 6 Response

I agree that assault is a serious crime and is not to be tolerated. It is a big step, however, to move from this statement to the statement that a football team should immediately and permanently remove a player accused of assault or that people should stop attending games if the team fails to do so. The key word to consider in this statement is accused.

I have read many books and articles about crime, and I have seen many news segments about people who have been accused of crimes but who have been found not guilty of having committed them. My aunt is a prosecuting attorney, and she has told me that people do sometimes file charges in cases in which a person is found to be not guilty. While it would be reasonable to suspend a player while there is an investigation and a trial regarding an assault, it would not be reasonable to remove a player permanently. It is possible that the player could be found not guilty or that the charges against the player could be dismissed.

It is also important to consider the variety of people other than players and team officials who benefit from football games. For example, people make incomes from working in the parking lot, preparing and serving food at the concession stands, maintaining the field, and cleaning after a game. When key players are removed from teams, this can have a huge impact on the number of people who attend the games. This in turn has an impact on the incomes of the people who work at the field. My neighbor sells sweatshirts and other team memorabilia at games, and she has told me that when attendance drops, her income also drops, and she needs her income to support her family. There is some risk in every job, and if a player is convicted of assault and removed, this is a risk the workers at the field face. It's not fair, though, for the players to face this risk due to just a charge without a conviction.

I agree that football is glorified in our country. Players are often looked upon almost as royalty, and

this can cause people to look the other way when a football player does something wrong, but I think it is a gross generalization to state that a player's morals, ethics, and common sense go out the window when the player steps onto the field. This might be true of some players, but it is certainly not true of all players. Many players show strong morals and ethics. Many are devoted to their families and participate in community service.

Like all people, football players must be looked upon as individuals who prove their true moral fiber through their actions. Certainly, if a football player is convicted of assault, then the player should be permanently removed from the team and the league, but until such a conviction, a permanent removal is unfair to the player and to others who make their living in ways related to football games.

About This Essay

This powerful response begins by clearly stating the writer's position, sharply focusing on the word *accused*. The essay continues with strong organization and support through reasons, details, and examples. After the introduction, the writer provides details of books she has read, as well as the example of an aunt who is a prosecuting attorney; the writer shares the explanation provided by her aunt, an explanation in which her aunt told her about cases in which the accused was found to be not guilty. The writer powerfully connects this example to the possibility of a football player being accused of assault but perhaps not being guilty.

The essay moves forward to discuss the impact of removal of a key player on others who earn an income through jobs related to football. This insightful example provides a dimension that other writers might not even consider, which elevates this essay's score. For support, the writer provides details related to specific types of jobs that could be affected, as well as the example of someone the writer knows personally. The writer also provides an insightful discussion of income risk and whether this risk should be anticipated simply due to an accusation. This again elevates the level of the essay.

The writer continues by stating agreement with the statement that football is glorified in our country. The writer connects this statement to the action of officials who look the other way when a player does something wrong; however, the writer clearly notes disagreement with the statement that a player's morals, ethics, and common sense go out the window when the player steps onto the field. The writer insightfully points out that this statement is a gross generalization, stating that many players are devoted to family and community.

The writer concludes by stating that football players are individuals and must be looked upon as such. The writer restates the position first asserted at the beginning of the essay.

Throughout the essay, the writer offers strong organization, as well as sentences of a variety of structures and lengths. This enhances the flow and readability of the essay. This strong essay is free from errors in mechanics, usage, and grammar. The power of all of these elements unquestionably brings the essay to a score of 6.

Sample Score 5 Response

It is not really fair to permanently remove a player who has been accused of assault, and it is not fair for fans to stop attending games if the team fails to take action, so I disagree with these parts of the prompt, but I do agree that assault is serious, and I do agree that football is glorified in our country.

For many years, I have seen news reports and read magazine articles detailing inexcusable behavior of football players. These reports have included many kinds of unacceptable behavior, including incidences of assault, disorderly conduct, and conducting dog-fighting rings. The football teams have generally looked in the other direction and refused to punish these players.

I read that one football player was convicted of conducting dog-fighting rings. He was unspeakably cruel to these living creatures. Then he later became a

football player again. A major team put him back on the field. Violence is at the heart of so many of these negative behaviors, and the violence is not acceptable. This player should never have been allowed to begin playing football again. Allowing him to do so sent a strong message to others, the message that violence is acceptable and should not have an impact on putting a person in a position of great income and influence. After all, many adults and children alike look up to football players as role models.

On the news, there have been videos of football players assaulting their girlfriends, and this action is rough and frightening. There have also recently been reports of football officials looking the other way when these players do something wrong, just as there have been such reports for many years. The players make a great deal of money for the teams and for those associated with football, so the people in charge just look the other way. This is not acceptable.

It is important for teams to stop looking the other way when this type of behavior occurs. Action must be taken to let players know that this kind of behavior will no longer be tolerated. When the status quo continues, when players are allowed to commit assaults and not suffer consequences, it sadly makes sense that many players will likely continue to engage in this behavior.

I do believe that a player charged with assault should be temporarily suspended from play, but I think this it is important for this suspension to be temporary until such time as it is determined whether the player actually committed the assault. At the company I work for, a worker was charged with having taken money from the company bank account for personal use. The worker was fired, but it was discovered later that the worker had not taken the money. The worker lost the job unfairly.

Of course, all of this said, I do not in any way condone assault, after a conviction, a player should definately be removed from a team. It is important to let these players know that that they cannot get away with assaults, just because the players are of value to the income of their teams. There should be a no-tolerance policy for assault across the board—no matter how important a person seems to be to the public and no matter how much money that person can generate for self and for others. Still, a player should not be removed permanently from play due to just an accusation.

About This Essay

The writer opens by stating a position on each of the key points of the prompt. The writer states disagreement with the act of permanently removing players accused of assault; the writer also states disagreement with fans refusing to attend games if the team fails to so remove the players. The writer states agreement, however, that assault is serious and that football is glorified in our country. The ability to sort out portions of the opinion expressed in the prompt is important, and this writer has clearly demonstrated the ability to do so.

After the introduction, the writer provides examples of players who have shown criminal behavior in their actions, such as the player who was running a dog-fighting ring. These examples are strong and powerful; however, it isn't until the writer has stated these examples that the reader learns that the writer is using these examples to support a position related to temporary suspension from play after an accusation of assault. The writer's ideas in the examples are powerful and effective; however, they would be much more effective if the writer had mentioned the position regarding temporary suspension prior to providing examples. As organized, this is a bit confusing, though the reader can look back through the examples to connect the ideas. A bit of change in organization here would have helped to elevate the essay to a score of 6.

The writer concludes by strongly disavowing any support of assault and again drawing a distinction between being accused of a crime and being convicted of a crime. This reinforces the position already stated by the writer.

The essay provides a variety of sentence types and lengths, though the effectiveness of the sentences fails to rise to a level of consistency. Some of the sentences are quite long, and a greater variety in length would be much more effective.

There are a couple of errors in grammar, mechanics, and usage, such as this run-on with a spelling error: *Of course, all of this said, I do not in any way condone assault, after a conviction, a player should definately be removed from a team.* With some work in these areas, this essay could be brought up to a score of 6.

Sample Score 4 Response

I agree that people should refuse to go to a team's games if the team fails to immediately and permanently remove a player who is accused of assault. When an assault occurs, the situation must be treated swiftly. A message must be sent right away that this kind of behavior is not to be accepted by anyone. If the team fails to do as it should. Then it is up to the fans to take matters into their own hands.

Football has always been glorified in our country, and I believe that the glorifying of the sport has led to inappropriate behavior being tolerated. There is a great deal of money to be made based on football play, and officials might sometimes allow this income to cloud their judgment. If this were not the case, then many players would allready have been seriously dealt with after committing assaults, and this has just not been the case. I have read newspaper articles about players who have committed assault and have then just been suspended for a game or two.

In those situations, the officials failed to act, but the fans could have, and they should have. The fans should not turn a blind eye. If the team fails to act, then the fans must act. This will hit the officials in the pocketbook, which will demand their attention.

It is sad that the pocketbook, rather than morals and ethics, seems to be the cause of change. This does not mean that all players' morals, ethics, and common sense go out the window when they step onto a football field, though. For some, it seems that this happens, but it is certainly not the case for all.

In conclusion, it is important to immediately and permanently remove a player accused of assault, and if a team fails to do so, people should refuse to attend the team's games. This will result in important changes that need to happen.

About This Essay

This essay shows competence. The writer opens by stating the clear position that people should refuse to go to games if a team fails to immediately and permanently remove a player accused of assault. The writer's message in the opening paragraph shows the writer's belief that fans can exert power over teams who fail to act appropriately.

There is control in the writer's organization and development of ideas. After the opening, the writer goes on to discuss agreement with the statement that football is glorified in our country and that this has led to inappropriate behavior being tolerated. The writer mentions a brief example, but clearer and more powerful reasons would have been more effective.

The writer continues by commenting on the fans having an obligation to act, which would "hit the officials in their pocketbook." Although this point is connected to the writer's position, elaboration on the point could have brought this essay up to a higher level.

As the essay goes on, it references morals and ethics, stating that some players suffer from a lack of morals and ethics but all players do not. This is a cogent statement, but it lacks the details and examples to give it great power.

The essay concludes by reiterating the writer's position, but it fails to end with any great insight or memorable statement for the reader.

Overall, the essay shows adequate use of language and general control of grammar, usage, and mechanics, but there are a few errors in these areas. For example, it includes a sentence fragment: *If the team fails to do as it should.* It also contains a spelling error: *allready.* This word is often misspelled, so it is one the writer should have studied prior to taking the exam.

Sample Score 3 Response

The issue of assault is a serious one. And it is important to take a serious look at it. Anyone commiting assault should be punished, it doesn't matter whether the offender is a famous football player or someone unknown.

Should a football team remove a player accused of assault? Where there is smoke, there is fire. If a person is accused of assault, chances are that the person did commit it. And the player might be able to get out of the charge after it is filed, so it doesn't make sense to wait until the charge go all the way through the courts. I know about these legal loopholes because my friend was assaulted, but the person who committed the assault got out of it because of a legal loophole. That just wasn't fair. Why was that person allowed to go free? There should have been strong and swift punishment. Anyone who thinks the legal system can find the truth is not thinking clearly.

Football is glorified in our country, but that is okay. It should be glorified. The players work hard. The people associated with the teams work hard. We should reward hard work. But glorifying football doesn't mean that players should be allowed to assault others. We have to get a handle on this immediately. Assault is just not okay.

About This Essay

This essay displays some competence; however, it is clearly flawed. It is limited in stating a position. It opens by discussing the seriousness of assault, but it does not state a position regarding the opinion expressed in the prompt.

The essay also shows limited control in the organization and development of ideas. In the second paragraph, the reader is given an idea of the writer's position through this statement: *Where there is smoke, there is fire.* Still, the writer does not clearly explain a position, and the example provided by the writer regarding the writer's friend is relevant but not clear.

In the final paragraph, the writer does state a position regarding whether football is glorified, and it provides a reason that relates to a reward for hard work, but this reason is not insightful or powerful. As the essay concludes, the writer makes this statement: *Assault is just not okay.* The prompt does not focus on whether assault is okay, so the writer is digressing in the conclusion.

This essay displays an accumulation of errors in the use of language and in mechanics, grammar, and usage. For example, the first paragraph contains this run-on with a spelling error: *Anyone commiting assault should be punished, it doesn't matter whether the offender is a famous football player or someone unknown.* Additionally, there is an error in subject-verb agreement in this phrase: *so it doesn't make sense to wait until the charge go all the way through the courts.*

Sample Score 2 Response

Should a team remove a player who is accused of assault? Should fans stop going to games? Who knows if the player really did it? Why should the player lose a job over something that mite not be true.

And I don't know why people complain that football is glorified. Its been part of country for so many years. It gives entertainment, and it makes money for lots of people. Its ok to glorify something that does that much good.

Assault is bad. Assault is a terrible thing. No one should put up with it, no one should have to go through it. And anyone who assaults someone else should be punished. But just because someone is accused of assault. This doesn't mean the person actually did it.

About This Essay

This essay is seriously flawed. It states no clear position, and it displays weak organization. It offers inadequate reasons, examples, and details for support, and it is riddled with errors in usage, mechanics, and grammar. The essay opens with a string of questions, one of which is incorrectly punctuated and contains a spelling error: *Why should the player lose a job over something that mite not be true.* This is confusing for the reader and shows a lack of organization.

In the second paragraph, the writer mentions the glorification of football and makes statements about football making money for lots of people. The paragraph references football as *something that does that much good.* This is unclear and offers a lack of support. Additionally, this paragraph contains errors in *Its* and *ok.*

As the essay concludes, it makes this statement: *Assault is bad.* The paragraph goes on to state that no one should put up with it and that no one should have to go through it. This doesn't relate to whether players should be removed immediately and permanently, as stated in the prompt. The final paragraph also includes a run-on and a fragment: *No one should put up with it, no one should have to go through it. But just because someone is accused of assault.*

Sample Score 1 Response

Yes. Do remove these palyers. And fans should stop going to games. Who do those palyers think they are? They can't get away with this. They can't behave this way.

I've seen peepul on tv who have been assaulted. They look scared, they look terribl. No one else is supposed to do this. Why can football palyers do it? The teams should take them out of the sport right away. Teams should keep others safe, and they shud show that assault is not ok. Better for the future.

About This Essay

This essay contains serious and persistent writing errors. It is incoherent. The reader cannot determine a true position. Examples, reasons, and details are sorely lacking, and this essay has errors in usage, grammar, spelling, and mechanics throughout its content. The writer opens by making this statement: *Do remove these palyers.* It's not clear exactly what the writer means here. The writer seems to be very emotional, as is clear through the following questions. *Who do those palyers think they are? They can't get away with this. They can't behave this way.* This emotion, however, drowns out rational statements the writer might have made to relate to the prompt.

Sample Responses for the Source-Based Essay

Sample Score 6 Response

Issues related to solar energy focus on renewability and sustainability, availability, environmentally friendly nature, and cost, as well as intermittent nature and noise. In Andrea Ling's piece, she wholeheartedly supports solar energy: "Solar energy is the wave of the future" (Energy: Crisis, Solutions, and Counterpoints). She begins by discussing the environmentally friendly nature of solar power, as compared to the pollution caused by burning fossil fuels. Ling further differentiates solar power from energy that comes from fossil fuels. Fossil fuels are not renewable; however, solar energy is a renewable resource (Ling).

Ling discusses the quiet nature of capturing and utilizing solar energy. This process does not create the noise that comes from the use of wind turbines (Ling).

As Ling discusses cost and availability of energy, she explains that solar energy can be made available in locations where other forms of energy would be too costly to develop. She provides the example of the vast infrastructure required to lay a grid for electricity. Insofar as cost, Ling points out that use of solar energy means no bills from an electricity provider. She goes on to mention government rebates and other economic incentives.

While Ling does make many good points, it is interesting to note the irony in the title of her book: Energy: Crisis, Solutions, and **Counterpoints***. Ling so avidly promotes solar energy that she fails to discuss the complexities of use of this energy source, complexities that necessarily indicate counterpoints to her position. In "The Truth about Solar Energy," Oscar Salazar cogently raises a number of these counterpoints. Ling's position would have been much stronger if she had acknowledged and addressed each of these.*

Salazar elaborates on the postured inexpensive nature of solar panels. The solar panels, also known as "solar cells," can cost more than $1,500 each, and one is generally not enough. There are installation fees to con-tend with—in addition to the costs of the cells (Salazar).

Insofar as a lack of electricity bills is concerned, Salazar points out that solar cells alone generally do not supply sufficient energy, so electricity bills, even though somewhat decreased, will remain in play. Salazar's credibility is bolstered by his acknowledgment that the electricity bills will likely be decreased due to the use of solar energy.

Salazar discusses the intermittent nature of solar energy, a fact overlooked by Ling, and Salazar also points out that obtaining solar energy does not occur without a pollution cost. Greenhouse gases might be emitted during production of solar cells, and pollution arises as cells are transported (Salazar).

Ling's position and Salazar's are at odds with one another; however, both raise interesting points. Salazar's are presented through a more balanced approach and so are more credible. Still, both authors make excellent points about the use of solar energy, and when analyzed together, these authors' pieces provide foundations from which readers can draw reasonable and valuable conclusions.

About This Essay

This essay demonstrates a high degree of competence. The writer opens by clearly elucidating the issues and their importance. The writer provides well-chosen reasons and examples and also offers powerful insight, which raises this essay to a score of 6. After discussing the position of Andrea Ling regarding solar energy, the writer points out the irony in the title of Ling's book, which includes the word *Counterpoints*. The writer is quick to note that Ling fails to provide and address counterpoints to her position, and the writer explains that doing so would have made Ling's position stronger.

The writer's insight continues as the writer points out Salazar's mention of a decrease—while not a total lack—of electricity costs with use of solar panels. The writer notes the bolstered credibility that Salazar garners through this balanced approach.

The writer organizes and develops ideas logically, beginning with a statement of the issue, continuing with specifics of Ling's position, and then addressing specifics of Salazar's position. Throughout these paragraphs, the writer weaves comments regarding the credibility of each of the authors. The writer concludes by acknowledging that both authors make valid points, while one author appears more credible than the other.

Throughout the essay, the writer offers great variety in sentence structure and length. The writer's development, organization, support, incorporation of links between the two sources, as well as proper citation when paraphrasing and quoting—in addition to the absence of errors in mechanics, usage, or grammar—easily warrant a score of 6.

Sample Score 5 Response

Primary issues related to solar energy focus on the availability and sustainability of this resource, as well as the expense, noise, and pollution linked to use of energy sources. As Andrea Ling points out, solar energy is renewable and does not result in the pollution caused by fossil fuels (Energy: Crisis, Solutions, and Counterpoints). Oscar Salazar is quick to point out, however, that solar energy has its own pollution costs, including possible greenhouse gases emitted during production and pollution that occurs through transportation of solar energy equipment ("The Truth about Solar Energy").

Ling discusses the distinction between quiet solar energy and the noisy alternative methods of energy production, such as wind turbines. This point is not addressed in Salazar's piece.

Ling discusses availability and cost of solar energy, explaining that solar energy can be provided in locations where traditional energy sources, such as electricity, are not available. This ties into her discussion of cost, as it would be too costly to provide the infrastructure for an electric grid in many locations. This point is not discussed in Salazar's piece.

In locations where electricity is available, solar energy can result in savings from living off of the grid, meaning "away from energy sources" (Ling). Salazar is quick to point out, though, that solar energy generally does not meet all the energy needs of a consumer, so having solar energy does not necessarily mean eliminating costs of electricity.

Ling points out that "rebates and other economic incentives area often available from state and local governments when consumers choose to use solar energy." Salazar makes his own point in this regard, he explains that local and federal officials often offer incentives for a variety of types of energy. Salazar also discusses a major negative aspect of solar energy, an aspect that Ling does not mention. Salazar points out the intermittent nature of solar energy, explaining that solar energy is generated only while the sun shines.

In conclusion. Ling and Salazar have very different viewpoints regarding solar energy. Aspects of both should be carefully considered by anyone studying energy sources or considering alternative energy sources.

About This Essay

Although this essay shows clear competence, it includes minor errors. The essay begins by explaining important issues. It incorporates information from both sources to identify and explain important concerns regarding solar energy. The ideas are organized and developed clearly. The writer presents information in a position-rebuttal format, first explaining Ling's position regarding a specific point and then immediately addressing Salazar's statements that rebut or clarify the point. This organizational structure is quite effective and allows the reader to clearly see how the two pieces relate to one another. The writer also addresses points that are covered in only one of the two pieces.

The writer does a very strong job of supporting points with examples and details from each of the pieces, for example: *In locations where electricity is available, solar energy can result in savings from living* off of the grid, meaning "away from energy sources" (Ling). Salazar is quick to point out, though, that solar energy generally does not meet all the energy needs of a consumer, so having solar energy does not necessarily mean eliminating costs of electricity.

Though it is true that the writer does a good job of linking the pieces and distinguishing between the two authors' positions in regard to specific points, the writer does not provide powerful insight and analysis regarding the positions of the authors. Had the writer done so, this piece would likely have been elevated to a score of 6.

Some sentence variety is demonstrated by the writer; however, the essay would have been stronger with greater variety. Both sources are cited by the writer when the writer paraphrases and quotes, and the essay is generally free from errors in grammar, usage, and mechanics, although the essay includes a fragment (*In conclusion.*) and a run-on (*Salazar makes his own point in this regard, he explains that local and federal officials often offer incentives for a variety of types of energy.*).

Sample Score 4 Response

There are many kinds of energy sources. Many people use electricity as an energy source for they're homes and businesses. Solar energy is an alternative type of energy that is being used. It is important to fine alternative energy sources, as fossil fuels are being burned and are not renewble. Once they are depleted, they are gone forever (Energy Crisis, Solutions, and Counterpoints).

"Solar energy is the wave of the future." This is what authur Andrea Ling believes. She believes that people should be using solar energy. She explains that solar power does not cause pollution. She also explains that solar energy is renewable.

Wind turbines is noisy, but solar power is quiet (Ling). This is a big advantage of solar power.

Solar power does not cost as much as electricity, and it can be easyer to get solar power than electricity in areas that are out in the middle of nowhere (Ling). It is

also much less expensive to have solar power than electricity. This is what Ling says. Ling also says that the government might give money to people who decide to use solar power.

Oscar Salazar has different ideas ("The Truth about Solar Energy"). He says that there is pollution from solar power. He says that there is pollution when solar cells are made, he says that solar cells have to be driven to places, and there is pollution during the transportation.

Salazar also writes about the cost of solar power. He mentions the high cost of the solar cells. He mentions the hi cost of installation. He also mentioned that the government might give money to people for using many types of power.

Salazar writes about some things that Ling does not mention. He writes about the intermittent nature of solar energy. He says that solar energy is produced only when the sun is shinning, so it is not being produced all the time.

Ling says that solar energy is the wave of the future, but Salazar says it is important to have a balanced viewpoint.

About This Essay

This essay adequately explains why the concerns are important, mentioning the issues of renewable resources, cost, noise, and intermittent availability of solar power. Even though adequate reasons are provided, these reasons are not powerful, and while some links between the sources are offered, these links are more regurgitation of statements in each article than cogent reasons that support specific positions.

The writer does show control in the organization and development of ideas, beginning by mentioning issues, continuing by mentioning some of Ling's points, and then mentioning some of Salazar's points. Overall, the writer does not include the depth of reasons, details, and examples that would be present in an essay warranting a higher score.

The essay displays adequate use of language and shows some control of grammar, usage, and mechanics, though there are a number errors. For example, the third paragraph contains an error in subject-verb agreement: *Wind turbines is noisy, but solar power is quiet.* The fifth paragraph contains a run-on: *He says that there is pollution from solar power. He says that there is pollution when solar cells are made, he says that solar cells have to be driven to places, and there is pollution during the transportation.* The sixth paragraph contains a tense shift: *He mentions the high cost of the solar cells. He mentions the hi cost of installation. He also mentioned that the government might give money to people for using many types of power.* There are many spelling errors throughout the essay.

Sample Score 3 Response

No, solar energy is not the answer to problems with energy, it costs a lot. It has to be put in. The govurment could offer money for this kind of energy. The govument couldd offer money for many other kinds of energy too. ("The Truth about Solar Eenrgy") But if you use solar energy. You could be using less electricity. (Salazar)

Solar energy is intermit. Sometimes you have it, sometimes you dont. This is a problem. You mite need it. But you mite not have it when you do. Even if you have solar energy, if there is pollution, your solar energy might not work as well. (Salazar)

Speaking of pollution, some people say there is no pollution form solar energy. This is not true. There can be pollution when solar cells are made. There is pollution when solar panels are driven to places. (Salazar)

About This Essay

This essay demonstrates some competence, but it is obviously flawed. The essay is limited in explaining why the concerns are important. While the essay mentions solar energy, it does not discuss clear reasons for the importance of considerations regarding solar energy. Only one source, the Salazar source, is

mentioned, and the reasons included in the essay are inadequate.

Still, the writer does explain that solar energy is expensive to install and that use of solar energy could mean use of less electricity. The writer also manages to explain, albeit weakly, the intermittent nature of solar energy, and the writer does make the point that solar energy might not be as effective when utilized during a time of pollution. The writer does also weakly make the point that pollution can be caused when solar cells are produced and transported. Thus, there is a small amount of merit gained for the points made, but there is only a small amount of merit, due to the weak manner in which the essay is written.

The writer demonstrates limited control in the organization and development of ideas, offering vague references to issues related to solar energy but clarifying none of them. The essay contains an accumulation of errors in the use of language and in grammar, usage, and mechanics. For example, the writer confuses the words *might* and *mite*. The writer omits the apostrophe in the word don't, and the writer begins the essay with a run-on.

Sample Score 2 Response

We need solar energy, it is a wave. It is for the future. It is important. It is clean. You don't have to burn things to get it. It doesnt pollute. Fosil fuels end, solar energy does not. Best idea ever.

Wind turbines are noisy. Solar energy is not. Solar energy is not expensive. Very cheap. People near wind turbines here the noise. Thermal energy comes from the sun, you can have solar energy in many places.

It is positive to have solar energy. You can save off of a grid. The goverment can give you money if you do. It is a good idee to use solar energy. It is sumthing everwon should do. "It should derinately be the top contender for satisfiing energy needs."

About This Essay

This essay is seriously flawed. It fails to clearly explain why specific issues related to solar energy are important. Instead, it appears to interject intended, but confused, restatements of content in the Ling piece, statements that often do not belong together and do not make sense in the order in which they are stated. Only one source, the Ling source, is utilized, and it is utilized quite weakly; there are no citations, and when a quote (the final sentence in the essay) is pulled from a source, it contains misspelled words. The organization is weak, and there is very little development.

The essay contains frequent serious errors in the use of language and in grammar, usage, and mechanics. There are many run-ons, fragments, and spelling errors.

Sample Score 1 Response

Power. Something we all need. Can come from sunlight. Can be expensive. But does not pollute, does not need electricity.

Sunny days gives more energie. Wind gives energy to. Neither one comes from fossils. Have to make "solar cells." Have to drive to get "solar cells" where their going. Solar cells sometimes works, sometimes doesn't.

About This Essay

This essay demonstrates fundamental deficiencies in writing skills. Although it vaguely references aspects of the topic, such as power, sunlight, wind power, and fossils, the essay is underdeveloped and almost incoherent. It is filled with serious and persistent writing errors, such as run-ons, spelling errors, lack of subject-verb agreement, and fragments.

Praxis® Core Academic Skills for Educators: Mathematics Practice Test 3

Time: 85 Minutes

Directions: Choose the best answer to each of the following questions.

1. Using the following diagram, find the length in inches of the arc subtended by the angle 240°.

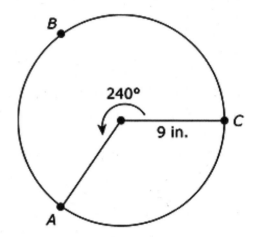

2. Which number is a multiple of 126?
   a. 14
   b. 63
   c. 200
   d. 326
   e. 630

3. Cynthia works 35 hours a week selling tennis equipment. She earns a base salary of $10 per hour and a 10% commission on her weekly sales. Cynthia wants to earn $700 before taxes each week. What is the total dollar value of sales she needs to have in order to reach that goal?

 a. $3,500
 b. $7,000
 c. $10,500
 d. $14,000
 e. $35,000

4. Ecologists are trying to determine what percentage of the fish population in a certain bay is infected with a new virus. They decide to rely on sampling to make their conclusion. Which of the following approaches is/are valid?

 I. Choose two fish at random from the bay and assess if they have the virus. Based on this information, conclude one of three things: The entire bay is infected, half the fish are infected, or none is infected.

 II. Choose a fish at random from the bay and determine if it has the virus. Throw it back into the water, and repeat the procedure 49 times. Use the percentage of the fish identified as having the virus as an estimate of the percentage of fish that have the virus in the bay overall.

 III. Send out 20 boats to different parts of the bay. At the same time, each boat selects 30 fish, determines the number of fish that are infected, and releases the fish back into the bay. Then tally how many of the 600 fish are infected, compute the percentage, and use this as an estimate of the percentage of the fish population in the bay overall that is infected.

 a. I only
 b. II only
 c. III only
 d. II and III only
 e. I, II, and III

5. A ladder is leaning against the side of a house. The top of the ladder rests on the house at a point 7 feet above the ground, and the bottom of the ladder forms an angle of 45° with the ground, as shown:

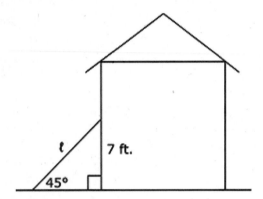

What is the approximate length, *l*, of the ladder?
  a. 4 feet
  b. 7 feet
  c. 9.9 feet
  d. 12.1 feet
  e. 14 feet

6. Find the value of *x* in this equation:
  $$\frac{x}{-4} = -5 + x$$
  a. $-\frac{20}{3}$
  b. 4
  c. 5
  d. 15
  e. no solution

7. Choose the answer that is equivalent to $\sqrt{600}$.
  a. $10\sqrt{6}$
  b. $6\sqrt{10}$
  c. 60
  d. $10\sqrt{60}$
  e. $60\sqrt{10}$

8. Your new house sits on a plot of land that is about one acre in size. There is a fence around the perimeter of the property, and you're curious how long the fence is. Which of the following would be the best unit of measurement to use when estimating the length of the fence?
  a. millimeters
  b. inches
  c. feet
  d. miles
  e. kilometers

9. Consider the function $f(x) = 12$. What is the value of $f(\pi^2)$ in inches?

10. This dot plot shows the number of Dean's Scholarship awardees in the senior class at a university from 2008 through 2014. Each dot represents 10 awardees.

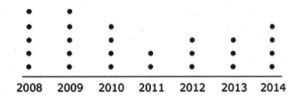

Select *all* of the correct statements for the seven-year period shown.
  a. The number of Dean's Scholarship awardees decreased steadily.
  b. 260 Dean's Scholarships were awarded.
  c. The dot plot is not symmetrical.
  d. The mode number of scholarships awarded annually is 20.
  e. The mean number of scholarships awarded annually is 37.

11. One brand of orange juice is sold in different sizes at a supermarket. Which size is the best deal based on the per-ounce price of juice?
   a. 24-ounce bottle for $1.72
   b. 18-ounce bottle for $1.35
   c. 6-ounce carton for $0.47
   d. 32-ounce jug for $2.91
   e. 8-ounce carton for $1.00

12. A closet shelf holds a collection of T-shirts: 7 purple, 4 blue, and 9 black. What is the probability of randomly selecting a T-shirt that is NOT purple from the shelf?

   a. $\frac{4}{20}$

   b. $\frac{7}{20}$

   c. $\frac{9}{20}$

   d. $\frac{13}{20}$

   e. 1

13. When building a model of the Titan 34D rocket, a model maker uses a scale of 0.6 inch for every 7.9 feet of the full-size device. If the length of a full-size Titan 34D rocket is 90.4 feet, what is the length of the model? Round your answer to the nearest hundredth of an inch.

14. Which of these scatterplots show(s) a positive trend? Choose *all* of the correct graphs.

a.

b.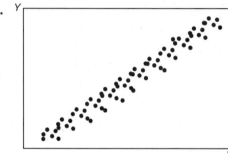

c.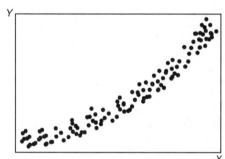

d.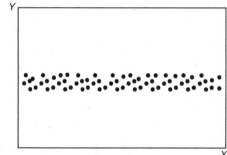

e.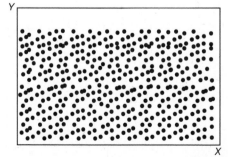

15. Which of the following is NOT equal to a whole number?

a. $5\frac{2}{3} - \frac{28}{6}$

b. 1.1×0.1

c. $1\frac{7}{8} \div \frac{3}{8}$

d. 16×0.5

e. 200% of $\frac{3}{2}$

16. Let $s(x) = \frac{3}{2} - 2x^2 + \frac{1}{3}x^4$ and $r(x) = 5x^2 - 10x^4$. Which of the following is equivalent to $6s(x) - \frac{1}{5}r(x)$?

a. $-11x^2 + 9$

b. $\frac{31}{3}x^4 - 3x^2 + 9$

c. $4x^4 - 13x^2 + 9$

d. $4x^4 - 13x^2$

e. $-4x^4 + 13x^2 - 9$

17. What is the solution of this system of equations?

$$\begin{cases} -x + 3y = -4 \\ -x + \ y = 6 \end{cases}$$

a. $x = 6, y = 12$

b. $x = 1, y = 2$

c. $x = 1, y = -1$

d. $x = -11, y = -5$

e. no solution

18. What is the area of the shaded region of circle Q?

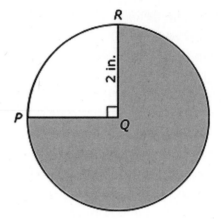

a. $\frac{\pi}{2}$ square inches

b. 3 square inches

c. π square inches

d. 3π square inches

e. 4π square inches

19. Suppose that a random variable x has the following probability distribution:

x	-2	-1	0	1	2
$P(X = x)$	$\frac{1}{8}$	$\frac{1}{8}$	$\frac{1}{8}$	$\frac{1}{8}$	$\frac{1}{2}$

What is the expected value of X?

a. -2

b. 0

c. $\frac{3}{4}$

d. 1

e. 2

20. Henry spends $\frac{3}{8}$ of his free time each week reading. Of this amount of time, he spends $\frac{4}{9}$ of it reading comic books. What fraction of his weekly free time does Henry spend NOT reading comic books?

21. Consider the intersecting graphs shown. To which of the following equations are the x-coordinates of the points of intersection the solutions?

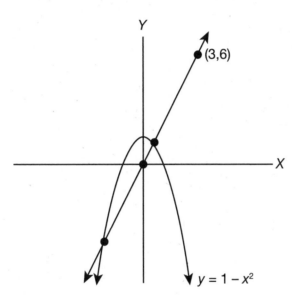

a. $1 - x^2 = x$
b. $x^2 - 2x = 0$
c. $x^2 + x = 0$
d. $x^2 + 2x - 1 = 0$
e. $1 - x^2 = 0$

22. If $x = \sqrt[3]{200}$, which of the following inequalities is true?
a. $2 < x < 4$
b. $3 < x < 5$
c. $6 < x < 6.5$
d. $4.5 < x < 5.5$
e. $5 < x < 6$

23. What type of transformation was used to map quadrilateral $WXYZ$ onto the image $W'X'Y'Z'$?

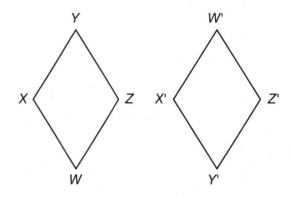

a. rotation
b. reflection
c. translation
d. translation followed by reflection
e. translation followed by rotation

24. Which of these is equivalent to $-3x(x^2 - 3x - 2)$?
a. $-3x^2 - 3x - 2$
b. $x^2 - 6x - 2$
c. $3x^3 - 9x^2 - 6x$
d. $-3x^3 + 9x^2 + 6x$
e. $-3x^2 + 9x + 6$

25. Let $y = f(x)$ be a given function and suppose the point $P(2,-3)$ lies on its graph. Consider the translation of this function given by $g(x) = f(x + 4) - 1$. What point would point P correspond to on the graph of $g(x)$?

26. Consider the set whose members are these geometric figures:

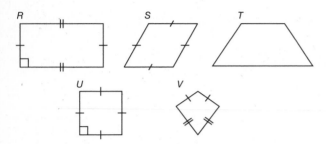

If a figure is selected at random, what is the probability of selecting a parallelogram?

a. 0
b. $\frac{1}{5}$
c. $\frac{2}{5}$
d. $\frac{3}{5}$
e. 1

27. A bike ramp is a right triangular prism with the dimensions shown:

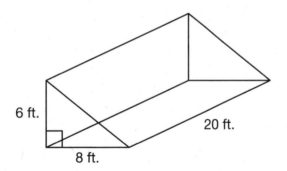

6 ft. 8 ft. 20 ft.

What is its total surface area?

a. 368 ft.^{2}
b. 408 ft.^{2}
c. 480 ft.^{2}
d. 504 ft.^{2}
e. 528 ft.^{2}

28. Which of the following statements is/are true? Select *all* of the correct statements.

a. An irrational number cannot be negative.
b. The difference of two rational numbers can be an irrational number.
c. The product of a rational number and an irrational number can be a rational number.
d. The sum of an irrational number and a rational number must be an irrational number.
e. The product of two irrational numbers must be an irrational number.

29. Suppose you spend $903 on a onetime cost for materials necessary to start a snow removal business. For each driveway you clear of snow, you earn $40, but it costs $5.25 in gas for each job. Determine the number of driveways you must clear order to break even.

a. 20
b. 25
c. 26
d. 52
e. 23

30. The length of a single lap at a university's pool is 200 feet. How many laps would you need to swim to swim a distance of 2.2 miles? Round your answer to the nearest lap. Note that 1 mile equals 5,280 feet.

31. Which of the following is an equation for this quadratic function?

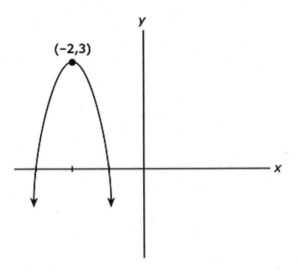

    a. $f(x) = -3(x - 2)^2 + 3$
    b. $f(x) = 3(x + 2)^2 + 3$
    c. $f(x) = -3(x + 2)^2 - 3$
    d. $f(x) = -3(x + 2)^2 + 3$
    e. $f(x) = -3(x + 3)^2 + 2$

32. Zelda, an event planner, is using a new catering hall for the first time. The catering hall is 45,000 square feet in area. For guests to be comfortable, her rule of thumb is to not exceed a population density of 0.03 people per square foot. What is the maximum number of people she thinks should occupy the new space?
    a. 135
    b. 450
    c. 1,350
    d. 4,500
    e. 45,000

33. What is the most reasonable correlation coefficient for the data set depicted by this scatterplot?

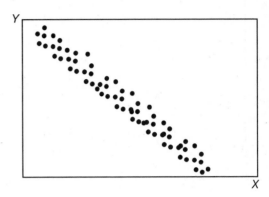

    a. −0.91
    b. −0.59
    c. 0.10
    d. 0.60
    e. 0.95

34. In 2014, the yearly average birth rate in China is 12.17 births for every 1,000 people. The population of China is 1.357 billion. Determine how many births are expected in one year.

35. Consider the function $f(x) = |x - h| + k$, where h and k represent real numbers. Select *all* of the following pairs of (h,k) for which the graph of $f(x)$ is obtained by translating the graph of $g(x) = |x|$ left by at least 3 units and up by at least 5 units.
    a. $h = 4, \ k = 5$
    b. $h = -4, k = 5$
    c. $h = -4, k = 7$
    d. $h = -4, k = -8$
    e. $h = -6, k = -6$

36. A rectangle is divided into six congruent squares, as shown:

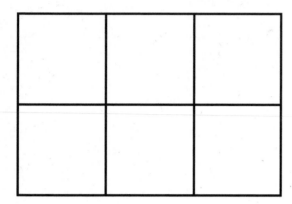

If the area of one of the squares is 9 square units, what is the perimeter of the rectangle?
a. 15 units
b. 24 units
c. 30 units
d. 36 units
e. 72 units

37. Which of these is equivalent to $\sqrt{(38+11)(60-11)}$?
a. 7
b. 14
c. 49
d. 343
e. 2,401

38. Which of the following collections of data has/have a mean of 44 and a variance of 0?
    I.   44, 44, 44, 44, 44, 44
    II.   44, 44, 0, 44, 44
    III. −44, −44, −44, 176, 176
a. I only
b. II only
c. III only
d. I and II
e. I, II, and III

39. Consider the data set {–4, –5, –4, –4, –2, –2, 5, 5, 5, 5, 6, 9}. Which of the following distributions best indicates the general shape of this data set?

a.

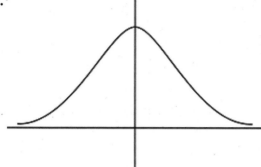

b.

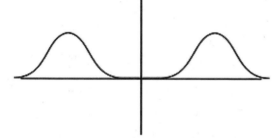

c.

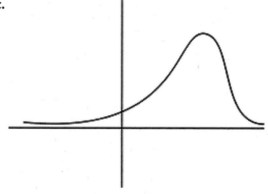

d.

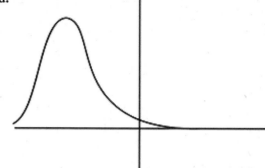

e.

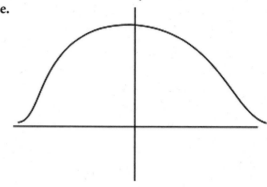

40. Which of the following lines could have an equation of the form $ax + 3y = 0$, where $a > 0$? Select *all* of the correct responses.

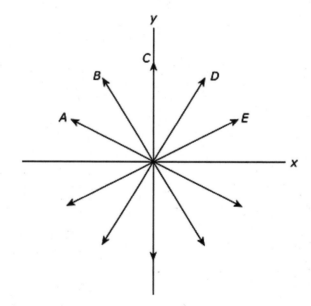

a. line A

b. line B

c. line C

d. line D

e. line E

41. If $\frac{3}{4} \div \frac{a}{a+1} = \frac{4}{3}$, then $a^2 = $ _____.

   a. $\frac{49}{81}$

   b. $\frac{7}{9}$

   c. $\frac{9}{7}$

   d. $\frac{81}{49}$

   e. $\frac{18}{7}$

42. Consider the set of whole numbers {8, 16, 24, 32}. Select *all* of the true statements.

   a. They are all prime numbers.

   b. All of the numbers are divisible by 4.

   c. None of the numbers is odd.

   d. All of the numbers are multiples of 8.

   e. All of the numbers are factors of 8.

43. Consider the triangle $\triangle ABC$ with vertices $A(-11,3)$, $B(-11,14)$, and $C(-21,5)$. If $\triangle ABC$ is reflected over the line $x = 2$, what are the coordinates of the image of vertex B?

   a. $(-11,-10)$

   b. $(15,14)$

   c. $(14,-11)$

   d. $(15,27)$

   e. $(-14,11)$

44. Which of the following is/are equivalent to $\dfrac{\frac{2}{x} - 4x}{\frac{1}{x}}$? Select *all* of the correct expressions.

   a. $2 - 4x$

   b. $\frac{1}{2 - 4x^2}$

   c. $4x^2 - 2$

   d. $\dfrac{\frac{2-4x^2}{x}}{\frac{1}{x}}$

   e. $2 - 4x^2$

45. What is the solution to the following equation?

$$5\ln(t+4) = 5$$

   a. -4

   b. $e - 4$

   c. 1

   d. $\frac{e}{4}$

   e. $4e$

46. The height of the right circular cone shown is twice the diameter of the base. If the diameter of the base of the cone is 20 inches, what is its volume?

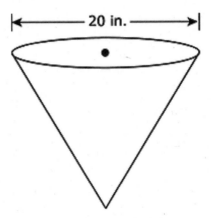

   a. $4{,}000\pi$ in.^{3}

   b. $\frac{400\pi}{3}$ in.^{3}

   c. $\frac{4{,}000\pi}{3}$ in.^{3}

   d. $\frac{16{,}000\pi}{3}$ in.^{3}

   e. 40π in.^{3}

47. At the turnpike tollbooth, the cashier-in-training, Meredith, handles fewer than one-third of the customers handled by two of the more experienced cashiers, Chris and Dana, combined. Assume that M represents the number of customers Meredith handles in a typical day, C represents the number Chris can handle in a typical day, and D represents the number Dana can handle in a typical day. Which of the following expressions correctly describes the relationship among M, C, and D?

   a. $D + C > \frac{1}{3}M$
   b. $C + D + M > 3$
   c. $M > 3(C + D)$
   d. $M < \frac{1}{3}DC$
   e. $C + D > 3M$

48. Segments JK and LK are radii of the circle. Each has a length of 8 cm. If the length of the arc extending from J to L is 2π feet, what is the value of x?

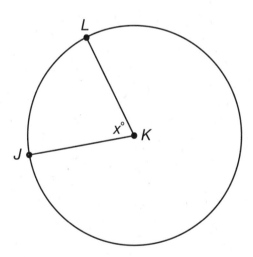

   a. 22.5°
   b. 45°
   c. 60°
   d. 90°
   e. 180°

49. The following shows the weight distribution in the average adult. The total average body weight is 75,000 grams.

ELEMENTS OF THE BODY	WEIGHT (IN GRAMS)
muscle mass	25,000
water	19,400
skeleton	12,000
blood	6,000
gastrointestinal tract	2,200
liver	1,800
brain	1,400
lungs	1,100

If the weight of a specific adult male's muscle mass is represented as m grams, which of the following expressions represents his total body weight B?

   a. $B = 75,000m$
   b. $B = 3m$
   c. $B = \frac{1}{3}m$
   d. $B = 30m$
   e. $B = 75,000m - 25,000$

50. Assume that a and b are positive integers. Which of the following statements is/are always true?

   I. $\frac{1}{b}$ is less than b.
   II. $\frac{a+b}{2b}$ equals $\frac{2a}{b+a}$ when a equals b.
   III. $\frac{a}{b}$ is greater than $\frac{b}{a}$.

   a. I only
   b. II only
   c. I and III only
   d. II and III only
   e. I and II only

51. What is the solution of this equation?
$$-2(3x - 2) = 4[8 - (2x - 1)]$$
- **a.** -8.5
- **b.** 17
- **c.** 32
- **d.** 34
- **e.** 68

52. Consider the following data set, where x is a positive integer:
$$\{x + 2, x + 4, x - 4, x - 3, x + 6\}$$
Which of the following statements is/are true?
   I. The mode is $x - 4$.
   II. The median is $x + 2$.
   III. The mean is $x + 1$.
- **a.** II only
- **b.** III only
- **c.** I and II only
- **d.** II and III only
- **e.** I, II, and III

53. A video game studio is considering two different promotions for its upcoming new release, as follows:

   Promotion X: The first 10,000 copies sold will include a code to download additional content worth $49.99. It is estimated that 40% of those receiving this offer will take advantage of it.

   Promotion Y: The first 25,000 copies sold will include a code to download additional content worth $29.99. It is estimated that 30% of those receiving this offer will take advantage of it.

Overall, the company expects to sell a total of 500,000 copies of this game for $69.99 each. Select *all* of the true statements.
- **a.** The cost of promotion X would be about $0.40 per game sold.
- **b.** The cost of promotion Y would be about $0.45 per game sold.
- **c.** The total cost of promotion Y would be $749,750.
- **d.** Promotion Y is more profitable than promotion X.
- **e.** Promotion X is more profitable than promotion Y.

54. The low temperature in Tucson on Tuesday was 11°F warmer than on Monday. Wednesday's low temperature was 5°F cooler than Tuesday's low temperature. Thursday's was 9°F warmer than Wednesday's low temperature. The average low temperature for these four days was 87°F. What was the low temperature on Tuesday?
- **a.** 94°F
- **b.** 90°F
- **c.** 85°F
- **d.** 79°F
- **e.** 70°F

55. A certain whole number w can be divided by 7 and 8 without a remainder. Which number is NOT a factor of w?

a. 4
b. 12
c. 14
d. 28
e. 56

56. Circles C_1 and C_2 both have a diameter of $6\sqrt{2}$. What is the sum of the solid lines in the diagram?

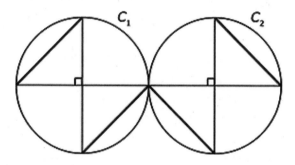

a. $12\sqrt{2}$
b. 24
c. $24\sqrt{2}$
d. $36\sqrt{2}$
e. 144

Praxis® Core Academic Skills for Educators: Mathematics Practice Test 3 Answers and Explanations

1. 12π **inches.** First, convert 240° to radians by multiplying it by $\frac{\pi}{180°}$. This yields $\frac{4\pi}{3}$ radians. Then apply the arc length formula ($S = r\theta$), where θ is measured in radians and r is the radius) to find the answer: $\frac{4\pi}{3} \cdot 9 = 12\pi$ inches.

2. e. A multiple of 126 is equal to the product of 126 and any whole number. (In other words: $126n$.) We can multiply 126 by 5 to get 630, which means 630 is a multiple of 126. Choices **a** and **b** are incorrect because 14 and 63 are factors of 126 (meaning a number that divides 126 evenly), not multiples of 126. Choices **c** and **d** are incorrect because a multiple of 126 is equal to the product of 126 and any whole number. In other words: $126n$. We know that $126 \times 1 = 126$ and $126 \times 2 = 252$. In order to create 200, n would have to be a number greater than 1 but smaller than 2—which means it would not be a whole number. Using the same logic, there is no whole number that we could multiply 126 by to arrive at 326.

3. a. To find the answer, let x represent the total of Cynthia's weekly sales, and rephrase her 10% commission as a rate of 0.10. Fill in the other facts supplied by the question, and then solve for x:

$$(35 \times 10) + 0.10x = 700$$
$$350 + 0.10x = 700$$
$$0.10x = 350$$
$$x = 350 \div 0.10 = 3,500$$

In order for Cynthia to earn $700 per week before taxes, her weekly sales must total $3,500. Excluding Cynthia's weekly base salary in your calculations, you arrived at the equation $700 = 0.10x$ (choice **b**). When solving the equation, subtract 350 from both sides to find x; adding 350 results in choice **c**, which is incorrect. Choice **d** is likely the result of an arithmetic error; $14,000 is four times the amount she needs. Choice **e** is also incorrect due to an arithmetic error when working with the rate. A 10% commission translates to a rate of 0.10.

4. c. This procedure uses a reasonable number of different fish from different parts of the bay to make a reasonable assessment of the entire population of fish in the bay. I is not valid since only two fish are used. This would not be representative of the population of fish in the bay. II is not valid because it is possible that the same fish are sampled multiple times. This would not be representative of the population of fish in the bay.

5. c. The triangle formed by the ladder, the wall, and the ground is a 45-45-90 triangle. The ladder is the hypotenuse of the triangle. For every 45-45-90 triangle, the length of the hypotenuse is $\sqrt{2}$ times the length of a side. Here, the side length is 7 feet, so the hypotenuse is $7\sqrt{2} \approx 9.9$ feet. Four feet (choice **a**) is way too short and likely the result of an arithmetic error. As a result of the triangle being 45-45-90, you can infer that the length of ground is the same length as the wall: 7 feet. But the hypotenuse—the ladder in this example—would be longer than each of these sides. In other words, choice **b** would be longer than 7 feet. Choice **d** is incorrect because in order to find the length of the hypotenuse, multiply one of the legs by $\sqrt{2}$, not by $\sqrt{3}$. Choice **e** is incorrect for a similar reason; to find the length of the hypotenuse, multiply one of the legs by $\sqrt{2}$, not by 2.

6. b. Begin by multiplying both sides by -4 to clear the fraction. Then gather the x terms on one side and the constants on the other, and simplify:

$$\frac{x}{-4} = -5 + x$$
$$x = -4(-5 + x)$$
$$x = 20 - 4x$$
$$5x = 20$$
$$x = 4$$

Choices **a** and **c** are incorrect due to arithmetic errors. To solve for x, divide both sides by the coefficient of x. You shouldn't subtract the coefficient, as was done in choice **d**.

7. a. Observe that $\sqrt{600} = \sqrt{10 \times 10 \times 6} = 10\sqrt{6}$. Choice **b** is incorrect because 6 and 10 should be switched. 60^2 does not equal 600, so $\sqrt{600}$ cannot equal 60 (choice **c**). In choice **d**, observe that $10\sqrt{60} = \sqrt{10 \times 10 \times 60} = \sqrt{6,000}$, not $\sqrt{600}$. Choice **e** is incorrect for a similar reason. Observe that $60\sqrt{10} = \sqrt{60 \times 60 \times 10} = \sqrt{36,000}$, not $\sqrt{600}$.

8. c. Of the five choices, millimeters is the smallest unit of measurement. There are more than 300 mm in 1 foot, so using millimeters to measure a fence of this size would give an extremely large figure that is too detailed for a general estimate. The next-smallest unit is inches, which would be an improvement over millimeters, since there are 12 inches to 1 foot, but of the options here, it is not the best unit of measurement. Miles and kilometers are not the best units to use for the opposite reason—they are too large to be useful to measure a fence that wraps around an acre of land. They'd produce a number that is too small. So, of the five choices, feet is the best option.

9. 12 inches. Constant functions such as $f(x)$ assign the same output for every input. Here, the value that the function $f(x)$ assigns to all real numbers x is 12.

10. b and c. Each dot represents 10 awardees and there are 26 dots, so 260 scholarships were awarded during the years shown (choice **b**). The year 2011 is in the middle of the dot plot. The dots on either side of that year would have to be the same in order for the dot plot to be symmetrical (choice **c**). But they're not. Choice **a** is incorrect because the number decreased during the first four years but then increased for three years. The number of scholarships in choice **d** is the *least* number of scholarships awarded annually. The average number of scholarships awarded annually for this period is $\frac{50+50+40+20+30+30+40}{7} = \frac{260}{7}$, which is approximately 37 (choice **e**).

11. a. You can use a proportion to find the price per ounce. For choice **a**, that would mean:
$$\frac{24 \text{ ounces}}{\$1.72} = \frac{1 \text{ ounce}}{x}$$
$$x = \frac{\$1.72}{24} \approx \$0.071 \text{ per ounce}$$
As you can see, the only arithmetic done here is dividing the price by the number of ounces. Since this is a simple procedure, you can skip setting up proportions for the rest of the choices and simply do the same division for each answer as a shortcut. Doing so yields \$0.075 per ounce for choice **b**, \$0.078 per ounce for choice **c**, \$0.091 per ounce for choice **d**, and \$0.125 per ounce for choice **e**. Since the cost per ounce is the smallest for choice **a**, that is the best buy.

12. d. There are 20 T-shirts on the shelf, and 13 of them are not purple. Because the shirt is selected at random, all T-shirts are equally likely to be chosen. So the probability that the shirt will not be purple is $\frac{13}{20}$.

13. 6.87 inches. This question requires a proportion to answer it. If x represents the length of the model, then:

$$\frac{0.6 \text{ inch}}{7.9 \text{ feet}} = \frac{x \text{ inches}}{90.4 \text{ feet}}$$

Cross multiplying yields $7.9x = 54.24$, which means that $x \approx 6.87$ inches.

14. b and c. The points rise from left to right, which shows a positive trend. Even though they do so along a curve, the points in choice **c** rise from left to right, which shows a positive trend. The points in choice **a** fall from left to right, which suggests a negative trend. The points in choice **d** take the shape, more or less, of a horizontal line. This does not show a positive—or negative—trend. Choice **e** does not show any trend at all.

15. b. $1.1 \times 0.1 = 0.11$, which is not a whole number. Choice **a** is an incorrect selection because this difference yields a whole number:

$$5\frac{2}{3} - \frac{28}{6} = \frac{17}{3} - \frac{28}{6}$$
$$= \frac{34}{6} - \frac{28}{6}$$
$$= \frac{34 - 28}{6}$$
$$= 1$$

The quotient in choice **c** also yields a whole number:

$$1\frac{7}{8} \div \frac{3}{8} = \frac{15}{8} \div \frac{3}{8} = \frac{15}{8} \times \frac{8}{3} = 5$$

Choice **d** is an incorrect selection because $10 \times 0.5 = 8$, which is a whole number. The phrase *200% of $\frac{3}{2}$* (choice **e**) is equivalent to $2.00 \times \frac{3}{2}$, which equals 3, a whole number.

16. c. To compute $6s(x) - \frac{1}{5}r(x)$, first distribute 6 through each term of $s(x)$ and distribute the $-\frac{1}{5}$ through each term of $r(x)$, and then add like terms:

$$6s(x) - \frac{1}{5}r(x) = 6(\frac{3}{2} - 2x^2 + \frac{1}{3}x^4) - \frac{1}{5}(5x^2 - 10x^4)$$
$$= (9 - 12x^2 + 2x^4) - (x^2 - 2x^4)$$
$$= 9 - 12x^2 + 2x^4 - x^2 + 2x^4$$
$$= 4x^4 - 13x^2 + 9$$

Choice **a** is incorrect because you used a coefficient of $\frac{1}{5}$ instead of $-\frac{1}{5}$ for $r(x)$, so you added the polynomials instead of subtracting them. In choice **b** you multiplied the first terms for $r(x)$ and $s(x)$ only by their respective coefficients. You must distribute the coefficient through all terms of these polynomial expressions. Choice **d** is incorrect because you applied the -1 only to the first term of $r(x)$ in the sense that you incorrectly computed $-\frac{1}{5}(5x^2 - 10x^4)$ as $-x^2 - 2x^4$. You must distribute it to all terms. In choice **e** you subtracted the polynomials in the wrong order; this should be multiplied by -1.

17. d. The method of substitution can be efficiently applied here by solving the second equation for y. Doing so yields $y = 6 + x$. Then substitute this expression for y into the first equation, and solve for x:

$$-x + 3(6 + x) = -4$$
$$2x + 18 = -4$$
$$2x = -22$$
$$x = -11$$

Substitute this value into the expression that is solved for y: $y = 6 - 11 = -5$. So, the solution is $x = -11$, $y = -5$. Choice **a** satisfies the second equation but not the first, choice **b** satisfies neither equation of the system, and choice **c** satisfies the first equation but not the second.

18. d. The area of the entire circle is $\pi \cdot 2^2 = 4\pi$ square inches. Angle *PQR* is a right angle, so the unshaded portion represents $\frac{1}{4}$ of the entire circle. This means that the shaded portion represents $\frac{3}{4}$ of the circle. So, the area of the shaded portion is $\frac{3}{4} \cdot 4\pi = 3\pi$ square inches. Choice **a** indicates that you forgot to square the radius when computing the area of the circle. You forgot to multiply by π in choice **b**. Remember, the area of a circle of radius *r* is πr^2. Choice **c** is the area of the *unshaded* portion, and choice **e** is the area of the entire circle.

19. c. To compute the expected value of such a random variable, multiply *x* times $P(X = x)$ and add all of them. Doing so yields:
$(-2)(\frac{1}{8}) + (-1)(\frac{1}{8}) + 0(\frac{1}{8}) + 1(\frac{1}{8}) + 2(\frac{1}{2}) = \frac{3}{4}$
Choice **a** shows the minimum value of the data set, not the expected value. In choice **b** you added the *x*-values but did not multiply each one by $P(X = x)$. Meanwhile in choice **d**, you added the probabilities, which must add to 1, but you must multiply each one by its respective value of *x*. Even though the value of *x* in choice **e** has the highest probability associated with it, the expected value is not this value. Rather, you must multiply each value of *X* by its probability of occurring and add those values to find the expected value.

20. $\frac{27}{40}$. Henry spends $\frac{4}{9}$ of his reading time with comic books, so he must spend $\frac{5}{9}$ of that time reading material other than comic books. To determine the fraction of his weekly free time spent reading material other than comic books, divide $\frac{3}{8}$ by $\frac{5}{9}$:
$$\frac{3}{8} \div \frac{5}{9} = \frac{3}{8} \times \frac{9}{5} = \frac{27}{40}$$

21. d. The equation of the parabola is given to be $y = 1 - x^2$. The slope of the graphed line is 2 and the *y*-intercept is 0, so that its equation is $y = 2x$. If we equate these equations, we get the equation $1 - x^2 = 2x$. The solutions of this equation would yield the *x*-coordinates of the points of intersection of the two graphs shown. Taking all terms to the right side yields the equivalent equation $x^2 + 2x - 1 = 0$. The left side of the equation in choice **a** is fine, but the right side is not correct because the equation of the line is not $y = x$. The $-2x$ is fine (choice **b**), but the x^2 term is not correct because the equation of the graphed parabola is $y = 1 - x^2$. So, $1 - x^2$ should replace $1 - x^2$. Neither term of the equation in choice **c** is correct. The equations of the shown graphs are $y = 1 - x^2$ and $y = 2x$. Equate these to get the desired equation. Choice **e** is incorrect because the solutions of this equation give the *x*-intercepts of the parabola, not the intersection points of the two graphs.

22. e. Looking at nearby third powers of integers, note that $53 = 125 < 200 < 216 = 63$. So, taking the cube root throughout this inequality yields $5 = \sqrt[3]{125} < \sqrt[3]{200} < \sqrt[3]{216} = 6$. Note that in choice **a**, $2^3 = 8 < x^3 < 64 = 4^3$. Since 200 does not lie between 8 and 64, it follows that $\sqrt[3]{200}$ cannot lie between 2 and 4. Note that $33 = 27 < x^3 < 125 = 5^3$. Since 200 does not lie between 27 and 125, it follows that $\sqrt[3]{200}$ cannot lie between 3 and 5 (choice **b**). Choice **c** is incorrect because $6^3 = 216 < x^3 < 274.625 = 6.53$. Since 200 does not lie between 216 and 274.625, it follows that $\sqrt[3]{200}$ cannot lie between 6 and 6.5. In choice **d**, $4.53 = 91.125 < x^3 < 166.375 = 5.53$. Since 200 does not lie between 91.125 and 166.375, it follows that $\sqrt[3]{200}$ cannot lie between 4.5 and 5.5.

23. d. Translate *WXYZ* so that *X* and *Z* line up with *X'* and *Z'*. Then draw the line passing through vertices *X* and *Z*, and reflect *WXYZ* across this line. The result will be *W'X'Y'Z'*. If you rotate (choice **a**) the figure *WXYZ* by any angle other than 360°, all four vertices move. Specifically, *X* and *Z* do not remain where they are once the transformation is performed. If you do not first translate *WXYZ*, a single reflection (choice **b**) cannot produce the given image. You must first translate *WXYZ* so that *X* and *Z* line up with *X'* and *Z'*. Then, draw the line passing through vertices *X* and *Z*, and reflect *WXYZ* across this line. Then, the result will be image *W'X'Y'Z'*. If you move the figure by any distance (choice **c**), all four vertices move and keep the same orientation. In the image shown, *X* and *Z* have the same orientation, but *Y* and *W* do not. Beginning with a translation is correct, but then it must be followed with a reflection (choice **d**), not a rotation (choice **e**).

24. d. Use the distributive property and multiply all terms in the parentheses:

$$-3x(x^2 - 3x - 2) = (-3x)(x^2) + (-3x)(-3x) + (-3x)(-2)$$
$$= -3x^3 + 9x^2 + 6x$$

In choice **a** you multiplied only the first term in the parentheses by $-3x$. You must distribute this to *every* term. Choice **b** is incorrect because you added the term outside the parentheses to the quantity enclosed within them, but you should have multiplied by it. You did not distribute the negative through the terms in the parentheses in choice **c**. In choice **e** you distributed only the -3 through the terms in the parentheses. You must also multiply by *x*.

25. **(–2,–4).** You need to translate the given point 4 units to the left and 1 unit down. So $(2,-3)$ would correspond to $(2 - 4, -3 - 1) = (-2,-4)$.

26. d. Quadrilaterals *R*, *S*, and *U* are all parallelograms, while *T* and *V* are not. Because a figure is being selected at random, the probability that it is a parallelogram is $\frac{3}{5}$. Choice **a** implies that none of the figures are parallelograms. Choices **b**, **c**, and **e** are incorrect because of the 5 figures, 3 are parallelograms, so there is a 3 in 5 chance of selecting a parallelogram. Additionally, choice **e** implies that all members of the set are parallelograms.

27. e. The ramp is made of five sides. The two triangular sides are congruent and each has an area of $\frac{1}{2}(6 \text{ ft.})(8 \text{ ft.}) = 24 \text{ ft.}^2$; so, their combined area is 48 ft.² The bottom of the ramp has an area of $(8 \text{ ft.})(20 \text{ ft.}) = 160 \text{ ft.}^2$. The front slanted side is a rectangle. Using the Pythagorean theorem, the hypotenuse of the right triangle is 10 ft., so the area of this rectangle is $(10 \text{ ft.})(20 \text{ ft.}) = 200 \text{ ft.}^2$. The back of the ramp is a rectangle with area $(6 \text{ ft.})(20 \text{ ft.}) = 120 \text{ ft.}^2$. Therefore, the total surface area is $(48 + 160 + 200 + 120) \text{ ft.}^2$ $= 528 \text{ ft.}^2$.

28. c and d. Note that zero is a rational number. So, for any irrational number *y*, $0 \times y = 0$, which is rational (choice **c**). Adding a rational number, which has a terminating or repeating decimal representation, to an irrational number cannot produce a decimal that is terminating or repeating (choice **d**). Choice **a** is not true because being a negative number does not affect a number's classification as rational or irrational. Because the set of rational numbers is closed under subtraction, choice **b** is also not true. Choice **e** is not true: the product of two irrational numbers may be a rational number, such as in $\sqrt{2} \times \sqrt{2} = 2$.

29. c. We must express profit as a function of the number of driveways cleared of snow. The $903 spent on materials yields <u>negative profit</u>, so we express it as –903 in our function. Next, since we earn $40 per driveway and it costs $5.25 per job, our net gain per job is $40 – $5.25 = $34.75. This is constant, so the profit gained from clearing x driveways is $34.75x$. This means that the function describing our profit is $P(x) = 34.75x - 903$. Computing the break-even point is an inverse problem. We know the output (the profit), but need to determine the input (the number of driveways cleared) that will yield it. This means we must solve the equation $0 = 34.75x - 903$. We do so as follows:

$$0 = 34.75x - 903$$
$$903 = 34.75x$$
$$x \approx 25.986$$

Rounding up, you see that you'll break even after clearing 26 driveways.

30. 59 laps. Since there are 5,280 feet in 1 mile, there are $5,280 \times 2.2 = 11,616$ feet in 2.2 miles. Now, to determine the number of laps needed to swim 11,616 feet, divide: $\frac{11,616}{200} = 58.08 \approx$ 59 laps.

31. d. Looking at the graph, you see that the parabola opens downward, and its vertex is (–2,3). Also, $f(-3) = f(-1) = 0$. If you graph the equation in choice **d**, you'd get a parabola with these characteristics. The equation in choice **a** would produce a parabola with a vertex of (2,3), but the parabola in the image has a vertex of (–2,3). The coefficient of x^2 in choice **b** is positive, so if you graphed the equation, you'd get a parabola that opens upward. The equation in choice **c** would produce a parabola with a vertex of (2,–3), but the parabola in the image has a vertex of (–2,3). The equation in choice **e** would produce a parabola with a vertex of (–3,2), but the parabola in the image has a vertex of (–2,3).

32. c. Multiply the square footage and the population density together to find the answer: $45,000 \times 0.03 = 1,350$ people. The answer in choice **a** is based on a population density of 0.003, not 0.03. In choice **b** it looks as if you divided the square footage by 100, which would correspond to a population density of 0.01, not 0.03. Choice **d** is the square footage divided by 10, which would correspond to a population density of 0.1, not 0.03. Choice **e** shows that there would be 1 person for every square foot (which would be very crowded!). Zelda prefers a maximum density of 0.03 people per square foot.

33. a. This correlation coefficient suggests a strong negative trend, which is what is illustrated in the scatterplot. Choice **b** describes a weak negative trend, and choice **c** describes a scatterplot with almost no trend. Choice **d** describes a scatterplot where the data rises from left to right, showing a weak positive trend, and choice **e** describes a strong positive trend.

34. 16,514,690 births. Let x represent the total number of births expected, and then set up the following proportion:

$$\frac{12.17}{1,000} = \frac{x}{1,357,000,000}$$

Solving for x yields:

$$(12.17)(1,357,000,000) = 1,000x$$
$$\frac{(12.17)(1,357,000,000)}{1,000} = x$$
$$16,514,690 = x$$

35. b and c. The graph in choice **b** is the graph of $g(x) = |x|$ shifted 4 units left and 5 units up. The graph in choice **c** is the graph of $g(x) = |x|$ shifted 4 units left and 7 units up. Choice **a** is incorrect because the graph is shifted 4 units to the right, while choices **d** and **e** are incorrect because the graph is shifted 8 units and 6 units down, respectively.

36. c. If the area of one square is 9 square units, then each side has length $\sqrt{9} = 3$ units. Using how the rectangle is subdivided into squares as shown, we multiply 3 by 2 to get 6 units as the height of the rectangle, and then multiply 3 by 3 to get 9 units as the length of the rectangle. The perimeter is $2(6) + 2(9) = 30$ units. In choice **a** you did not count both sides twice when calculating the perimeter of the rectangle. Choices **b** and **d** are incorrect because you mistakenly assumed that the rectangle was itself a square by assuming all four sides had the same length. Choice **e** is incorrect because you multiplied the perimeter of one square by the number of squares: 12×6. This answer is incorrect because it mistakenly includes the segments that are inside the rectangle.

37. c. Observe that $\sqrt{(38 + 11)(60 - 11)} = \sqrt{49 \times 49} = 49$. Choice **a** represents the square root of only one factor of the product under the radical sign. Choice **b** is incorrect because you added the square roots of the two individual factors rather than multiplying them. In choice **d** you found the square root of one of the factors, but not the other, before multiplying the results. Choice **e** is incorrect because you forgot to take the square root.

38. a. When all the data points are the same, the mean is the same as that data value, and the variance (average distance from the mean) is 0. In II, the mean is not 44 because you must divide the sum by the number of data points, which is 5. The variance is not 0 because all of the points are measurable distances from the mean. The only time the variance can be 0 is if all the data points are equal to the mean. In III, the mean is 44, but the variance is not 0 because all of the points are measurable distances from the mean.

39. b. The data can be displayed along the number line using a dot plot as follows:

Observe that the data set is bimodal with nothing occurring in between those two clusters. This is the general shape described by this distribution.

40. a and b. The equation $ax + 3y = 0$ is equivalent to $y = -\frac{a}{3}x$. The slope of this line is $-\frac{a}{3}$ and, since $a > 0$, the slope is negative. The lines in choices **a** and **b** have a negative slope since they fall from left to right. Choice **c** is incorrect because the line is vertical; such lines have no slope. Choices **d** and **e** are incorrect because the lines rise from left to right and so have a positive slope.

41. d. Rewrite the left side as a multiplication problem and simplify. Then, cross multiply and solve the resulting equation for a, as follows:

$$\frac{3}{4} \div \frac{a}{a+1} = \frac{4}{3}$$
$$\frac{3}{4} \times \frac{a+1}{a} = \frac{4}{3}$$
$$\frac{3a+3}{4a} = \frac{4}{3}$$
$$9a + 9 = 16a$$
$$9 = 7a$$
$$a = \frac{9}{7}$$

Finally, square this fraction by squaring the top and bottom separately to get $a^2 = \frac{81}{49}$.

42. b, c, and d. All members of the set are of the form $8n$, for some whole number n. Thus, each one is divisible by 4 (choice **b**). Choice **a** is incorrect because none of the members of this set is prime, since they are all multiples of the composite number 8. Choice **c** is a true statement because all members of this set are even. Choice **d** is a true statement because all members of the set are of the form $8n$, for some whole number n. This is precisely what it means to be a multiple of 8. In choice **e** you are confusing the term *factor* with *multiple*. In order for the members of this set to be factors of 8, they must all divide *into* 8 evenly. The only one for which this is true is 8 itself because all of the other members are larger than 8.

43. b. When reflecting a point across the line $x = 2$, the y-coordinate will stay the same, but the x-coordinate will change. Subtract $2 - (-11) = 13$ and *add* this to 2 to get the new x-coordinate. So, the image of vertex B is $(15,14)$. Choice **a** shows the image across the line $y = 2$, not $x = 2$. Choice **c** is incorrect because it shows the image across the line $y = x$. The x-coordinate is correct in choice **d**, but the y-coordinate should not change when reflecting across the line $x = 2$. Choice **e** is incorrect because this is the image across the origin (which means reflection about the y-axis, and then the x-axis).

44. d and e. Rewriting the fractions in the numerator of the complex fraction with the common denominator x and then combining them yields this form (choice **d**):

$$\frac{\frac{2}{x} - 4x}{\frac{1}{x}} = \frac{\frac{2}{x} - \frac{4x^2}{x}}{\frac{1}{x}} = \frac{\frac{2 - 4x^2}{x}}{\frac{1}{x}}$$

In choice **e**, rewrite the fractions in the numerator of the complex fraction with the common denominator x, and combine them. Then cancel by a factor of $\frac{1}{x}$:

$$\frac{\frac{2}{x} - 4x}{\frac{1}{x}} = \frac{\frac{2}{x} - \frac{4x^2}{x}}{\frac{1}{x}} = \frac{\frac{2 - 4x^2}{x}}{\frac{1}{x}} = \frac{2 - 4x^2}{\not{x}} \cdot \frac{\not{x}}{1} = 2 - 4x^2$$

Choice **a** is not equivalent because you cannot cancel the term $\frac{1}{x}$ in the numerator and denominator. You can only cancel like factors. Neither choices **b** nor **c** are equivalent: choice **b** is the reciprocal of the final simplified form and choice **c** needs to be multiplied by -1 in order for it to be equal to the given complex fraction.

45. b. Solve for t, as follows:

$$5\ln(t + 4) = 5$$
$$\ln(t + 4) = 1$$
$$t + 4 = e$$
$$t = e - 4$$

Choice **a** cannot be the solution, because $\ln(0)$ is not defined. Choice **c** is incorrect because you ignored "5 ln" and solved the linear equation $t + 4 = 5$. In the process of solving the logarithmic equation, you did not solve the equation $e = t + 4$ correctly; you should have subtracted 4, not divided by 4 (choice **d**). Choice **e** is incorrect because in the process of solving the logarithmic equation, you did not solve the equation $e = t + 4$ correctly; you should have subtracted 4, not multiplied by 4.

46. c. The height is 2(20 in.) = 40 in. and the radius is $\frac{1}{2}$(20 in.) = 10 in. So, the volume of the cone is $V = \frac{1}{3}\pi r^2 h = \frac{1}{3}\pi(10 \text{ in.})^2(40 \text{ in.})$ $= \frac{4{,}000\pi}{3}$ in.^{3}. Choice **a** is incorrect because you need to multiply by $\frac{1}{3}$. In choice **b** you forgot to square the radius; in choice **d** the diameter was used in place of the radius; and in choice **e** the answer given is the circumference of the base.

47. e. The phrase *Meredith handles fewer than* is translated symbolically into "M <"; the phrase *one-third of the customers* translates to "$\frac{1}{3}$"; and the phrase *Chris and Dana combined* translates to "C + D." So, the correct relationship is M < $\frac{1}{3}$(C + D). Multiplying both sides by 3 yields the equivalent inequality C + D > 3M. Choice **a** is incorrect because the $\frac{1}{3}$ should be replaced by 3. The inequality in choice **b** does not make sense because "3" has no contextual meaning here. The inequality in choice **c** means that Meredith handles more than three times the total customers handled by Chris and Dana in a typical hour. The product DC should be replaced by the sum C + D (choice **d**).

48. b. The length of the entire circle (or its circumference) is $2\pi \cdot 8 = 16\pi$ cm. The ratio of the length of arc *JL* to the circumference is $\frac{2\pi}{16\pi} = \frac{1}{8}$. Sector *JKL* accounts for $\frac{1}{8}$ of the circle. So, the central angle x should be $\frac{1}{8} \times 360° = 45°$.

49. b. Let *B* represent the body weight of this adult male. Since the quantities are in proportion, we have the following:
$$\frac{25{,}000 \text{ grams}}{m \text{ grams}} = \frac{75{,}000 \text{ grams}}{B \text{ grams}}$$
Solving for *B* yields
$$25{,}000B = 75{,}000m$$
$$B = \frac{75{,}000m}{25{,}000} = 3m$$

50. b. Observe that statement I is not correct because $\frac{1}{b}$ is not less than b if b equals 1. Next, II is correct because "$\frac{a+b}{2b}$ equals $\frac{2a}{b+a}$" is equivalent to $\frac{2b}{2b} = \frac{2b}{2b}$ when $a = b$. Also, III is incorrect because if b is greater than a, then the reverse inequality is true.

51. b. Simplify both sides of the equation, then gather the x terms on one side and the constants on the other, and then divide by the resulting coefficient of x:
$$-2(3x - 1) = 4[8 - (2x - 1)]$$
$$-6x + 2 = 4(8 - 2x + 1)$$
$$-6x + 2 = 4(9 - 2x)$$
$$-6x + 2 = 36 - 8x$$
$$2x = 34$$
$$x = 17$$
Choice **a** is incorrect because when simplifying the right side of the equation, you did not distribute the 4 through all terms in the brackets. Choice **c** is incorrect because in the final step the coefficient of x was subtracted from both sides, rather than divided. Similarly, choice **e** is incorrect because the coefficient of x was multiplied by both sides, rather than divided. Choice **d** is incorrect because the final step was omitted: both sides need to be divided by the coefficient of x, which is 2.

52. d. Statement I is not true because the mode is not $x - 4$, as this value occurs only once, just like every other value in this set. II is true, because when you order the values from least to greatest, the middle value is $x + 2$. III is true because the mean is the sum of the values divided by the number of values. Here the sum is $5x + 12 - 7 = 5x + 5$. The number of values is 5, so the mean is $x + 1$.

53. a, b, and e. The probability that a person who buys the game will download the additional content is $\frac{4,000}{500,000}$ (since 40% of the 10,000 eligible are expected to download the content) and the probability that they won't is $\frac{496,000}{500,000}$. Thus, the expected cost of the promotion is $(\frac{4,000}{500,000})(49.99) + (0)(\frac{496,000}{500,000}) \approx 0.40$ (choice **a**). The probability that a person who buys the game will download the additional content is $\frac{0.30(25,000)}{500,000} = 0.015$ (since 30% of the 25,000 eligible are expected to download the content) and the probability that they won't is 0.985. Thus, the expected cost of the promotion is $(0.015)(29.99) + (0)(0.985) \approx 0.45$ (choice **b**). Promotion X costs the company less per game than does Promotion Y. So, it is more profitable (choice **e**).

54. b. Let x represent Monday's low temperature. Then, Tuesday's low can be represented by $x + 11$, since we know that Tuesday's low was 11°F warmer than the low on Monday. Likewise, Wednesday's low temperature equals $x + 11 - 5 = x + 6$, since it was 5°F cooler than Tuesday's low temperature. Also, Thursday's low temperature can be represented by $x + 15$ since it was 9°F warmer than Wednesday's low temperature. Now, we must set up an equation to solve for x. Multiply the average low temperature by 4 since there are 4 days ($87 \times 4 = 348$) and set the sum of the expressions for the low temperatures for Monday through Thursday equal to 348. Doing so yields

$$x + (x + 11) + (x + 6) + (x + 15) = 348$$

This simplifies to $4x + 32 = 348$, so that solving yields $x = 79$. Finally, we substitute this in for x into the expression for Tuesday's temperature, $x + 11$, to see that Tuesday's low temperature was 90°F. Choice **a** is Thursday's low temperature. Choice **c** is Wednesday's low temperature. Choice **d** is Monday's low temperature. Choice **e** is too low and is likely the result of an arithmetic error.

55. b. Since 7 and 8 each divide evenly into w, we know that all products of factors of 8 and 7 must also divide evenly into w. Specifically, we know that w must be divisible by each of the following numbers:

$$2 \times 4 = 8$$
$$2 \times 7 = 14$$
$$4 \times 7 = 28$$
$$2 \times 4 \times 7 = 56$$

Note that choices **a**, **c**, **d**, and **e** are included in this list, whereas choice **b** is not. Consequently, we conclude that the answer is choice **b**.

56. b. Since the diameter of each circle is $6\sqrt{2}$, the radius is half this, or $3\sqrt{2}$. Each of the solid lines is the hypotenuse of a 45-45-90 triangle that has legs that are each $3\sqrt{2}$ long. Using the Pythagorean theorem with h being the length of the hypotenuse, we see that $2(3\sqrt{2})^2 = h^2$, which simplifies to $36 = h^2$, so that $h = 6$. Since there are four such triangles and they are all congruent, we can conclude that each of the four solid lines has this length, so the sum of the lengths is 24. Choice **a** is incorrect because the solid lines are not radii of the circle and therefore do not have a length equal to half the diameter. Choice **c** implies that the length of each solid line is $6\sqrt{2}$, which is not the case. Choice **d** is likely the result of an arithmetic error. The radical should not be part of the solution. Choice **e** is likely the result of forgetting to take the square root of 36 when using the Pythagorean theorem. The length of each solid line is 6 units, not 36 units.

6 ▶ PRAXIS® CORE ACADEMIC SKILLS FOR EDUCATORS: PRACTICE TEST 4

CHAPTER SUMMARY
Here is your final set of full-length tests for each Praxis® Core Academic Skills for Educators test: Reading, Writing, and Mathematics. Now that you have completed three total tests, take these exams to see how much your score has improved.

As you take this final set of practice tests, you should once again simulate the actual test-taking experience as closely as you can. Find a quiet place to work where you won't be disturbed. Follow the time constraints noted at the beginning of each test.

After you finish taking your tests, review the answer explanations. (Each individual test is followed by its own answer explanations.) See **A Note on Scoring** on page 375 to find information on how to score your test. Good luck!

Praxis® Core Academic Skills for Educators: Reading Practice Test 4

Time: 85 Minutes

Directions: Read the following passages and answer the questions that follow.

Refer to the following passage for questions 1 through 5.

Thirty years ago, the northern spotted owl was one of the most common owls in the Pacific Northwest. However, these owls live in old-growth forest, and much of their habitat has
5   been lost to logging and natural disasters. In 1991, the federal government passed laws to protect the land where the owls live. Now, though, the owls face a new threat—competition with the barred owl. Barred owls are larger
10   and more aggressive, and their activity results in the spotted owls leaving nesting and hunting grounds.

    Scientists have tried several ways to protect the endangered spotted owl. Some track
15   the owl nests as they monitor activity to determine when eggs hatch. Some scientists have even tried to reduce the population of barred owls. Environmental specialists are working hard to protect spotted owls, but more research
20   is needed. In addition to the myriad other dangers, the northern spotted owl is threatened by climate change and competition with other birds of prey. Given all of these significant hazards, scientists must do whatever they can to
25   save the northern spotted owl species.

1. Which is NOT stated or implied by the passage as a threat to the northern spotted owl?
  a. logging
  b. scientific research
  c. forest fires caused by lightning
  d. climate change
  e. barred owls in the environment

2. Which statement based on information from the passage represents a statement of opinion, rather than a statement of fact?
  a. Thirty years ago, the northern spotted owl was one of the most common owls in the Pacific Northwest.
  b. In 1991, the federal government passed laws to protect the land where the owls live.
  c. Barred owls are larger and more aggressive, and their activity results in the spotted owls moving away from nesting and hunting grounds.
  d. Activity is monitored to determine when eggs hatch.
  e. Given all these significant hazards, scientists must do whatever they can to save the northern spotted owl species.

3. What is the purpose of the phrase *Now, though* in lines 7–8 within the context of the passage?
  a. to contrast the author's opinion with the actual facts
  b. to reverse the decision that a species must be protected
  c. to question the reasonableness of a government bill
  d. to contrast an earlier protection with current threats
  e. to compare a variety of threats to an endangered species

4. Which sentence provides the best summary of the reading selection?
   a. The northern spotted owl suffers from a loss of habitat.
   b. The northern spotted owl faces severe threats and must be protected.
   c. Scientists are struggling to identify ways to protect the northern spotted owl.
   d. The northern spotted owl was once common in the Pacific Northwest.
   e. The northern spotted owl is an endangered species.

5. Which detail from the reading selection provides the least support for the main idea?
   a. However, these owls live in old-growth forest, and much of their habitat has been lost to logging and natural disasters.
   b. Now, though, the owls face a new threat—competition with the barred owl.
   c. Barred owls are larger and more aggressive, and their activity results in spotted owls leaving nesting and hunting grounds.
   d. Owl nests are monitored to determine when eggs hatch.
   e. In addition to the myriad other dangers, the northern spotted owl is also threatened by climate change and competition with other birds of prey.

Refer to the following passage for questions 6 through 8.

In recent years, it is clear that the local minor league baseball team, the Dowshire Ducks, has truly become standard weekend entertainment for hundreds of families. On summer after-
5 noons, the bleachers in Hulldown Stadium are teeming with cheering fans. But this hasn't always been the case. Even ten years ago, ticket sales were limited, and the team was largely ignored. The Ducks rarely won games or placed

10 well in regional tournaments. The arrival of manager Duncan Brin in 2004, however, started a new era of success and fame for the Ducks.

6. Which sentence best states the main idea of the passage?
   a. The Dowshire Ducks were once an unsuccessful baseball team.
   b. Throughout the years, there have been many managers of the Dowshire Ducks.
   c. The Dowshire Ducks play their games in Hulldown Stadium.
   d. Due to the work of Duncan Brin, the status of the Dowshire Ducks has risen.
   e. Attending a Dowshire Ducks game is popular family entertainment.

7. Which best describes the organizational structure of the passage?
   a. Details are provided through contrasts, and then a main idea is provided.
   b. A main idea is provided, and then supporting details are listed.
   c. A handful of comparisons are given, and then several dissimilarities are provided.
   d. Definitions are provided for several unknown terms, and then a main idea is stated.
   e. A problem is posed, and then potential solutions are discussed.

8. The word *teeming* in line 6 could be replaced with which of the following words to result in the least change in meaning of the sentence?
   a. crowded
   b. rooting
   c. energized
   d. vacant
   e. teaming

Refer to the following graph for questions 9 through 11.

This graph provides data regarding purchases made by three students during the month of July.

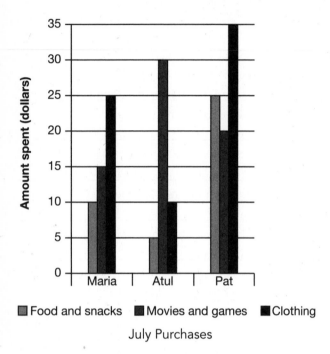

Purchases of Three Students in July

July Purchases

Food and snacks Movies and games Clothing

9. Based on information in the graph, which inference could reasonably be drawn?
   a. Pat will spend more on clothing in August than María or Atul will.
   b. Of the three students whose expenditures are detailed in the graph, it is clear that Atul is saving the most money for large purchases.
   c. María spent the same amount on clothing as she spent on movies and games during July.
   d. Atul's parents cook his meals and prepare snacks for him.
   e. Of the three students whose expenditures are detailed in the graph, Atul spent the most on movies and games during the month of July

10. During July, who spent the greatest total amount for the three types of expenditures identified in the graph?
   a. María
   b. Atul
   c. Pat
   d. María and Pat tied for the greatest amount spent.
   e. Pat and Atul tied for the greatest amount spent.

11. Which statement(s) about expenditures is/are supported by data in the bar graph? Choose all that apply.
   a. Clothing prices were higher during July than during other months of the year.
   b. María and Atul shopped together during the month of July.
   c. There were more sales on food and snacks during July than during other months of the year.
   d. Atul spent the same amount for the combination of food and snacks, movies and games, and clothing as María spent for movies and games only.
   e. Pat spent as much for the combination of food and snacks and movies and games as Atul spent for clothing only.

Refer to the following passage for questions 12 and 13.

Laughter is always the laughter of a group. It may, perchance, have happened to you, when seated in a railway carriage, to hear travelers relating to one another's stories, which must
5   have been comic to them, for they laughed rapturously. Had you been one of their company, you would have laughed like them, but, as you were not, you had no desire whatsoever to do so. However spontaneous it seems, laughter
10   always implies a kind of complicity with other laughers, real or imaginary. How often has it been said that the fuller the theater, the more uncontrolled the laughter of the audience! On the other hand, how often has the remark been
15   made that many comic effects are incapable of translation from one language to another, because they refer to the customs and ideas of a particular social group!

12. The anecdote about the travelers in the railway carriage supports the author's main argument, as stated in the first sentence of the passage. Which most clearly states how this support occurs?
  a. The anecdote demonstrates through personal experience that laughter is an isolated phenomenon.
  b. The anecdote illustrates how the specific customs and ideas of a person's society dictate what is and what is not funny.
  c. The anecdote accentuates that an individual who is not part of an intended audience might lack a necessary connection to find humor in a situation.
  d. The anecdote shows the significant impact of railway travel on a humorous situation.
  e. The anecdote demonstrates that laughter is an inexplicably spontaneous event.

13. In the context of the passage, the word *rapturously* in line 6 could be replaced with which of the following words to have the least impact on the meaning of the sentence?
  a. enthusiastically
  b. painfully
  c. morosely
  d. awkwardly
  e. ridiculously

Refer to the following passage for questions 14 through 20.

Mounting conflict between the colonies and England during the 1760s and 1770s reinforced growing conviction that Americans should be less dependent on England for manufacturing.
5   Manufacture of homespun cloth was encouraged as a substitute for English imports. But manufacturing of cloth outside the household was associated with relief for the poor. Houses of Industry employed poor families at spinning
10   for their daily bread.

     Such practices made many pre-Revolutionary Americans dubious about manufacturing. After independence, many unsuccessful attempts to establish textile
15   factories occurred. Americans needed access to British industrial innovations, but England had passed laws forbidding export of machinery or emigration of those who could operate it. Nevertheless, an English immigrant, Samuel Slater,
20   introduced British cotton technology to America.

     Slater had worked his way up from apprentice to overseer in England. Drawn by American bounties for introduction of textile
25   technology, he passed as a farmer and sailed for America after memorizing details of a revolutionary cloth-making machine. In 1790, he started the first permanent American cotton-spinning mill. Employing a workforce of young

30   children, Slater successfully mechanized crucial
     processes.

         A generation of workers trained under
     Slater. Thus began the rapid proliferation of
     textile mills during the early nineteenth cen-
35   tury. From the trained workforce in Slater's first
     mill, the industry spread across New England.
     For two decades, before mills modeled on Fran-
     cis Cabot Lowell's factory system offered com-
     petition, the "Rhode Island System" of small,
40   rural spinning mills set the tone for early
     industrialization.

14. The primary purpose of the passage is to
   a. account for the decline of rural America.
   b. contrast political views held by the British
   and the Americans.
   c. summarize British laws forbidding the
   export of industrial machinery.
   d. describe the introduction of textile mills to
   New England.
   e. provide a cogent argument in support of
   industrial development.

15. The passage refers to the work of Houses of
   Industry to illustrate
   a. an early successful program to support
   international travel.
   b. the perception of cloth production outside
   the home as a social welfare measure.
   c. the preference for the work of individual
   artisans over that of spinning machines.
   d. the first textile factory to be established
   within the United States.
   e. the utilization of technological advances
   being made in England at the time.

16. Based on the passage, it can reasonably be
   inferred that early American manufacturing
   was
   a. entirely beneficial.
   b. politically and economically necessary.
   c. symbolically undemocratic.
   d. environmentally destructive.
   e. spiritually corrosive.

17. The explanation of Slater's immigration to the
   American colonies best helps to support the
   author's claims in the passage by
   a. demonstrating Slater's craftiness in evading
   British export laws.
   b. showing the attraction of farming
   opportunities in the American colonies.
   c. explaining the details of British
   manufacturing technologies.
   d. illustrating American efforts to block
   immigration to the colonies.
   e. describing the willingness of British factories
   to share knowledge with the colonies.

18. The passage infers that Slater viewed child
   labor as
   a. available workforce.
   b. necessary evil.
   c. unpleasant reality.
   d. established institution.
   e. outdated.

19. The author implies that the catalyst behind the
   spread of American textile mills during the
   early 1800s was
   a. Slater's voyage on a ship to America.
   b. the decline in the ideal of the self-sufficient
   American farm family.
   c. the expertise of the workforce trained in
   Slater's prototype mill.
   d. an increased willingness to support families.
   e. the support of British manufacturers who
   owned stock in American mills.

20. The word *modeled* in line 37 most closely means
   a. posed.
   b. displayed.
   c. arranged.
   d. illustrated.
   e. fashioned.

Refer to the following passage for question 21.

Despite an innocuous appearance that brings to mind an oversized pig or water-dwelling cow, the hippopotamus is capable of great viciousness. Short legs and hefty bodies (on average, adults weigh in the neighborhood of 3,000 lbs.) do not slow the hippo, which can run up to 19 miles per hour in short spurts. That weight, coupled with tusks that may measure more than a foot long and a generally aggressive attitude, makes for an unexpected danger. People would be wise to steer clear of the beasts, and though young hippos might fall prey to the lions, crocodiles, and hyenas with which they share their habitat, full-grown hippos are more likely to be the aggressors in confrontations with such notoriously deadly animals.

21. Which description of a hippopotamus best represents a statement of opinion rather than a fact?
   a. It looks like an oversized pig or water-dwelling cow.
   b. It is often aggressive to lions, hyenas, and crocodiles.
   c. It can weigh in the neighborhood of 3,000 lbs.
   d. It is capable of running 19 miles per hour in short spurts.
   e. It has tusks that may measure more than a foot long.

Refer to the following passage for questions 22 through 24.

Wilma Rudolph, a child who contracted polio and went on to become an Olympic running champion, is an inspiration for us all. Born prematurely in 1940, Wilma spent her childhood
5   battling illness, including measles, scarlet fever, chicken pox, pneumonia, and polio, a disease for which there was no cure at the time. At the age of four, Rudolph was told she would never walk again. But Rudolph and her family refused
10   to give up. After years of special treatment and physical therapy, 12-year-old Rudolph was able to walk normally again. But walking wasn't enough for her; she was determined to be an athlete. Little time passed before her talent
15   earned her a spot in the 1956 Olympics, where she won a bronze medal. In the 1960 Olympics, the zenith of her career, she won three gold medals.

22. Which statement provides the best summary of the main idea of the reading selection?
   a. Rudolph had a great desire to become an athlete, despite challenges she faced.
   b. Rudolph was an Olympic champion who won a bronze medal and three gold medals.
   c. Rudolph overcame extreme difficulty to rise to great accomplishment.
   d. Chicken pox, pneumonia, and polio are very serious diseases contracted by Rudolph.
   e. Many inspirations, such as Rudolph, exist in the annals of history.

23. Which of the following is most analogous to the life of Wilma Rudolph?

a. After contracting what was believed to be polio at age 39, President Franklin Roosevelt suffered partial paralysis and was forced to spend much of the rest of his life in braces or in a wheelchair.

b. Diagnosed with the degenerative nervous system disorder Parkinson's disease in 1991, actor Michael J. Fox took a break from full-time acting in 2000.

c. Following his fall from a horse in 1995, actor Christopher Reeve was confined to a wheelchair until his death in 2004.

d. Nicknamed the "Iron Horse" for his durability, New York Yankee Lou Gehrig retired at age 36 due to advanced amyotrophic lateral sclerosis (ALS).

e. Although he suffered from severe asthma as a child, Theodore Roosevelt became a U.S. president and an avid outdoorsman.

24. What is the meaning of *zenith* as it is used in line 17 of the passage?

a. peak

b. nadir

c. conclusion

d. epilogue

e. midpoint

Refer to the following passage for questions 25 and 26.

For many students juggling a heavy scholarly workload and numerous extracurricular activities, school is tough enough without worrying about what to wear and how to look cool every
5 day. Much of the clothing students choose to wear to school of their own accord, such as stylized jeans or tee-shirts that promote personal beliefs or favorite musical artists, can be a distraction within the classroom's walls. Further-
10 more, allowing students the freedom to select their own attire presents an outward inequality; students who have the financial resources to buy designer-labeled clothing will frequently do so, resulting in a flaunting of financial disparity
15 among students.

25. Which adjective best describes the author's attitude toward an enforced student dress code?

a. resistant

b. cautious

c. ambivalent

d. concerned

e. sympathetic

26. Which statement, if it were true, would most significantly weaken the author's main argument?

a. An education study recently demonstrated that dress codes enhance students' ability to learn.

b. A school that employs a stringent dress code provides a safer educational environment.

c. Restricting students' right to choose their clothing limits their independence and creativity.

d. Tolerance across social groups is improved through use of a formal dress code.

e. Schools frequently differ as to the style and color of a mandatory school uniform.

Refer to the following passage for questions 27 through 29.

In the long history of soccer, no single player has changed the game as much as Pelé. Born Edison Arantes do Nascimento in Brazil in 1940, Pelé played professional soccer for 20
5   years, including in four World Cups for his native Brazil. Toward the end of his career, he also played for a North American soccer league. Though he was well past his prime, Pelé helped to significantly increase American interest in
10   soccer. Counting his time in the American league, Pelé scored a total of 1,281 goals—the largest number of goals scored by any professional soccer player. Pelé's athletic skills were some of the most impressive in history. He was
15   awarded the title "Athlete of the Century" by the International Olympic Committee. By the time he retired, no one had helped increase the popularity of soccer more.

27. Which statement from the passage represents a statement of opinion, rather than a statement of fact?
   a. In the long history of soccer, no single player has changed the game as much as Pelé.
   b. Born Edison Arantes do Nascimento in Brazil in 1940, Pelé played professional soccer for 20 years, including in four World Cups for his native Brazil.
   c. Toward the end of his career, he also played for a North American soccer league.
   d. Counting his time in the American league, Pelé scored a total of 1,281 goals—the largest number of goals scored by any professional soccer player.
   e. He was awarded the title "Athlete of the Century" by the International Olympic Committee.

28. Which detail from the passage least supports the main idea?
   a. Pelé was born Edison Arantes do Nascimento in Brazil in 1940.
   b. Pelé played professional soccer for 20 years, including in four World Cup competitions.
   c. Pelé helped significantly to increase American interest in soccer.
   d. Pelé scored a total of 1,281 goals.
   e. Pelé earned the title "Athlete of the Century."

29. Based on information provided in the passage, which of these athletes is most similar to Pelé?
   a. Cristiano Ronaldo, a Portuguese soccer player who is the highest-paid soccer player in history
   b. Dilma Rousseff, the 36th president of Brazil and the first woman to hold the country's highest office
   c. Babe Ruth, who helped make baseball the most popular sport in America by breaking home-run records
   d. Charles Haley, who was a member of five Super Bowl–winning football teams from 1986 through 1999
   e. Landon Donovan, who scored multiple goals in the 2010 World Cup for the American soccer team

Refer to the following passage for questions 30 through 36.

Gray wolves once roamed the U.S. Yellowstone area but were gradually displaced by human development and hunting by farmers and ranchers who were trying to protect livestock.

5　By the 1920s, wolves had practically disappeared from the area, migrating north, into Canadian forests.

Disappearance of wolves had many consequences. Deer and elk populations—major

10　food sources for wolves—grew rapidly without this predator. The deer and elk consumed large amounts of vegetation, reducing plant diversity. Without wolves, coyote populations also grew quickly. Coyotes killed many red foxes and

15　completely eliminated the park's beavers.

By 1966, biologists asked the government to consider reintroducing wolves to Yellowstone Park. The biologists hoped wolves would be able to control elk and coyote populations.

20　Many ranchers and farmers opposed the plan; they feared that wolves would kill livestock or pets. Other people feared that wolves would no longer be protected in Yellowstone.

The government spent almost 30 years

25　developing a reintroduction plan. Although wolves were technically an endangered species, Yellowstone's wolves were classified as an "experimental" population. This allowed greater governmental control over wolf packs.

30　To counteract potential resistance, the government pledged to pay ranchers for livestock killed by wolves. Today, debates continue as to how well the gray wolf is fitting in at Yellowstone. Elk, deer, and coyote populations have

35　decreased, while beavers and red foxes have made a comeback.

30. What is the main idea of the first paragraph of the passage?

  a. Gray wolves were unfairly treated by the ranchers and farmers.

  b. Canada provided a better habitat for gray wolves than Yellowstone did.

  c. Gray wolves were displaced from their original homes by humans.

  d. Gray wolves were a threat to ranchers.

  e. It was important to reintroduce the gray wolves to Yellowstone.

31. According to the passage, biologists asked the government to reintroduce wolves in Yellowstone principally in order to

  a. control the elk and coyote populations

  b. restore the park's plant diversity

  c. control the local livestock

  d. protect the wolves from extinction

  e. increase tourism revenue

32. In the fourth paragraph, the author references the gray wolf as being a technically endangered species. This reference most helps to support the author's claims in the passage by

  a. emphasizing the legal definition of *endangered.*

  b. showing that the government controls the wolves' status.

  c. explaining why the wolves are endangered.

  d. highlighting the fact that the Yellowstone wolves are a special population.

  e. accentuating the scientific usage of the reintroduction.

33. Which most closely identifies the primary organizational structure of the second paragraph of the passage?
   a. compare and contrast
   b. cause and effect
   c. chronological order
   d. order of importance
   e. classification

34. What is the implied main idea of the article?
   a. Yellowstone's wolf program was a mistake.
   b. The government is responsible for reintroducing wolves
   c. Wolves are an important part of our national parks.
   d. Yellowstone's wolf program has been beneficial for the wolves and the park.
   e. It is important not to disrupt the delicate balance of life in nature.

35. Which statement, if it were true, would most significantly weaken the author's main argument?
   a. The government continues to monitor the populations of gray wolves, elk, and coyotes.
   b. The introduction of the gray wolf has increased the population diversity of the Yellowstone area.
   c. Yellowstone has been a protected area since its founding as a national park in 1872.
   d. The introduction of the gray wolf allowed scientists to consider reintroducing beavers to Yellowstone.
   e. The reintroduction of the gray wolf at this time could ultimately result in a decrease of beneficial gray wolf characteristics.

36. Which species endured the most similar experience to that of the gray wolves in Yellowstone?
   a. the polar bear, whose northern habitat is threatened by warming air temperatures and the resulting reduction of sea ice
   b. the possum, which was introduced in non-native New Zealand in an effort to create a fur industry but resulted in overpopulation of the land
   c. the muskox, which was hunted to extinction in Alaska by about 1900 but brought back to repopulate the land during the 1930s
   d. the moa, a series of large New Zealand birds that were hunted to extinction in about A.D. 1400
   e. the house cat, whose introduction to Australia has resulted in the extinction of dozens of other species

Refer to the following passage for questions 37 and 38.

It is a statistical anomaly that Barack Obama is generally recognized as the 44th president of the United States, yet only 42 other people held the presidency before he did. This is due to the
5   fact that Grover Cleveland served two non-consecutive terms in office, one from 1885 to 1889 and the other from 1893 to 1897. As the only president to serve nonconsecutive terms, Cleveland is counted twice in the numbering of the presidents and is therefore considered both
10   the 22nd and 24th president of the United States. Given the resulting disparity, it would be more rational to number the presidents based solely on the first term, ignoring any secondary
15   tenures that could complicate the sequence.

37. Which best describes the author's opinion regarding the current numbering system for U.S. presidents?
a. clever
b. illogical
c. reverential
d. presidential
e. rational

38. Which word has the closest meaning to *anomaly* as it appears in line 1 of the passage?
a. data
b. irregularity
c. representation
d. conclusion
e. indiscretion

Refer to the following passages for questions 39 through 45.

Passage 1

The first bicycle, the fragile wooden draisienne, was invented in Germany in 1818 by Baron Karl de Drais de Sauerbrun. Riders moved it by pushing their feet against the ground. In 1839,
5 Kirkpatrick Macmillan, a Scottish blacksmith, developed an improved model with tires that had iron rims to keep them from getting worn down. He also used foot-operated cranks, similar to pedals, as an instrument for faster riding.
10 His didn't look much like the modern bicycle; its back wheel was substantially larger than its front wheel. Although Macmillan's bicycles could be ridden easily, they were never produced in great numbers.

Passage 2

15 In 1861, Pierre and Ernest Michaux invented a popular bicycle, the velocipede ("fast foot"), with an improved crank mechanism that connected to the front wheel. Ten years later, English inventor James Starley revolutionized

20 bicycle design. He made the front wheel much larger than the back wheel, put a gear on pedals to make the bicycle more efficient, and lightened wheels with wire spokes. Although this bicycle was much lighter and less tiring to
25 ride, it was still clumsy and top-heavy. In 1874, the first truly modern bicycle appeared. Invented by another Englishman, H.J. Lawson, the safety bicycle had equal-sized wheels; it was much less prone to toppling over. Lawson
30 attached a chain to pedals to drive the rear wheel; by 1893, he further improved the bicycle with air-filled rubber tires, a diamond-shaped frame, and easy braking.

39. Which sentence summarizes the information from *both* passages?
a. Lawson was focused on the safety of the bicycle when he developed his 1874 version.
b. From the early 1800s to the end of the century, many improvements were made to the bicycle.
c. Bicycles that were manufactured in 1850 and 1860 shared numerous similarities.
d. The 1818 bicycle could be described as a rudimentary version of Macmillan's bicycle.
e. Iron rims created problems for Macmillan's bicycles, while Starley's smaller front wheel was a positive advance.

40. Kirkpatrick Macmillan affected the development of the bicycle by
a. improving the overall energy efficiency of the design.
b. increasing the durability of the bicycle.
c. allowing the bicycle to be ridden by the masses.
d. making the bicycle lighter and easier to ride.
e. adjusting the size of the wheels to make the front wheel larger.

41. Based on information in the passages, which series of improvements to the bicycle represents the sequence of changes in chronological order?
   a. iron rims, improved crank mechanism, wire spokes, rubber tires, equal-sized wheels
   b. iron rims, gears on pedals, improved crank mechanism, equal-sized wheels, diamond-shaped frame
   c. iron rims, improved crank mechanism, wire spokes, easy braking, chain to the pedals
   d. diamond-shaped frame, easy braking, equal-sized wheels, iron rims, wire spokes
   e. iron rims, improved crank mechanism, wire spokes, equal-sized wheels, diamond-shaped frame

42. The development of the bicycle was most similar to the development of the
   a. hot-air balloon, because it helped transport many passengers great distances without an engine.
   b. automobile, because its design was improved upon by many inventors during a long period of time.
   c. space station, because its components were constructed during a period of several years.
   d. atomic bomb, because a specific technological advance allowed for its development.
   e. radio, because it improved the method and speed of communication.

43. The word *instrument* as it is used in line 9 most nearly means
   a. item to produce musical sound.
   b. tool.
   c. formal document.
   d. impediment.
   e. monitoring device.

44. Based on information in the passage, which prediction for the future of bicycle development is most reasonable?
   a. The development of the bicycle will cease, as all potential improvements have been achieved.
   b. The design will regress to the conditions of the nineteenth-century bicycle, including unequal wheel sizes.
   c. Future modifications to the bicycle will further enhance the design and specifications.
   d. Added weight to the framework design will improve stability and control.
   e. The advent of jet propulsion and safety features will allow for potential air travel.

45. Who invented the earliest bicycle discussed in the two passages?
   a. Pierre and Ernest Michaux
   b. James Starley
   c. Baron Karl de Drais de Sauerbrun
   d. H.J. Lawson
   e. Kirkpatrick Macmillan

Refer to the following passage for questions 46 and 47.

Plato, the famous Greek philosopher, taught the premise that the things of the world around us are merely copies, or "shadows," of greater, eternal realities. He used a metaphor, alluding to
5   people living inside a cave, to convey his ideas. The people inside the cave could not see the world outside the cave; they could see only shadows of people and animals passing by. Plato's position was that the shadows would
10   seem very real and alive to the people inside the cave—because that was all they had ever seen of the outside world. But these shadows were not the real, living creatures of the outside world; they were merely reflections of them.

15 Plato held that this temporal world was a narrow picture of some greater, eternal reality.

46. Which best explains the way in which the following sentence from the passage supports the author's claims?

> The people inside the cave could not see the world outside the cave; they could see only shadows of people and animals passing by.

a. The sentence provides concrete evidence of a philosophical truth.

b. The sentence offers a look at the world outside of a cave.

c. The sentence illustrates a concept through use of an understandable context.

d. The sentence describes the geographic location and setting of a story.

e. The sentence shows a vision of an illogical future.

47. As it appears in line 9 of the passage, the word *position* most nearly means
a. situation.
b. location.
c. movement.
d. opinion.
e. style.

Refer to the following passage for questions 48 through 51.

A cursory glance at a globe will reveal a fascinating observation: the continents of South America and Africa, separated by thousands of kilometers of open ocean, seem to fit together
5 like pieces of a jigsaw puzzle. The eastern edge of South America, part of modern-day Brazil, juts out into the Atlantic Ocean at about the same latitude where the coast of northern Africa shrivels toward the east. The reason for
10 this geological phenomenon is not pure happenstance. Both massive land masses were once connected in a supercontinent called Gondwana, which also contained most of the land found today in India, Australia, and Antarctica,
15 about 200 million years ago.

The process responsible for Gondwana splitting into the two separate continents as they now stand in their current positions is "continental drift." The significant hypothesis,
20 put forth by German geologist Alfred Wegener in 1915, states that parts of Earth's crust can shift above the planet's liquid core as time progresses. A later theory of plate tectonics expanded on Wegener's discovery, conjecturing
25 that Earth's continental plates move in different directions, which affects the positions of the continents and explains why South America and Africa seem to fit like puzzle pieces, despite their locations on opposite sides of an ocean.

48. The description of the continents of South America and Africa as pieces of a jigsaw puzzle best helps to support the author's claims in the passage by
a. contrasting the significant difference between the land masses.
b. detailing the mystery of the continental shapes as a puzzle.
c. minimizing the geological importance of the continents.
d. reinforcing the corresponding physical relationship of the continents.
e. illustrating the problems scientists faced in determining the causes of continental drift.

49. The word *cursory* in line 1 could be replaced with which of the following words to result in the least change in meaning?
   a. investigative
   b. hasty
   c. internal
   d. offensive
   e. cursive

50. Which statement, if it were true, would most significantly strengthen the author's main argument?
   a. Gondwana was once part of a much larger supercontinent called Pangaea.
   b. Fossils of the same type of plant have been found in parts of South America and Africa.
   c. The African island of Madagascar was once part of the supercontinent Gondwana.
   d. There are countless species of animals that exist in only South America or Africa, but not on both continents.
   e. Scientists have studied Africa and South America for decades, arriving at many theories.

51. According to the passage, which statement can most reasonably be made?
   a. Alfred Wegener developed the theory of plate tectonics.
   b. There was a time on planet Earth when there were no oceans.
   c. South America and Africa are roughly the same size.
   d. There is scant evidence that supports the "continental drift" theory.
   e. South America and Africa are located on two different plates.

Refer to the following graph for questions 52 and 53.

The United States is one of the most culturally diverse nations on Earth. This is clear from the "melting pot" moniker so proudly sported by the nation. The United States is also one of the
5 most climatically diverse nations. The climate of the United States ranges from very low temperatures to very high temperatures. These very high temperatures are often described as "torrid." Some areas of Alaska rarely get warm
10 enough to melt an ice cube. The weather in Hawaii is perfect throughout the year. A temperature once recorded in northern Alaska was −79.8°F, while Hawaii has never recorded a sub-zero temperature.

52. Which of the following sentences from the passage is an example of an opinion?
   a. The United States is one of the most culturally diverse nations on Earth.
   b. The climate of the United States ranges from very low temperatures to very high temperatures.
   c. Some areas of Alaska rarely get warm enough to melt an ice cube.
   d. The weather in Hawaii is perfect throughout the year.
   e. A temperature once recorded in northern Alaska was −79.8°F, while Hawaii has never recorded a sub-zero temperature.

53. Within the context of the passage, the word *torrid* in line 9 can be replaced with which word to incur the smallest change in meaning?
   a. sweltering
   b. dissimilar
   c. glacial
   d. lukewarm
   e. uncomfortable

Refer to the following passage for questions 54 through 56.

If you frequently feel drowsy during the day or fall asleep within five minutes of lying down, you might be experiencing sleep deprivation. Microsleeps, very brief episodes of sleep in an
5 otherwise awake person, are another mark of sleep deprivation. The widespread practice of "burning the candle at both ends" in Western industrialized societies has created so much sleep deprivation that abnormal sleepiness is
10 now almost the norm.

Studies prove that sleep deprivation is dangerous. Sleep-deprived people tested with a driving simulator perform as badly as or worse than those who are intoxicated. Driver fatigue is
15 responsible for an estimated 100,000 motor vehicle accidents and 1,500 deaths each year. Since drowsiness is the brain's last step before falling asleep, drowsy driving can often lead to disaster. The National Sleep Foundation says
20 that if you have trouble keeping your eyes focused, can't stop yawning, or can't remember driving the last few miles, you are too drowsy to drive safely.

54. The primary purpose of the passage is to
 a. offer preventive measures for sleep deprivation
 b. explain why sleeplessness has become a common state in Western cultures
 c. recommend the amount of sleep that is needed by individuals of a variety of ages
 d. alert readers to the signs and risks of failure to obtain a sufficient amount of sleep
 e. discuss the effects of alcohol on a sleep-deprived person

55. The phrase *burning the candle at both ends* in line 7 illustrates
 a. an unrelenting schedule that affords little rest
 b. an ardent desire to achieve
 c. the flames that can ignite when a flammable item is burned
 d. a latent period before a conflict or collapse
 e. a state of extreme agitation

56. The term *norm* in line 10 could be replaced with which of the following words to result in the most minimal change in meaning?
 a. outlier
 b. standard
 c. danger
 d. oddity
 e. ideal

Praxis® Core Academic Skills for Educators: Reading Practice Test 4 Answers and Explanations

1. b. The passage mentions that more research is needed to try to protect the northern spotted owl, but the research is not a threat to the owl. The passage states that a great deal of the spotted northern owl's habitat has been lost to logging and natural disasters (choice **a**). Forest fires are not mentioned explicitly in the passage as a threat to the northern spotted owl, but the passage does mention that a great deal of the owl's habitat has been lost as a result of natural disasters—and forest fires caused by lightning are natural disasters (choice **c**). Climate change (choice **d**) is specifically mentioned as a threat to the northern spotted owl. Barred owls (choice **e**) are specifically mentioned as a threat to the northern spotted owl.

2. e. It cannot be proven or disproven that scientists should do all they can for this purpose. This is a matter of opinion, not fact. The statements in choices **a**, **b**, **c**, and **d** can all be proven or disproven.

3. d. Within the context of the passage, the phrase *Now, though* is used to describe an additional threat to the northern spotted owl, despite the protection provided by a 1991 law. Choices **a**, **b**, **c**, and **e** are incorrect because they are not supported by the context of the passage.

4. b. The crux of the passage references the many threats faced by the northern spotted owl, as well as the need for the protection of the species. Choices **a**, **c**, and **d** are incorrect because they discuss supporting details, not main ideas. The statement in choice **e** is too general to summarize the passage.

5. d. The main idea of the passage relates to the northern spotted owl being in need of protection, as it faces many threats. This answer choice shows that scientists are trying to monitor the owls' nests; this alone provides the least support for the main idea. Choices **a**, **b**, **c**, and **e** mention specific threats, so they do not provide the least support for the main idea, the need for protection of the owl from threats.

6. d. The passage focuses on the rise of the team as a result of the work of Duncan Brin. Choices **a**, **c**, and **e** are incorrect because they are supporting details. Additionally, there is no evidence in the passage to suggest the position mentioned in choice **b**.

7. a. The passage opens with details about the team today, and then the passage contrasts these details with details about the team's earlier problems. The passage then concludes with the main idea. Choice **b** is incorrect because the passage does not begin with the main idea. The organization of the passage is not based on a handful of comparisons and then several dissimilarities, so choice **c** is incorrect. Choice **d** is incorrect because definitions are not provided. Additionally, choice **e** is incorrect because the passage does not open by stating a problem.

8. a. The word *teeming* is being used to describe the population of the bleachers of a baseball stadium, to address the number of cheering fans, so the best word to replace *teeming* also relates to the many people in the (*crowded*) bleachers. Choices **b** and **c** are incorrect because *rooting* and *energized* do not show the meaning of the word *teeming*. In choice **d**, *vacant* is an antonym, not a synonym, of *teeming*. The word *teeming* in choice **e** has a spelling that is similar to the spelling of *teeming*, but *teaming* is not a synonym of *teeming*.

9. e. The graph key identifies the bar that corresponds to movies and games. In the graph, this bar rises higher for Atul than for the other students. Choice **a** is incorrect because the data in the chart do not address the month of August, and it's not reasonable to infer that just because Pat spent more on clothing in July, Pat will also spend more on clothing in August. In fact, it could reasonably be argued that the converse is true, that Pat would not need to spend money on clothing in August after the clothing purchases in July. Based on data in the graph, choice **b** is incorrect because it is not possible to tell how much money each student is saving. Choice **c** is incorrect because Maria spent $25 on clothing and $15 on movies and games. Based on data in the graph, it is not possible to discern whether Atul's parents provide meals and snacks (choice **d**).

10. c. The total of the amounts for each type of expenditure is the greatest for Pat. Choices **a**, **b**, **d**, and **e** are not supported by the data in the graph.

11. d. Atul spent $5 on food and snacks, and he spent $10 for clothing—for a total of $15. María spent $15 for clothing. The graph depicts only expenditures of three students. Based on the data, it is not possible to know whether clothing prices were higher during July than during other months of the year, so choice **a** is incorrect. The graph does not supply data regarding students shopping together, making choice **b** incorrect. Choice **c** is incorrect because, based on the data, it is not possible to know whether clothing prices were higher during July than during other months of the year. For the combination of food, snacks, movies, and games, Pat spent $45. For clothing, Atul spent $10. Therefore choice **e** is incorrect.

12. c. The author shows support for the statement in choice **c** in the anecdote about the group of laughing travelers on the railway; because you were not part of the group, you lacked a connection and did not find the humor funny. The statement in choice **a** is contradicted throughout the passage. The final sentence in the text supports choice **b**, but the railway anecdote not does relate specifically to the customs and ideas of a society. Railway travel is not central to the argument, so choice **d** is incorrect. Choice **e** is incorrect because the author is not using the anecdote to show that laughter is spontaneous.

13. a. The adverb *rapturously*, as it appears in the passage, describes the way the travelers in the railway carriage are laughing. Laughing rapturously equates to laughing enthusiastically. The travelers' laughter is true because the context of the sentence states that they were laughing at something comic. Choices **b**, **c**, **d**, and **e** are not supported by the context.

14. d. The passage describes the introduction of British cotton technology to America, specifically to New England. The passage does not account for the decline of rural America or contrast political views, so choices **a** and **b** are incorrect. While the passage does mention British laws forbidding the export of industrial machinery (choice **c**), this is a supporting detail, not the primary purpose of the passage. Choice **e** is incorrect because the passage does not provide a cogent argument in support of industrial development.

15. b. The passage references Houses of Industry as an example of the association of cloth manufacturing with relief of the poor. Choices **a**, **c**, **d**, and **e** are incorrect because they are not supported by evidence in the passage.

16. b. The mounting conflict between the colonies and England—referenced in the first sentence of the passage—suggests that America had political and economic reasons for developing its own textile industry. While there were certainly beneficial results from the manufacturing, it cannot be inferred that there were no negative effects (choice **a**). Choices **c**, **d**, and **e** are incorrect because it is not suggested in the passage that early American manufacturing was symbolically undemocratic, environmentally destructive, or spiritually corrosive.

17. a. The description of Samuel Slater's immigration to America shows the deceptive measures necessary to evade British export laws and introduce cotton technology to the colonies. Slater posed as a farmer in order to immigrate to America after committing to memory the cotton technology he had learned in an English factory. Choices **b** and **c** are incorrect because the reason for including this information was not primarily to show the attraction of farming opportunities in the American colonies or to explain the details of British manufacturing technologies. Americans were not trying to block immigration to the colonies, so choice **d** is incorrect. The British were attempting to prevent the knowledge from being shared with the colonies, making choice **e** incorrect.

18. a. The author does not offer Slater's personal viewpoint on child labor, instead stating only the fact that Slater hired young children to work in his Rhode Island mill. Therefore, based on evidence in the passage, it can be inferred that he viewed child labor as an available workforce. Because there is no opinion regarding child labor expressed, it cannot be inferred that Slater identified the labor as a necessary evil; therefore choices **b** and **c** are incorrect. Choices **d** and **e** are incorrect because there is no evidence in the passage to support either inference.

19. c. According to the passage, the trained workers were instrumental in beginning the spread of cotton mills in New England. Slater did sail to America (choice **a**), but his voyage was not the main catalyst. Choices **b**, **d**, and **e** are not supported by any evidence in the passage.

20. e. This response is supported by passage context. Choices **a**, **b**, **c**, and **d** are incorrect because passage context does not support these meanings.

21. a. A statement of opinion is a statement that cannot be proven with facts; not everyone may agree that a hippopotamus looks like a pig or a cow, so choice **a** is merely an opinion. However, it can be scientifically proven that the hippo is aggressive to predators (choice **b**), weighs around 3,000 lbs. (choice **c**), can run 19 miles per hour in short spurts (choice **d**), and has tusks that measure more than a foot long (choice **e**). These statistics are all facts, not opinions.

22. c. The passage details Rudolph's difficulties and shows how she overcame those difficulties to rise to great accomplishments. Choices **a**, **b**, and **d** are incorrect because they provide details about Wilma Rudolph but do not summarize the main idea of the passage. While choice **e** provides an accurate statement, it does not summarize the passage.

23. e. The fact that Theodore Roosevelt suffered from severe asthma as a child, but overcame it as an adult, and then rose to great heights makes his life most analogous to that of Wilma Rudolph. While the situation stated in choice **a** is similar to that identified in the question, the fact that Roosevelt acquired his illness as an adult makes his situation less analogous than the situation detailed in answer choice **e**. Choice **b**, **c**, and **d** do not present scenarios analogous to that of a child overcoming a debilitating illness to become successful as an adult.

24. a. The passage states that at the 1960 Olympics, Rudolph won three gold medals. This is the greatest accomplishment that Rudolph achieved as a runner; therefore, it was her zenith, or peak. A zenith is a high point. Choice **b** is an antonym and would suggest that this was the low point of Rudolph's career. Although the high point might be a conclusion to a great deal of hard work, the words *zenith* and *conclusion* are not synonymous (choice **c**). Choices **d** and **e** are incorrect because they do not show the meaning of *zenith*.

25. e. The word *sympathetic* can be defined as *favorably inclined*. Because the author presents details that support the need for a student dress code, the adjective *sympathetic* best describes the author's attitude. Choices **a**, **b**, and **c** are incorrect because the author is supportive of a dress code. Additionally, choice **d** is incorrect because being sympathetic is not the same as being concerned about a dress code.

26. c. The author holds the position that a dress code is a good idea. This answer choice offers the only statement that weakens this argument. The statements in choices **a**, **b**, and **d** strengthen the author's argument. Meanwhile, choice **e** is not relevant to the author's argument.

27. a. It cannot be proven that one player changed the game of soccer more than any other player. The statements in choices **b**, **c**, **d**, and **e** could be proven true or false.

28. a. The main idea of the passage focuses on Pelé being an amazing soccer player who helped transform the sport. His name, place of birth, and year of birth do not support this main idea. The details mentioned in choices **b**, **c**, **d**, and **e** greatly help to support the main idea, which relates to Pelé being an amazing soccer player who helped transform the sport. The question asks which detail supports the main idea the least.

29. c. The passage focuses on Pelé's talent and his impact on the game of soccer. Because he transformed his sport in a similar way, Babe Ruth is most similar to Pelé. Choice **a** is incorrect because while Cristiano Ronaldo was a great soccer player, there is no indication in the statement that he transformed the sport in the way Pelé did. Dilma Rousseff (choice **b**) is from Brazil, but it is not indicated that she influenced a sport in the way Pelé did. Charles Haley was a successful athlete, but there is no indication that he had a lasting impact on his sport (choice **d**). Landon Donovan (choice **e**) was a great soccer player, but there is no indication in the statement that he transformed the sport in the way Pelé did.

30. c. The passage explains that wolves once lived in the Yellowstone area—until conflict with humans caused them to disappear. Choices **a** and **e** are not the main idea of the paragraph. Choices **b** and **d** are too narrow to be the main idea; they are supporting details.

31. a. Biologists hoped that wolves would help balance the elk and coyote populations. Restoring the park's plant diversity (choice **b**) was a factor, but it is not stated as the principal motive, so this answer is incorrect. Ranchers and farmers objected to the wolves killing their livestock (choice **c**). Choice **d** is not stated as the principal motive. Additionally, there is no evidence to suggest that wolves were reintroduced to increase tourism (choice **e**).

32. d. This answer is supported by evidence in the passage. The passage suggests the legal definition of *endangered* (choice **a**) but does not explain it. Choice **b** is a true statement but is not the best answer. The passage does not explain why the wolves are endangered or how science is utilized during the reintroduction, so choices **c** and **e** are incorrect.

33. b. The second paragraph describes the result of the wolf's disappearance. The paragraph is not structured to compare and contrast, and is not organized by classification, so choices **a** and **e** are incorrect. Although the events occur in chronological order, choice **c**, they are organized to show cause and effect. Events are not provided in order of importance, making choice **d** incorrect.

34. d. The author concludes the article by listing some of the positive effects of the wolf's return: beaver and red fox populations are being restored, and elk and coyote populations are balancing to normal levels. There is no indication that the program was a mistake (choice **a**). Choice **b** is a supporting detail and is not sufficiently broad to be the main idea; on the other hand, choice **e** is too broad. Choice **c** is too general; the article addresses only Yellowstone Park and does not reference reintroduction in other national parks.

35. e. The author's argument focuses on the reintroduction of the gray wolf as being beneficial. The only statement that provides a definitively negative result of the reintroduction would be a decrease of beneficial gray wolf characteristics. Choices **a** and **c** fail to strengthen or weaken the argument. Choices **b** and **d** provide a positive effect of the reintroduction, so it would strengthen the author's argument. The question asks for the statement that would most *weaken* the argument.

36. c. Like the gray wolf, the muskox was driven to extinction within a particular geographic area; it was then reintroduced to those lands at a later date. The polar bear is threatened, but the statement does not indicate that it has been reintroduced (choice **a**). The possum (choice **b**) was introduced to New Zealand, causing environmental havoc, but the statement does not indicate that it was reintroduced there. The moa was hunted to extinction centuries ago; however, the statement does not indicate that it was ever reintroduced (choice **d**). The statement does not indicate that the house cat has been in danger of extinction (choice **e**).

37. b. The author discusses the numbering system for U.S. presidents; then the author provides a more rational numbering system. Therefore, the author most likely believes that the current system is illogical. Choices **a** and **e** represent the opposite of the author's opinion, and choices **c** and **d** are not supported by evidence in the passage.

38. b. An anomaly is an abnormality or irregularity. Choices **a**, **c**, **d**, and **e** are not synonyms of anomaly.

39. b. The two passages provide details about the development of the bicycle from 1818 (the early 1800s) through 1893 (the late 1800s). Choice **a** includes only some of the details from Passage 2. Neither passage includes the details from choice **c**. Choice **d** includes information from only Passage 1. Choice **e** includes information that contradicts information in the passages.

40. b. The passage states that the iron rims kept the tires from getting worn down. This is in contrast to the earlier fragile model from 1818. Therefore, Macmillan increased the durability of the bicycle. It might be tempting to suggest that Macmillan's improvements to the bicycle improved its efficiency, but there is no direct correlation in the passage from his improvements to energy efficiency (choice **a**). The passage states that Macmillan's bicycles were never produced in large numbers; therefore, there is no indication that he helped the bicycle to be ridden by the masses (choice **c**). Although the passage says that Macmillan's bicycles could be ridden easily, lighter weight (choice **d**) is not a clear correlation. One of the wheels in Macmillan's bicycle design was much larger than the other, but it was not the front wheel that was larger (choice **e**).

41. e. Based on the passage, this was the order of the improvements. Choice **a** does not show the correct order. The inclusion of gears on pedals did not occur until 10 years after Pierre and Ernest Michaux created the improved crank mechanism (choice **b**). According to details, the *easy braking* represents a further improvement that Lawson made only *after* attaching a chain to the pedals to drive the rear wheel (choice **c**). The list of improvements to the bicycle's design in choice **d** is provided in alphabetical order, rather than chronological order.

42. b. Like the automobile, the bicycle was developed during a long period of time and through the contributions of many inventors. Choice **a** is incorrect, because unlike a hot air balloon, a bicycle does not transport multiple passengers over long distances. The space station (choice **c**) might have been constructed throughout several years, but the bicycle was not; it was improved upon, not built, during a long time period. There was no single specific technological advance (choice **d**) that led to the development of the bicycle. Transporting many passengers was not instrumental in the development of the bicycle (choice **e**).

43. b. The instrument referenced in the passage is a foot-operated crank that improved the riding experience, so the crank is a tool. The word *instrument* can mean *item to produce musical sound*, such as a guitar or a piano; however, the passage does not relate to music, so context indicates that the definition of *instrument* in choice **a** is incorrect. Choices **c** and **e** each show one definition of *instrument*; however, the context does not support these meanings. Choice **d** is not a correct meaning of *instrument*.

44. c. Details of a series of modifications made to the design of the bicycle throughout the years are chronicled. These modifications improved its usability. Therefore, it would be reasonable to predict that additional modifications would be made to continue development. Based on details, it can be inferred that additional changes will likely occur, making choice **a** incorrect. Choices **b**, **d**, and **e** are not supported by evidence in the passage.

45. c. The passages state that Baron Karl de Drais de Sauerbrun invented the earliest bicycle. Pierre and Ernest Michaux invented the earliest bicycle discussed in the second passage, but the question asks for the earliest bicycle discussed in both passages, so choice **a** is incorrect. Choices **b**, **d**, and **e** are incorrect simply because these people did not invent the earliest bicycle.

46. c. The sentence that precedes this statement in the text suggests that Plato used a metaphor to convey his ideas. This sentence then provides details of the metaphor, describing the people inside the cave as seeing only the shadows of those passing by. The concept of living in a world of shadows might be difficult to grasp without a description to provide perspective. The illustrative concept of living within the walls of the cave does provide an understandable context. Choice **a** is incorrect because the sentence does not provide any sort of concrete evidence—no indisputable proof or confirmation—that Plato's philosophical idea was, in fact, true. Choice **b** is a literal interpretation that does not support the author's claims. The description of a cave is not offered to provide a setting (choice **d**) for a story. Choice **e** also does not logically support the author's claims.

47. d. The word *position* has more than one meaning. Context makes it clear that in this sentence, the word *position* refers to Plato's argument, his point, which is his opinion. Choices **a** and **b** are incorrect because these meanings of *position* are not supported by context. Choices **c** and **e** do not show the correct meaning of *position*.

48. d. The author follows the portrayal of the continents as puzzle pieces with a physical description of their shapes. This shows that the author is supporting the description of the physical relationship between the continents. The author does not make claims to contrast significant differences of the continents, making choice **a** incorrect. Choice **b** is incorrect because the author is not detailing a mystery. The author does not minimize the geological importance of the continents, so choice **c** is incorrect. Additionally, the author is not focusing on problems that scientists faced in determining causes of continental drift, so choice **e** is incorrect as well.

49. b. The author uses the word *cursory* to suggest that it would not take much time to notice an obvious pattern in the globe's continental patterns. Choice **a** is an antonym, not a synonym, so it is incorrect. Choices **c, d,** and **e** do not show meanings of *cursory* and are not supported by passage context.

50. b. The author makes the argument that the African and South American continents were once joined. If the same plant were found to have lived on both continents, this would lend support to that argument. Choice **a** does not relate closely enough to the author's main argument that the African and South American continents were once joined. Choice **c** is not relevant to the author's main argument. If species were unique to each continent alone, choice **d** would not strengthen the author's argument. Choice **e** is too general to significantly strengthen the author's main argument.

51. e. The final sentence of the passage states that plates can move in different directions, which has resulted in the current positions of the continents. Therefore, this answer choice provides a reasonable statement. Alfred Wegener developed the theory of continental drift, but the theory of plate tectonics followed later; the passage does not suggest who proposed the theory of plate tectonics, but the statement in choice **a** cannot be inferred. Although the passage states that at one point no ocean existed between Africa and South America, this does not indicate that Earth had no oceans (choice **b**). The passage does not compare the sizes of the continents (choice **c**); it compares their shapes. Passage evidence does not support choice **d**.

52. d. An opinion is a statement that cannot be proven true or false. It cannot be proven true or false that Hawaii has perfect weather, as perfect weather is a matter of opinion. Some people might like cold weather. Some people might like warm weather. Choices **a, b, c,** and **e** can be proven true or false, so they are statements of fact.

53. a. The passage contrasts the climate extremes in the United States, comparing very cold temperatures to torrid temperatures. Therefore, *torrid* must have the opposite meaning of *very cold*; the best answer choice to describe that opposite temperature is *sweltering*. The temperatures might be dissimilar (choice **b**), but the word *torrid* does not mean *dissimilar*. The word *glacial* in choice **c** does not describe hot weather. The word *lukewarm* does not describe hot weather (choice **d**). While a torrid temperature might be uncomfortable, the word *torrid* does not mean *uncomfortable* (choice **e**).

54. d. The first paragraph of this short passage deals with the symptoms of sleep deprivation, and the second paragraph discusses the dangers of failure to obtain a sufficient amount of sleep. Choices **a** and **e** do not show the primary purpose of the passage. Choice **b** is too narrow to reflect the passage's primary purpose. Choice **c** is not supported by the passage.

55. a. The image of burning the candle at both ends connotes a state of working hard without adequate rest. Evidence in the passage does not support choices **b**, **d**, or **e**. Choice **c** shows the literal meaning of the phrase; the author is using the phrase to offer a figurative meaning.

56. b. The word *norm* most nearly means *custom* or *normal*. Therefore, the word *standard* would result in the most minimal change in meaning. Choices **a** and **d** are antonyms, not synonyms. While sleep deprivation is dangerous (choice **c**), the word *norm* does not mean *danger*. Context makes it clear that abnormal sleepiness is not ideal (choice **e**).

Praxis® Core Academic Skills for Educators: Writing Practice Test 4

Part I: Multiple-Choice
Time: 40 Minutes

Directions: Each of the following 15 questions consists of a sentence that contains four underlined portions. Read each sentence, and decide whether any of the underlined parts contains an element that would be considered incorrect or inappropriate in carefully written English. The error or concern may be in grammatical construction, word use, punctuation, or capitalization. Select the underlined portion that must be revised to produce a correct sentence. If a sentence contains no errors, select "No error." **No sentence contains more than one error.**

1. I have <u>all ways</u> been enamored of the concept
   a
   that <u>through</u> computer <u>modeling, we</u> can create
   bc
   <u>an executable model</u> to test a complex system.
   d
   <u>No error</u>
   e

2. <u>During World War II,</u> the Allies stormed
   a
   <u>Italy and</u> then <u>would launch</u> a <u>massive assault.</u>
   bcd
   <u>No error</u>
   e

3. Lin and Morgan shared a <u>their</u> daily nutrition
   a
   <u>plan,</u> we weren't surprised to discover that <u>it</u>
   bc
   <u>included</u> fiber, fruit, and protein. <u>No error</u>
   de

4. <u>In my opinion,</u> watching a <u>psychological thriller</u>
   ab
   is <u>more interesting</u> <u>than a general drama film.</u>
   cd
   <u>No error</u>
   e

5. Not only did the <u>unexpected blizzard</u> prevent
a
<u>us</u> from leaving the house <u>to go to work</u>, <u>and</u>
b   c   d
the frigid conditions also resulted in burst
pipes. <u>No error</u>
e

6. <u>Peoples' interests</u> <u>differ substantially</u> regarding
a   b
careers and <u>hobbies; otherwise,</u> this <u>would be</u> a
c   d
boring world. <u>No error</u>
e

7. Oscar and Pat did <u>good</u> in the dance
a
<u>competition; they</u> were confident that <u>they</u>
b   c
would continue their winning streak in the
<u>few</u> dance competitions remaining in the
d
season. <u>No error</u>
e

8. Last <u>week, the Hollywood trainer</u> <u>lead</u> the dogs
a   b
<u>through the exercises</u> to prepare <u>them</u> for the
c   d
movie scene. <u>No error</u>
e

9. <u>Our cousins are</u> from <u>Italy and speak</u> fluent
a   b
<u>Italian, and they also speak</u> <u>English, French,</u>
c   d
and Portuguese. <u>No error</u>
e

10. Stunned by the <u>audacity</u> of <u>the coworker</u>, <u>it</u>
a   b   c
was turning into a <u>volatile workplace. No error</u>
d   e

11. The other <u>Senators</u> listened to <u>their</u> colleague,
a   b
who advocated filibusters for the purpose of
drawing attention <u>to</u> <u>specific causes.</u> <u>No error</u>
c   d   e

12. <u>Believe it or not</u>, several of our revered
a
<u>artists, such as</u> Michelangelo and Leonardo
b
da Vinci, lived and <u>created</u> their masterpieces
c
during the <u>Middle Ages.</u> <u>No error</u>
d   e

13. Just <u>among</u> the three of us, <u>I'd</u> have to say that
a   b
the surprise party is a big <u>mistake; however,</u> I
c
know that most of <u>our friends</u> disagree.
d
<u>No error</u>
e

14. Ana's sisters arrived to drive the carpool home
from soccer <u>practice,</u> so Ana and her friend
a
grabbed their <u>backpacks</u> and extra gear because
b
<u>their</u> sisters <u>were</u> in a hurry. <u>No error</u>
c   d   e

15. The journalist <u>reported</u>, "Of the four people
a
running for the governorship, Reynolds is the
<u>less likely</u> to <u>win</u>; this is <u>due</u> to progressive
b   c   d
views that do not appeal to a broad base of the
electorate." <u>No error</u>
e

Directions: In each of the following questions, part of the sentence or the entire sentence has been underlined. Beneath each sentence, the underlined words are written in five ways. The first option repeats the original underlined content, but the other four differ. If the original sentence is the best option, select the first choice; otherwise, select one of the other choices.

This part of the test measures correctness and effectiveness of expression. Pay particular attention to usage in grammar, word choice, sentence construction, capitalization, and punctuation. Select the option that best expresses information presented in the original sentence. Your answer should be free of awkwardness, ambiguity, and redundancy.

16. Keisha and Lara worked out the project details <u>themself</u>.
   a. themself
   b. herselves
   c. themselves
   d. herself
   e. ourselves

17. The teaching assistant asked them to take the books to <u>her and I</u>.
   a. her and I
   b. she and I
   c. her and me
   d. she and we
   e. we and I

18. My <u>mother who is a film director is</u> teaching a seminar for film students attending New York University.
   a. mother who is a film director is
   b. mother, who is a film director, is
   c. mother who is a film director, is
   d. mother, whom is a film director, is
   e. mother, who is a film director is

19. As soon as they came in from the icy temperatures, the <u>children put away their jacket and hat</u>.
   a. children put away their jacket and hat
   b. children put away their jacket's and hat's
   c. children put away their jackets and hats
   d. children puts away their jackets and hats
   e. children's put away their jacket and hat

20. <u>We cant recall why the mistakes were made, but were certain</u> we will not repeat those mistakes in the future.
   a. We cant recall why the mistakes were made, but were certain
   b. We can't recall why the mistakes we're made, but we're certain
   c. We cant recall why the mistakes we're made, but we're certain
   d. We can't recall why the mistakes were made, but we're certain
   e. We can't recall why the mistakes we're made, but were certain

21. The students <u>joined together with</u> their teachers for an assembly in the gymnasium.
   a. joined together with
   b. joined with
   c. joining
   d. will be joining together with
   e. joined

22. Currently playing the lead role in a new televi-sion series, you should give a warm round of applause for Daniella, a rising star.
- **a.** Currently playing the lead role in a new television series, you should give a warm round of applause for Daniella, a rising star.
- **b.** You should give a warm round of applause, currently playing the lead role in a new television series, for Daniella, a rising star.
- **c.** Currently playing the lead role in a new television series, you should give a warm round of applause for a rising star, Daniella.
- **d.** You should give a warm round of applause for Daniella, a rising star currently playing the lead role in a new television series.
- **e.** Currently play the lead role in a new television series. You should give a warm round of applause for Daniella, a rising star in a television series.

23. It had been a decade since his Grandmother had published a new Bestseller, but she had continued to prove herself a prolific author.
- **a.** his Grandmother had published a new Bestseller
- **b.** his Grandmother had published a new bestseller
- **c.** His grandmother had published a new Bestseller
- **d.** his grandmother had published a new bestseller
- **e.** His Grandmother had published a new Bestseller

24. The sun shining on the ocean, dappling ocean waves with golden dots.
- **a.** The sun shining on the ocean, dappling ocean waves with golden dots.
- **b.** The sun, shining on the ocean; dappling ocean waves with golden dots.
- **c.** The sun, shining on the ocean. Dappling ocean waves with golden dots.
- **d.** The sun. Was shining. On the ocean, dappling ocean waves with golden dots.
- **e.** The sun was shining on the ocean, dappling ocean waves with golden dots.

25. He hadn't been expecting the change in per-sonnel, so when the change was announced, he was shocked and said, "You could have knocked me over with a feather."
- **a.** "You could have knocked me over with a feather."
- **b.** "That's the way the cookie crumbles."
- **c.** "Take the tiger by the tail."
- **d.** "What a ball of fire!"
- **e.** "Stop bugging me!"

26. Not only did we inadvertently write the wrong address on the invitations, but we also forgot to include a telephone number.
- **a.** but
- **b.** nor
- **c.** or
- **d.** and
- **e.** neither

27. <u>We never knew anybody who could finish a test so quickly.</u>
   a. We never knew anybody who could finish a test so quickly.
   b. We've never knew nobody who could finish a test so quickly.
   c. We never knew nobody who could finish a test so quickly.
   d. We never knew anybody who could finish a test so quick.
   e. We never knew nobody who could finish a test so quick.

28. When my cousin arrived for a visit last month, <u>we see friends, go to a play, and eat at our favorite restaurant.</u>
   a. we see friends, go to a play, and eat at our favorite restaurant
   b. we saw friends, went to a play, and ate at our favorite restaurant
   c. we seen friends, went to a play, and eaten at our favorite restaurant
   d. we will see friends, go to a play, and eat at our favorite restaurant
   e. we sees friends, goes to a play, and eats at our favorite restaurant

29. Each of the ten musical artists in the <u>men's choral group believed their group</u> would take top honors at the competition.
   a. men's choral group believed their group
   b. men's choral group believed there group
   c. men's choral group believed his group
   d. mens' choral group believed their group
   e. mens choral group believed his group

Directions: Some parts of the following passage need to be improved. Read the passage and then answer the questions about specific sentences. In choosing your answers, pay attention to development, organization, word choice, tone, and the standards of written English.

(1) Moving can be a stressful endeavor; however, with the proper preparation, all can go smoothly.
(2) Initially, it is important to base decisions on whether the move is a local move or one that will take you across the country—or perhaps to a different country—as it can be the most difficult of moves.
(3) This article covers national moves, but not international moves.

(4) Are you moving within the same city? You might try some good ideas: consider asking friends to help you pack and move. (5) If you are moving a great distance, however, you will likely need to hire a moving company. (6) To do a good job of locating a moving company to best meet your needs, ask friends, colleagues, and neighbors. (7) Additionally, perform Web searches to find others' comments about movers. (8) The National Moving, Packing, and Transportation Organization maintains a list of recommended movers and pertinent questions to ask as you are considering a move.

(9) If you are packing your own items for a local move, if you are taking some of the items to the new location yourself, the packing likely will not require as much cushioning and wrapping paper. (10) Your items will not be jostled in a large truck for a long period of time. (11) The basic fundamentals of environmental responsibility give rise to an idea you might not have considered. (12) Be certain to advise others of your new address. (13) Instead of the traditional cardboard boxes, you might consider obtaining plastic reusable moving crates from a company specializing in this environmentally friendly option. (14) This option will allow you to have the crates delivered, and you can pack them yourself. (15) Then you can have them picked up from your new location.

30. Which is the most effective way to write sentence 2 (reproduced here)?

Initially, it is important to base decisions on whether the move is a local move or one that will take you across the country—or perhaps to a different country—as it can be the most difficult of moves.

a. As it is now.
b. Initially, it is important to base decisions on whether the move is a local move or one that will take you across the country. Difficult.
c. Initially, it is important to base decisions on whether the move is a local move or one that will take you across the country or to a different country, as it can be the most difficult of moves.
d. Initially, it is important to base decisions on whether the move is a local move or one that will take you across the country—or perhaps to a different country—as an international move can be the most difficult of moves.
e. Initially, it is important to make decisions. On whether the move is a local move or one that will take you across the country. Some moves are difficult.

31. How can sentence 6 (reproduced here) best be written?

To do a good job of locating a moving company to best meet your needs, ask friends, colleagues, and neighbors.

a. As it is now.
b. To do a good job of locating a moving company, ask others.
c. Do a good job of locating a moving company to meet your needs.
d. To do an effective job of locating a moving company to best meet your needs, ask friends, colleagues, and neighbors.
e. To locate a moving company, talk to other people who you think might have information that could possibly help you as you look to find a moving company.

32. What is the correct and most effective way to write sentence 8 (reproduced here)?

> The National Moving, Packing, and Transportation Organization maintains a list of recommended movers and pertinent questions to ask as you are considering a move.

a. As it is now.

b. The National Moving, Packing, and Transportation organization maintains a list of recommended movers and pertinent questions to ask as you are considering a move.

c. The national Moving, Packing, and Transportation Organization maintains a list of recommended movers and pertinent questions to ask as you are considering a move.

d. The National moving, Packing, And Transportation Organization maintains a list of recommended movers and pertinent questions to ask as you are considering a move.

e. the National Moving, Packing, and Transportation Organization maintains a list of recommended movers and pertinent questions to ask as you are considering a move.

33. What is the most effective way to write sentence 9 (reproduced here)?

> If you are packing your own items for a local move, if you are taking some of the items to the new location yourself, the packing likely will not require as much cushioning and wrapping paper.

a. As it is now.

b. If you are packing your own items for a local move if you are taking some of the items to the new location yourself the packing likely will not require as much cushioning and wrapping paper.

c. If you are packing your own items for a local move. If you are taking some of the items to the new location yourself, the packing likely will not require as much cushioning and wrapping paper.

d. If you are packing your own items for a local move, if you are taking. Some of the items to the new location yourself, the packing likely will not require as much cushioning and wrapping paper.

e. If you are packing your own items for a local move, and if you are taking some of the items to the new location yourself, the packing likely will not require as much cushioning and wrapping paper.

34. What is the most effective way to write sentence 11 (reproduced here)?

The basic fundamentals of environmental responsibility give rise to an idea you might not have considered.

a. As it is now.
b. The basic fundamentals of environmental responsibility give rise to an idea you might knot have considered.
c. The fundamentals of environmental responsibility give rise to an idea you might not have considered.
d. The environmental responsibility give rise to an idea you might not have considered.
e. The fundamentals of environmental responsibility, an idea you might not have considered.

35. To eliminate an irrelevant sentence, which sentence in the final paragraph should be deleted?

a. Your items will not be jostled in a large truck for a long period of time.
b. Be certain to advise others of your new address.
c. Instead of the traditional cardboard boxes, you might consider obtaining plastic reusable moving crates from a company specializing in this environmentally friendly option.
d. This option will allow you to have the crates delivered, and you can pack them yourself.
e. Then you can have them picked up from your new location.

36. Which sentence would be the most effective concluding sentence to add to the passage?

a. Organizations are available to help with moving.
b. Local moves are easier than international moves.
c. Careful preparation can result in effective packing and moving.
d. Friends and neighbors can be important resources as you plan a move.
e. The environment is an important consideration when you prepare to move.

Research Skills

Directions for questions 37 through 40: The questions that follow will measure your basic research skills. Read each question and then select the best option.

37. Read the following citation.

Salazar, Joanne, Dinah Feldstein, and Michael Johnston. *Analyzing the Supreme Court Justices: 1950–Present.* 3rd ed. New York: National Considerations Publishing, 2015. Print.

Based on the citation, which of the following is accurate?

a. There are three authors of this work.
b. The work has been published online.
c. The work was first published in 1950.
d. Supreme Court justices wrote the work.
e. This is the second edition of the work.

38. Which information would be most relevant to and provide the strongest support of the opinion stated here?

> Opinion:
> Admission to the city's neighborhood swimming pools should be free on Thursdays through Sundays during the summer.

    a. All pools allow for ample parking.
    b. Exercise and a place to gather for activities are important to all families, and this service is provided by the pools.
    c. All pool cleaning systems are currently in working order.
    d. Lifeguards have been hired to staff pools for the season, and pools will be safe for all people in the neighborhood.
    e. All pools are in serious need of repair.

39. Which would be the most effective and credible for obtaining primary source, in-depth evidence for a research project focused on a recently discovered rare local plant?
    a. photograph of the rare local plant
    b. interview with a local botanist who specializes in rare plants
    c. print or electronic encyclopedia article regarding rare plants
    d. questionnaire that has been completed by a local official in the parks department
    e. discussion with students regarding completed fact-finding about the rare plant

40. Which best explains why a narrowing triangle can be an important tool in the process of completing a research paper?
    a. Specific sources for research are clarified through a narrowing triangle.
    b. Content for the middle of a research paper can be quickly formulated through a narrowing triangle.
    c. Information can be drawn from the outline to apply to the research paper while using the narrowing triangle.
    d. Unnecessary time can be invested when in-depth research is conducted for broad topics prior to developing a narrowing triangle.
    e. A conclusion for the research paper can easily be generated through a narrowing triangle.

Part IIa: Argumentative Essay
Time: 30 Minutes

Directions: Read the opinion stated here. To what extent do you agree or disagree with this opinion? Support your views with specific reasons and examples from your own experiences, observations, or reading. Allow 30 minutes for your essay.

> Paparazzi, roving photographers of celebrities, are lazy slackers. They should be subject to civil fines and criminal penalties when they take photographs while celebrities are participating in activities for their personal lives. There should also be fines and criminal penalties when the paparazzi approach young children of celebrities to take their photos.

Source-Based Essay
Time: 30 Minutes

Directions: The following essay assignment asks that you to use information from two different sources to discuss the most important concerns that relate to a specific issue. Allow 30 minutes to write your essay.

Travel to the Moon by humans has been an ongoing source of debate in the United States for many decades. On July 20, 1969, Neil Armstrong, Buzz Aldrin, and Michael Collins traveled to the Moon. Armstrong became the first human to step onto the lunar surface. Since that time, proponents and opponents of human lunar travel have firmly stood their ground. Each side has made compelling arguments regarding the potential return of humans to the Moon. During his tenure as U.S. president, Barack Obama made the decision to suspend plans for future human lunar missions, including the goal of again sending a human to the Moon by 2015. He referenced the expense of this endeavor and the current needs of people on Earth.

Read the two passages carefully and then write an essay in which you identify the most important concerns regarding the issue and explain why they are important. Your essay must draw on information from BOTH of the sources. In addition, you may draw on your own experiences, observations, or reading. Be sure to CITE the sources whether you are paraphrasing or directly quoting.

Source 1

The United States should reinstate programs for human missions to the Moon. There is a great deal to be learned from such travel. Humans can much more effectively conduct research than the research conducted by robotic probes and rovers. There simply is no replacement for human analytical skills and decisions to be made as research is being conducted. A robotic rover simply lacks this capability, and the clunky "arms" of a robotic rover are not able to carefully and delicately extract and examine samples from the lunar surface.

Earlier lunar missions explored only an infinitesimally small quantity of the Moon's surface. There is a great deal more area to explore.

The Moon holds many possibilities for people on Earth. For example, human colonies on the Moon might one day be possible. Without initial human travel to the Moon and research regarding the conditions, however, such colonization would not be possible. There are many risks of cataclysmic events on Earth, including massive volcanic eruptions and asteroid strikes. It is important to begin now to explore potential human habitation of locations other than Earth. . . . It is true that lunar travel and exploration are expensive; however, what price is too steep to place on the potential survival of humanity in the face of potential epic disaster?

The United States must maintain its position at the forefront of other nations in the world. This is important for a variety of reasons, not the least of which is security. It is believed that China, Japan, India, and other nations are working to develop programs for human lunar exploration. While it is not now known exactly what types of weapons or other resources might be developed from a lunar stronghold, it is certainly important that the United States not place itself behind other countries by giving up on lunar exploration. . . .

Adapted from: Patel, Sanjeev. *Research and Frontiers: The Moon.* New York: Powerful Travel Publishing, 2014. 303–312. Web. 5 Oct. 2014.

Source 2

President Obama made the right decision when he suspended plans for human lunar missions, including suspending the goal of sending another human to the Moon by 2015. Human lunar missions cost millions of dollars, and there are so many needs here on Earth for those funds.

A human can spend only a short time on the Moon. It makes a great deal more sense to send a robotic rover to the Moon, just as the United States did with the Mars Rovers for Mars exploration. A robotic rover is able to perform many functions that a scientist can perform, and it can remain on a planet for many years without the expense of a return mission. It can feed data back to scientists on Earth. And the cost of sending a robotic rover to the Moon is substantially less than the cost of sending a human to the Moon.

The assertion that humans might colonize the Moon is so remote a possibility as to be laughable. In order for humans to live on the Moon, it would be necessary to devise and develop some sort artificial atmosphere under a dome or similar structure. This is far beyond the technology available today or at any point in the foreseeable future.

Certainly, these comments are not meant to pummel any and all ideas of human travel to the Moon. It is feasible for private companies to send humans to the Moon. Indeed, private companies have already begun launches into space from Earth. Should a private U.S. company be motivated by vanity or potential revenue to continue such endeavors, this activity should not be denigrated. Such activity does not dip into the pocketbooks and needs of Americans. Such activity does not require revenue from the U.S. government, revenue that would be better spent in taking care of more pressing needs. . . .

Adapted from: Chin, Midori. "Balancing Priorities: Earth and Moon." *Standard Observation Legal Analysis.* 14.3 (2012): 168. Web. 5 Oct. 2014.

Praxis® Core Academic Skills for Educators: Writing Practice Test 4 Answers and Explanations

1. a. The phrase *all ways* refers to a number of methods. The word *always* is the adverb that tells when, so this phrase would correctly be written *always been enamored*. The preposition *through* (choice **b**) is correct in the sentence. A comma must follow the introductory clause, as is done in choice **c**. The article *an* and adjective *executable* in choice **d** correctly modify the noun *model*.

2. c. The phrase *would launch* represents a shift in tense from the past-tense verb in the preceding clause. The capitalization and comma are required in choice **a**. In choice **b** the proper noun *Italy* must be capitalized, and no comma is required preceding the word *and*, as it does not connect two independent clauses. There are no errors in the adjective and noun in choice **d**.

3. b. This is a run-on, as a comma has been placed to separate two independent clauses. A semicolon would be the correct punctuation. The possessive adjective *their* in choice **a** is correct, as it agrees with its antecedent, *Lin and Morgan*. The pronoun *it* in choice **c** references *plan*, so *it* is correct. The verb *included* in choice **d** does not represent a shift in tense, as it is in the same tense as the verb *shared* in the preceding clause.

4. d. The sentence lacks parallel structure. For the sentence to be correct, parallelism would be required: *watching a psychological thriller is more interesting than watching a general drama film.* The introductory phrase in choice **a** is correctly punctuated by a comma. The adjective *psychological* correctly modifies the noun *thriller* in choice **b**. The phrase *more interesting* in choice **c** correctly follows the verb *is*.

5. d. The phrase *not only* appears in the first clause, so *but*, not *and*, is the correct conjunction in the second clause. The adjective in choice **a**, *unexpected*, and noun *blizzard* are correct. The pronoun *us* is correct in choice **b**. The phrase *to go to work* is correct in choice **c**.

6. a. The word *people* is the plural form of the word *person*. The apostrophe to form the possessive form of *people* must precede the letter *s*, not follow it: *people's*. The verb *differ* agrees with the subject *interests*, and the adverb *substantially* is correct in choice **b**. The semicolon in choice **c** correctly separates two independent clauses, and the comma correctly follows *otherwise*. The phrase *would be*, conditional, is correct in choice **d**.

7. a. The word *good* modifies the verb *did*. *Good* is an adjective, so it is incorrect. An adverb is required to modify a verb. The correct word would be the adverb *well*. The semicolon in choice **b** is the correct punctuation to join two independent clauses. The antecedent of the pronoun *they* is *Oscar and Pat*, so *they* is the correct pronoun to use in choice **c**. The adjective *few* in choice **d** is correct, as it modifies *competitions*.

8. b. The correct word would be *led*, the past tense of *to lead*. The introductory clause *last week* makes it clear that the action in the sentence occurred in the past. The comma must appear after the introductory phrase, and *Hollywood* must be capitalized, as it is a proper adjective (choice **a**). The preposition and its object are correct as used in choice **c**. The pronoun *them* agrees with its antecedent: *dogs* (choice **d**).

9. e. There are no errors in the conventions of standard grammar and usage in this sentence. The plural form of the verb, *are*, agrees with the plural subject, *cousins* (choice **a**). The word *Italy* is correctly capitalized, as it names a country. No comma is required before the word *and* (choice **b**). The comma must precede the word *and*, as the word *and* joins two independent clauses as it does in choice **c**. Commas are required to separate the items in the list (choice **d**).

10. c. The pronoun *it* is vague in this sentence. Based on the content of the sentence, it is not possible to determine the antecedent. To correct the sentence, it would be necessary to first determine what is being referenced by the pronoun *it*. The noun *audacity* is used and spelled correctly in choice **a**. In choice **b** the word *coworker* is correctly spelled. Additionally, the comma that follows *coworker* is correct, as it follows an introductory clause. The adjective *volatile* is correctly spelled and used in choice **d**, and *workplace* is a single compound word.

11. a. The word *senators* is a common noun, not a proper noun. It does not name specific senators, so it should not be capitalized. The possessive pronoun *their* (choice **b**) agrees with the plural noun *senators*. The word *to* is correctly spelled in choice **c**. The adjective *specific* is spelled correctly and correctly modifies the noun *causes* in choice **d**.

12. e. The sentence is free of errors. The comma is correctly placed in choice **a**. The clause in choice **b**, *such as Michelangelo and Leonardo da Vinci*, must be set off by commas, as it is a nonessential clause. The verb created as used in choice **c** is in the same tense as the verb *lived*. The proper noun *Middle Ages* names a specific period in history, so it must be capitalized (choice **d**).

13. e. The sentence is free of errors. *Among* is correct, as three people are referenced in choice **a**. The apostrophe in choice **b** is correctly placed in the contraction *I'd*. Two independent clauses are joined by *however* in choice **c**. The semicolon preceding and comma following *however* provide the correct punctuation. The plural possessive pronoun *our* agrees with *the three of us* in choice **d**.

14. c. The possessive pronoun must agree with *Ana*, so the possessive pronoun must be singular: *her*, not *their*. The comma used in choice **a** is correctly placed before *so*. The word *backpack* is a compound word; it is spelled and used correctly in choice **b**. The verb does not represent a shift in tense in choice **d**.

15. b. The adjective *less* would be correct in comparison of two people or things. In this sentence, four people are being compared, so *least* would be the correct adjective. The punctuation that precedes the spoken words in choice **a** (a comma with an opening quotation mark) is correct. A semicolon correctly separates the two independent clauses in choice **c**. The word *due* is spelled and used correctly in choice **d**.

16. c. The correct intensive pronoun agrees with *Keisha and Taylor*, so the correct word is *themselves*. Because choices **a**, **d**, and **e** do not agree, they are incorrect. *Herselves* (choice **b**) is not a word. The correct intensive pronoun agrees with *Keisha and Taylor*, so the correct word is *themselves*.

17. c. The direct objects are in the correct case—objective case. The pronoun *her* in choice **a** is correct, as it is in the objective case (the case for a direct object), but the pronoun *I* is incorrect, as it is in the nominative case (the case for a subject). In choices **b**, **d**, and **e** the direct objects are in nominative case, rather than objective case (*her and me*).

18. b. The clause *who is a film director* is a nonessential clause, so it must be set off from the rest of the sentence by commas. If the writer had several mothers, only one of whom was a film director, and if this information were essential to the meaning of the sentence, then the commas would not be required.

19. c. The noun in the subject, *children*, is plural. The nouns in the predicate must agree with the plural subject. The nouns in the predicate, *jackets* and *hats*, are plural, so they agree with the plural subject.

20. d. An apostrophe is required for *can't recall* and *we're certain* but not for *were made*, as *were* is a verb in the phrase *were made*.

21. e. The phrase *joined together with* is redundant. The word *joined*—without the word *together* or *with*—is correct. Choice **a** is incorrect because the phrase *joined together with* is redundant. Additionally, choices **b** and **d** are also redundant. Choice **c** is incorrect because the word *joining* does not provide the verb required by the sentence.

22. d. As originally written, the sentence means that *you* are currently playing the lead role in a new television series. The modifier is misplaced. The sentence in choice **d**, however, corrects the problem by properly placing the modifier. Choices **a**, **b**, **c**, and **e** are incorrect because the modifiers are misplaced.

23. d. The noun *grandmother* is a common noun; it does not name a specific grandmother, so the word *grandmother* is not capitalized. The word *bestseller* is also a common noun; it does not name a specific bestseller, so it is not capitalized.

24. e. This is a complete sentence. The remaining answer choices are fragments.

25. a. This idiom means that someone was very surprised. The remaining choices do not indicate shock.

26. a. The phrase *not only* appears in the first clause, so *but* is the correct coordinating conjunction in the second clause. Due to use of *not only* and *also*, using *nor* (choice **b**) and *neither* (choice **e**) is incorrect. *Or* (choice **c**) is not the correct coordinating conjunction for use with *not only* and *also*. Use of the phrase *not only* in the first clause and use of the word *also* in the second clause requires a different coordinating conjunction than used in choice **d**.

27. a. Grammar and usage in the sentence are correct. The past participle that should be used in choice **b** is *known*, not *knew*. Additionally, this sentence and choice **c** include a double negative: *never* and *nobody*. Choices **d** and **e** are incorrect because the word *quick* in the sentence modifies the verb *finish*, so this modifier should be an adverb (*quickly*), not an adjective (*quick*). Additionally, the use of *never* and *nobody* in choice **e** creates a double negative.

28. b. The verbs in the independent clause must comport to the verb in the dependent clause in number and tense. The verbs *saw*, *went*, and *ate* comport to the verb *arrived* in person and number. Due to the phrase *last month* and the verb *arrived*, the verbs in the independent clause must be in the past tense, which isn't the case in choice **a**. The verbs in the independent clause must comport to the verb *arrived* in the dependent clause. In choice **c**, the verb *went* comports to *arrived*, but the words *seen* and *eaten* are participles, so this answer choice is incorrect. The verbs in the independent clause must comport to the verb in the dependent clause in number and tense, so choice **d** is incorrect. The verbs in choice **e** do not agree with the subject.

29. c. The possessive pronoun *he* agrees with the singular *each*. The possessive pronoun *their* in choice **a** is plural, not singular. The possessive pronoun is misspelled as *there* in choice **b**. Even if it were spelled correctly (*their*), it would still be incorrect, as the possessive pronoun must agree with the singular *each*. The possessive pronoun *their* is plural, not singular. Choice **d** includes *mens'*, which is not a word. Additionally, it includes *their*, which is the plural possessive pronoun. This sentence requires the singular possessive pronoun—to agree with *each*. While choice **e** includes the possessive pronoun *his*, which agrees with the singular *each member*, the answer choice also includes *mens*, which is not a word.

30. d. This revision clarifies the sentence, as the vague pronoun *it* has been replaced by *an international move*. This revision makes it clear that international moves can be the most difficult moves. Choices **b** and **e** create fragments. Additionally, these choices and choice **c** fail to clarify the vague pronoun *it*.

31. d. The adjective *good* is vague and overused. Replacing the adjective *good* with the adjective *effective* provides more specific information. Choices **a**, **b**, and **c** are incorrect because they continue to use the word *good*. Additionally, choices **b** and **c** delete important information that appears in the original sentence. Choice **e** is wordy and fails to provide valuable information.

32. a. All of the words in the organization's name—other than the minor word *and*—must be capitalized. This reasoning makes all the other answer choices incorrect.

33. e. The word *and* has been added, which cures the run-on and creates a complete sentence. Choices **b** and **d** are incorrect because they do not contain complete sentences. Choice **c** contains a run-on and a fragment.

34. c. The phrase *basic fundamentals* is redundant. Deleting the word *basic* cures the redundancy. Choice **b** includes the mistake of *knot* for *not*. The revision in choice **d** changes the meaning of the sentence. Additionally, the verb (*give*) does not agree with the subject (*responsibility*). Choice **e** does not contain a complete sentence.

35. b. The main idea of the paragraph relates to packing, and advising others of a new address is not relevant to packing. The remaining answer choices are relevant to the main idea of the paragraph, which relates to packing.

36. c. The entire passage relates to preparation for packing and moving, so this sentence summarizes the information in the passage and provides a strong conclusion. While the passage does reference an organization, choice **a** does not summarize the passage and would not provide a strong conclusion. While the passage does reference local and international moves, this is only a small part of the passage. Choice **b** does not summarize the ideas in the passage and would fail to provide a strong conclusion. The help of friends and neighbors is mentioned in the passage, but this is only a small part of the passage. Choice **d** does not summarize the ideas in the passage and would fail to provide a strong conclusion. Environmental considerations are mentioned in the passage but are not the main focus of the passage. Choice **e** fails to summarize the ideas in the passage, and it would not provide a strong conclusion.

37. a. The authors are Salazar, Feldstein, and Johnston. The word *Print* indicates that this work has been published in hardcopy. There is no indication within the citation that the work has been published online (choice **b**). The 1950 date in choice **c** is part of the title of the work. The phrase *Supreme Court Justices* is part of the work's title; Supreme Court justices are not the authors of the work (choice **d**). Choice **e** is incorrect because this is the third edition of the work, as indicated by *3rd ed.*

38. b. Free admission would mean that all families, regardless of ability to pay admission, would have a place to participate in activities and exercise. Ample parking could be relevant, but choice **a** does not provide the strongest support for the opinion. While pools would need to be in working order for families to be able to swim, choice **c** does not strongly support the opinion. It does not relate to free admission. Safety is important, but choice **d** does not strongly support the opinion. It does not relate to free admission. Choice **e** is incorrect because it does not support the opinion.

39. b. The botanist would provide primary source information from an expert. While a photograph (choice **a**) would be a primary source, it would not provide in-depth information. The sources in choice **c** and **e** would not provide primary source material. While the responses in choice **d** would provide primary source material, there is insufficient information in this answer choice to show that the local park officials would have in-depth information regarding the rare plant that is the subject of the research.

40. d. A narrowing triangle is used for the purpose of narrowing a broad idea to a topic that is sufficiently narrow for a project. If in-depth research is conducted prior to narrowing, unnecessary time can be invested. A narrowing triangle is used for the purpose of narrowing a broad topic to one that is sufficiently narrow and suitable for a research project; it is not used to clarify resources (choice **a**). The middle of a research paper (choice **b**) is not developed until after the topic has been narrowed, research has been conducted, and organizational pattern has been determined. The outline strategy (choice **c**) is not used until after the topic has been narrowed and research has been conducted. The conclusion (choice **e**) of a research paper is not developed until after the topic has been narrowed, research has been conducted, organizational pattern has been determined, and drafts are being written.

Sample Responses for the Argumentative Essay

Sample Score 6 Response

I do not agree that there should be civil and criminal penalties when paparazzi snap photos of celebrities, nor do I agree that paparazzi are lazy slackers; however, I do agree that paparazzi should be subject to civil fines and criminal penalties when they approach young children of celebrities to take their photos. These children have not asked for celebrity status. They have not asked for fame. Even if they have a parent who is a celebrity, they are just children.

I know from my own experience that my young children are often frightened when they experience sudden movement and loud noises when we are out. I have seen the clips on television of paparazzi racing toward the children of celebrities, shouting at these children as photographers swirl all around them. The children look absolutely terrified. Some sob and bury their faces in a parent's shoulder as the paparazzi shout at them. It does not matter how much money the paparazzi can make from these photographs. Income does not warrant this type of behavior.

Civil fines and criminal penalties are a step in the right direction to show that this type of fear-inducing behavior around children will not be tolerated; these sanctions will punish intolerable behavior. Additionally, these sanctions will serve as a strong deterrent. If the paparazzi realize they will have to give up the money they make from the photos, and if they discover that they could spend time in jail and then have a criminal record for frightening these children, then they will think twice before engaging in this behavior. I would even go so far as to say that the same penalties that apply to paparazzi for photographing children of celebrities should be extended to the magazines and websites that publish the photos, as it is important to make the punishment stringent across the board.

While it is clear that approaching children of celebrities to snap their photos is unacceptable, it is not accurate to refer to the paparazzi as "lazy." This behavior of the paparazzi is not to be condoned; however, these photographers race from location to location to try to get photographs, so it is not truly accurate to characterize them as "lazy slackers."

While I believe that paparazzi should be subject to civil fines and criminal penalties for approaching celebrity children to snap photos, I do not believe this should also be the case when paparazzi approach celebrities to take their photos when celebrities' children are not present. Celebrities make millions of dollars. The price I pay for a movie ticket is becoming more astronomical all the time; it is currently ten dollars or more and is funneled in the direction of the celebrities. There is a price the celebrities pay for fame. This price is being recognizable and being the target of constant adoration by fans, fans who want to see the celebrities' photos as the celebrities go about their everyday lives. This is part and parcel of inviting fame, and celebrities know this as they take on such status.

I do not have to tolerate photographers racing toward me and snapping my photo as I go to work, head to the cleaners, or spend time at a local restaurant; however, I also do not garner the income of a celebrity. If I did, I would know that fame has many facets and that one of these is tolerating constant adoration. We all have negative and positive consequences of our life choices, and a cadre of photographers is a negative consequence for celebrities who have chosen their life pursuits; however, it should never be anticipated as a negative consequence for their young children, who have not chosen this life pursuit.

About This Essay

This extremely strong response begins by explaining the parts of the prompt with which the writer agrees and disagrees, explaining the distinction between photographs taken of celebrities and photos taken of their children. The essay continues by providing personal examples of the fear young children can experience when faced with loud noises and sudden movement while out in public. The essay also provides a clear, strong example of children's reactions to the paparazzi when the children are out with their parents.

The essay continues by stating the reasons for civil and criminal penalties, and the writer provides support by stating that the paparazzi would lose income. The essay also points out the deterrent effect of criminal penalties. The writer takes the argument and support one step further by suggesting that websites and magazines publishing the photos should also face penalties.

As the essay continues, the writer refutes the position in the prompt that paparazzi are lazy. The essay provides a strong example, explaining that paparazzi must race from location to location, which contraindicates laziness.

The essay then makes a clear and strong point of elaborating on the position that while paparazzi should be punished for taking photos of celebrities' children, the paparazzi should not be punished for taking photos of the celebrities when their children are not present. The essay supports this position by detailing the huge incomes garnered by celebrities.

The essay concludes by drawing a distinction between the life of the writer and the lives of celebrities. The writer cogently points out that people experience negative and positive consequences for their life choices. The writer elaborates by providing details to explain that the writer does not have to tolerate hordes of paparazzi when the writer goes through the daily routine; however, the writer also does not have the income of a celebrity. As the writer notes, due to the income of celebrities, a positive consequence that comes to them through their life choices, the celebrities must also tolerate the negative consequence of being constantly approached for photos. The essay's final sentence pulls the essay together, reiterating the distinction between a life chosen by celebrities and a life that is not chosen by their children.

The writer offers strong organization, providing clear development of the writer's position. This is accomplished through a focus on the writer's position and support for this position through clear details and examples. The writer also provides a variety of sentence lengths and types, which adds interest and credibility to the essay. The essay is free from errors in mechanics, usage, and grammar. All of these qualities result in the essay clearly deserving a score of 6.

Sample Score 5 Response

I agree that paparazzi should not be allowed to take photos of celebrities or their children, but I do not agree that paparazzi are lazy. They do a great deal of work to take the photos they take from day to day. Even though these are photos they should not be taking, it does not logically follow that the paparazzi are lazy.

It is very sad when human beings are not able to go about their daily lives without having photographers mob them and snap photos of them every time they walk a few feet down the sidewalk. I've even seen photos taken by the paparazzi that showed celebrities doing workout exercises in places where the celebrities clearly thought no cameras were nearby. It isn't fair that celebrities' never have the chance to relax and just be themselves without the necessity to be performing every minute of every day.

It is true that celebrities make a great deal of money, but so do people in many other walks of life, and all of them don't have to push past huge groups of photographers coming at them to take their photographs. There is no reason to assume that just because a person makes large sums of money, that person should lose the right to live a daily life like a normal person. One of neighbors has a friend who is an actor and lives in New York. My neighbor told me that his friend was actually injured by paparazzi who just wouldn't stop coming closer and closer to try to snap her photo. This was a terrifying experience for her just as being pursued by paparazzi must be a terrifying experience for all celebrities.

As bad as it is for paparazzi to race to celebrities to take their photos, it is even worse when paparazzi race toward children of celebrities. At least the adult celebrities understand what is happening. The children likely do not understand. No matter how many times the paparazzi approach them, screaming and snapping photos, the experience is a scary one for young children. Celebrities have even testified before Congress about the fear their children feel when paparazzi approach.

The real problem here is not with the paparazzi. It is with the magazines and Web sites that purchase these photos. If the magazines and Web sites refused to buy the photos, the paparazzi would stop taking them, as they would not make any money from the photos they snapped. Until the purchases of the photos stop, though, it is necessary to punish the people who are constantly approaching the celebrities and their children. Civil penalties and criminal charges are strong admonitions that show this type of behavior will not be tolerated.

About This Essay

The essay opens by clearly stating the writer's position. The writer agrees with part of the prompt but not with the entire prompt. The writer explains agreement with the statement that paparazzi should not be permitted to take photos of celebrities and their children; however, the writer points out disagreement with the statement that paparazzi are lazy.

The essay continues by pointing out that celebrities are humans and should have the opportunity to go about their daily lives without having paparazzi constantly snapping photos of them. The essay provides an example of paparazzi managing to snap photos at workout facilities.

As the essay continues, the writer points out that celebrities do make great amounts money—as a number of people do. The essay explains that all people who earn substantial incomes do not have to tolerate paparazzi constantly coming at them. This comparison provides strong support for the writer's position.

The essay goes on to make the point that as bad as it is for adult celebrities to be approached by paparazzi, it is even worse for the paparazzi to approach celebrities' children. To strongly exemplify the seriousness of the problem, the writer details the work of celebrities to bring this issue before members of Congress.

In the conclusion, the writer details the cause of the paparazzi problem, stating that if magazines and websites refused to purchase the photos, the paparazzi would stop taking them. Short of that event, however, the writer states that civil penalties and criminal punishment would show that this type of behavior would not be tolerated. This clearly shows that the writer has come full circle in the essay—by opening with the position, supporting the position, and reiterating the position.

The writer does have clear organization throughout the essay; however, the examples and details, while applicable, would be stronger if they were to offer greater perception about the depth of the issue. The essay does offer a variety of sentence types and lengths; however, the effectiveness of the sentences is not consistent. Additionally, the vocabulary could be more powerful. While the response has few errors in grammar, usage, and mechanics, it does contain a couple of errors, such as the use of the possessive *celebrities'* rather than the plural noun *celebrities* in the second paragraph and the lack of a comma after the word *her* in this sentence: *This was a terrifying experience for her just as being pursued by paparazzi must be a terrifying experience for all celebrities.* These issues keep the essay from rising to the level of an essay scored at 6.

Sample Score 4 Response

I agree that paparazzi should suffer consequences for taking photos of celebrities' young children; however, I do not agree that paparazzi should suffer consequences for taking photos of the celebrities, and I do not think paparazzi are lazy.

Young children of celebrities can be vulnerable, and they can be frightened by photographers, they can be especially frightened when they are just walking out the front door of a home.

Celebrities, on the other hand, should be used to fame, he should be accustomed to having their photographs taken all the time. After all, celebrities sign on for fame. This is what they ask for, so it only makes sense that they must accept the constant attention that comes along with this fame.

While I disapprove of the way paparazzi make their living, I do not think it is correct to say that they are lazy. They do their work, just as so many other people do their work.

So, it is clear that paparazzi should suffer penalties for going after the children of celebrities to take their photos, but they should not be punished for taking photos of the celebrities.

About This Essay

This essay demonstrates competence. The writer clearly states positions, including agreement with the position that paparazzi should be punished for photographing celebrities' young children and disagreement with the position that paparazzi should be punished for photographing celebrities. The writer also expresses disagreement with the position that paparazzi are lazy. The essay is organized, beginning with the position regarding celebrities' young children, continuing with discussion of the position regarding photographing celebrities, going on to state a position regarding whether the paparazzi are lazy, and then wrapping up by restating two of the positions.

The writer explains some key ideas with adequate support; however, additional key ideas and stronger, insightful support would make the essay rise to a higher score. The essay is also in need of more examples to support the positions stated by the writer.

Overall, the writer shows control of grammar, usage, and mechanics; however, there are some errors in these areas. For example, the writer includes a run-on in the second paragraph: *Young children of celebrities can be vulnerable, and they can be frightened by photographers, they can be especially frightened when they are just walking out the front door of a home.* The writer also makes an error in parallelism in the third paragraph: *Celebrities, on the other hand, should be used to fame, he should be accustomed to having their photographs taken all the time.*

Sample Score 3 Response

It is true that these photographers should note be taking pictures. Celebrities have rights. They're children have rights. But the papparzi are given too many rights. They should suffer serious penalties for taking pictures of celebrities and their children. They should be punished for doing this. Don't they ever think about how the people they are taking pictures of feel. I don't think they do, I don't think they care at all.

What happens to the celebrities after someone takes the picture? What happens to they're children? There should be more caring about the feelings they have, their should be more laws to stop papparzi from behaving this way.

I don't get why the papprazi get to make money. Theyre kind of like a herd of elephants always stampeding after others. They should be punished because they fail to respect the rights of the people they are photographing.

About This Essay

While there is some competence in this essay, it contains serious flaws. It limits itself to stating that paparazzi are given too many rights and should suffer serious penalties; however, it fails to detail what these rights and penalties might be. The organization is weak, and there is very little development of ideas. While the writer indicates a disdain for the action of paparazzi, the writer does not fully develop the reasons for this disdain. The essay includes many errors in grammar, usage, and mechanics.

Sample Score 2 Response

Papparrazzi who take photos of celebrities and children are ridiculous. They run around taking photos and bothering people all day long. Why should they get real jobs when all they have to do is take pictures? They are just lazy and irritating.

You can see how scared the children are when paparazzi take photos, but do the paparazzi care? No, they don't care about the children, they don't care about the celebrities. They only care about themselves.

In conklusun, the paparazi just take advantage of celebrities and children to make money. They should not be aloud to do this.

About This Essay

This essay is seriously flawed; it contains only the most minimal of development. It states no clear position, and it lacks organization. The essay emotionally states a lack of approval for the action of the paparazzi; however, it fails to include examples and strong details and it contains many errors in mechanics, grammar, and usage.

Sample Score 1 Response

No, I don't think the paparazi shud take photos of people who are celebrities. And they shouldn't take pitchers of their children. They are just lazy, they should get a reel job. They should wurk for a living just lik we all do.

Who do they think they are anyway? Their not important, they just want to take pitchers and make lots of money. Everywon wants to make lots of money. That is true. They just should never take these fotos. They should have respect for others. Those poor children!

About This Essay

This essay is underdeveloped; it alludes loosely to the topic, but it fails to develop an argument. The essay shows fundamental deficiencies in writing skills. It contains serious and persistent writing errors, displaying issues with usage, mechanics, language facility, and development. All of these issues make the essay very confusing.

Sample Responses for the Source-Based Essay

Sample Score 6 Response

There is a clear division of opinion regarding whether human missions to the Moon should be resumed. This is an important issue, as resuming such travel could result in millions of government dollars being spent. A failure to resume such travel, however, could result in the United States falling behind other nations in research, potential alternative colonization, and potential weaponry for protection.

Sanjeev Patel believes human lunar missions should resume (*Research and Frontiers: The Moon*). Patel offers clear reasons, while countering potential arguments against his stance. "Humans can much more effectively conduct research than the research conducted by robotic probes and rovers." Humans can do delicate work and critical analysis that cannot be accomplished by robots (Patel).

Another reason for space exploration is that on prior missions, only a very small quantity of the Moon was explored (Patel). In examining the potential of the Moon, Patel discusses possible colonization of the Moon, which could be valuable in the event of a cataclysmic Earth event; however, Patel offers almost no specifics regarding feasibility.

As referenced by Patel, the security of the United States is an important concern. It is thought that many nations are planning human lunar missions. Patel admits that types of future weaponry might not be known at the current time but that it is important that the United States not fall behind other nations.

Midori Chin articulates her support for Obama's decision to suspend plans for human lunar missions. Millions of dollars would have been spent for these human lunar missions, "and there are so many needs here on Earth for those funds" (Chin).

In referencing the argument of robotic rover versus a human on the Moon, Chin states that a human can live only a short time on the Moon, while a rover could remain there for a long period of time. The Mars Rovers provide strong support regarding this longevity (Chin). Still, Chin fails to reference the delicate work and analytical skills of a human. This damages the credibility of her position.

There are strong opposing views to Patel's statements regarding lunar colonization. "The assertion that humans might colonize the Moon is so remote a possibility as to be laughable." Such colonization is far beyond the technology available at the present time (Chin). Chin discusses the possibility of private companies sending humans to the Moon, an interesting alternative to government funding.

In conclusion, there are strong pros and cons regarding human lunar travel. Based on the arguments and support presented in these two pieces, the benefits of human lunar travel at the present time are not worth the expense such travel would incur.

About This Essay

This essay demonstrates a high degree of competence. The writer explains why the concerns are important, immediately identifying the issues upon opening the essay: *This is an important issue, as resuming such travel could result in millions of government dollars being spent. A failure to resume such travel, however, could result in the United States falling behind other nations in research, potential alternative colonization, and potential weaponry for protection.*

In addition to identifying the issues, the writer provides insight into the importance of the issues and the positions of each author. For example, the writer notes Patel's lack of support regarding feasibility of human lunar colonization. The writer also recognizes the failure of Chin to address the delicate and analytical nature of human work: *Still, Chin fails to reference the delicate work and analytical skills of a human. This damages the credibility of her position.* The writer's insight is an important element in elevating the essay to a score of 6.

The writer incorporates information from both sources, and the writer organizes and develops ideas logically. The writer opens by stating the important issues. The writer continues by discussing Patel's positions and then discussing Chin's positions. The writer compares the positions of the two authors.

The writer offers substantial variety in sentence structure and length throughout the essay. The writer also cites both sources when paraphrasing and quoting. The writer clearly displays facility in the use of language, offering strong grammar, usage, and mechanics. For all of these reasons, the essay most certainly deserves a score of 6.

Sample Score 5 Response

There is a clear division of opinion regarding human lunar space travel by the United States government. Some believe this type of travel is essential, others believe it should not be pursued. The issues related to human lunar travel are of great merit. Such travel could add to the knowledge base of scientists. It could offer the potential of lunar colonization, and it could provide a base for weapons that could one day protect the security of the United States.

In consideration of research. Some believe that robotic probes and rovers could do a more effective job than humans could ("Balancing Priorities: Earth and Moon"). Midori Chin states that humans would be able to live only a short time on the Moon, while rovers, such as the Mars Rovers could remain on the Moon for many years.

Not everyone agrees that rovers are the most effective vehicles for research. In Research and Frontiers: The Moon, Sanjeev Patel explains that humans could much more effectively move forward with research than rovers could. "There simply is no replacement for human analytical skills and decisions to be made as research is being conducted. A robotic rover simply lacks this capability, and the clunky 'arms' of a robotic probe are not able to carefully and delicately extract and examine samples from the lunar surface" (Patel).

As Patel explains, humans might one day need to leave Earth as the result of a disaster, such as a volcanic eruption or asteroid strike. Patel states that the Moon holds the key to potential human colonization. Chin

strongly disagrees with this statement. "In order for humans to live on the Moon, it would be necessary to devise and develop some sort of artificial atmosphere under a dome or similar structure" (Chin). Chin states that his simply would not be possible, based on the technology currently available.

Patel makes a strong point of discussing the security of the United States, explaining that many nations are believed to be developing human lunar missions. Chin does not reference this point; however, national security is vital.

Chin makes a very strong point in her piece. She points out that private companies could fund human lunar space travel. This idea makes sense, and it takes the onus off of the United States to expend the funds for human lunar space travel.

In summary, there is a clear split of opinion regarding whether the United States should resume human lunar space travel. While there are cogent ideas on both sides of the argument, the idea that is most reasonable is for human lunar space travel to continue through the funding of private companies, not through the funding of the United States government.

About This Essay

This essay demonstrates clear competence; however, it contains minor errors. The writer provides clear organization by comparing the positions of Patel and Chin when relevant throughout the essay. This method of organization is effective, and it shows clear links between the two pieces, while incorporating information from both sources to identify and explain important concerns. This is just one strong example from the essay:

In consideration of research. Some believe that robotic probes and rovers could do a more effective job than humans could ("Balancing Priorities: Earth and Moon"). Midori Chin states that humans would be able to live only a short time on the Moon, while rovers, such as the Mars Rovers could remain on the Moon for many years.

Not everyone agrees that rovers are the most effective vehicles for research. In Research and Frontiers: The Moon, *Sanjeev Patel explains that humans could much more effectively move forward with research than rovers could. "There simply is no replacement for human analytical skills and decisions to be made as research is being conducted."*

While it is true that the writer clearly identifies the opposing views of the two authors, the writer does not offer keen insight and analysis regarding these positions. Such insight and analysis would have helped to elevate the essay to a score of 6.

The writer provides some sentence variety; however, the essay would have been more powerful with greater variety. The writer cites both sources when paraphrasing and quoting, and the essay is generally free from errors in grammar, usage, and mechanics, although the essay includes this fragment: *In consideration of research.* The essay also contains this run-on: *Some believe this type of travel is essential, others believe it should not be pursued.*

Sample Score 4 Response

The United States has stoped programs for human lunar space travel. Some people think this is a bad idea. Some people think this is a good idea. People could one day live on the Moon. Researchers could do more research on the Moon. There might be weapons the United States could use from the Moon for protection.

Sanjeev Patel wrote Research and Frontiers: The Moon. *He thinks the United States should start sending people to the Moon again. He says scientists could do research there. He says robots can't do this kind of research.*

There is more of the Moon to explore (Patel). People could colonize the Moon. At least, that's what Patel thinks. Midori Chin does not agree ("Balancing Priorities: Earth and Moon"). She thinks it would be hard to colonize the Moon.

It would be less expensive to send a rover to the Moon than to send a person. The rover would not need to come back (Chin).

The United States needs to be protected. Other nations might send people to the Moon (Patel). What if those other countries start putting weapons on the Moon before the United States does. This could be disastrous. The United States might no longer be secure. Chin does not discuss this issue in her piece.

It's possible that someone could still go to the Moon and the United States would not have to pay. Private companies could send people to the Moon (Chin). Then people would still be going to the Moon, but the money would not have to come from the budget of the U.S. governemetn. Many people on Earth need things. It takes money to pay for those things. If private companies send people to the Moon, then the people on Earth could still get the things they need from the goverment.

About This Essay

This essay adequately explains why the concerns are important. The essay also supports the explanation with some links between the two sources. Although the reasons and examples provided are adequate, they are not powerful. For example, the writer skims the surface of sending rovers rather than humans to the Moon; however, the writer does not provide strong reasons or in-depth analysis in this regard. More powerful reasons and examples, as well as a stronger explanation regarding the importance of the concerns, could be instrumental in elevating this essay to a higher score.

The essay cites both sources when paraphrasing, and the writer shows some control in the organization and development of ideas. The writer opens with a rudimentary summary of the issues and then continues by discussing opposing viewpoints regarding issues. The writer also mentions the lack of an opposing viewpoint: *The United States needs to be protected. Other nations might send people to the Moon (Patel). What if those other countries start putting weapons on the Moon before the United States does. This could be disastrous. The United States might no longer be secure. Chin does not discuss this issue in her piece.*

The essay demonstrates adequate use of language and shows some control of grammar, usage, and mechanics, though there are a number of errors (e.g., the misspelling of *stoped* for *stopped* and a period rather than a question mark at the end of a question).

Sample Score 3 Response

There are no more missions scheduled by the U.S. government for humans to travel to the Moon. There are costs to think about. There is research to think about, there is national security to think about. There is another place for people to one day live to think abowt.

Robots could go to the Moon insted of humans. But these robots could not do the kind of work humans could do (Research and Frontiers: The Moon). We've looked at only part of the Moon (Patel). People could live on the Moon if something teribul happens.

The United States has to stay safe. That's why the United States needs to send peepul to the Moon. This is important.

About This Essay

This essay shows some competence, but it contains many flaws. The essay is limited in explaining why the concerns are important. The writer opens by essentially providing a list of things to "think about" but gives little detail about explaining why these are important concerns.

The writer uses a single source, the Patel source, to identify concerns regarding the issue. Reasons and details are inadequate. The writer fails to clearly establish why human lunar space travel is important.

The writer has limited control in the organization and development of ideas. The essay never fully develops any ideas; instead, it states unclear references regarding human lunar travel.

The essay contains an accumulation of errors in the use of language and in grammar, usage, and mechanics. For example, the writer includes run-ons, such as the following: *There is research to think about,*

there is national security to think about. The writer also includes many spelling errors, including *abowt, insted, teribul,* and *peepul.*

Sample Score 2 Response

It is ridiculus to think about spending money to go to the Moon. A person can't breath the air. A robot could live they're. A robot lives on Mars, it do good work. We need money here. Not on the Moon.

How could even won person live on the Moon? Why even think about lots of people living there. Its just silly. The president said we wouldnt send people to the Moon now. This makes sense. Money is to bee spent here. Maybe we could go to live on the Moon in the future, or maybe a companie could send people there now.

About This Essay

This essay is seriously flawed. It does not explain why human lunar travel is an important issue. Instead, it rambles on about the air on the Moon and how ridiculous it is to think about spending money to travel there. Only one source, the Chin source, is used, and its use is weak and unclear. No source is cited. The organization is weak, and there is very little development.

The essay contains frequent serious errors in the use of language and in grammar, usage, and mechanics. For example, the essay contains this error in subject-verb agreement: *it do good work.* The essay contains this fragment: *Not on the Moon.* The essay also includes many spelling errors, such the following: *ridiculus, breath* (for breathe), *won* (for one), *wouldnt,* and *companie.*

Sample Score 1 Response

Travel to space? Maybe good idea. Maybe not a good idea. People could go. Robots could work there. Costs a lot. Peepul couldnt live there for long times.

Country could protect from the Moon, people cud live on the Moon. People needs money here and now.

This is not whut they need later on the Moon. Maybe company would send people to the Moon, that cud wurk. That wud cost less money.

About This Essay

This essay demonstrates fundamental deficiencies in writing skills. Although it alludes to portions of the topic, such as robots on the Moon, the essay is under-developed and almost incoherent. It is filled with serious and persistent writing errors (e.g., run-ons, spelling errors, lack of subject-verb agreement, and fragments).

Praxis® Core Academic Skills for Educators: Mathematics Practice Test 4

Time: 85 Minutes

Directions: Choose the best answer to each of the following questions.

1. Select all of the statements that are true for the regular pentagon *ABCDE*:

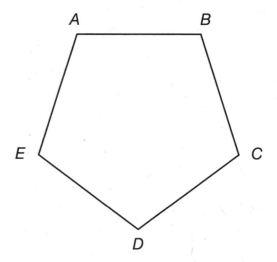

   a. There is at least one line of symmetry.
   b. It has rotation symmetry with vertex *E* being the center of rotation.
   c. There is a glide reflection that maps *ABCDE* onto itself.
   d. It has at least three angles of rotational symmetry about the center of the pentagon.
   e. There is a transformation that maps vertex *A* to vertex *D*.

2. Which sentence best describes the data in the scatterplot?

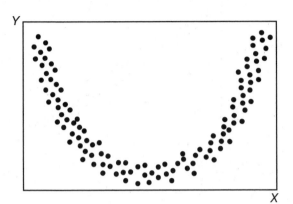

a. The data have a strong positive correlation.
b. The correlation is weak.
c. There is a moderate negative correlation between the variables.
d. There is a strong nonlinear relationship between the two variables.
e. There is no relationship between the data.

3. Let $f(x) = 2x^3 - 3x + 4$ and $g(x) = -2x^2 - 3x - 1$. What is $f(x) - 3x \cdot g(x)$?
a. $8x^3 + 9x^2 + 4$
b. $8x^3 + 6x + 4$
c. $-8x^3 + 9x^2 - 4$
d. $(2x^3 - 6x + 4)(-2x^2 - 3x - 1)$
e. $2x^3 + 2x^2 + 5$

4. The length of a rectangular room is 4 feet less than 3 times the width of the room. The perimeter of the room is 56 feet. What is the length of the room?
a. 8 feet
b. 14 feet
c. 15 feet
d. 41 feet
e. 20 feet

5. On the map of a national park, 1 inch corresponds to 2.4 miles. If the length of a hiking trail on the map is 4.9 inches, what is the length of the real trail?
a. 2.04 miles
b. 7.30 miles
c. 11.76 miles
d. 24.01 miles
e. 30.00 miles

6. Select all of the solutions to this system of equations:
$$\begin{cases} 5x - 3y = 3 \\ 20x = 12y + 12 \end{cases}$$
a. $x = 1, y = 1$
b. $x = 0, y = -1$
c. $x = \frac{3}{5}, y = 0$
d. $x = -1, y = \frac{5}{3}$
e. $x = 2, y = -3$

7. Suppose that a random variable X has the following probability distribution:

x	-2	0	1	3	4
$P(X = x)$	$\frac{1}{6}$	$\frac{1}{4}$	$\frac{1}{8}$	$\frac{5}{24}$	$\frac{1}{4}$

What is the expected value of X as a simplified improper fraction?

8. Which of the following numbers is equivalent to $\frac{8\sqrt{3}}{16\sqrt{15}}$?

   a. $\frac{10}{\sqrt{5}}$

   b. $\frac{1}{2\sqrt{12}}$

   c. $\frac{\sqrt{5}}{10}$

   d. $2\sqrt{5}$

   e. $\frac{\sqrt{5}}{40}$

9. A chairlift at a ski resort carries skiers from the base of the mountain to the top, as shown in this diagram:

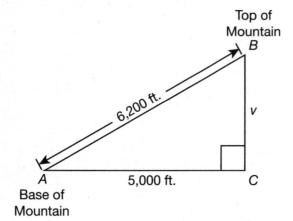

The distance a skier travels while on the chairlift is 6,200 feet. The horizontal distance a skier travels as she moves on the chairlift is 5,000 feet. What is the approximate height of the mountain, rounded to the nearest foot?

   a. 1,200 feet

   b. 3,666 feet

   c. 5,000 feet

   d. 7,965 feet

   e. 11,200 feet

10. Which of these scatterplots illustrates a moderate positive relationship between X and Y?

   a.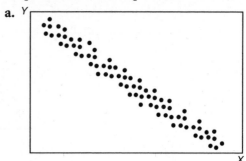

   b.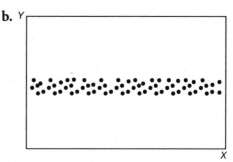

   c.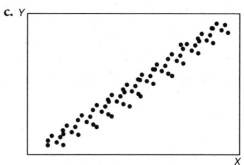

   d.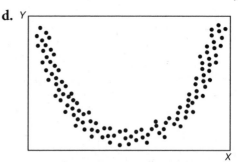

   e.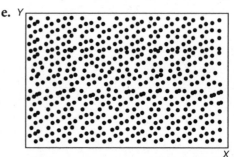

11. Consider this recursively defined function:

$$\begin{cases} f(1) = 5 \\ f(n+1) = 3 - 2f(n), n \ge 1 \end{cases}$$

What is $f(4)$?

12. Which of these statements is true?
   a. $\pi = 3.14$
   b. $\sqrt{\frac{1}{\pi^2}} = \frac{1}{\pi}$
   c. $\sqrt{2} + \sqrt{14} = \sqrt{16}$
   d. $\sqrt{e} \approx 2.718$
   e. $\sqrt{\frac{e}{\pi}} > \sqrt{\frac{\pi}{e}}$

13. Which of these numbers is/are greater than 2? Choose all that apply.
   a. $\pi - 1$
   b. e^{-1}
   c. $\sqrt{3}$
   d. e
   e. $\sqrt{e}$

14. Choose the expression that is equivalent to $8x^2y^3 - 4xy^2 - 2x^2y$.
   a. $2xy(4xy^2 - 2y - x)$
   b. $-2xy(-2y + 4xy^2 - x)$
   c. $2xy^2(4xy - 2y - x)$
   d. $8x^2y^3 - 2xy(2y - x)$
   e. $8x^2y^3 - 6x^3y^3$

15. Consider the triangle ABC:

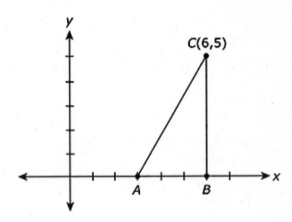

Which of the following transformations creates an image of triangle ABC where A' is at $(-5,0)$, B' is at $(-8,0)$, and C' is at $(-8,5)$?
   a. Rotate triangle ABC around the origin counterclockwise by 90 degrees.
   b. Translate triangle ABC to the left 14 units.
   c. Reflect triangle ABC across the x-axis.
   d. Reflect triangle ABC across the line $x = -1$.
   e. Reflect the triangle ABC across the line $x = 3$.

16. What is the median of the data set represented by this box-and-whisker plot?

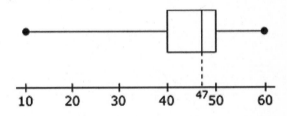

   a. 35
   b. 40
   c. 47
   d. 50
   e. 60

17. Which of these numbers is a prime factor of 504?
   a. 7
   b. 9
   c. 11
   d. 17
   e. 21

18. Which of these is a reasonable estimate for the height of a full-grown cherry tree?
   a. 150 mm
   b. 1.5 km
   c. 35 cm
   d. 12 ft.
   e. 20 in.

19. What is the solution to this system of equations?
$$\begin{cases} y - x = -5 \\ 4y - x = 40 \end{cases}$$

20. Which of the following distributions appears(s) to have a mean that is NOT positive? Select all of the correct answers.

a.

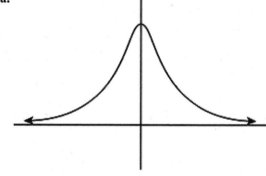

b.

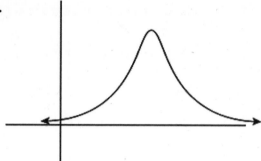

c.

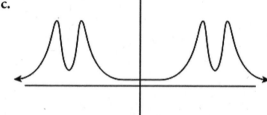

d.

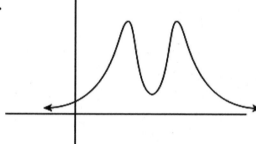

e.

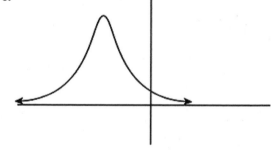

21. Bob's favorite recipe for cake frosting calls for 1.5 cups of sugar and 0.5 cups of butter, but he has only 1 cup of sugar in his pantry. If he wants to produce the same type of frosting as in the recipe, how much butter should he use with his 1 cup of sugar?

   a. 3 cups

   b. 1 cup

   c. $\frac{1}{3}$ cup

   d. $\frac{1}{4}$ cup

   e. $\frac{1}{6}$ cup

22. Find the value of x:
$$\frac{3}{4}x - 1 = -\left(\frac{3}{8}x - 2\right)$$

   a. $-\frac{8}{9}$

   b. $\frac{9}{24}$

   c. $\frac{17}{9}$

   d. $\frac{24}{9}$

   e. 15

23. If the radius of a circular garden is three times the radius of a circular flower bed, the area of the garden is how many times the area of the flower bed?

   a. $\frac{1}{9}$

   b. 3

   c. 6

   d. 9

   e. 27

24. What is the slope of the line graphed here?

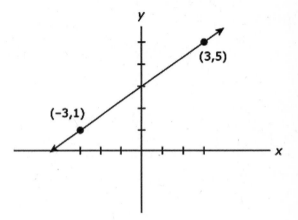

   a. $-\frac{2}{3}$

   b. 0

   c. $\frac{2}{3}$

   d. $\frac{3}{2}$

   e. 2

25. Jeannette has $7\frac{2}{5}$ gallons of paint and wishes to paint as many panels of her fence as possible. Each panel requires $\frac{7}{8}$ gallon of paint. How many complete panels can she paint?

26. Frank has $140 to spend at a cookware store. A specialty kitchen gadget costs $9.50 and a container of spices averages $4.25. If G represents the number of gadgets and S represents the number of containers of spices, which of the following inequalities accurately describes the relationship between G and S?

   a. $140 - 9.50G \le 4.25S$

   b. $140 \ge G + S$

   c. $9.50S + 4.25G \le 140$

   d. $9.50G + 4.25S \le 140$

   e. $(9.50G)(4.25S) < 140$

27. Consider the parallelogram *WXYZ* shown here. What is the value of *d*?

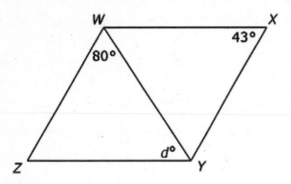

a. 43°
b. 57°
c. 60°
d. 80°
e. 137°

28. The diameter of a spherical oil tank is 2 meters. What is the volume of the tank?

a. $\frac{1}{3}\pi$ cubic meters
b. $\frac{4}{3}\pi$ cubic meters
c. 4π cubic meters
d. $\frac{32}{3}\pi$ cubic meters
e. 32π cubic meters

29. Consider the following distribution, and then choose all of the true statements:

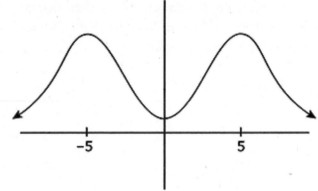

a. The distribution is symmetric.
b. The distribution is bimodal.
c. The distribution is skewed left.
d. The mean of this distribution is positive.
e. The median is greater than the mean.

30. The directions on a can of frozen orange-juice concentrate read, "Mix contents with two cans of water." How many 8-ounce cans of concentrate are needed to make 384 fluid ounces of juice?

31. A sixth-grade teacher is going to select a student to serve as this month's hall monitor. To do this, he randomly selects a letter from the alphabet and then chooses the first student in his roster whose last name begins with that letter. Which statement is true?
   a. This would be fair for a class of 50, but not for a class of 20.
   b. The selection is unfair because there may not be an equal number of students for each letter.
   c. The selection is fair because students with an uncommon last name will not be singled out.
   d. The selection is fair because each letter has an equal chance of being selected.
   e. The selection is unfair because he did a random selection of letters instead of numbers.

32. Which of the following quadratic equations has/have imaginary solution(s)? Select all that apply.
   a. $2x^2 + 8 = 0$
   b. $-2x^2 - 6x = 0$
   c. $x^2 + 9x + 2 = 0$
   d. $2x^2 - 15 = 0$
   e. $2x^2 + x + 3 = 0$

33. A professional tennis player can serve the ball at 110 miles per hour. Which of the following numerical expressions is the speed of her serve in feet per second? (Note that 1 mile = 5,280 feet.)
   a. $\frac{110}{60 \times 60}$ feet per second
   b. $\frac{110}{60}$ feet per second
   c. $\frac{110 \times 5,280}{60 \times 60}$ feet per second
   d. $\frac{110 \times 60 \times 60}{5,280}$ feet per second
   e. $\frac{110 \times 5,280}{60}$ feet per second

34. A tool shed is shaped like a cube. The surface area, including the floor and ceiling, is 294 square meters. What is the volume of the shed?
   a. 7 cubic meters
   b. 49 cubic meters
   c. 216 cubic meters
   d. 294 cubic meters
   e. 343 cubic meters

35. A single card is selected from a standard deck of 52 playing cards. Which of the following statements is/are true?
   I. P(getting a black card or getting a jack) $= \frac{7}{13}$
   II. P(getting a 4 or getting a red 8) $= \frac{3}{26}$
   III. P(getting a king and a club) $= \frac{16}{52}$

   a. I only
   b. I and II only
   c. II and III only
   d. III only
   e. I, II, and III

36. Suppose that f is an invertible function. Look at the table of values for $f(x)$.

x	-4	-2	-1	0	1	2
$f(x)$	0	2	3	5	1	-1

What is the value of the expression $f^{-1}(f^{-1}(-1))$, where f^{-1} represents the inverse function of f?

37. Which of these is equivalent to the expression $\frac{7}{12} \times 2^3 + \frac{1}{12} \times 2^4$?

   a. $\frac{2}{3} \times 2^3$

   b. $\frac{3}{4} \times 6$

   c. $\frac{1}{2} \times 2^3$

   d. $\frac{3}{4} \times 2^4$

   e. $\frac{3}{4} \times 2^3$

38. Two brothers are reading the same book, but one of them is 4 pages behind the other. If they add their current page numbers together, the sum is 408. On what page is the slower reader?

   a. 98

   b. 102

   c. 202

   d. 210

   e. 206

39. There are 80 questions on a test. How many questions must you answer correctly to score 70%?

40. The side *AC* of the triangle *ABC* is the diameter of the pictured semicircle. If the radius of the circle is 3, what is *AB*?

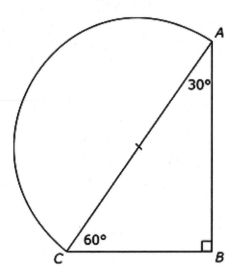

   a. $\sqrt{3}$

   b. 3

   c. $3\sqrt{3}$

   d. 6

   e. $6\sqrt{3}$

41. One hundred college freshmen were asked if they intended to transfer to another university for their sophomore year. The responses are tabulated here:

	MALE	FEMALE
Yes	8	21
No	16	20
Maybe	22	13

What is the probability that the student is male given that the answer is yes?

   a. $\frac{8}{100}$

   b. $\frac{8}{29}$

   c. $\frac{29}{100}$

   d. $\frac{46}{100}$

   e. $\frac{26}{29}$

42. In the diagram, if segment *DF* is a diameter of circle *E*, and segment *DG* is congruent to segment *EG*, what is the value of 2*y*?

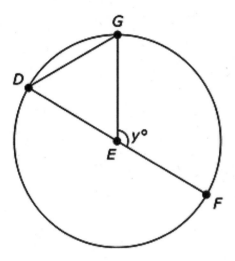

    a. 30°

    b. 60°

    c. 120°

    d. 240°

    e. 360°

43. Choose the expression that is equivalent to the following:

$$\frac{9 - x^2}{(x + 5)^2} \div \frac{(x + 5)(3 - x)}{x}$$

    a. $\frac{(x + 3)x}{x + 5}$

    b. $\frac{(x + 3)(x - 3)^2}{(x + 5)\,x}$

    c. $\frac{x(x + 3)}{x^2 + 10x + 25}$

    d. $\frac{x(x + 3)}{(x + 5)^3}$

    e. $\frac{x^2 + 3x}{x^3 + 125}$

44. Which equation has solutions that correspond to the *x*-intercepts in the following graph?

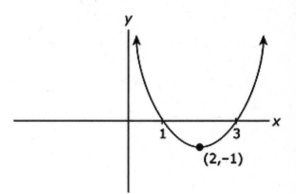

    a. $(x + 2)^2 - 1 = 0$

    b. $(x - 2)^2 + 1 = 0$

    c. $(x - 2)^2 - 1 = 0$

    d. $(x + 2)^2 + 1 = 0$

    e. $3(x - 2)^2 + 1 = 0$

45. What is the value of $\frac{1 + x^2}{1 - x^2}$ when $x = \frac{3}{4}$?

    a. $\frac{7}{25}$

    b. $\frac{175}{256}$

    c. 1

    d. $3\frac{4}{7}$

    e. $4\frac{3}{7}$

46. What is the greatest common factor of 30, 45, and 60?

    a. 5

    b. 10

    c. 15

    d. 20

    e. 180

47. A room measures 12 feet by 15 feet, and the ceiling is 9 feet high. One gallon of paint is needed to apply one coat of paint to 250 square feet of surface area. How many gallons will it take to paint all but the floor of the room if two coats of paint must be applied? Round your answer to the nearest tenth of a gallon.

48. Which of these is equivalent to $\sqrt{121y^{16}z^{36}}$?

    a. $11y^4z^6$

    b. $11y^8z^{18}$

    c. $121y^8z^{18}$

    d. $121y^4z^6$

    e. $11y^{32}z^{72}$

49. Consider the set of geometric figures shown:

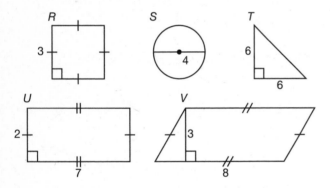

If a shape is selected at random, what is the probability of selecting one whose area is at least 10 square units?

    a. $\frac{4}{5}$

    b. $\frac{3}{5}$

    c. $\frac{2}{5}$

    d. $\frac{1}{5}$

    e. 0

50. Beth wishes to build three identical, adjacent rectangular pens on her farm so that the back of all three pens is against the barn.

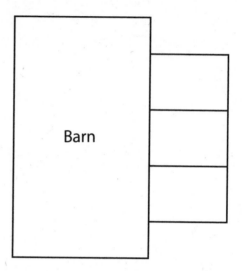

She will use 1,500 feet of fencing to construct the pens, and fencing is not needed along the side that touches the barn. The combined area of all three pens is 65,000 square feet. What is the width of each pen? Assume the width is the longer side.

    a. 25 feet

    b. 50 feet

    c. 200 feet

    d. 325 feet

    e. 433.3 feet

51. A cross section parallel to the ground of an oil tank is as follows:

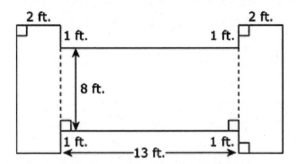

The tank is 5 feet high throughout. One cubic foot of oil equals about 7.85 gallons. How many gallons of oil can the tank hold?
   a. 720 gallons
   b. 1,130.4 gallons
   c. 5,652 gallons
   d. 4,867 gallons
   e. 7,200 gallons

52. Suppose p and q are different prime numbers. What is the least common multiple of 4, $2p$, and $16q$?
   a. 2
   b. $4p$
   c. $4pq$
   d. $148pq$
   e. $2^4 \times p \times q$

53. Suppose that a company's profits (in millions of dollars) for a 10-year period are shown in this graph, where $t = 0$ corresponds to 2004 and $t = 10$ corresponds to 2014.

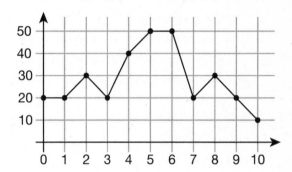

Select all of the true statements.
   a. The maximum profit during this 10-year period occurred in the years 2005 and 2006.
   b. The profit never dipped below $10 million.
   c. Profit increased from 2011 through 2014.
   d. Profit never increased for a period longer than one year.
   e. There are consecutive years during which the profit remained the same.

54. Choose the expression that is equivalent to:
$$-\frac{1}{(x-3)^2} + \frac{1}{x+3}$$
   a. $\dfrac{1}{(x+3)(x-3)^2}$
   b. $\dfrac{-6}{(x+3)(x-3)^2}$
   c. $\dfrac{1}{(x^2-9)(x-3)}$
   d. $\dfrac{x^2-5x+12}{(x+3)(x-3)^2}$
   e. $\dfrac{(x-6)(x-1)}{(x+3)(x-3)^2}$

55. Consider these two sets of data:

$$A = \{5, 5, 5, 5, 5\}$$
$$B = \{4, 4, 4, 4\}$$

Which of the following statements is/are true?

I.   The mean of set A is greater than the mean of set B.

II. The standard deviation of set A is greater than the standard deviation of set B.

III. The median and mean of set A are equal.

a. I only

b. II only

c. I and III only

d. II and III only

e. None of the statements is true.

56. Assume that $0 < x < 1$ and y is a negative integer less than -1. Which of these must be greater than 1? Select all answers that apply.

a. $\dfrac{1}{x}$

b. $-y$

c. $-\dfrac{1}{y}$

d. x^2

e. y^4

Praxis® Core Academic Skills for Educators: Mathematics Practice Test 4 Answers and Explanations

1. a, d, and e. There are, in fact, five lines of symmetry (choice **a**). If you connect each vertex to the midpoint of the opposite side, you will get a line of symmetry. There are also four angles of rotational symmetry (choice **d**) about the center of the pentagon, and a rotation of 144 degrees about the center would accomplish the transformation suggested in choice **e**. Choice **b** would rotate the figure around vertex E and move the pentagon from its current location. Once the figure is moved, any reflection (choice **c**) would change the orientation of the vertices. So this is not possible.

2. d. The points are closely grouped together, so the correlation is strong. And a quadratic function describes the relationship, which is nonlinear. The data do not rise from left to right throughout the scatterplot, so the trend is not positive, as is suggested in choice **a**. The points are closely grouped together, which suggests a strong, not a weak, correlation, so choice **b** is incorrect. Choice **c** is incorrect because, as already mentioned, the points suggest a strong correlation. Additionally, the points do not fall from left to right, so the trend is not negative. There is a proven relationship as well, so choice **e** is incorrect.

3. a. Distribute $-3x$ through all terms of $g(x)$, and then simplify:

$$f(x) - 3x \cdot g(x) = (2x^3 - 3x + 4) - 3x(-2x^2 - 3x - 1)$$
$$= 2x^3 - 3x + 4 + 6x^3 + 9x^2 + 3x$$
$$= 8x^3 + 9x^2 + 4$$

4. e. Let w represent the width of the room. That means that the length is $3w - 4$. The perimeter of a rectangular room is twice the length plus twice the width. Based on this information, you'll come to the following equation:

$$2w + 2(3w - 4) = 56$$

Then solve for w:

$$2w + 2(3w - 4) = 56$$
$$2w + 6w - 8 = 56$$
$$8w = 64$$
$$w = 8$$

So, the length of the room is $3(8) - 4 = 20$ feet.

Choice **a** is the width of the room, not the length. If w represents the width of the room, then the length is $3w - 4$, not $3w + 4$ (choice **b**). If you chose **c** or **d**, you did not multiply the width and length each by 2 when setting up the perimeter equation.

5. c. Let x represent the length of the real trail. Then set up a proportion:

$$\frac{1 \text{ inch}}{2.4 \text{ miles}} = \frac{4.9 \text{ inches}}{x \text{ miles}}$$

$$(1 \text{ inch})(x \text{ miles}) = (2.4 \text{ miles})(4.9 \text{ inches})$$

$$x = \frac{(2.4 \text{ miles})(4.9 \text{ inches})}{1 \text{ inch}} = 11.76 \text{ miles}$$

So, $x = 11.76$ miles.

Choice **a** is incorrect because after setting up a proportion, you need to multiply 4.9 by 2.4, not divide 4.9 by 2.4. If you chose choice **b** it looks like you simply added 2.4 miles to 4.9 inches, which is incorrect. If you picked choice **d** you may have multiplied 4.9 by itself. This would mean that 1 inch on the map represents 4.9 miles, which is not true. Choice **e** is incorrect because of an arithmetic error.

6. b and c. Notice that the two equations are equivalent. (To see this, move the y-term to the left in the second equation and divide both sides by 4—you'll get the first equation.) Since the equations are equivalent, you need to test out a pair of x and y values only once—if they work in one equation, they'll work in the other. This is the case for $x = 0$, $y = -1$ and $x = \frac{3}{5}$, $y = 0$. Through this logic, all other answer choices are incorrect.

7. $\frac{17}{12}$. To compute the expected value of a random variable such as this, multiply x times $P(X = x)$ and add all of them. Doing so yields:

$$(-2)(\tfrac{1}{6}) + 0(\tfrac{1}{4}) + 1(\tfrac{1}{8}) + 3(\tfrac{5}{24}) + 4(\tfrac{1}{4}) = \tfrac{17}{12}$$

8. c. Use the properties of radicals and multiplying fractions to simplify the expression:

$$\frac{8\sqrt{3}}{16\sqrt{15}} = \frac{8}{16} \cdot \frac{\sqrt{3}}{\sqrt{15}} = \frac{1}{2} \cdot \frac{\sqrt{3}}{\sqrt{3} \cdot \sqrt{5}} = \frac{1}{2\sqrt{5}}$$

Then rationalize the expression by multiplying the numerator and denominator by $\sqrt{5}$ to get

$$\frac{1}{2\sqrt{5}} = \frac{1}{2\sqrt{5}} \cdot \frac{\sqrt{5}}{\sqrt{5}} = \frac{\sqrt{5}}{10}$$

Choice **a** is the reciprocal of the correct answer. If you picked choice **b** you subtracted the radicands instead of dividing them. The correct answer is 1 over the quantity in choice **d**. Choice **e** is incorrect because $\frac{8}{16} = \frac{1}{2}$, not $\frac{1}{8}$.

9. b. Use the Pythagorean theorem to determine the vertical distance v. Doing so produces this equation:

$5{,}000^2 + v^2 = 6{,}200^2$, which simplifies to $v^2 = 13{,}440{,}000$, so $v = \sqrt{13{,}440{,}000} \approx 3{,}666$ feet.

Choice **c** is incorrect because 5,000 is the horizontal distance, not the vertical height. In choice **a**, you forgot to square the sides. In choice **d**, you treated AB as a leg instead of the hypotenuse. The same applies to choice **e**, but you also forgot to square the sides.

10. c. In this scatterplot, the data points rise from left to right, showing a positive relationship. And while they aren't packed extremely tightly near a line with positive slope, such a line is visible and shows a trend—meaning that *moderate* describes the relationship. The scatterplot in choice **a** shows a moderate negative relationship, since the data points fall from left to right. The scatterplot in choice **b** shows a nearly constant relationship, since the data points are packed together in what looks like a horizontal line. Choice **d** shows a nonlinear relationship between X and Y. A positive relationship is shown when data points are clustered near a line with positive slope. The scatterplot in choice **e** does not show a clear relationship between X and Y.

11. −31. Since the function is recursively defined, start by computing f of the integer values, starting at 2, as follows:

$$f(2) = f(1 + 1) = 3 - 2f(1) = 3 - 2(5) = -7$$
$$f(3) = f(2 + 1) = 3 - 2f(2) = 3 - 2(-7) = 17$$
$$f(4) = f(3 + 1) = 3 - 2f(3) = 3 - 2(17) = -31$$

12. b. Recall that $\sqrt{x^2} = x$, if x is a nonnegative real number. Here, $x = \frac{1}{\pi}$. Choice **a** is incorrect because π is an irrational number; 3.14 is only an approximation of it. The left side of the equation in choice **c** is the sum of two positive irrational numbers, so it must be irrational, but the right side equals 4, which is rational. Choice **d** is incorrect because the number e itself is approximately equal to 2.718, whereas $\sqrt{e}$ is smaller, around 1.648. Recall that $e \approx 2.718$ and $\pi \approx 3.14$. Therefore, $\frac{e}{\pi} < 1$ (so that $\sqrt{\frac{e}{\pi}}$ is also less than 1), whereas $\frac{\pi}{e} > 1$ (so that $\sqrt{\frac{\pi}{e}}$ is also greater than 1). This means that the inequality in choice **e** is false.

13. a and d. Observe that $\pi - 1 \approx 3.14 - 1 = 2.14$ and $e \approx 2.718$, which are both greater than 2. The remaining answer choices are all less than 2.

14. a. The greatest common factor of the three terms in the original expression is $2xy$. Factor it out, and you find that $8x^2y^3 - 4xy^2 - 2x^2y = 2xy(4xy^2 - 2y - x)$. If you factor out -1, you must change all of the signs of the terms in the parentheses, making choice **b** incorrect. Choice **c** is incorrect because you cannot factor a y^2 out of the last term in the expression without creating a fraction. Notice that $2xy^2(-x) = -2x^2y^2$, not $-2x^2y$. Choice **d** is almost right, but there is a mistake at the end of the expression: $(2y - x)$ should be $(2y + x)$. You incorrectly added the last two terms of the expression to arrive at choice **e**. These expressions are not like terms, so they can't be added.

15. d. Imagine drawing the line $x = -1$ on the graph. It's a vertical line that runs 1 unit to the left of the y-axis. Point A sits 4 units to the right of that vertical line, at $(3,0)$, which means that if you reflect triangle ABC across the line, A' would fall 4 units to the *left* of the line, at $(-5,0)$. Doing a similar conversion for the other two points of the triangle also gives the correct coordinates. Remember that the origin (choice **a**) is the center point of the graph, where the x- and y-axes intersect. When a figure is rotated around the origin counterclockwise by 90 degrees, (x,y) becomes $(-y,x)$, which means that A' would fall on $(0,3)$, B' on $(0,6)$, and C' on $(-5,6)$. This is not what the question asks for. Here is a more informal way to understand this: In the image, the triangle is "sitting" on the x-axis, 3 units to the right of the origin. If we rotate it by 90 degrees counterclockwise, it will now "sit" on the y-axis, 3 units above the origin. (If we rotate it again by 90 degrees counterclockwise, it will "sit" on the x-axis, 3 units to the left of the origin, and so on.) With the transformation in choice **b**, B' and C' would have the correct coordinates, but A' would fall on $(-11,0)$, which is not what the question asks for. With the transformation in choice **c**, the triangle $A'B'C'$ would appear in the fourth quadrant (the bottom right corner of the graph), but based on the coordinates in the question, we know that $A'B'C'$ should appear in the second quadrant (the upper left corner). Reflecting the triangle across the line created by $x = 3$ (choice **e**) would give A' the same coordinates as A, which is not what the question asks for. Furthermore, B' would fall on $(0,0)$ and C' would fall on $(5,0)$, which are also incorrect.

16. c. The median is shown in a box-and-whisker plot as the vertical line segment occurring within the box portion of the plot. Here, that line occurs at the value 47, which means the median of the data set is 47. Although 35 (choice **a**) is the midpoint between the outer boundaries of the plot (which occur at 10 and 60), it is not the center of the data set; the median of the data set is shown by the vertical line within the box, and this occurs at 47. Choice **b** represents the lower (or 25th) percentile, not the 50th percentile, or median. Choice **d** represents the upper (or 75th) percentile, not the 50th percentile, or median. Choice **e** is the maximum value of any data point in the data set, not the middle (or median) of the data set.

17. a. The number 7 is prime and it divides 504 evenly. So 7 is a prime factor of 504. Although 9 (choice **b**) is a factor of 504, it is not a prime number. In choice **c**, 11 is a prime number, but it does not divide 504 evenly. Choice **d** is incorrect because, although 17 is a prime number, it does not divide 504 evenly. Although 21 (choice **e**) is a factor of 504, it is not a prime number.

18. d. Of all the choices listed, this is the most reasonable. It is about twice the height of an adult person. There are 100 mm in 1 cm. So, 150 mm = 1.5 cm (choice **a**), which is less than 2 inches. This is not a reasonable estimate for a full-grown cherry tree. Choice **b** would exceed a mile, which is much too tall for the height of a tree. Choice **c** is less than 30 inches, or 2.5 feet. This is too small for the height of a full-grown cherry tree. Choice **e** is less than 2 feet, which is too small for the height of a full-grown cherry tree.

19. $x = 20, y = 15$. First, find out what y equals in terms of x. Do this by isolating y in the first equation: $y = x - 5$.

Now use this information to change the y in the second equation to $x - 5$. Doing this transforms the second equation into an equation that has only one type of variable: x. This allows us to find out the number value of x, which is the key to learning the number value of y. Here is the math behind this process:

$$4(x - 5) - x = 40$$
$$4x - 20 - x = 40$$
$$3x - 20 = 40$$
$$3x = 60$$
$$x = 20$$

Now that we know that x equals 20, we can replace x with 20 in either one of the equations to solve for y.

20. a, c, and e. The means of choice **a**'s and choice **c**'s distributions are zero, which is not positive. The mean of the distribution in choice **e** is negative. The means of the remaining distributions are both positive.

21. c. Let b be the portion of butter needed in the reduced recipe. To keep the same balance of butter and sugar as in the original recipe, set up the following proportion:

$$\frac{1.5 \text{ cups of sugar}}{0.5 \text{ cups of butter}} = \frac{1 \text{ cup of sugar}}{b \text{ cups of butter}}$$

Then solve for b:

$$1.5 \times b = 1 \times 0.5$$
$$1.5b = 0.5$$
$$b = \frac{1}{3}$$

So, to make his favorite frosting, Bob will need to use $\frac{1}{3}$ cup of butter with his 1 cup of sugar. If you arrived at choice **a**, you used a proportion to solve the problem, which is correct, but you inverted one of the fractions by mistake. Choice **b** is incorrect because the recipe does not call for equal parts of sugar and butter. Choice **d** is less than how much is needed. Choice **e** is half as much as the amount needed.

22. d. First, simplify the right side and multiply both sides by 8 to clear the fractions. Then gather the x-terms on one side and the constants on the other to solve for x:

$$\tfrac{3}{4}x - 1 = -(\tfrac{3}{8}x - 2)$$
$$\tfrac{3}{4}x - 1 = -(\tfrac{3}{8}x - 2x - 1 = -\tfrac{3}{8}x + 2$$
$$6x - 8 = -3x + 16$$
$$9x = 24$$
$$x = \tfrac{24}{9}$$

It looks as if you forgot to distribute the -1 through the parentheses on the right side of the equation if you picked choice **a**. Choice **b** is the reciprocal of the correct answer. To arrive at choice **c**, you forgot to multiply the 1 by 8 when clearing the fractions. If you picked choice **e**, it looks as if you subtracted both sides by 9 rather than dividing by 9 in the final step.

23. d. Let r be the radius of the flower bed, which means the radius of the garden is $3r$. The area of the flower bed is πr^2, while the area of the garden is $\pi(3r)^2 = 9\pi r^2$. So, the area of the garden is 9 times the area of the flower bed. Choice **a** is the reverse comparison. This is what you would multiply the area of the garden by to find the area of the flower bed. If you picked choice **b**, it looks as if you forgot to square the 3 when computing the area of the garden. If you chose **c**, you multiplied 3 by 2 instead of raising 3 to the second power when squaring $3r$. Note that $3^2 = 9$. If you chose choice **e**, you cubed 3 instead of squaring it.

24. c. Use the two labeled points (–3,1) and (3,5) to compute the slope:
$$m = \frac{5-1}{3-(-3)} = \frac{4}{6} = \frac{2}{3}$$
The slope is positive, since the line rises from left to right, and choice **a** shows a negative slope, making it incorrect. The slope should not be zero (choice **b**) because the line is not horizontal. Choice **d** is the reciprocal of the slope. Choice **e** is incorrect because you subtracted the *x*-coordinate from the *y*-coordinate of each point rather than computing the change in *y* over the change in *x*.

25. 8 panels. First, divide $7\frac{2}{5}$ gallons by $\frac{7}{8}$ gallon:
$$\frac{7\frac{2}{5}}{\frac{7}{8}} = \frac{\frac{37}{5}}{\frac{7}{8}} = \frac{37}{5} \times \frac{8}{7} = \frac{296}{35} = 8\frac{16}{35}$$
Then round down, since we need the number of *complete* panels. Jeannette can paint 8 complete panels.

26. d. The cost of *G* gadgets is $9.50*G* and the cost of *S* containers of spices is $4.25*S*. So the total cost of *G* gadgets and *S* containers of spices is 9.50*G* + 4.25*S*. Since Frank has $140 to spend, this total cannot exceed 140. So the inequality 9.50*G* + 4.25*S* ≤ 140 accurately describes the relationship between *G* and *S*. The inequality sign is reversed in choice **a**. In choice **b**, you did not multiply the quantities *G* and *S* by the cost per unit. The *S* and *G* should be interchanged in choice **c**. The expressions enclosed within parentheses on the left side should be added, not multiplied, making choice **e** incorrect.

27. b. In a parallelogram, the measures of opposite angles are equal. This means that the measure of angle *X* is equal to the measure of angle *Z*, and therefore the measure of angle *Z* is 43°. Use the sum of the measures of the angles in a triangle equaling 180° on triangle *WYZ* to set up an equation, and then solve for *d*:
$$43 + 80 + d = 180$$
$$123 + d = 180$$
$$d = 57$$
These angles in a parallelogram are not necessarily equal, so choice **a** is incorrect. Choices **c** and **d** are incorrect because angle *Z* measures 43° and angle *ZWY* measures 80°, so *d* cannot be 60° because this would make the sum of three angles in a triangle greater than 180°. Choice **e** shows the measure of angle *Y*, which is not the value of *d*.

28. b. The radius of the tank is 1 meter. The volume of a sphere with radius *r* is $\frac{4}{3}\pi r^3$. Substituting *r* = 1 meter into this formula gives a volume of $\frac{4}{3}\pi$ cubic meters. Choice **a** is incorrect because you need to multiply by 4. Choice **c** is the surface area, not the volume. In choice **d** you used the diameter instead of the radius when computing the volume. Choice **e** is the surface area of a sphere with a radius of 2 meters, but we're looking for the volume of a sphere with a diameter of 2 meters.

29. a and b. If you fold the distribution over the *y*-axis, the graph lines up perfectly, which implies that it is symmetric (choice **a**). There are two identical peaks in the distribution, so it is bimodal (choice **b**). If choice **c** were true, most of the values would occur to the left and taper down toward the right. The mean occurs at 0, which is not positive, making choice **d** incorrect. For symmetric distributions, the mean and median are equal, so choice **e** is incorrect.

30. 16 cans. Let x represent the total number of 8-ounce cans needed. Note that each 8-ounce can of concentrate is combined with two 8-ounce cans of water. So each 8-ounce can creates 24 fluid ounces of orange juice. Based on this, set up the following proportion:

$$\frac{1 \text{ can of concentrate}}{24 \text{ fluid ounces of juice}} = \frac{x \text{ cans of concentrate}}{384 \text{ fluid ounces of juice}}$$

Then solve for x:

$$24x = 384$$
$$x = 16$$

31. b. A fair selection would result in each student having an equal chance of being selected. However, if 5 students have last names starting with the letter S while 10 have last names starting with the letter D, then the students do not have an equal chance of being selected. The size of the class (choice **a**) is not the deciding criterion about the fairness of the method. Rather, there may not be an equal number of students for each letter. To be fair, each student should have an equal chance of being selected whether their name is common or uncommon, making choice **c** incorrect. While each letter has an equal chance of being selected (choice **d**), there may be different numbers of students for each letter. Choice **e** is incorrect because random selection can be done with letters or numbers.

32. a and e. Since $2x^2 + 8$ is always positive (in fact, no less than 8), the equation in choice **a** has no real solutions. In fact, the solutions are $\pm 2i$. In choice **e**, the discriminant is $1^2 - 4(2)(3) = -23 < 0$, so the solutions are imaginary. The solutions for choice **b** are -3 and 0, which are real. The discriminant is $9^2 - 4(1)(2) = 73 > 0$, so the solutions for choice **c** are real. The solutions for choice **d** are $\pm\sqrt{5}$, which are real.

33. c. There are 60 minutes in an hour and 60 seconds in a minute. So, there are 60×60 seconds in an hour. Also, there are 5,280 feet in a mile. Using these two facts allows us to convert from miles per hour to feet per second as follows:

$$\frac{110 \text{ miles}}{1 \text{ hour}} = \frac{110 \text{ miles}}{1 \text{ hour}} \times \frac{1 \text{ hour}}{60 \times 60 \text{ seconds}} \times \frac{5,280 \text{ feet}}{1 \text{ mile}}$$

$$= \frac{110 \times 5,280}{60 \times 60} \text{ feet per second}$$

Choices **a**, **b**, and **e** are incorrect because you did not account for the fact that there are 5,280 feet in 1 mile and 360 seconds in 1 hour. Choice **d** is incorrect because you inverted both fractions, namely the ratio of hours to seconds and the ratio of feet to miles, when setting up the conversion.

34. e. Let s represent the length of an edge of this shed. Because the shape is a cube, each of the edges has the same length. This means that each of the faces has the same area, namely s^2 square meters. Because a cube has six faces, the surface area is $6s^2$. And since we know that the surface area is 294 square meters, we know that $6s^2 = 294$, so $s = 7$ meters. Now we can find the volume of the shed: $s^3 = 7^3 = 343$ cubic meters. Choice **a** is the length of an edge. You must raise this to the third power to get the volume. You must raise a side to the third power, not second, when finding the volume of a cube, so choice **b** is incorrect. You incorrectly computed the length of an edge as 6 meters in choice **c**. It should be 7 meters. Generally, surface area and volume are not the same. They are not equal for this figure, making choice **d** incorrect.

35. b. This is the correct answer. For I, there are 26 black cards and 4 jacks. But 2 of the jacks are also black, and we don't want to count them twice in the total count. So, there are 28 possibilities, all of which are equally likely. This means that the probability that the card is black or a jack is $\frac{28}{52} = \frac{7}{13}$. For II, there are four 4s and two red 8s. These conditions are mutually exclusive, so there are 6 possibilities, all of which are equally likely. So, the probability that the card is a 4 or a red 8 is $\frac{6}{52} = \frac{3}{26}$. For III, this is the probability that the card is either a king or a club. The remaining answer choices are incorrect following this logic.

36. –2. We must use the fact that $y = f(x)$ if and only if $x = f^{-1}(y)$. Using this with the table values, notice that $f^{-1}(-1) = 2$. So, $f^{-1}(f^{-1}(-1)) = f^{-1}(2) = -2$.

37. e. First, use the distributive property to factor 2^3 from both terms of the sum. Then simplify the resulting quantity enclosed within parentheses, as follows:

$$\frac{7}{12} \times 2^3 + \frac{1}{12} \times 2^4 = 2^3\left(\frac{7}{12} + \frac{1}{12} \times 2\right)$$
$$= 2^3\left(\frac{7}{12} + \frac{2}{12}\right)$$
$$= 2^3\left(\frac{9}{12}\right)$$
$$= 2^3\left(\frac{3}{4}\right)$$

By commutativity, this is equivalent to $\frac{3}{4} \times 2^3$.

The fractional part is incorrect in choice **a**: factoring 2^3 from the product $\frac{1}{12} \times 2^4$ leaves you with $\frac{1}{12} \times 2$, not $\frac{1}{12}$. In choice **b** you simplified 2^3 incorrectly as 2×3. The fractional part is incorrect in choice **c**. The power of 2 is incorrect in choice **d**. You can only factor 2^3 from both terms of this sum.

38. c. Let x represent the page number of the faster reader. This means that the slower reader is on page $x - 4$. We translate the second sentence of the problem into the equation $x + (x - 4) = 408$. This simplifies to $2x - 4 = 408$, which yields $x = 206$. Because x is the page of the faster reader, the slower reader is on page 202. Choices **a** and **b** are incorrect because when solving the equation for x, you divided both sides by 4, not 2. It looks like when you determined that $x = 206$, you mistakenly interpreted that as the slower reader's page. In fact, this was the page for the faster reader, making choice **d** incorrect. Choice **e** is the current page of the faster reader.

39. 56 questions. Rewrite 70% as 70 out of 100, and then set up a proportion to see how many questions q out of 80 must be answered correctly:

$$\frac{70}{100} = \frac{q}{80}$$

Then solve for q:

$$5,600 = 100q$$
$$q = 56$$

So, you must answer 56 questions correctly to score 70%.

40. c. A 30-60-90 triangle will always have sides in the ratio of $1x : 2x : \sqrt{3}x$, where $2x$ is the length of the hypotenuse and $\sqrt{3}x$ is the length of the side opposite the 60-degree angle. The radius is 3, so the diameter must be 6. The hypotenuse is $2x$, so $2x = 6$; thus $x = 3$. This means that $AB = 3\sqrt{3}x$. Choice **a** is incorrect because of the ratio of the sides. Choice **b** shows the length of BC, not AB, and choice **d** shows the length of the hypotenuse. Choice **e** is incorrect because it is double the correct answer.

41. b. This is a conditional probability. Let A be the event that the student is male, and B be the event that the answer is yes. We are asked to compute $P(A|B)$. Do so as follows:

$P(A|B) = \frac{P(A\cap B)}{P(B)}\ \frac{\frac{8}{100}}{\frac{29}{100}} = \frac{8}{29}$. Choice **a** shows the probability that a student is male and answers yes, but since *the answer is yes* is given information, the answer should be computed as a conditional probability. Choice **c** also shows the probability that the answer is yes, but it does not account for whether the student is male or female. Choice **d** shows the probability that a student is *not* male given that the answer is yes, and choice **e** shows the probability that the student is male, but it does not account for only those who answered yes.

42. d. Because segment DF is a diameter, it follows that segment DE is a radius. Furthermore, since segment EG is also a radius (connecting the center to a point on the circle), it follows that segments DG, GE, and DE are all congruent. So triangle DGE is an equilateral triangle. Thus, angle DEG has a measure of 60°. Because angle DEF is a straight angle, $y° + 60° = 180°$, so that $y = 120°$. Therefore, $2y = 240°$. Choices **a** and **b** are incorrect because angle DEF is a straight angle, $y° + 60° = 180°$, not 90°. Choices **c** and **e** are incorrect because those answer choices do not show the value of $2y$.

43. d. This is the correct answer. First, factor the numerator of the first rational expression. Then rewrite the division problem as a multiplication problem using the reciprocal of the divisor, and cancel like factors in the numerator and denominator:

$$\frac{9-x^2}{(x+5)^2} \div \frac{(x+5)(3-x)}{x} = \frac{(3+x)(3-x)}{(x+5)^2} \div \frac{(x+5)(3-x)}{x}$$
$$= \frac{(3+x)(3-x)}{(x+5)^2} \cdot \frac{x}{(x+5)(3-x)}$$
$$= \frac{(3+x)\cancel{(3-x)}}{(x+5)^2} \cdot \frac{x}{(x+5)\cancel{(3-x)}}$$
$$= \frac{x(x+3)}{(x+5)^3}$$

It looks as if you incorrectly canceled a factor of $x + 5$ in choice **a**. If you arrived at choice **b**, you multiplied when you should have divided. Remember that when converting a division problem into a multiplication problem, you take the reciprocal of the divisor. You are missing a factor of $x + 5$ in the denominator for choice **c**. Choice **e** is incorrect because once you had the factored form, it looks as if you incorrectly simplified the denominator. In general, $(a + b)^3 \neq a^3 + b^3$.

44. c. We must determine the equation of the parabola. Its vertex is $(2,-1)$, so the form of the equation is $y + 1 = a(x - 2)^2$. In order to determine a, substitute one of the points, say $(3,0)$, into this equation. Doing so yields $a = 1$. So the equation of this parabola is $y + 1 = (x - 2)^2$. Solving for y yields the equivalent statement $y = (x - 2)^2 - 1$. In this form, the x-intercepts occur when $y = 0$, which results in the equation $(x - 2)^2 - 1 = 0$. Choice **a** is incorrect because the quantity within the parentheses should be $x - 2$. Choices **b** and **e** are incorrect because the 1 should be replaced by -1. Additionally, in choice **e**, the 3 should not be there. Both plus signs should be minus signs, making choice **d** incorrect.

45. d. Substitute the value of x, simplify the numerator and denominator separately, and then divide the resulting fractions as follows:

$$\frac{1+x^2}{1-x^2} = \frac{1+(\frac{3}{4})^2}{1-(\frac{3}{4})^2} = \frac{1+\frac{9}{16}}{1-\frac{9}{16}} = \frac{\frac{25}{16}}{\frac{7}{16}}$$

$$= \frac{25}{16} \times \frac{16}{7} = \frac{25}{7} = 3\frac{4}{7}$$

Choice **a** is the reciprocal of the correct answer. After simplifying the fraction on the top and bottom, you may have divided incorrectly if you arrived at choice **b**. Remember, to convert a division problem into a multiplication problem, multiply the top portion of the fraction by the reciprocal of the bottom (the divisor). You cannot cancel like terms in the numerator and denominator of a fraction; you can only cancel like factors, so choice **c** is incorrect. If you picked choice **e**, you made a mistake when converting the answer into an improper fraction in the final step.

46. c. The greatest common factor of a set of whole numbers is the largest whole number that divides evenly into all of them. Notice that 30 equals 15×2, 45 equals 15×3, and 60 equals 15×4. The number 15 divides evenly into 30, 45, and 60, and no other number can do the same. The next candidate would be 30, but 30 does not divide evenly into 45. The number in choice **a** is a factor of all three numbers, but it is not the greatest common factor. The number in choice **b** is not a factor of 45, so it cannot be the greatest common factor of all three numbers. The number in choice **d** not a factor of either 30 or 45, so it cannot be the greatest common factor of all three numbers. Choice **e** is the least common multiple of the three numbers, not the greatest common factor of the three numbers.

47. 5.3 gallons. Two of the walls have dimensions of 12 feet by 9 feet each; the combined area of these two walls is $12 \times 9 \times 2 = 216$ square feet. The other two walls have dimensions of 15 feet by 9 feet each; the combined area of these two walls is $15 \times 9 \times 2 = 270$ square feet. The ceiling has dimensions of 12 feet by 15 feet, so its area is 180 square feet. This means that the total square footage that must be painted is $216 + 270 + 180 = 666$ square feet. Since two coats of paint are needed, this number must be doubled, making 1,332 square feet. The last step is to divide 1,332 by 250, which yields 5.328 gallons of paint, or 5.3 gallons when rounded to the nearest tenth.

48. b. Rewrite the radicand as a quantity squared, and then use the fact that $\sqrt{a^2} = a$ if $a \geq 0$, as follows:

$$\sqrt{121y^{16}z^{36}} = \sqrt{(11y^8z^{18})^2} = 11y^8z^{18}$$

In choices **a** and **d** you mistakenly took the square roots of the exponents. Additionally, in choice **d** as well as choice **c**, you forgot to take the square root of 121. In choice **e** you multiplied the exponents by 2 instead of dividing them by 2.

49. a. First, compute the areas of each of the geometric figures:

Area(R) = $3 \cdot 3 = 9$ square units

Area(S) = $\pi \cdot 2^2 = 4\pi$ square units

≈ 12.6 square units

Area(T) = $\frac{1}{2} \cdot 6 \cdot 6 = 18$ square units

Area(U) = $2 \cdot 7 = 14$ square units

Area(V) = $3 \cdot 8 = 24$ square units

Since a geometric figure is being selected at random, they are all equally likely. Since four of them have an area that is at least 10 square units, the probability of selecting such a figure is $\frac{4}{5}$. The remaining answer choices are incorrect following this logic.

50. d. Because the three pens are identical and no fencing is needed along the side that touches the barn, there are four sides of width w and three sides of length l that need fencing. She will use 1,500 feet of fencing to construct all three pens, so the sum of the lengths of all sides of the three pens must be 1,500. This leads to the following equation: $4w + 3l = 1,500$. The area of the three pens combined is $w \cdot (3l)$. To get an expression in terms of only w, solve the perimeter equation for l and substitute it in:

$$4w + 3l = 1,500 \Rightarrow l = \tfrac{1,500 - 4w}{3}$$

So, the combined area of the pens is:

$$w \cdot (3l) = w \cdot 3 \cdot \tfrac{1,500 - 4w}{3}$$
$$= w(1,500 - 4w)$$
$$= -4w^2 + 1,500w$$

The combined area of the pens will be 65,000 square feet. To find the width of each pen, set the expression for the area equal to 65,000 and solve for w:

$$-4w^2 + 1,500w = 65,000$$
$$4w^2 - 1,500w + 65,000 = 0$$
$$4(w^2 - 375w + 16,250) = 0$$
$$4(w - 50)(w - 325) = 0$$

There are two solutions: $w = 50$ and $w = 325$. The first solution would yield a value of l that was larger than w, which cannot be the case since we are assuming the width is the longer side. So, the width must be 325 feet, and choice **b** is incorrect. Choice **a** is half of the correct value of the width. Choice **c** is the sum of the four segments needed to construct the pens. You should have divided this by 4. Choice **e** is approximately the length of one pen, not the width.

51. c. Divide the tank into three simpler parts—the two rectangles on either side and the middle rectangle. Compute the volume of each part, and then add the volumes and multiply the sum by the number of gallons equivalent to 1 cubic foot.

> Volume of each of the outer rectangular parts:
> 10 ft. × 2 ft. × 5 ft. = 100 cubic feet
> Volume of middle rectangular portion:
> 13 ft. × 8 ft. × 5 ft. = 520 cubic feet

So, the volume of the entire tank is 720 cubic feet. Multiplying by 7.85 gallons per cubic foot yields 5,652 gallons. Choice **a** is incorrect because you forgot to multiply by 7.85 (the conversion between cubic feet and gallons). In choice **b** you forgot to multiply by the height of the tank, which is 5 feet throughout. Choice **d** is incorrect because you accounted for only one of the two side rectangles. In choice **e** you multiplied the volume by 10, not 7.85.

52. e. The least common multiple of a group of whole numbers is the smallest whole number into which they all divide evenly. Take a look at the prime factorizations of each of the numbers in question:

> $4 = 2^2$
> $2p = 2p$
> $16q = 2^4 \times q$

Now take the highest power of every prime number that occurs anywhere in these prime factorizations. You'll arrive at $2^4 \times p \times q$ as the least common multiple. Choice **a** is the greatest common factor of the three quantities, not the least common multiple. Choice **b** cannot be the least common multiple, because q is not included in the product. The coefficient in choice **c** is incorrect because 16 is not a multiple of 4. Choice **d** is a common multiple, but not the *least* common multiple.

53. b and e. The lowest y-value shown on this graph is indeed $10 million (choice **b**). Profit remained constant at $20 million in 2004 and 2005 and remained constant at $50 million in 2009 and 2010 (choice **e**). The points on the graph at which the largest y-value occurs have a t-coordinate of 5 and 6, which correspond to the years 2009 and 2010, making choice **a** incorrect. Profit increased from 2011 to 2012, but decreased from 2012 through 2014, so choice **c** is incorrect. The intervals on which the profit increases are (1,2), (3,5), and (7,8). The second of these intervals shows two consecutive years with an increase in profit; therefore choice **d** is incorrect.

54. e. First, rewrite each fraction with the least common denominator $(x + 3)(x - 3)^2$. Then subtract the numerators by simplifying each expression and combining like terms, as so:

$$-\frac{1}{(x-3)^2} + \frac{1}{x+3} = \frac{1}{x+3} - \frac{1}{(x-3)^2}$$
$$= \frac{(x-3)^2}{(x+3)(x-3)^2} - \frac{x+3}{(x+3)(x-3)^2}$$
$$= \frac{(x-3) - (x+3)}{(x+3)(x-3)^2}$$
$$= \frac{(x^2 - 6x + 9) - (x+3)}{(x+3)(x-3)^2}$$
$$= \frac{x^2 - 6x + 9 - x - 3}{(x+3)(x-3)^2}$$
$$= \frac{x^2 - 7x + 6}{(x+3)(x-3)^2}$$
$$= \frac{(x-6)(x-1)}{(x+3)(x-3)^2}$$

In choice **a**, the denominator is correct, but the numerator is not. If you arrived at choice **b**, it looks as if you multiplied the numerator and denominator of the first term by $x - 3$ only, when you need to multiply by $(x - 3)^2$. In choice **c**, you forgot to include the numerator in your final answer. If you arrived at choice **d** it appears that you added the fractions instead of subtracting them.

55. c. The mean of set A is computed by adding the five entries and dividing the sum by 5; this yields a mean of 5. Similarly, the mean of set B is computed by adding the four entries of B and dividing the sum by 4; this yields a mean of 4. Therefore the mean of set A is larger than the mean of set B, and statement I is true. The standard deviation of both sets is 0 because for each set all of the data points are equal to the mean, and there is no variation among the data points. So statement II is false. Finally, the median and mean are both equal to 5 in set A, so III is true. Following this logic the remaining answer choices are incorrect.

56. a, b, and e. The reciprocal of any number between 0 and 1 must be larger than 1 (choice **a**). Because y is a negative integer less than -1, the least value of $-y$ is $-(-2) = 2$. So for all values of y, the expression in choice **b** is greater than 1. Because y is a negative integer less than -1, the least value of y^4 is $(-2)^4 = 16$. So for all values of y, the expression in choice **e** is greater than 1. Choice **c** is incorrect because y is a negative integer less than -1, and the greatest value of $-\frac{1}{y}$ is $\frac{1}{2}$, which is not greater than 1. Choice **d** is incorrect because squaring a number between 0 and 1 always yields an answer that is less than the original number.

A NOTE ON SCORING ▶

I n order to evaluate how you did on the Praxis Core diagnostic and practice tests, first count the number of questions you answered correctly on each test. You will recall that your scores on the multiple-choice and fill-in segments of the tests are based on only the number of questions you answered correctly; there is no guessing penalty or penalty for unanswered questions. You will also recall that the Educational Testing Service has not set passing scores for these tests; this is left up to the institutions, state agencies, and associations that utilize the tests. Therefore, the interpretation of your score depends on the purpose for which you are taking the test.

If you are unsure of the passing score you will need, you can set yourself a goal of at least 70% of the answers right on each multiple-choice/fill-in section of the Praxis Core. To find the percentage of questions you answered correctly, add up the number of correct answers and then divide by the total number of questions to find your percentage.

Even if you have scored well on the Reading test, the Mathematics test, and the multiple-choice subsections of the Writing test, don't forget that you must receive a passing score on the essay portion of the Praxis Core Writing test. On this portion, your essay will be scored by at least two writing experts, and their combined score will be used to evaluate how you did. The scoring criteria are outlined in detail in the answer explanations. The best way to see how you did on the essay portion of the exam is to give your essay and the scoring criteria to a teacher or other reader whom you trust to see what scores he or she would assign.

- If you scored below 60% on any subject, you should seriously consider whether you are ready for the Praxis Core test in this subject at this time. A good idea would be to take some brush-up courses, either at a university or community college nearby or through correspondence, in the areas you feel less sure of. If you don't have time for a course, you might try private tutoring.
- If your score is in the 60% to 70% range, you need to work as hard as you can to improve your skills. It might also be helpful to ask friends and family to make up mock test questions and quiz you on them.

- If your score is between 70% and 90%, you could still benefit from additional work by brushing up your reading, writing, and general math skills before the exam.
- If you scored above 90%, that's great! This kind of score should make you a success in the academic program of your choice or in a teaching position.

Once you have honed your test-taking skills, study again the areas that gave you the most trouble. The key to success in almost any pursuit is to prepare for all you are worth. By taking the practice tests in this book, you have made yourself better prepared than other people who may be taking the test with you. You have diagnosed where your strengths and weaknesses lie and learned how to deal with the various kinds of questions that will appear on the test. So go into the tests with confidence, knowing that you're ready and equipped to do your best!

Using the codes below, you'll be able to log in and access additional online practice materials!

Your free online practice access codes are:

FVEQMD52JD0N3SV7C5468

FVEUPK7NNXX11LVFBWLJ

FVE3I6067V3M1Q612YT1

Follow these simple steps to redeem your code:

- Go to **www.learningexpresshub.com/affiliate** and have your access code handy.

If you're a new user:

- Click the **New user? Register here** button and complete the registration form to create your account and access your products.
- Be sure to enter your unique access code only once. If you have multiple access codes, you can enter them all—just use a comma to separate each code.
- The next time you visit, simply click the **Returning user? Sign in** button and enter your username and password.
- Do not re-enter previously redeemed access codes. Any products you previously accessed are saved in the **My Account** section on the site. Entering a previously redeemed access code will result in an error message.

If you're a returning user:

- Click the **Returning user? Sign in** button, enter your username and password, and click **Sign In**.
- You will automatically be brought to the **My Account** page to access your products.
- Do not re-enter previously redeemed access codes. Any products you previously accessed are saved in the **My Account** section on the site. Entering a previously redeemed access code will result in an error message.

If you're a returning user with a new access code:

- Click the **Returning user? Sign in** button, enter your username, password, and new access code, and click **Sign In**.
- If you have multiple access codes, you can enter them all—just use a comma to separate each code.
- Do not re-enter previously redeemed access codes. Any products you previously accessed are saved in the **My Account** section on the site. Entering a previously redeemed access code will result in an error message.

If you have any questions, please contact Customer Support at Support@ebsco.com. All inquiries will be responded to within a 24-hour period during our normal business hours: 9:00 A.M.–5:00 P.M. Eastern Time. Thank you!